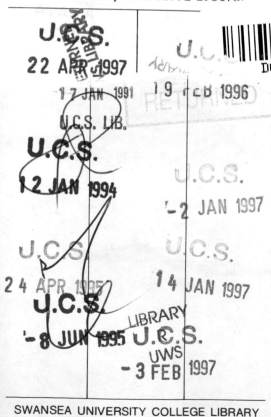

M·E·L·V·I·L·L·E'·S

MAJOR FICTION

M·E·L·V·I·L·L·E'·S

MAJOR FICTION

· POLITICS, THEOLOGY, AND IMAGINATION ·

JAMES DUBAN

NORTHERN ILLINOIS UNIVERSITY PRESS · DEKALB 1983

Library of Congress Cataloging in Publication Data

Duban, James, 1951–
    Melville's major fiction.

    Includes bibliographical references and index.
    1. Melville, Herman, 1819–1891—Criticism and
interpretation. 2. Melville, Herman, 1819–1891—
Knowledge—United States. 3. United States in litera-
ture. 4. Civilization, Modern—19th century. I. Title.
PS2387.D8   1983   813'.3   83-2432
ISBN 0-87580-086-6

Published by the Northern Illinois University Press, DeKalb, Illinois 60115

Manufactured in the United States of America

Design by Joan Westerdale

In memory of my father, Edmund I. Duban, 1908–1956, Doctorat d'État, Sorbonne, 1952

In honor of my mother, Sylvia Mould Duban

C O N T E N T S

A B B R E V I A T I O N S
Critical Editions Cited

The abbreviations in the left-hand column are those used for parenthetical references in the text and notes.

These works are quoted by permission of the publishers.

BB · *Billy Budd, Sailor (An Inside Narrative)* (1924), ed. Harrison Hayford and Merton M. Sealts, Jr. (Chicago: Univ. of Chicago Press, copyright © 1962).

CM· *The Confidence-Man: His Masquerade* (1857), ed. Hershel Parker (New York: W. W. Norton, copyright © 1971).

L · *The Letters of Herman Melville*, ed. Merrell R. Davis and William H. Gilman (New Haven: Yale Univ. Press, copyright © 1960).

M · *Mardi and A Voyage Thither* (1849), ed. Harrison Hayford, Hershel Parker, and G. Thomas Tanselle (Evanston, Ill.: Northwestern Univ. Press; Chicago: Newberry Library, copyright © 1970).

MD· *Moby-Dick; or, The Whale* (1851), ed. Harrison Hayford and Hershel Parker (New York: W. W. Norton, copyright © 1967).

Om· *Omoo: A Narrative of Adventures in the South Seas* (1847), ed. Harrison Hayford, Hershel Parker, and G. Thomas Tanselle (Evanston, Ill.: Northwestern Univ. Press; Chicago: Newberry Library, copyright © 1968).

P · *Pierre; or, The Ambiguities* (1852), ed. Harrison Hayford, Hershel Parker, and G. Thomas Tanselle (Evanston, Ill.: Northwestern Univ. Press; Chicago: Newberry Library, copyright © 1971).

RB · *Redburn, His First Voyage: Being the Sailor-boy Confessions and Reminiscences of the Son-of-a-Gentleman, in the Merchant Service* (1849), ed. Harrison Hayford, Hershel Parker, and G. Thomas Tanselle (Evanston, Ill.: Northwestern Univ. Press; Chicago: Newberry Library, copyright © 1969).

T · *Typee: A Peep at Polynesian Life* (1846), ed. Harrison Hayford, Hershel Parker, and G. Thomas Tanselle (Evanston, Ill.: Northwestern Univ. Press; Chicago: Newberry Library, copyright © 1968).

WJ · *White-Jacket; or, the World in a Man-of-War* (1850), ed. Harrison Hayford, Hershel Parker, and G. Thomas Tanselle (Evanston, Ill.: Northwestern Univ. Press; Chicago: Newberry Library, copyright © 1970).

All parenthetical references to *Clarel* (1876) are from *Clarel: A Poem and Pilgrimage in the Holy Land,* ed. Walter E. Bezanson (New York: Hendricks House, copyright © 1960).

ACKNOWLEDGMENTS

During the decade in which this study was conceived and developed, I have benefited from the encouragement and intellectual exchange of several colleagues and friends. In this respect, special thanks are due Michael J. Colacurcio, of Cornell University, and William J. Scheick, of The University of Texas at Austin. I have also received generous responses to my work from Edwin T. Bowden, Wayne Lesser, Walter L. Reed, Anthony Hilfer, Richard Ryan, Stanley J. Idzerda, Warner Barnes, Don Graham, William Goetz, Merton M. Sealts, Jr., Thomas Scorza, H. Bruce Franklin and the late Gordon Mills. Acknowledgment is also due Ann Bates Congdon, of Northern Illinois University, for her fine editorial suggestions. I am grateful, as well, to The University of Texas Research Institute and the American Council of Learned Societies, both of which provided grants to assist my research. And to my wife, Karen Carlisle Duban, whose companionship I cherish and whose interest in this project has so often found expression in perceptive and helpful commentary, I extend the most heartfelt love and gratitude.

P R E F A C E

Scholars who address the writings of Herman Melville in the 1980's will doubtless find themselves caught between Emerson's lament that "[m]an is timid and apologetic; ... he ... quotes some saint or sage" and Channing's belief that "few among us can be said to have followed out any great subject of thought patiently, laboriously, so as to know thoroughly what others have discovered ... concerning it, and thus to occupy a ground from which new views may be gained."[1] While holding in esteem Emerson's self-reliant dictum, I have nonetheless arrived at the ideas in this book after a series of liberating encounters with the scholarship of my predecessors. On the political milieus of Melville's life, fiction, and heritage there are Hershel Parker's still-essential dissertation; Nicholas Canaday, Jr.'s, study of Melville and authority; John Bernstein's work on pacifism and rebellion; and Joyce Sparer Adler's book on Melville's imaginative encounter with war. Also, Alan Heimert and Charles H. Foster make us aware of American political symbolism in Melville's works; Milton R. Stern, of the horological and generally conservative outlook of Melville's fiction; and Thomas Scorza, of Melville's quarrel with both modernity and the insufficiency of all political outlooks.[2] Important, as well, to Melville's political concerns

---

1. Emerson, "Self-Reliance" (*Essays, First Series*), in *The Complete Works of Ralph Waldo Emerson*, ed. Edward Waldo Emerson, 12 vols. (Boston and New York: Houghton Mifflin, 1903–04), II: 67; Channing, "Remarks on National Literature" (1823), in *The Works of William E. Channing, D.D.* (Boston: American Unitarian Assoc., 1895), p. 128.

2. Hershel Parker, "Melville and Politics: A Scrutiny of the Political Milieux of Herman Melville's Life and Works," Diss. Northwestern Univ., 1963; Nicholas Canaday, Jr., *Melville and Authority* (Gainesville: Univ. of Florida Press, 1968); John Bernstein, *Pacifism and Rebellion in the Writings of Herman Melville* (The Hague: Mouton, 1964); Joyce Sparer Adler, *War in Melville's Imagination* (New York: New

are the questions of race, primitivism, and "civilization"; and here one may draw on the observations of Edward S. Grejda, Carolyn L. Karcher, James Baird, and T. Walter Herbert, Jr.[3] And by no means unrelated to these issues are many theological concerns that William Braswell, Nathalia Wright, Lawrance Thompson, T. Walter Herbert, Jr., and Rowland A. Sherrill have shown to characterize Melville's fiction.[4]

Still, as Redburn says, each generation must write its own guidebooks. Given the wealth of scholarship already devoted to every phase of Melville's literary genius, a new guidebook is here offered mainly for those uncharted political, theological, and philosophical byways of his longer narratives. In fact, the dramatic impact of these works hinges, in large degree, on such previously overlooked or underemphasized contexts. For instance, I shall show how, in *Typee* through *Mardi*, categories derived from Jonathan Edwards and Samuel Hopkins concerning the "nature of true virtue" allow us to appreciate the process by which Melville structures his critiques of "civilization," Manifest Destiny, and the Mexican War. And even though Melville disparaged *Redburn* and *White-Jacket* as being "two *jobs*, which I have done for money" (L, 91), *Redburn*, I maintain, evokes political and theological concerns that assist our perception of how that work dramatizes what Alexis de Tocqueville defined as the isolationist tendencies of Jacksonian "individualism." Following this, my chapter

---

York Univ. Press, 1981); Alan Heimert, "*Moby-Dick* and American Political Symbolism," *American Quarterly*, 15 (Winter 1963), 498–543; Charles H. Foster, "Something in Emblems: A Reinterpretation of *Moby-Dick*," *New England Quarterly*, 34 (March 1961), 3–35; Milton R. Stern, *The Fine Hammered Steel of Herman Melville* (Urbana, Ill.: Univ. of Illinois Press, 1957), and "Introduction" to *Billy Budd, Sailor: An Inside Narrative*, ed. Milton R. Stern (Indianapolis, Ind.: Bobbs-Merrill, 1975), pp.vii–xliv; Thomas Scorza, *In the Time before Steamships: "Billy Budd," the Limits of Politics, and Modernity* (DeKalb, Ill.: Northern Illinois Univ. Press, 1979).

3. Edward S. Grejda, *The Common Continent of Men: Racial Equality in the Writings of Herman Melville* (Port Washington, N.Y.: Kennikat Press, 1974); Carolyn L. Karcher, *Shadow Over the Promised Land: Slavery, Race, and Violence in Melville's America* (Baton Rouge: Louisiana State Univ. Press, 1980); James Baird, *Ishmael: The Art of Melville in the Contexts of International Primitivism* (Baltimore, Md.: Johns Hopkins Press, 1956); T. Walter Herbert, Jr., *Marquesan Encounters: Melville and the Meaning of Civilization* (Cambridge, Mass.: Harvard Univ. Press, 1980).

4. William Braswell, *Melville's Religious Thought: An Essay in Interpretation* (Durham, N.C.: Duke Univ. Press, 1943); Nathalia Wright, *Melville's Use of the Bible* (Durham, N.C.: Duke Univ. Press, 1949); Lawrance Thompson, *Melville's Quarrel with God* (Princeton, N.J.: Princeton Univ. Press, 1952); T. Walter Herbert, Jr., "*Moby-Dick*" and Calvinism: A World Dismantled* (New Brunswick, N.J.: Rutgers Univ. Press, 1977); Rowland A. Sherrill, *The Prophetic Melville: Experience, Transcendence, and Tragedy* (Athens, Ga.: Univ. of Georgia Press, 1979).

on *White-Jacket* raises the question of whether aristocratic and anti-slavery overtones make that book's narrative something of a "Conscience Whig" enterprise having a good deal in common with Charles Sumner's *White Slavery in the Barbary States* (1847). Also new in emphasis is a discussion of Ishmael's use of covenant psychology and Christian apologetical strategies to structure his abolitionist narrative. These religious interests serve to ally Ishmael with Ahab's militant racism and implicate him in a tradition of providential historiography evident in narratives of American aggression ranging from the Pequot Massacre of 1637 to the Mexican War of 1846–48. In a similar contextual vein, my exploration of *Pierre* suggests that Melville criticizes "subjective Transcendentalism" in a manner recalling Henry Norman Hudson's outrage with the licentious tendencies of the by now nearly forgotten *Festus: A Poem*, by Philip James Bailey. My reexamination of *The Confidence-Man* demonstrates how that book's satire of liberal Christianity depends upon a previously unexplored definition of "confidence" and thereby opens up new possibilities for apprehending the skeptical interplay of theology and epistemology aboard the *Fidèle*. Finally, I shall reassess *Billy Budd* by showing how its narrator appropriates the thoughts of Thomas Carlyle, Matthew Arnold, and conservative Whig apologists of Captain Mackenzie's conduct in the *Somers* affair to create, in Captain Vere, a heroic persona whose uncompromising conservatism actually mirrors the narrator's own failure to confront what Jean-Paul Sartre would later call the "possible possibilities" of existence. The probable source materials of *Billy Budd*, I argue, are subordinate in importance to the philosophical implications of the narrator's use of these historical documents in "bad faith."

Behind my interest in these new contexts rests something like the Emersonian premise that in the creation of Art, "no man can quite emancipate himself from his age and country, or produce a model in which the education, the religion, the politics, usages and arts of his times shall have no share."[5] To arrive, therefore, at my conclusions about Melville's works, I have made use of several nineteenth-century newspapers, periodicals, and congressional publications. Melville was a voracious reader of these and of numerous other items that we shall never be able to trace. While a resident of New York, he had access to Evert Duyckinck's private library of over sixteen thousand titles, and he spent an average of one to two hours a day at the New York Society Library, the reading room of which an 1840 issue of the *New Yorker* described as having "four commodious tables covered with rich food

---

5. Emerson, "Art" (*Essays, First Series*), in *Works*, II: 352–53.

for the literary appetite. One contains the city journals; another those from different parts of the United States; and the other two are loaded with English and American periodicals—weekly, monthly, quarterly; literary, scientific, religious, and political."[6] Of major importance to my study is the *American Whig Review* (16 vols., 1845–52). The chief political writer of the *Whig*, Daniel Dewey Barnard, was an associate of Herman's uncle Peter; its main editor during its first three years, George H. Colton, met Melville at least as early as 1847; and a coeditor, Alexander W. Bradford, was a close friend of the Melvilles.[7] In the *Whig*, Melville would have encountered ideas for White-Jacket's aristocratic outlook, as well as the sort of complacency on the issue of slavery to which the "Conscience Whig" dimension of *White-Jacket* has reference. The *Whig* also contains columns which facilitate our assigning political significance to Ahab's Shakespearian postures; and in the *Whig* is Hudson's critique of *Festus*, which casts light upon the focus of *Pierre*.

Also crucial for its bearing upon Melville's imagination is the *Congressional Globe*, in which Melville probably read quoted portions of his brother Gansevoort's 1844 speech calling for the New York Democrats to ratify the nomination of James K. Polk for the Presidency.[8] My inquiry extends as well to *Yankee Doodle* (Oct.

---

6. Quoted in an informative discussion of Melville's reading habits by Luther Stearns Mansfield, "Herman Melville: Author and New Yorker," Diss. Univ. of Chicago, 1936, p. 170. Also see Merton M. Sealts, Jr., *Melville's Reading: A Check-List of Books Owned and Borrowed* (Madison: Univ. of Wisconsin Press, 1966), pp. 3–26, 117–20. Sealts shows how, from 1835 to 1836, Melville had access to the thousand volumes of the Young Men's Association of Albany; in 1838, to the library of the Lansingburgh Academy; and in 1850–51, to the Pittsfield Library Association. In addition, Melville's father-in-law, Chief Justice Lemuel Shaw, perhaps for Melville, borrowed a good number of books from the Boston Athenaeum.

7. For the intimacy of Barnard and Bradford with the Melvilles, see Parker, pp. 93 (n. 2), 128, 145, 154–55. On Melville's encounter with Colton, see Donald Yannella and Kathleen Malone Yannella, eds., "Evert A. Duyckinck's 'Diary: May 29–November 8, 1847,'" in *Studies in the American Renaissance, 1978*, ed. Joel Myerson (Boston: Twayne, 1978), p. 241. Parker (p. 180) shows that "many of the ideas in the Scroll chapter of *Mardi* are restatements of the pronouncements of the *Whig Review*." Melville doubtless would have consulted this journal after it reviewed *Typee* (3 [April 1846], 415–24) and harshly criticized *Omoo* (6 [July 1847], 36–46). Thereafter, Melville and his works are either referred to or discussed in several other issues of the *Whig*: 4: 539; 5: 210; 9: 565; 10: 218, 329; 11: 442, 495; 15: 89, 234–35, 356; 16: 311, 446–54. The best summaries of the *Whig*'s contributors and aesthetic outlook are Frank Luther Mott's *A History of American Magazines, 1741–1850* (Cambridge, Mass.: Harvard Univ. Press, 1939), pp. 750–54, and James E. Mulqueen's "Conservatism and Criticism: The Literary Standards of American Whigs, 1845–1852," *American Literature*, 41 (Nov. 1969), 355–72.

8. See *Congressional Globe*, 28th Cong., 1st sess., Appendix, pp. 662–63 (June,

1846–Oct. 1847), the weekly satiric newspaper containing Melville's "Authentic Anecdotes of 'Old Zack.' "[9] Melville's contributions to this publication, with their emphases on the Mexican War and slavery, foreshadow both the Vivenza chapters of *Mardi* and one of the paramount political considerations of *Moby-Dick:* the relation of American expansionism to the extension of slavery into the new territories acquired from Mexico. My study makes use of such newspapers as the New York *Evening Post,* the New York *Herald,* the New York *Morning News,* and the *Brooklyn Daily Eagle,* all of which would have been available to Melville before he moved to Pittsfield; each of which has engaging columns about American nationalism and Manifest Destiny; and the last of which was edited between 1846 and 1847 by Walt Whitman, whose editorials we shall see to figure in the worlds of *Mardi, Redburn, White-Jacket, Moby-Dick,* and *The Confidence-Man.* Also consulted is *The Law Reporter* (1838–66), a journal distant from Melville studies but significant for a fuller understanding of both *Moby-Dick* and *Billy Budd.* We shall immerse ourselves in these and many other books and journals that Melville is known to have either read or owned; that internal evidence suggests he used to fashion the political, religious, and philosophical dimensions of his fiction; or that deal with matters prominently discussed in his day and generally compatible with the concerns of his works. Perhaps Perry Miller said it best in remarking, "I am wary of becoming over-historical, but we need help in understanding how Melville's masks become pasteboard; no reader can be let off the duty of striking through them with whatever harpoon he can handle, if only one of the period."[10]

Still, my book seeks to meet what Wesley Morris has defined as the challenge of "a new historicism"—that is, "to dissolve the distinc-

---

1844). Heimert, p. 507, first noticed this passage, the larger context of which is clarified with reference to Hershel Parker's "Gansevoort Melville's Role in the Campaign of 1844," *New-York Historical Society Quarterly,* 49 (April 1965), 143–73, esp. 157–58.

9. See Luther Stearns Mansfield, "Melville's Comic Articles on Zachary Taylor," *American Literature,* 9 (Jan. 1938), 411–18. Although Melville's commitment to *Yankee Doodle* occurred after Cornelius Mathews assumed its editorship on 10 July 1847, I shall still utilize early issues of the paper, since these would have been available to Melville in 1846. As Mansfield ("Melville's Comic Articles," pp. 32, 411 [n. 2]) shows, Melville had made the acquaintance of Duyckinck, a member of *Yankee Doodle's* original editorial board, at least as early as March 1846; and Duyckinck, we know, owned the complete run of *Yankee Doodle.* See "Duyckinck Collection," *Lenox Library Short-Title Lists,* 8 (1887), 66. For the pertinence of *Yankee Doodle's* early and later themes for Melville's thought, see my "Satiric Precedent for Melville's 'The Two Temples,' " *American Transcendental Quarterly,* 42 (Spring 1979), 137–45.

10. Perry Miller, "Melville and Transcendentalism," *Virginia Quarterly Review,* 29 (Autumn 1953), 558.

tion between aesthetics and historical interpretation."[11] In most of Melville's longer narratives one would be hard-pressed to distinguish completely between contextual concerns and such aesthetic elements as structure, genre, and point of view, because the latter are often extensions of the former. For instance, existing scholarship on *Typee* and *Omoo* illustrates how Tommo's shifting point of view about native regeneracy and depravity reflects Melville's critique of the prevailing nineteenth-century notion of "civilization"; also, a beachcomber perspective conveyed in a travel book has been shown to combine the narrative outlook and the conventional genre best suited to Melville's subversions of his era's anthropological assumptions.[12] Similarly, we shall see how the quasi-"romance" genre of *Mardi* parodies the American political romanticism that the narrative ultimately undermines. And to this end Melville draws upon ideas derived from Jonathan Edwards's *The Nature of True Virtue* (1765), a treatise that helps to clarify the evasive unity between *Mardi*'s early emphasis on Taji's rescue of Yillah and the book's later political concerns. The gap between aesthetic preoccupation and historical reflection in Melville's fiction further diminishes once we realize that Redburn's shifting point of view is indebted to Irvingesque and Jeffersonian notions about "the Old World and the New," as well as to the traditions of typology and millennialism that lead him to regard his stroll through Liverpool as an anguishing march along Jerusalem's Via Dolorosa. Of course, Redburn fancies himself something of an autobiographer, but even this genre-related impulse merges into historical context when we recall the tradition of American autobiographies that appropriate and mirror the mythic dimensions of American culture.[13] Historical context and narrative form likewise mingle interdependently in the way the narrator of *White-Jacket* defines and structures his perceptions within categories like those involved in debates between Cotton Whigs and Conscience Whigs; moreover, White-Jacket's ambivalent democratic outlook wavers between "anticipatory" and "antipathetic" perspectives on the democratic experience. Yet nowhere is the union between Melville's reflection upon history and his preoccupation with literary form more pronounced than in *Moby-Dick*, the narrative structure of which I shall show to be inseparably linked

---

11. Wesley Morris, *Toward a New Historicism* (Princeton, N.J.: Princeton Univ. Press, 1972), p. 30.

12. Herbert, *Marquesan Encounters*, pp. 147–48; Janet Giltrow, "Speaking Out: Travel and Structure in Herman Melville's Early Narratives," *American Literature*, 52 (March 1980), 30–31.

13. See William C. Spengemann and L. R. Lundquist, "Autobiography and the American Myth," *American Quarterly*, 17 (Fall 1965), 501–19.

to the American jeremiad, to the argumentative strategy of Bishop Butler's *Analogy of Religion* (1736), and to debates articulating the relation between American expansionism and the extension of slavery into the new territories. In *Moby-Dick*, historical instance and imaginative vision coalesce; they also sustain one another in *Pierre*, whose achievement becomes apparent once we understand how the concept of "authorship" relates to Transcendental ideas about intuition. On the other hand, *The Confidence-Man*'s protean form mirrors the skeptical philosophy that operates throughout the book; I shall argue, moreover, that the abbreviated and interpolated form of that narrative's "Story of the Gentleman-Madman" comprises an important thematic commentary on the reductionist and diminutive effects upon Christian revelation of the *Fidèle*'s predominantly liberal atmosphere. And while the narrator of *Billy Budd* defines his aesthetic in terms of an "Inside Narrative," his manipulation and appropriation of conservative Whig assessments of the *Somers* affair cast his point of view into the existential abyss of "bad faith." In these ways I seek interpretively to enhance our understanding of Melville's major fiction. Still, my book does not primarily pursue the "meanings" of Melville's longer narratives; rather, it aims to elucidate their *subject matters* and the processes of thinking and imagining whereby Melville negotiated these issues in ideological and aesthetic terms simultaneously.

The closing section of this book accounts, as well, for an even more important relation between aesthetic preoccupation and historical reflection—the form of Melville's career as a writer when judged against as many historical contexts and debates as there are islands in *Mardi*. To this end, I shall envision the polemical instances of Melville's thought within their governing framework: the author's desired projection of his political and theological concerns into a world-serving imaginative realm. Indeed, his fiction violates the status quo of nineteenth-century assumptions about political, religious, and social matters; and each violation transcends the limitations of the context that it evokes to suggest that imagination, consciousness, and the anguish of confronting *alternatives* are the enduring mandates and mental exercises that Melville prescribes for posterity. Melville, we shall see, is not as concerned with history as he is with something like a Nietzschean "historical sense," which, as Lionel Trilling has said, "is to be understood as the critical sense, as the sense which life uses to test itself."[14]

---

14. Lionel Trilling, "The Sense of the Past," in *The Liberal Imagination: Essays on Literature and Society* (1950; rpt. New York: Doubleday, 1953), p. 191.

M·E·L·V·I·L·L·E'·S

MAJOR FICTION

C H A P T E R   I

The Nature of True Virtue: *Typee* through *Mardi*

The place to start is with *Typee, Omoo,* and *Mardi,* which contain Melville's first protest against messianic nationalism and which anticipate several other political, religious, and philosophical concerns of his later fiction. For instance, the narrator of *Typee* offers an early statement of the difference between "Chronometricals and Horologicals," or heavenly and earthly standards of behavior and morality. Tommo says that "against the cause of missions in the abstract no Christian can possibly be opposed; it is in truth a just and holy cause. But if the great end proposed by it be spiritual, the agency employed to accomplish that end is purely earthly; and, although the object in view be the achievement of much good, that agency may nevertheless be productive of evil" (T, 197). This observation foreshadows what Plinlimmon might consider Pierre's folly in seeking to live by abstract and absolutist standards of morality and holiness; but in *Typee* and *Omoo* Melville explores primarily national rather than personal modes of presumptuous conduct, which turn out to resemble something of a confidence game practiced by civilization's sanctimonious emissaries:

> An unwarranted confidence in the sanctity of [missionaries]—a proneness to regard them as incapable of guile—and an impatience of the least suspicion as to their rectitude as men or Christians, have ever been prevailing faults in the Church. Nor is it to be wondered at: for subject as Christianity is to the assaults of unprincipled foes, we are naturally disposed to regard everything like an exposure of ecclesiastical misconduct as the offspring of malevolence or irreligious feeling. (T, 198)

But here, as aboard the *Fidèle,* suspicion is more than justified since Tommo regards missionaries as the vanguard of exploitative westerners who have civilized the natives into "draught horses," have evangelized them into "beasts of burden" (T, 196), have exasperated them into "savages" (T, 27), and have poisoned their physical and social systems with venereal disease and apartheid (Om, 191, 188).[1] "In a word," says Tommo, "here, as in every case where Civilization has in any way been introduced among those whom we call savages, she has scattered her vices, and withheld her blessings" (T, 198). Thus, the missionaries' rhetoric of redemption notwithstanding, the tendency of their efforts seems antimessianic: "Lies, lies!" yell the natives in *Omoo*, "you tell us of salvation; and, behold, we are dying. We want no other salvation, than to live in this world. Where are any saved through your speech? ... [W]e are all dying with your cursed diseases" (p. 191). As Tommo says elsewhere, "[W]ere civilization itself to be estimated by some of its results, it would seem perhaps better for what we call the barbarous part of the world to remain unchanged" (T, 17).

Still, Tommo's portrait of primitivism is ambiguous, since he sometimes regards the natives as remarkably noble and virtuous; other times, as depraved and cannibalistic. Yet Melville is not to be faulted for inconsistency here; as T. Walter Herbert, Jr., has recently shown, in Tommo's shifting perspective Melville parodies the western habit of imposing a wide range of interpretive presuppositions upon native character, and these tell us more about western attitudes than about Typean culture: "Melville becomes fascinated by the ways in which factual information is taken up by exponents of various interpretive perspectives and made into a symbolic carrier of the world view they embrace."[2] Moreover, in sometimes lauding native virtue, but occasionally repudiating Typean savagery, Tommo shifts back and forth between what Charles Roberts Anderson has shown to be the opposing attitudes about Marquesans espoused by the Reverend Charles Stewart and Captain David Porter. For example, in *A Visit to the South Seas* ... (1831) the Calvinistic Stewart asserts that the natives' inability to transcend their "republic *en sauvage*" justifies missionary efforts. On the other hand, Porter's *Journal of a Cruise Made to the Pacific Ocean* ... (1815) records that "an honester or more friendly and better disposed people do not exist under the sun...; they rank high in the scale of human beings, whether we consider them morally

---

1. That *Typee* and *Omoo* share the same narrator is evident from *Omoo*'s first chapter and from the way the narrator of *Omoo* pens the name "Typee" (Om, 77) to the round robin.

2. T. Walter Herbert, Jr., *Marquesan Encounters: Melville and the Meaning of Civilization* (Cambridge, Mass.: Harvard Univ. Press, 1980), pp. 158–59. Cf. Edward S.

or physically."[3] To the degree, then, that Tommo wavers between these outlooks, he neither completely affirms nor denies any one impression of the natives but rather participates in the full range of stereotypes with which westerners structured their Marquesan encounters. Insofar as Tommo sometimes concurs with Porter, however, *Typee* undermines the premise about native depravity to which the missionaries appealed in justifying their redemptive and messianic crusades. And the precise strategy by which Tommo seeks to convince us of Typean virtue deserves further comment at this juncture. As we shall see, Tommo defends native virtue by combining the philosophy of Shaftesbury and Hutcheson with the theology of Jonathan Edwards and his New Divinity disciples. Melville's use of these previously unrecognized borrowings foreshadows contextual strategies operating in all of his major works, and especially in *Mardi*, the structural unity of which picks up where *Typee*'s encounter with New Divinity theology leaves off.

Tommo's defense of native virtue is most evident in the way he hints that Typee is a sort of prelapsarian refuge devoid of crime (T, 195, 201). Not surprisingly, then, Tommo regrets having "once heard it given of an instance of the frightful *depravity* of a certain tribe in the Pacific, that they had no word ... to express the idea of *virtue*" (T, 126; emphasis added); and he responds to this charge by claiming that "civilization does not engross all the virtues of humanity," which often "flourish in greater abundance and attain greater strength among many barbarous people" (T, 202). Moreover, with rhetoric resembling the thoughts of Shaftesbury and Hutcheson about a moral sense that belies theories concerning "the inborn lawlessness of the human race," Tommo defends native virtue by describing both the Typeans' "inherent principle of honesty and charity towards each other" and their "indwelling, universally diffused perception of what is *just* and *noble*" (T, 201).

Yet the full impact of Tommo's apologia for Typean character becomes evident only if we recall that many eighteenth- and nineteenth-century missionary societies justified their undertakings by appealing to the Hopkinsian idea that Christians ought to engage in acts of "disinterested benevolence" as sanctifying evidences of their own regeneracy—and especially in the areas of domestic and international social reform. They were to embrace "the poor, the illiterate,

---

Grejda, *The Common Continent of Men: Racial Equality in the Writings of Herman Melville* (Port Washington, N.Y.: Kennikat Press, 1974), p. 25.

3. Quoted in Charles Roberts Anderson, *Melville in the South Seas* (1939; rpt. New York: Dover Publications, 1966), pp. 130–31.

the slaves, the down-trodden everywhere, even the untold millions of heathens in Asia, Africa, and the South Sea Islands. These blind worshippers of gods of wood and stone were perishing because of the neglect of professing Christians to practice disinterested benevolence."[4] Melville, I shall argue presently, was familiar with the notion of disinterested benevolence that helped to shape the outlook of America's first generation of foreign missionaries. He likewise seems to have known about Jonathan Edwards's definition of "true virtue" as a "love to being in general," from which Hopkins derived his more socially minded doctrine.[5] Edwards, we should remember, had responded to his era's moralistic theologians by insisting that "benevolence to being in general" was a disposition limited exclusively to regenerate Christians. The merely apparent virtue of unregenerates, he said, was traceable either to selfish motives or to amoral "particular instincts of Nature, which in some respects resemble virtue." For example, "the love of parents to their children," though seemingly virtuous and benevolent, could be "referred to instinct"; therefore this "limited private benevolence, not *arising* from, not being *subordinate* to benevolence to being in general, cannot have the nature of true virtue."[6] Assumptions such as these anticipate those of missionaries who, believing in native degeneracy, hoped to imbue Polynesians with "true virtue."

Yet a somewhat different application of ideas indebted to Ed-

---

4. Oliver Wendell Elsbree, "Samuel Hopkins and His Doctrine of Benevolence," *New England Quarterly*, 8 (Dec. 1935), 541. (Also see p. 548.)

5. Jonathan Edwards, *The Nature of True Virtue*, in *The Works of President Edwards*, ed. Sereno E. Dwight, 10 vols. (New York: S. Converse, 1829–30), III: 95. For an informative study of Hopkins's modification of Edwards's doctrine, see Joseph A. Conforti, "Samuel Hopkins and the New Divinity: Theology, Ethics, and Social Reform in Eighteenth-Century New England," *William and Mary Quarterly*, 34 (Oct. 1977), 572–89.

6. Edwards, III: 94–95, 136–37. Melville's familiarity with Edwards's and Hopkins's thought is evident in a section of *Omoo* where Captain Guy reprimands Tommo for refusing to man the *Julia* after that ship rescues him from the Typeans: "It is you," says Guy, "who owe your life to my humanity." But Tommo draws upon logic similar to that of Edwards and Hopkins in remarking, "I was perfectly acquainted with his motives in sending a boat into the bay; his crew was reduced, and he merely wished to procure the sailor whom he expected to find there. The *ship* was the means of my deliverance, and no thanks to the benevolence of its captain" (Om, 140). Equally reminiscent of Edwards is the way White-Jacket exposes the true nature of military valor by tracing its seemingly virtuous inspiration to natural instincts shared by animals: "Courage is the most common and vulgar of *virtues*; the only one shared with us by the beasts of the field.... But in a naval officer, animal courage is exalted to the loftiest merit, and often procures him a distinguished command" (WJ, 314; emphasis added). Also, in *Moby-Dick* Ishmael draws more lightheartedly upon Hopkins's rhetoric in

wards and Hopkins surfaces in Tommo's remark that, among the natives, "I formed a higher estimate of human nature than I had ever before entertained," especially since the Typeans deal "more kindly with each other, and are more humane, than many who study essays on virtue and benevolence" (T, 203). Indeed, with rhetoric approaching Edwards's definition of "true virtue," Tommo observes that "the natives appeared to form one household whose members were bound together by the ties of strong affection. The *love to kindred I did not so much perceive*, for it seemed blended in the *general love*; and where all were treated as brothers and sisters, it was hard to tell who were actually related to each other by blood" (T, 204; emphasis added). Thus, while Marquesan domestic relationships actually emphasized the household rather than the immediate family, this arrangement does not necessarily "def[y] the categories with which the missionaries were equipped";[7] rather, Tommo's description shows how communal living corresponds to Hopkinsian and Edwardsian ideas about disinterestedness that render missionary efforts redundant. Moreover, Tommo elsewhere capitalizes upon Hopkins's logic to argue that the missionaries have "exaggerated the evils of Paganism, in order to enhance the merit of their own disinterested labors" (T, 169). Cannibalism notwithstanding, says Tommo, "[T]hose who indulge in it are in other respects humane and virtuous" (T, 205). When natives are left to themselves, "virtue, without being clamourously invoked, is as it were, unconsciously practiced" (T, 192). Corrupted, however, by westerners, the Marquesans lose much of their indiscriminate and general love—a point illustrated in *Omoo's* reference to "Tayo," a native ritual of selfless friendship that western mercantile forces have corroded to "a mere mercenary relation" (Om, 152).[8] Thus, far from imbuing natives with disinterested benevolence, Christianity "has given birth to ignorance, hypocrisy, and hatred of all other modes of faith, which was once foreign to the open and *benevolent* character of the Tahitian" (Om, 186; emphasis added).

This general protest of Tommo's against western efforts to con-

---

remarking that Tashtego and Daggoo exercise a "disinterested and benevolent" (MD, 272) frame of mind in protecting Queequeg from sharks. Existing scholarship, moreover, suggests that Edwards's essay on *True Virtue* functions in "Bartleby." See Allan Moore Emery, "The Alternatives of Melville's 'Bartleby,'" *Nineteenth-Century Fiction*, 31 (Sept. 1976), 182–83.

7. Herbert, *Marquesan Encounters*, p. 36.

8. For Melville's encounter with "Tayo," and its disintegration under western influence, see James Baird, *Ishmael* (Baltimore, Md.: Johns Hopkins Press, 1956), pp. 205–11; A. N. Kaul, *The American Vision: Actual and Ideal Society in Nineteenth-Century Fiction* (New Yaven: Yale Univ. Press, 1963), pp. 237–38.

vert Polynesians sheds light, as well, upon his reluctance to have his face tattooed. Factually, of course, Tommo errs in believing that "the whole system of tattooing was ... connected with their religion; and it was evident, therefore, that they were resolved to make a convert of me" (T, 220).[9] But since Melville's artistic modification of the facts allows Tommo to become the reluctant object of one culture's effort to impose its religious customs upon another, the tattooing motif inversely corresponds to the largest concern of *Typee* and *Omoo*, summarized by James Baird as "the confusion set up in an indigenous symbolic system when the symbols of an alien culture are imposed upon the native religious expression of the Tahitian." And something like this, as D. H. Lawrence early noted, also characterizes the significance of Tommo's leg infection, indicative of civilized man's reckless effort to return to Eden.[10] Moreover, as we shall see directly, Tommo's effort first to abandon his own culture, and then to impose its values upon the Typeans, only accelerates the decline of a people whose corruption by westerners he nominally laments.

Crucial to Tommo's complicity in changing Typean culture is the frame of mind that has allowed him to abandon the *Dolly* under the pretext of "resistance to unmitigated tyranny" (T, 21); for Tommo here seems to echo the Declaration of Independence.[11] Of course, Tommo purports to loathe westerners who, while abusing the natives, profess brotherly love and natural rights; but Tommo himself, in the process of securing Fayaway's affections and favors, is guilty of applying republican standards of equality in opposition to the Typean religious stricture barring women from canoes: "[F]or the life of me I could not understand why a woman should not have *as much right* to enter a canoe as a man" (T, 133; emphasis added). Although Tommo prides himself in having extended the area of this particular freedom, Milton R. Stern is probably correct in suggesting that Tommo here effects "the beginning dissolution of native order."[12] Moreover, Tommo compounds his dereliction by introducing into Typee Valley ideas relating to regimental warfare; indeed, protest as he may against civilization's

---

9. Anderson, pp. 149–51, notes Tommo's error in associating tattooing with religious conversion.

10. Baird, p. 191; D. H. Lawrence, *Studies in Classic American Literature* (New York: Thomas Seltzer, 1923), pp. 203–4.

11. See Thomas Scorza, "Tragedy in the State of Nature: Melville's *Typee*," *Interpretation: A Journal of Political Philosophy*, 8 (Jan. 1979), 105–7.

12. Milton R. Stern, *The Fine Hammered Steel of Herman Melville* (Urbana: Univ. of Illinois Press, 1957), p. 40. Cf. Edgar Dryden's critique of Tommo in *Melville's Thematics of Form: The Great Art of Telling the Truth* (Baltimore, Md.: Johns Hopkins Press, 1968), p. 45.

"fiend-like skill ... in the invention of all manner of death-dealing engines" (T, 125), Tommo later fashions a toy popgun for one native child, and before long initiates the entire valley into strategies of modern warfare: "For three or four hours I was engaged in manufacturing popguns, but at last made over my good-will and interest in the concern to a lad of remarkable quick parts, whom I soon initiated into the art and mystery. Pop, Pop, Pop, Pop, now resounded all over the valley. Duels, skirmishes, pitched battles, and general engagements were to be seen on every side" (T, 145). This incident recalls the way that Gulliver introduces the King of Brobdingnag to mechanized warfare and anticipates the innovative reforms of a Connecticut Yankee in a society more primitive than his own. But whether the transgression is individual or national, Melville renders obvious the moral inconsistencies and general harm which result from the misguided effort of civilization to rehabilitate so-called primitive and barbarous societies.

Of course, as T. Walter Herbert, Jr., suggests, the idea of "civilization" is actually the main conceptual accessory to this process. Civilization is a "structural feature" of the western outlook, a "frame of mind" that generates the idea of barbarism to affirm its own validity.[13] Thus, whatever Tommo's seemingly admirable relativism in pronouncing that "civilization does not engross all the virtues of humanity.... They flourish in greater abundance and attain greater strength among many barbarous people" (T, 202–3), he nonetheless perpetuates the very concepts that sustain the messianic outlooks of both missionary societies and their financial benefactors.[14] And precisely this category of "civilization" allows Tommo sometimes to speak condescendingly about "the savage nature of the beings at whose mercy I was" (T, 232), to refer to the Typeans as "nothing better than a set of cannibals" (T, 118), to remark that "there are no wild animals of any kind on the island, unless it be decided that the natives themselves are such" (T, 212), and to call them "fiends incarnate" (T, 95), thereby indulging in the stereotype central both to missionary efforts in Polynesia and to his own country's incursion upon

---

13. Herbert, *Marquesan Encounters*, pp. 18, 116, 125.

14. In attributing this chauvinistic outlook to Tommo, I differ from Herbert, who sometimes takes the narrative's references to barbarism and heathenism as evidence "that Melville has not broken out of the conceptual framework whose validity he is implicitly challenging" (*Marquesan Encounters*, p. 173). That Melville was fully aware of the condescending and exploitative tendencies of Tommo's rhetoric is evident from a section of *Mardi* that describes how, whenever King Bello "found a rich country, inhabited by a people, *deemed by him barbarous* and incapable of wise legislation, he sometimes relieved them from their political anxieties, by assuming the dictatorship over them" (M, 468; emphasis added).

the territories of supposedly diabolical Indians and Mexicans. Somewhat self-defeating, then, are Tommo's laments that "the Anglo-Saxon hive have extirpated Paganism from the greater part of the North American continent: but with it they have likewise extirpated the greater portion of the Red Race. Civilization is gradually sweeping from the earth the lingering vestiges of Paganism, and at the same time the shrinking forms of its unhappy worshippers" (T, 195). Indeed, no huge conceptual gap exists between efforts to "civilize" Polynesia and expropriationist outlooks that dominated American continentalism in the nineteenth century.[15]

In fact, even *Yankee Doodle*, the weekly satiric newspaper to which Melville contributed his "Authentic Anecdotes of 'Old Zack,'" demonstrated as much in regard to Mexico:

> Hon. Mr. Cushing, who studied political economy under the celebrated HUM-HUM in China, recently said in a lecture delivered in Newbury-port that he "did not doubt that Mexico would be ultimately benefitted by the detachment and occupation effected by our troops of a large portion of that country." If the Mexicans are not duly sensible of the efforts which YANKEE DOODLE and Gen. TAYLOR are making in their behalf, they are a set of the most ungrateful, kinky-headed, copper-colored rapscallions in the universe, and ought to be "civilized" off the face of the earth. (12 Dec. 1846, p. 117)

Much the same point is evident in *Yankee Doodle*'s satire of General Stockton, whose California campaign is said to recall a line from *Don Quixote:* "My master, said Sancho, will have a good many governments to dispose of in the Pagan countries he conquers with his lance" (19 Dec. 1846, p. 127). And that rhetoric such as this actually corresponds to contemporary expansionist attitudes about "civilization" and "barbarism" is evident from the way one magazine described how America would bring California "under the immediate moral power of ur [*sic*] institutions and prevent a lapse to barbarism—will keep it as bone of our bone and flesh of our flesh."[16] Char-

---

15. Edwin Fussell, in *Frontier: American Literature and the American West* (Princeton, N.J.: Princeton Univ. Press, 1955), p. 236, remarks that Toby and Tommo resemble "'pioneers,' who hack their way through a forest of cane (as if Nukuheva were Kentucky), encounter Niagaras of waterfalls, and are shaken with ague, for their invasion of the happy valley is by simple correspondence and obvious geographic extension the archetypal American behavior epitomized." Cf. Herbert's *Marquesan Encounters*, pp. 26, 27, 60, 83, 102, 122, for the way endeavors of Polynesian missionaries corresponded to expansionist attitudes in America.

16. "California," *American Literary Magazine*, 3 (Dec. 1848), 340.

acteristic of most Locofoco outlooks on America's mandate in the West, this passage has an added feature: its reference to the creation of Eve in Genesis implies a link between the quest for new territories and the pursuit of female partnership. Such a link is evident in much of America's outlook on its "virgin land" and helps to explain the structural unity in *Mardi* between Taji's westward search for Yillah and the concerns of the Vivenza chapters, which address the American political scene. We shall see that these two emphases pick up where *Typee* leaves off in casting a peculiarly Edwardsian judgment upon the seemingly disinterested endeavors of messianic nationalism.

Although *Mardi* is concerned primarily with the world of mind, Babbalanja's reference to "consciousness" as "an empire boundless as the West" (M, 397) provides a category with which to link the book's epistemological and expansionist inquiries. Indeed, in a chapter titled "Dreams" even Taji shows the great American West somehow to correspond with the boundless domain of mind:

> DREAMS, DREAMS! golden dreams: endless, and golden, as the flowery prairies, that stretch away from Rio Sacramento, in whose waters Danae's shower was woven;—prairies like rounded eternities: jonquil leaves beaten out; and my dreams herd like Buffaloes, browsing on the horizon, and browsing on round the world; and among them, I dash with my lance, to spear one, ere they all flee. (M, 366; cf. 368)

Western references such as these, as Edwin Fussell has shown, are innumerable in *Mardi*, Taji many times reminding us that he and his companions always head "Westward," where lie "numerous groups of islands, loosely laid down upon the charts, and invested with all the charms of dream-land" (M, 7).[17] Like an explorer, moreover, Taji sets out for *"Terra Incognita"* (M, 51) and remarks that "though America be discovered, the Cathays of the deep are unknown" (M, 39). Also, references to "our Northwest Passages" (M, 575), "Arkansas' boundless prairies" (M, 39), Davy Crockett's rifle (M, 105), Michigan wigwams (M, 372), and numerous comparisons of objects to bison (M, 117, 458, 586) are consistent with the way Taji regards his participa-

---

17. See Fussell, pp. 240–48, for a discussion of western references and symbols in *Mardi*. Taji's westward course is also mentioned on pp. 17, 18, 26, 96, 108, 144, 160, 499, 549, 582, and 617 of *Mardi*.

tion in Yillah's liberation as something akin to the rescue of a white maiden from Indian captivity. In fact, after slaying Aleema for his pursuance of a "barbarous [sacrificial] custom," Taji boasts in explicitly western American terms of his and Yillah's escape: "Let the Oregon Indian through brush, bramble, and brier, hunt his enemy's trail, far over the mountains and down in the vales; comes he to the water, he snuffs idly in air" (M, 141).[18] Not unrelated to these references are, first, the fact that Taji and Jarl embark upon their "Westward" course "without chart or quadrant" (M, 17); second, the manner in which Taji compares their "chartless" voyage to the way the sun wends its way through the zodiac (M, 557); and third, the book's concern with "the world of mind; wherein the wanderer may gaze round, with more of wonder than Balboa's band roving through the golden Aztec glades" (M, 557). These passages all pertain on at least one level to the idealistic inspiration that, in the nineteenth century, helped to generate America's sometimes reckless course of empire. Timely, indeed, for the way Taji ends up racing over "an endless sea" (M, 654) are the *American Whig Review*'s words of caution about a too-energetic expansionist policy: "It were great folly in us that we should fancy ourselves still riding at ease in our own well-chosen and capacious land-locked harbor, when in truth we have gone to sea, where we never were before, and may never see land again—having taken care to leave our *best chart behind us*."[19] To understand Taji's "chartless" (M, 556) voyage, let us begin by exploring the idealistic and political nature of Vivenza's.

The concern of the Vivenza chapters with America's romanticized vision of democracy is evident in the way her patriots rejoice in the disruptive volcanoes of Porpheero (Europe): "Hurrah!" shout the Vivenzans, "another kingdom is burnt down to the earth's edge; another

---

18. For a review of the Indian captivity narrative, see Richard Slotkin, *Regeneration Through Violence: The Mythology of the American Frontier, 1600–1860* (Middletown, Conn.: Wesleyan Univ. Press, 1973), pp. 74–75, 247–59. See especially pp. 446–48 of Slotkin's text for Melville's familiarity with this genre.

19. "The Constitution; Written and Unwritten," *American Whig Review*, 6 (July 1847), 5; emphasis added. Melville most likely saw this issue of the *Whig Review*, since it also contains (pp. 36–46) George Washington Peck's scathing attack on *Omoo*. Also worth noting is another issue of the *Whig*, which traces the "chart" metaphor to Polk's inaugural address and then shows his Mexican War policy to be a transgression of his constitutional powers: "So much for Mr. Polk's observance of the solemn promise which he made to the nation in his inaugural address, and to which he had just then bound himself by a solemn oath. 'The Constitution,' said he, 'will be the chart by which I shall be directed. It will be my first care to administer the government in the true spirit of that instrument, and to assume no power not expressly granted, or clearly implied in its terms'" ("The President and His Administration," 7 [May 1848], 445).

demi-god is unhelmed; . . . Ere we die, freemen, all Mardi will be free"
(M, 524). Still, Media's anonymous scroll warns the Vivenzans that the
misguided fervor of the French Revolution owes much to America's
erroneous view that republicanism and democracy comprise worldwide
millennial mandates: "[T]he grand error of your nation, sovereign-
kings! seems this:—The conceit that Mardi is now in the last scene of
the last act of her drama; and that all preceding events were ordained,
to bring about the catastrophe you believe to be at hand,—a universal
and permanent Republic" (M, 525).[20] While Melville may not have
espoused all of Media's sentiments, he probably would have agreed
that a too-zealous democratic enthusiasm informed what America
considered her "manifest destiny" to extend her republican values and
institutions over North America. And since he wrote so much of *Mardi*
in 1848, this concern probably has reference to American hostilities
against Mexico.

Melville, however, prepares us for *Mardi*'s encounter with the
Mexican War by exploring the inception of the American messianic
outlook in New England's seventeenth- and eighteenth-century habit
of contrasting "New World" regeneracy with the religiously and
politically decrepit character of "Old World" Europe:

> Did not their bards pronounce them a fresh start in the Mardian
> species; requiring a new world for their full development? . . .
> Vivenza might be likened to St. John, feeding on locusts and
> wild honey, and with prophetic voice crying to the nations from
> the wilderness. Or, child-like, standing among the old robed
> kings and emperors of the Archipelago, Vivenza seemed a young
> Messiah, to whose discourse the bearded Rabbis bowed. (M, 472)

Since the Vivenzans' pride in their landscape and physical prowess
(M, 514) seems to echo "Query VI" of Thomas Jefferson's *Notes on
the State of Virginia*, the Vivenzan notion of a depraved Old World
probably owes something to Jefferson's well-known sentiments, which
Cushing Strout summarizes as "the mythical conception of a Europe
whose every charm is the vicious opposite of an American virtue."[21] Of

---

20. For an informative reading of this aspect of Melville's satire, see John Gerlach,
"Messianic Nationalism in the Early Works of Herman Melville: Against Perry Miller,"
Arizona Quarterly, 28 (Spring 1972), 5–26. Because of the anonymous scroll's monarchical
tone, I assign its authorship to Media. Indeed, since Media claims to be a demigod, the
scroll playfully hints at his identity: "[Y]ou may ascribe this voice to the gods: for never
will you trace it to man" (M, 524).

21. Cushing Strout, *The American Image of the Old World* (New York: Harper and
Row, 1963), p. 28.

course, Jefferson's view of Old World depravity is itself indebted to the still older and more explicitly religious outlook of the Puritan separatists (de facto or otherwise), who thought themselves the inheritors of God's covenant with Israel. Thus, William Bradford could view the Pilgrim migration as a symbolic Exodus; Edward Johnson could insist that "because every corner of England was filled with the fury of malignant adversaries, Christ creates a New England to muster up the first of his Forces in"; and, nearly a century later, Jonathan Edwards could reaffirm America's messianic identity by arguing that inasmuch as the "old continent" had "crucified Christ, they shall not have the honour of communicating religion in its most glorious state to us, but we to them." Therefore, said Edwards, the millennium *"is probably to begin in America"* and "the most glorious renovation of the world shall originate from the new continent."[22]

Probably just as relevant, however, to the heritage of Vivenza's sense of mission is the way America defined her messianic identity in the years immediately preceding 1776 in terms of an independent political community—and, after the Revolution, in terms of the dissemination of her democratic principles.[23] Nowhere was this outlook more evident than in America's nineteenth-century habit of thinking it her destiny to manifest the blessings of democracy, by means of acquisitive territorialism, to neighboring nations. Americans sanctioned this policy by claiming that they were "extending the area of freedom" and practicing a "destined use of the soil" by those whose labor would give it value. These, we should recall, were rationales upon which the Polk administration and such newspaper editors as John L. O'Sullivan and Walt Whitman drew in disavowing that America's expansionist or Mexican War policies were selfishly motivated. "Nor is it the much condemned lust of power and territory," claimed Whitman in his 6 June 1846 editorial in the *Brooklyn Daily Eagle,* "that

---

22. William Bradford, *Of Plymouth Plantation, 1620–1647,* ed. Samuel Eliot Morison (New York: Modern Library, 1952), pp. 19, 63; Edward Johnson, *Wonder-Working Providence of Sions Saviour in New-England (1628–1651),* ed. J. Franklin Jameson (New York: Charles Scribner's Sons, 1910), p. 23; Edwards, *Some Thoughts Concerning the Present Revival of Religion,* in *Works,* IV: 128, 130. The evolution of America's messianic identity is discussed by Ernest Lee Tuveson, *Redeemer Nation: The Idea of America's Millennial Role* (Chicago: Univ. of Chicago Press, 1968); Sacvan Bercovitch, *The Puritan Origins of the American Self* (New Haven: Yale Univ. Press, 1975), pp. 35–86.

23. See John F. Berens, *Providence and Patriotism in Early America, 1640–1815* (Charlottesville: Univ. Press of Virginia, 1978), pp. 51–80; Ralph H. Gabriel, *The Course of American Democratic Thought,* 2nd ed. (New York: Ronald Press, 1956), pp. 34–37.

makes the popular heart respond to the idea of these new acquisitions. Such greediness might very properly be the motive of widening a less liberal form of government; but such a greediness is not ours. We pant to see our country and its rule far-reaching, only inasmuch as it will take off the shackles that prevent men the even chance of being happy and good." "We have lofty views of the scope and destiny of our American Republic," Whitman elsewhere remarked; "it is for the interest of mankind that its territory should be extended—the farther the better."[24] Still, Melville would later point out the hypocritical tendency of remarks such as these in a chapter of *White-Jacket* where the narrator patriotically pronounces "national selfishness . . . unbounded philanthropy; for we can not do a good to America but we give alms to the world" (WJ, 151). As Norman Graebner has remarked, "Morality among individuals is a rationale for self-sacrifice; among nations it often serves as a cloak for self-aggrandizement."[25]

Of course a truly enlightened policy of self-interest was not universally disparaged; Tocqueville, in fact, thought it one of the most admirable features of the American experiment: "The Americans . . . are fond of explaining almost all the actions of their lives by the principle of interest rightly understood"; "if it does not lead men straight to virtue by the will, it gradually draws them in that direction by their habits."[26] But in America's effort to disavow self-interest by redefining lustful territorialism as beneficent expansionism, Melville most likely saw his country regressing from Tocqueville's standards of enlightened self-interest to what Albert Gallatin denominated a hypocritical justification for outright greed: "The allegation that the subjugation of Mexico would be the means of enlightening the Mexicans, of improving their social state, and of increasing their happiness, is but the

---

24. The latter quotation is from Whitman's column on "Mr. Gallatin's Plan for Settling Our Dispute with Mexico" (2 Dec. 1847). The text of both editorials is from *The Gathering of the Forces by Walt Whitman: Editorials, Essays, Literary and Dramatic Reviews . . . Written by Walt Whitman as Editor of the "Brooklyn Daily Eagle" in 1846 and 1847*, ed. Cleveland Rodgers and John Black, 2 vols. (New York: G. P. Putnam's Sons, 1920), I: 244, 266. For a fine overview of American appeals to "extending the area of freedom" and to "the destined use of the soil," see Albert K. Weinberg, *Manifest Destiny: A Study of Nationalist Expansionism in American History* (Baltimore, Md.: Johns Hopkins Univ. Press, 1935), pp. 72–129, 160–89.

25. Norman Graebner, *Manifest Destiny* (New York: Bobbs-Merrill, 1968), p. xxii. Cf. John William Ward's account, in *Andrew Jackson: Symbol for an Age* (London: Oxford Univ. Press, 1953), p. 141, of the habit of nineteenth-century Americans of perceiving "national selfishness as international good will." For Melville's self-conscious parody of this idea in the statement quoted above from *White-Jacket*, see Gerlach, p. 12.

26. Alexis de Tocqueville, *Democracy in America* (1835–40), trans. Henry Reeve, part II (New York: J. & H. G. Langley, 1840), pp. 130, 131.

shallow attempt to disguise unbounded cupidity and ambition."[27]

By the time he wrote *Mardi*, then, Melville no longer had to look as far away as Polynesia either to find messianic rhetoric justifying political and economic exploitation or to peer with Edwardsian scrutiny at national pretensions to benevolence. In fact, Media challenges the disinterestedness of policies involved in "the destined use of the soil" by remarking that Vivenzan "freemen are engaged in digging down other lands, and adding them to their own, piece-meal. And this, they call extending their dominions agriculturally, and peaceably" (M, 536). Melville similarly exposes the greed behind appeals to "extending the area of freedom" in his portrait of Vivenza's Temple of Freedom, "a lofty structure,... supported by thirty pillars [i.e. states] of palm; four quite green; as if recently added." Perhaps realizing that annexation would not stop with Florida, Texas, Iowa, and Wisconsin (not to mention the territories of Oregon, New Mexico, and California), Melville relates that "beyond these [pillars was] an almost interminable vacancy, as if all the palms in Mardi, were at some future time, to aid in upholding that fabric" (M, 514–515). However benevolent Vivenza's rhetoric, Media knows that she "lusts for empire like any czar" (M, 542), and Melville caricatures the self-serving bellicosity involved in so-called regenerative expansionism by depicting President Polk "holding the spear in one hand, and striking the bargain with the other" (M, 536). The text also exposes the Polk administration's acquisitive interpretation of the Monroe Doctrine: "Vivenza owned no garden [in South America or Cuba]; yet longed and lusted.... 'Mardi's half is ours;' said they. 'Stand back invaders!' Full of vanity; and mirroring themselves in the future; they deemed all reflected there, their own" (M, 539).[28] Justly, then, Media's scroll warns Vivenza against being "too grasping, nearer home" and against conflating potential areas of liberation with her own republican boundaries: "Expand not your area too widely, now. Seek you proselytes? Neighboring nations may be free, without coming under your banner" (M, 529).[29] As Media

---

27. Gallatin, "Peace with Mexico" (1847), in *The Writings of Albert Gallatin*, ed. Henry Adams, 3 vols. (Philadelphia: J. B. Lippincott, 1879), III: 586.

28. Merrell R. Davis, in *Melville's "Mardi": A Chartless Voyage* (New Haven: Yale Univ. Press, 1952), pp. 158–59, 79–99, 157–59, offers an informative overview of *Mardi*'s political concerns. I shall use his discussion as a point of departure in advancing an Edwardsian reading of the tie between Vivenzan politics and Taji's quest after Yillah. For a review of Polk's expansionist interpretation of the Monroe Doctrine, see Frederick Merk, *The Monroe Doctrine and American Expansionism, 1843–1849* (New York: Alfred A Knopf, 1966), esp. pp. 181–82, 208, 232.

29. Here Media expresses views similar to those of James Pollock, Pennsylvania Whig, on the "Annexation of Texas": "[W]hilst I am desirous of extending the enjoy-

elsewhere observes, Vivenza's efforts to achieve its "marvelous destiny" entail a hunger for empire rivaled only by earlier Roman conquest (M, 527). Appropriately, then, Media points out how "the maxims once trampled under foot, are now imprinted on [Vivenza's] front; and he who hated oppressors, is become an oppressor himself" (M, 526).

Of course, nowhere is oppression more evident than in Vivenza's institution of slavery, the territorial extension of which in America highlighted the hypocrisy of the rhetoric about enlarging the area of freedom. "[I]t has been said here and elsewhere," remarked James Pollock, "that the annexation of Texas would extend the 'area of freedom.' It would be a matter of curious inquiry whether this new-born zeal for the extension of 'freedom' has not its origin in a still stronger desire to extend the 'area of slavery?' "[30] In *Mardi*, Melville emphasizes a similar inconsistency between America's democratic rhetoric and her institution of slavery when Media observes that Vivenza's Temple of Freedom is "the handiwork of slaves" (M, 528), with Taji elsewhere comparing the slaves' flayed backs to the Temple's "correspondingly striped" flag (M, 515). Therefore, far from meriting a self-imposed messianic identity, Vivenza sanctions this national sin to guarantee her perpetuity as a union of states: "The first blow struck for [the slaves]," cries Nulli (evoking John C. Calhoun, the nullificationist), "dissolves the union of Vivenza's vales. The Northern Tribes know it" (M, 533). Aptly, then, Media would have Vivenza reassess her pretensions to national regeneracy and also her mandate to redeem *others;* for while the republican Vivenza might fancy herself liberated from the harsh caste systems and severe poverty of Media's Odo (ch. 63), from the sloth and dissipation resulting from hereditary succession to a throne (chs. 73–78), from the imperialist outlook of Kings Uhia and Bello (chs. 91, 145), from the Old World priestcraft and intolerance of pontifical Maramma (chs. 105–110), and from the Malthusian economies of Lords Hello and Piko (chs. 139–140), she is, nonetheless, hardly in a position to cast stones. Other countries may not merit Vivenza's esteem, "yet by abstaining from criminations," says Babbalanja, "Vivenza should ever merit its own" (M, 519).

Mardi's satirical inquiry into American expansionism and slavery finds ample precedent in such literary works as Washington Irving's *A*

---

ment and the blessings of liberty to the farthest limits of our world, and while I believe its extension and triumphs cannot be restrained,... still, I am not for extending the boundaries of our country along with it." (*Congressional Globe*, 28th Cong., 2nd sess., [22 Jan. 1845], Appendix, p. 355.)

30. *Cong. Globe*, 28th Cong., 2nd sess. (22 Jan. 1845), Appendix, p. 356. The best study of the relation between expansionism and slavery is Frederick Merk's *Slavery and the Annexation of Texas* (New York: Alfred A. Knopf, 1972).

History of New York (1809), James Russell Lowell's first series of *The Biglow Papers* (1846–48), Seba Smith's "Downing Letters" (1847–56), and *Yankee Doodle*, the last of which exposed the self-seeking aspect of America's mission of regeneration in the Southwest by describing how funds are gathered "for the benevolent purpose of cutting the throats of the Mexicans" (19 Dec. 1846, p. 123). These Mexicans, says *Yankee Doodle*, "fight like devils—the pertinacity with which they insist upon repelling the benevolent designs of myself and General TAYLOR, to disseminate the inestimable blessings of enlightened liberty among them is indeed surprising" (12 Dec. 1846, p. 111). Also, Melville probably knew that, as early as 1837, William Ellery Channing had described how " 'the generous zeal for freedom,' which has stirred and armed so many of our citizens to fight for Texas" was actually "a passion for unrighteous spoil." Moreover, Channing even anticipated the emancipationist concerns of the Vivenza chapters by asking whether America dared "extend and perpetuate an institution, the grand feature of which is, that it tramples private rights in the dust." Clearly, Melville did not have to look toward the Marquesas to witness the corrupting influence of "civilization"; he had merely to consider the Mexican War and Channing's earlier concern whether the time would ever come "when the neighborhood of a more powerful and civilized people will prove a blessing, instead of a curse, to an inferior community."[31]

Suggestive, too, for Melville's satire is Channing's use of Hopkinsian rhetoric to define the virtuous outlook that might cause America to abandon her imperialist ambitions. In one paragraph, for instance, Channing solicits the sort of "disinterested considerations" that would incline a senator to indulge in the "virtue" of "looking above himself" and thereby to achieve a "generous self-oblivion" when "acting on the vast and permanent interests of a nation." Obviously, Channing here adapts Edwards's and Hopkins's definitions of virtue to his own conception of an ideal foreign policy.[32] But some twelve years

---

31. Channing, "A Letter to the Hon. Henry Clay, on the Annexation of Texas to the United States" (1837), in *The Works of William E. Channing, D.D.* (Boston: American Unitarian Assoc., 1895), pp. 757, 767, 762. Merton M. Sealts, Jr., in *Melville's Reading: A Check-List of Books Owned and Borrowed* (Madison: Univ. of Wisconsin Press, 1966), item 130, shows that Melville's wife owned an 1848 set of Channing's *Works*.

32. Channing, pp. 777–78. Channing's enthusiastic encounter with the doctrine of disinterested benevolence is mentioned in John Greenleaf Whittier's sketch of "Samuel Hopkins" (1847), in *The Writings of John Greenleaf Whittier*, 7 vols. (Cambridge, Mass.: Riverside Press, 1888), VI: 143–44. Channing knew how Hopkins had modified an essentially Edwardsian tenet to achieve his theory of "disinterested benevolence"; for Channing mentions Hopkins's friendship with Edwards (*Works*, p. 428) and attacks the idea that so-

later, Melville seems to have sensed that America's southwestern outlook was no more disinterested than it had been in 1837; messianic
rhetoric aside, North America was still "the spoil of any vagabonds
who may choose to settle therein" (M, 512). That Melville dramatizes
this point in Taji's murder of Aleema and abduction of Yillah we are
now in a position to see; for while *Mardi*'s political satire may seem unrelated to Taji's more personal quest, the two plots correspond insofar
as Yillah typifies man's general aspirations toward happiness, which
are so often associated with recognizably political contexts.[33] Moreover,
insofar as Yillah might "be at last found in Vivenza's vales" (M, 501; cf.
523), we shall again evoke Edwards's ideas about "true virtue"—this
time to show that the Hautia-like sensuality behind Taji's nominally
benevolent abduction of Yillah finds an analog in the rapacious outlook that characterized America's supposedly regenerative policies of
territorialism both before and during the Mexican War of 1846-48.

P ertinent to this analog is the suggestively phallic nature
of Taji's comparison of his search party's canoes to elephants'
trunks and sea-serpents: "But what monsters of canoes!
Would they devour an innocent voyager? their great black
prows curling aloft, and thrown back like the trunks of elephants;
and a dark, snaky length behind, like the sea-serpent's train" (M, 199).
As scholarship shows, Melville would have known that *Yankee Doodle* had popularized the expression "seeing the elephant" as a metaphor for frustrated idealism—and especially in relation to the Mexican War (see Figure A). Moreover, in 1847 Evert Duyckinck thought
of having Melville publish in *Yankee Doodle* a series of sketches on
"the sea serpent," another comic symbol of America's political
designs, including the implications of the Mexican War for the extension of slavery into the Southwest (see Figure B).[34] We shall see that

called unregenerate persons are incapable of either "real virtue" or "disinterested benevolence" (*Works*, p. 393).

33. William Ellery Sedgwick, in *Herman Melville: The Tragedy of Mind* (Cambridge,
Mass.: Harvard Univ. Press, 1944), p. 41, remarks that Yillah becomes "truth in the sense
of a standard of righteousness by which nations and institutions are judged." Cf. Nicholas Canaday, Jr., *Melville and Authority*, Univ. of Florida Monographs in the Humanities, no. 28 (Gainesville: Univ. of Florida Press, 1968), p. 14. My sense of the continuity
of *Mardi*'s "romantic" and political concerns is consistent with scholarship that, on the
basis of the book's imagery, argues a case for *Mardi*'s unity. See J. Michael Sears, "Melville's *Mardi:* One Book or Three?" *Studies in the Novel*, 10 (Winter 1978), 411-19.

34. See Donald Yannella, " 'Seeing the Elephant' in *Mardi*," in *Artful Thunder:
Versions of the Romantic Tradition in American Literature in Honor of Howard P.*

MEXICAN VOLUNTEERS "SEEING THE ELEPHANT."

Figure A. *Yankee Doodle*, 27 February 1847, p. 229. Courtesy of the Newberry Library, Chicago.

these allusions aptly characterize Taji's ultimately self-serving enthusiasm; for however admirable his wish to rescue Yillah from certain harm, his subsequent effort to enslave her both psychologically and physically corresponds to the way territorial lust and the cultivation of slavery in lands freed from the allegedly tyrannical Mexicans rendered hypocritical America's nominally libertarian rhetoric concerning westward expansion.

Taji's behavior, paralleling Vivenzan hypocrisy, is closely related to his effort to claim what Milton R. Stern calls an "ideal origin, with all the transcendent cosmic status attendant thereon,... which rejects

Vincent, ed. Robert J. De Mott and Sanford E. Marovitz (Kent, Ohio: Kent State Univ. Press, 1975), pp. 106–7, 114. Alan Heimert, in *"Moby-Dick* and American Political Symbolism," *American Quarterly*, 15 (Winter 1963), pp. 504–5, discusses the popularity of the serpent metaphor as a political symbol among the Duyckinck circle, remarking that "the 'Serpent' was to have been the subject of Melville's articles for *Yankee Doodle* ... ; but Duyckinck ordered instead a lampoon of Zachary Taylor's dispatches" (p. 505). See, in this respect, Jay Leyda, ed., *The Melville Log: A Documentary Life of Herman Melville, 1819–1891*, 2 vols. (New York: Harcourt, Brace, 1951), I: 250–51; and an anonymous item titled "The Sea Serpent Again," in *The Prompter*, ed. Cornelius Mathews, no. 3 (1 July 1850), 68–69, which explicitly links this monster with such concerns as "the war with Mexico" and "the great Clay Compromise" concerning slavery in the new territories.

Figure B. Eugene Batchelder, *A Romance of the Sea-Serpent* (Cambridge, Mass.: John Barlett, 1849), p. 100.

historical origins, with all [their] dullnesses, deaths, duties and limitations."[35] Of course, the Redeemer Nation did not disclaim history but redefined it idealistically by conflating civil government and nationalist growth with God's scheme of universal fitness: John Winthrop spoke of a "city upon a hill"; the Polk administration proclaimed America's destiny to manifest her democratic ideal throughout North America; and Walt Whitman popularized the idealistic premise of expansionism by remarking, "It is to us a cheering and *grand idea,* that the agricultural and *domestic* West must eventually outtopple in means, extent and political power, all the rest of this Republic—and carry sway in what it listeth. The boundless democratic free West!— We love well to contemplate it."[36] Is not a similar idealism evident both in Taji's westward search for Yillah and his paean about the "West, West, West, West! ... Whitherward mankind and empires— flocks, caravans, armies, navies; worlds, suns, and stars all wend! ... Oh boundless boundary!" (M, 551)? Indeed, whereas *Typee* and *Omoo* show the *idea* of civilization to be a conceptual accessory to self-aggrandizing modes of foreign policy, *Mardi* explores the idealistic and romantic impulses behind western territorial imperatives.

35. Stern, p. 112.

36. Whitman, "Where the Great Stretch of Power Must Be Wielded" (2 April 1847), in *Gathering of the Forces*, I: 25; emphasis added to the first and second of the italicized words. For the idealistic impulse behind nineteenth-century American expansionism and democracy, see Graebner, pp. xviii, xxxi; Ephraim Douglass Adams, *The Power of Ideals in American History* (New Haven: Yale Univ. Press, 1913), pp. 65–67, 81.

Note, for instance, how Taji abandons the *Arcturion* because he loathes boredom and monotony (M, 4), the very title of chapter 2 ("A Calm") standing in vivid contrast to his earlier fascination with Pitcairn's Island, the Enchanted Islands, Spanish buccaneers (M, 3), and the Alhambra of the West: "In the distance what visions were spread! The entire western horizon high piled with gold and crimson clouds; airy arches, domes, and minarets; as if the yellow, Moorish sun were setting behind some vast Alhambra. Vistas seemed leading to worlds beyond" (M, 7–8). Here and elsewhere *Mardi* hints at the romance of ideas inherent in all visions of empire. And as we shall see, the "romance" (M, xvii) convention of *Mardi* is more than suited to a book having concerns such as those entailed in Vivenza's somewhat chivalric outlook on expansionism.

In this respect, Taji's identity as a sun god travelling west merits extended comment; for to the degree that he conflates the area of the sunset with the general course of "mankind and empires" (M, 551), there is major significance in the way he later compares his westward travels through Mardi with the progress of the sun through the zodiac: "And, as the sun, by influence divine, wheels through the Ecliptic; threading Cancer, Leo, Pisces, and Aquarius; so, by some mystic impulse am I moved, to this fleet progress, through the groups in white-reefed Mardi's zone" (M, 556). However romantic or fanciful, Taji's analogy corresponds both to Bishop Berkeley's theory of a destined western succession of world states and to William Gilpin's related ideas about the function of the zodiac in expansionist thought. As for the first, Henry Nash Smith remarks how, in advancing the concept "Westward the course of empire takes its way," Berkeley implied that "the empire of Greece had given way to that of Rome, Rome had yielded preeminence to northern Europe, the empires of France and Spain had waned as Britain had waxed in power. Was America fated to be the next inheritor of universal sway?"[37] Taji's travels may conform to this pattern insofar as he and his friends proceed westward through many waning political states before arriving in Vivenza. Further, Taji's comparison of Mardi's zones to the divisions of the zodiac finds an expansionist analog in the thinking of William Gilpin, who synthesized Berkeleyan and Humboldtian thought in suggesting the existence of an isothermal zodiac that dictated the westward progress of mankind and, in the nineteenth century, specifically toward the Pacific coast of America:

It is within this belt ... that the majority of the human race is

---

37. Henry Nash Smith, *Virgin Land: The American West as Symbol and Myth* (Cambridge, Mass.: Harvard Univ. Press, 1950), p. 8.

assembled, and that the civilized nations ... have succeeded one
another, commencing at the further extremity of Asia, and forming a zodiac towards the setting sun. This succession has flowed
onward with an uneven course, until in our time the ring is
about to close round the earth's circumference by the arrival of
the American nation on the coast of the Pacific, which looks over
on to Asia. ... It is in this channel that the affairs of mankind are
sweeping onward in their legitimate forward career.

Not surprisingly, Gilpin lauds pioneers and explorers who seek to
fulfill this mandate by striving "unceasingly to overtake the distant
horizon, which as unceasingly eludes [them] by an eternal flight,"[38] a
remark that may invite a second glance at Taji's statement, "[W]as not
the sun a fellow-voyager? were we not both wending westward? But
how soon he daily overtook and passed us; hurrying to his journey's
end" (M, 38). Unlike Gilpin, however, Melville questions the integrity
of the westward quest. In the same chapter in which Taji compares his
journey to the sun's wending westward through the zodiac, he also
says that "this new world here sought ... is the world of mind; wherein
the wanderer may gaze round, with more of wonder than Balboa's band
roving through the golden Aztec glades." And then comes the suggestion that all such idealistic visions of empire are, like the zodiac itself,
grounded in psychological projection: "[F]iery yearnings their own
phantom-future make, and deem it present" (M, 557). As we have already seen, this is specifically true of the Vivenzans, who, "full of vanity; and mirroring themselves in the future[,] deemed all reflected [in
South America] their own" (M, 539).

   Mardi, then, defines as narcissistic the idealistic and romantic
mandates with which America justified her westward course of empire.

---

38. William Gilpin, in *Senate Documents* (ser. 474), 29th Cong., 1st sess., no. 306
(20 April 1846): Report of the Committee on the Post Office and Post Roads, pp. 29–30,
40. Gilpin's essay was written at the invitation of the Congress, which solicited his
thoughts on all possible "information ... in relation to our trade in the Pacific and
Oregon" (p. 19). As I show below (chapter IV) in my discussion of this document's
importance for *Moby-Dick*, Gilpin's aims are entirely expansionist. For Gilpin's synthesis of notions derived from Bishop Berkeley and Alexander von Humboldt, and for
his application of such ideas to America's westward course of empire, see Smith, pp.
35–43; and Thomas L. Karnes, *William Gilpin, Western Nationalist* (Austin: Univ. of
Texas Press, 1970). My aim in applying Gilpin's thought to our discussion of *Mardi* is
to add a specifically political dimension to what scholars have more generally sensed to
be the importance of the zodiac as a device that helps to structure the progress of Taji's
voyage. See, for example, William B. Dillingham, *An Artist in the Rigging: The Early
Works of Herman Melville* (Athens: Univ. of Georgia Press, 1972), pp. 113–15; Maxine
Moore, *That Lonely Game: Melville, "Mardi," and the Almanac* (Columbia: Univ. of
Missouri Press, 1975), pp. 38, 115–19.

Since, moreover, Taji concludes his thoughts about the zodiac with the confession that "I've chartless voyaged" (M, 556), the text may hint at the breach of constitutional powers to which such self-serving idealism can lead. In fact, since Taji likens the tattoos of Aleema's sons to "two broad cross-stripes ... [of] a foot soldier's harness" (M, 130), we might well compare Media's thoughts about Polk's invasion of Mexico ("You yourselves were precipitated upon a neighboring nation, ere you knew your spears were in your hands" [M, 528]) with Taji's overzealous response to Aleema's defensive thrusts: "Ere I knew it, my cutlass made a quick lunge. A curse from the priest's mouth; red blood from his side" (M, 133).[39] And if in its tendency to redefine selfishness as humanitarianism, Vivenzan politics negates the possibility of disinterested benevolence, then in the uncertainty about his motives in killing Aleema, Taji makes explicit the true nature of his seemingly virtuous resolve: "I asked myself whether the death-deed I had done was sprung of a *virtuous motive,* the rescuing a captive from thrall; or whether beneath that pretense, I had engaged in this fatal affray for some other, and *selfish purpose*" (M, 135; emphasis added). Melville even has Taji emphasize the Edwardsian context of his "evil deed" (M, 423) in murdering Aleema: "Sifted out, my motives to this enterprise justified not the mad deed, which in a moment of rage, I had done: though, those motives had been *covered with a gracious pretense; concealing myself from myself*" (M, 140; emphasis added). Yet the point to be addressed

---

39. Here I concur with Joyce Sparer Adler, who, in *War in Melville's Imagination* (New York: New York Univ. Press, 1981), p. 21, remarks that "Taji's murder of the Polynesian priest is not part of a personal story but a symbol of the wars of white civilized man." Moreover, what I take to be the Mexican War significance of this encounter possibly gains support from the way Taji elsewhere uses expansionist rhetoric in speaking of the newly discovered planet of Neptune: "[I]ncrease of dominion seems increase of power; and day by day new planets are being added to elder-born Saturns" (M, 229–30). In fact, insofar as Melville may have "charted the voyage through *Mardi* to coincide with the mathematical quest for the new world Neptune" (Moore, p. 9; cf. Davis, pp. 68–69), we would do well to recall that in 1847 *Yankee Doodle* actually satirized the Mexican exploits of Zachary Taylor with a full-page cartoon and two articles equating the renown and political prospects of Old Zack with Leverrier's new planet. (See Figure C, and *Yankee Doodle,* 24 April 1847, p. 24; 8 May 1847, p. 47.) Melville was probably familiar with the latter issue of *Yankee Doodle,* since it also spoke satirically of "Omboog, or three months residence in the Moon ... [by] ... HERMAN MELVILLE" (p. 44). Worth recalling, too, in this comparison of Taji and Taylor is the fact that a widely circulated pamphlet, quoted at length in the *Congressional Globe* (30 Cong., 1st sess. [16 Feb. 1848], p. 366), had compared Taylor's Mexican exploits to those of the "hired assassin" Dick Crowningshield. See Henry C. Wright, *Dick Crowningshield, the Assassin, and Zachary Taylor, the Soldier: The Difference Between Them* (Hopedale, Mass.: Non-resistant and Practical Christian Office, 1848).

DISCOVERY OF A NEW PLANET AT THE WASHINGTON OBSERVATORY

PROFESSOR POLK.   BENTON, MY BOY, IT'S VERY ASTONISHING THAT A STAR OF SUCH BRILLIANCE AND MAGNITUDE SHOULD HAVE BEEN OVERLOOKED BY ALL THE ASTRONOMERS.   WE'LL CALL IT TAYLOR, IN HONOR OF MONTEREY AND BUENA VISTA.

Figure C. *Yankee Doodle*, 24 April 1847, p. 25. Courtesy of the Newberry Library, Chicago.

is that the specifically sexual impulses which inspire Taji's self-deception correspond to America's lust for empire.

The American idea of conquering a "virgin land" assists this comparison of Taji's pursuit of a maiden and Vivenza's territorial imperative. Taji himself compares Yillah's beauty to "a crystal lake in a fathomless wood" (M, 152), and he later uses the metaphor of an "arbor" (M, 189) to characterize his seclusive ecstasy with Yillah.[40] Moreover, from *The Confidence-Man* we know that Melville understood how "step by step [the pioneers] had been lured to their lonely resting-place by the ever-beckoning seductions of a fertile and virgin land" (CM, 128). The point is that Americans had always regarded the wilderness "as essentially feminine—that is, not simply the land as mother, but the land as woman, the total female principle of gratification—enclosing the individual in an environment of receptivity, repose, and painless and integral satisfaction."[41] That the American West served as an arena for the expression of sublimated desires is evident as well from the way "sleeping on the ground, chasing wild game, making love to Indian maidens, and reading Homer's Iliad" were celebrated activities of pioneers otherwise praised for their "love of liberty" and their concern about the "political regeneration" of neighboring peoples.[42] Appropriately, therefore, chapter 91 of *Mardi* illustrates the sometimes interchangeable nature of sexual and territorial impulses in its description of how King Uhia, believing "himself foreordained to the dominion of the entire Archipelago" (M, 276), sets about "to the accomplishment of the [manifest] destiny believed to be his." He does so as a way of preserving and enhancing his masculinity: "Springing from syren embrace—'They shall sap and mine me no more,' he cried; 'my destiny commands me. I will don my manhood. By Keevi! no more will I clasp a waist'" (M, 275). Still, everywhere evident is the way Uhia transfers his clasp from women to territory, and in a manner which might bring to mind the European charge that "the government of the United States have passed their arm down the waist of the

---

40. With a different but related emphasis, Adler (p. 18) remarks that Taji regards Yillah as "his 'arbor,' his retreat from reality and conscience."

41. Annette Kolodny, *The Lay of the Land: Metaphor as Experience and History in American Life and Letters* (Chapel Hill: Univ. of North Carolina Press, 1975), p. 4. As Slotkin (p. 29) shows, the idea is indebted to myths in which "the hero-king achieves sexual union with the goddess of nature in the wilderness, thus ensuring the seasonal renewal of human and vegetable life. Underlying the myth and its attendant rituals is the psychological quest of the *anima*, the feminine principle of passivity, passion, and acceptance within the reasoning, cold, masculine consciousness." Cf. Slotkin, pp. 208–9, 218, 227, 306.

42. Charles Edwards Lester, *Sam Houston and His Republic* (New York: Burgess, Stringer, 1846), pp. 13, 105. Worth quoting is a passage in which Lester makes explicit the tie between pioneering and sexual impulses:

It was the moulding period of life, when the heart, just charmed into the fevered hopes and dreams of youth, looks wistfully around on all things for light and beauty—"when every idea of gratification fires the blood and flashes on the fancy—when the heart is vacant to every fresh form of delight, and has no rival engagements to withdraw it from the importunities of a new desire." (pp. 12–13)

continent, and, now that they have got it there, they will not hesitate to pass it round.''[43]

However, most nineteenth-century expansionists disowned their Hautia-like impulses; like Taji, they instead fancied themselves the disinterested saviors of maidens in distress. For example, in a 1 December 1845 editorial for the New York *Morning News*, John L. O'Sullivan, who had earlier coined the term "manifest destiny," spoke of continentalism in conspicuously chivalric terms. Evoking America's "philanthropic" extension of democracy into North American territories threatened by Great Britain, he compares his country's expansionist motives to those of a man who should observe "some unprotected female exposed to the insults of the libertine. . . . [H]umanity or gallantry would impel him to interfere. . . . He would interfere with good motives and for a good, and so would our country, in discharging what we maintain to be its duty." In *Mardi*, however, Media more frankly charges that Vivenza "*lusts* for empire like any czar" (M, 542; emphasis added), an assertion that finds ironic corroboration in nineteenth-century debates about America's rights to Texas on the grounds that all territory west of the Sabine River belonged to the United States by virtue of the Louisiana Purchase of 1803.[44] Sam Houston's exploits in Texas had already been compared to "the story of Romulus, who . . . planted the foundation of a mighty empire"; yet the New York *Morning Herald*, a paper to which Melville may have subscribed, drew more tellingly upon Romulus's rape and seizure of the Sabine women (in peopling his Palatine settlement) to celebrate America's "gorgeous prospect" of annexing all of Mexico: "It were more desirable that she should come to us voluntarily; but as we shall have no peace until she be annexed, let it come, even though force be necessary, at first, to bring her. Like the Sabine virgins, she will soon learn to love her ravisher."[45] Quite justly, then, the *American Whig Review* referred to the "Executive Usurpation" entailed in Polk's designs upon Mexico as a form of rape: "Our hand is on her neck; our knee is on her prostrate bosom"; "his real designs from the beginning towards that country were those of the Oppressor and the Spoiler. He has dragged the coun-

---

43. From the *Dublin Freeman*, reprinted by the Washington *Union* (25 Aug. 1845), quoted by Frederick Merk, *Manifest Destiny and Mission in American History: A Reinterpretation* (New York: Alfred A. Knopf, 1963), p. 83.

44. See Merk, *Monroe Doctrine*, pp. 135–36.

45. For the comparison of Houston to Romulus, see Lester, p. 13. The newspaper quotation is from the New York *Morning Herald* (8 Oct. 1847). Melville mentions the "New York Herald" in *White-Jacket* (p. 244), and the "morning . . . Herald" in *Redburn* (p. 306). Sealts (p. 25) says that, "as reported by Mrs. Metcalf, [Melville] subscribed to the New York *Herald* because it contained the best shipping news."

try after him in a bold career of rapacity and conquest."[46]

Which—if any—of these items Melville read is not as important as the fact that such statements were common in the contemporary press. Moreover, Melville had already dramatized the connection between rape and imperialism in *Typee*,[47] and would do so again in a section of *Clarel* where Ungar describes American expansionism as a form of rapine—the only available outlet for an Anglo-Saxon community unable to win the love of other peoples:

> The Anglo-Saxons—lacking grace
> To win the love of any race;
> Hated by myriads dispossessed
> Of rights—the Indians East and West.
> These pirates of the sphere! grave looters—
> Grave, canting, Mammonite freebooters,
> Who in the name of Christ and Trade
> (Oh, bucklered forehead of the brass!)
> Deflower the world's last sylvan glade! (IV. ix. 118–26)

And to some degree, I would suggest, this indictment extends to the motives that inspire Taji's pursuit of Yillah. For whatever Taji's good will in wishing to help a maiden in distress, and whatever his efforts to disown passionate interest in her, his subconscious motives resemble the same feelings aroused by "the night-blowing Cereus" (M, 640) of Hautia. We need only be alert to the pun involved in Taji's confessing that "such was the scene; so still and witching that the hand of Yillah in mine seemed no hand, but a touch. Visions flitted before me and in me; something hummed in my ear; all the air was *a lay*" (M, 144; emphasis added).[48] Moreover, like expansionists who flaunted rhetoric about extending the area of freedom, but who then sought to

---

46. "Executive Usurpation," *American Whig Review*, 5 (March 1847), 229; "The President and His Administration," *American Whig Review*, 7 (May 1848), 452.

47. Adler (p. 11) is probably right in suggesting that "what the composite canvas of *Typee* and *Omoo* depicts is the rape of Polynesia—its conquest and occupation by brute Force."

48. *The Oxford English Dictionary* (1933; rpt. Oxford: Clarendon Press, 1961), I: 940, shows the words "blowen" and "blowing" to have been used pejoratively in the nineteenth century as references to prostitution. The *OED* (VI: 129) also shows sexual connotations of "lay" to have existed as early as Shakespeare's *Henry VIII* (I,iii.40). In Melville's time, the pun is conspicuous in the choice of words used by Poe's narrator to describe the incestuous lineage of Roderick Usher's family: "[T]he entire family lay in the direct line of descent, and had always ... so lain" (*Collected Works of Edgar Allan Poe: Tales and Sketches, 1831–42*, ed. Thomas Ollive Mabbott [Cambridge, Mass.: Harvard Univ. Press, 1978], p. 399).

introduce slavery into the American Southwest, Taji subjects Yillah, whom he has recently liberated, to a form of bondage reminiscent of ideas surrounding proslavery *stewardship*: "I contemplated the extinguishment in her heart of her own spirituality. For as such thoughts were chased away, she clung the more closely to me, as unto one without whom she would be desolate indeed." That Taji thereby finds the means to satiate his sexual appetite is evident from his somewhat romanticized remark that "we lived and we loved; life and love were united" (M, 159). As Channing had already warned, the true motive which inspired many cries about extending the area of freedom was the dissemination of slavery, an institution where "one human being is placed powerless and defenceless in the hands of another,... to live as his tool, the instrument of his pleasure."[49]

Taji, however, persists in evading the complexity of his motives: "Again that phantom obtruded; again guilt laid his red hand on my soul. But I laughed. Was not Yillah my own? by my arm rescued from ill? To do her a good, I had periled myself. So down, down, Aleema" (M, 145). Of course, to some extent Taji justly lauds himself for rescuing this woman from sure death—just as Vivenza's messianic impulse potentially stands to benefit humanity. But Melville's treatment of both Taji and Vivenza dramatizes the self-deceit and hypocrisy into which mere mortals lead themselves when seeking to embody ideality. As Plinlimmon later says,

> For, hitherto, being authoritatively taught by his dogmatical teachers that he must, while on earth, aim at heaven, and attain it too, in all his earthly acts, on pain of eternal wrath; and finding by experience that this is utterly impossible; in his despair, [a person] is too apt to run clean away into all manner of moral abandonment, self-deceit, and hypocrisy (cloaked, however, mostly under an aspect of the most respectable devotion). ... (P, 215)

---

49. Channing, "A Letter ... on the Annexation of Texas," in *Works*, p. 766. The proslavery significance that I attribute to Taji's efforts to smother Yillah's spirituality is consistent with Melville's exploration, in chapter 162 of *Mardi*, of ideas surrounding southern "stewardship." There Nulli (Calhoun) asks, "are they [i.e. the slaves] not fed, clothed, and cared for? Thy [northern] serfs pine for food: never yet did these; who have no thoughts, no cares" (M, 533). But a slave whom Babbalanja questions hints at the tie between a dignified sense of selfhood and man's inner spirituality: "Under the lash, I believe my masters, and account myself a brute; but in my dreams, bethink myself an angel" (M, 532). In *Moby-Dick*, as we shall see, Melville explores much the same issue in relation to Pip. That Melville was aware of the tie between slavery and sexual exploitation has been shown by Carolyn L. Karcher, in *Shadow Over the Promised*

Whereas, then, Taji seeks to acquit himself of criminality by defining passionate motives as disinterested virtue, Melville has Aleema's avenging sons and Hautia's alluring heralds appear more or less alternately— the first seeking to avenge their father's murder, the latter extending sensual invitations to Taji, reminders of the motives that initially led him to kill Aleema as a way of securing the favors of Yillah.[50] But by refusing to acknowledge Hautia, Taji fails to confront the true nature of his virtue: "Tell your Hautia, that I know her not; nor care to know. I defy her incantations; she lures in vain. Yillah! Yillah! still I hope!" (M, 423; cf. 268, 310, 313). Hautia, however, knows that "through me, perhaps, thy Yillah may be found" (M, 640)—suggesting that in Taji's mind and heart the two women are more intimately related than he will admit. And partly for this reason, Taji finally dreams of finding some sort of Ligeian synthesis of Yillah's virgin spirit and Hautia's inviting passion: "One, openly beckoned me here, the other dimly allured me there. Yet now was I wildly dreaming to find them together" (M, 643). Taji seems not to understand the significance of this conflation. Yet in rescuing and then seducing Yillah he has all along championed Hautia-like impulses which have led him to misconstrue self-gratification as virtue. Similarly, Melville exposes the true nature of American virtue by showing Vivenza's rhetoric of regenerative expansionism to be inspired by self-serving outlooks which are more hypocritical than redemptive. And by thus illustrating the harmony between *Mardi*'s early and later concerns, the historically definable context of "true virtue" casts light, as well, upon *Mardi*'s structural unity, sometimes regarded as evasive and fragmented.

Still, the degree to which debates concerning human nature figure so significantly in *Mardi* mandates a brief review of some of the theological assumptions that helped to shape Melville's attitudes about humanity and, by implication, several concerns of both his early and later fiction.

Land: Slavery, Race, and Violence in Melville's America (Baton Rouge: Louisiana State Univ. Press, 1980), pp. 134, 243–52.

50. The sequential appearance of the avengers and the heralds is evident on pp. 308–9, 364, 423, 450, 568, 638. James E. Miller, Jr., in "The Many Masks of *Mardi*," *Journal of English and Germanic Philology*, 58 (July 1959), 411–13, anticipates elements of the psychological significance that I assign to this repetitive pattern.

I t is well known that Melville's mother espoused Calvinistic beliefs, but that both his father's side of the family and his wife were Arminian and Unitarian. More recent discoveries reveal that two years after their marriage in 1847, Herman and Elizabeth paid a pew rental fee in Dr. Henry Whitney Bellows's New York congregation of the Church of the Divine Unity (later, All Souls). Also, after moving to Pittsfield in 1850, they had three of their children baptized by Dr. Orville Dewey, a retired Unitarian minister. The Melvilles returned to New York in 1863 and in 1865 renewed their tie to All Souls, where they rented pews on and off until Herman's death in 1891—and then Elizabeth rented one herself until 1906.[51] However, from Hawthorne's remark in 1856 that Melville "can neither believe, nor be comfortable in his unbelief," and from Frances Melville Thomas's statement that she could remember her father attending church only twice, we may assume that Elizabeth constituted the real tie to Bellows's congregation (especially with regard to Bellows's interest in her marital problems) and that Herman's affiliation was largely nominal.[52] But however perfunctory the nature of Melville's membership at All Souls, one scholar seems to err in arguing that Melville became altogether skeptical about Unitarianism after his father's bankruptcy and death in 1832.[53] In fact, probably between 1846 and 1850 Melville espoused liberal Christian ideas about human regeneracy that, as we

---

51. For the religious background of Melville's family, see William H. Gilman, *Melville's Early Life and "Redburn"* (New York: New York Univ. Press, 1951), pp. 21–23, 38; and Newton Arvin, *Herman Melville* (New York: Sloane, 1950), pp. 30–35. *The Dictionary of American Biography*, ed. Dumas Malone (New York: Charles Scribner's Sons, 1943), notes that Lemuel Shaw, Melville's father-in-law, "attended Unitarian services, though he was never a communicant." That he raised his daughter as a Unitarian is suggested by his 1848 gift to her of Channing's *Works* (Sealts, item 130). My summary of Melville's affiliation with All Souls is based upon Walter D. Kring and Jonathan S. Carey, "Two Discoveries Concerning Herman Melville," *Proceedings of the Massachusetts Historical Society*, 87 (1975), 137–41; and Kring, *Henry Whitney Bellows* (Boston: Skinner House, 1979), pp. 96–97, 274–75, 480–81.

52. Hawthorne's remark is from *The English Notebooks by Nathaniel Hawthorne*, ed. Randall Stewart (London: Oxford Univ. Press, 1941), p. 433. For Frances Melville Thomas's recollection of her father's infrequent church attendance, see Baird's *Ishmael*, p. 78, n. 40. Moreover, as Walter D. Kring has more recently suggested, a letter from Elizabeth Shaw Melville to the church treasurer may indicate that the formal tie to All Souls was hers alone. See Kring's "Introduction," and his reproduction of this letter in *The Endless, Winding Way in Melville: New Charts by Kring and Carey*, Donald Yannella and Hershel Parker, eds. (Glassboro, N.J.: Melville Society, 1981), pp. 4, 49–51. For Bellows's attention to Elizabeth's problems, see Kring and Carey, pp. 139–41.

53. T. Walter Herbert, Jr., *"Moby-Dick" and Calvinism: A World Dismantled* (New Brunswick, N.J.: Rutgers Univ. Press, 1977), pp. 45–56.

have already seen above, suggest several possibilities for the interplay of politics and theology in his fiction.

Melville's adult allegiance to at least some liberal Christian ideas is evident from two unattributed quotations that he transcribed on the inside covers of a *New Testament and Psalms* given him in 1846:

"In Life he appears as a true
Philosopher—as a wise man in the highest
sense. He stands <u>firm to his point;</u> he
<u>goes on his way inflexibly;</u> and while he
exalts the lower to himself, while he makes
the ignorant, the poor, the sick, partakers of
his wisdom, of his riches, of his strength, he, on
the other hand, in no wise conceals his divine
origin; he dares to equal himself with God;
nay, to declare that he himself is God.
In this manner is he wont from
youth upwards <u>to astound his familiar</u>
<u>friends;</u> of these he gains a part to his
own cause; irritates the rest against
him; and shows to all men, who are
aiming at a certain elevation in doctrine
and life, <u>what they have to look for from</u>
<u>the world.</u>
And thus, for the nobler portion
of mankind, his walk and conversation are
even more instructive and profitable than
his death; for to those trials every one is
called, to this trial but a few."

"If we can conceive it possible, that the
creator of the world himself assumed the form
of his creature, and lived in that manner for
a time upon earth, this creature must seem
to us of infinite perfection, because sus-
ceptible of such a combination with his maker.
Hence, in our idea of man there can be
no inconsistency with our idea of God: and
if we often feel a certain disagreement with
Him & remoteness from Him, it is but the
more on that account our duty, not like
advocates of the wicked Spirit, to keep our
eyes continually on the nakedness and
wickedness of our nature; but rather
to seek out every property & beauty, by

"In Life he appears as a true Philosopher — as a wise man in the highest sense. He stands firm to his point; he goes on his way inflexibly; and while he exalts the lower to himself, while he makes the ignorant, the poor, the rich, partakers of his wisdom, of his riches, of his strength, he, on the other hand, in no wise conceals his divine origin; he dares to equal himself with God; nay, to declare that he himself is God.

In this manner is he wont from youth upwards to astonid his familiar friends; of these he gains a part to his own cause; irritates the rest against him; and shows to all men, who are aiming at a certain elevation in doctrine and life, what they have to look for from the world.

And thus, for the nobler portion of mankind, his walk and conversation are even more instructive and profitable than his death; for to those trials every one is called, to this trial but a few. "

Inscription on the inside front cover of Melville's *New Testament and Psalms*. By permission of the Houghton Library, Harvard University.

which our pretension to a similarity with
the Divinity may be made good.''

Melville probably would not have transcribed such passages in his own Bible unless he felt some loyalty to these possibly Unitarian and

> " If we can conceive it possible, that the creator of the world himself assumed the form of his creature, and lived in that manner for a time upon earth, this creature must seem to us of infinite perfection, because susceptible of such a combination with his maker. Hence, in our idea of ~~God~~ man there can be no inconsistency with our idea of God: and if we often feel a certain disagreement with Him & remoteness from Him, it is but the more on that account our duty, not like a disciple of the wicked Spirit, to keep our eyes continually on the nakedness and wickedness of our nature; but rather to seek out every property & beauty, by which our pretension to a similarity with the Divinity may be made good. "

Inscription on the inside back cover of Melville's *New Testament and Psalms*. By permission of the Houghton Library, Harvard University.

Transcendental views on the imitableness of Christ's character and the innate goodness of man.[54] Obvious, moreover, are the implications of such liberal Christian ideas for Melville's fiction. The protest against messianic nationalism in *Typee* and *Omoo* is predicated, in part, upon a regenerate view of human nature, as is Media's insistence that

---

54. Cf. Channing's "The Imitableness of Christ's Character," in *Works*, pp. 310–16. The Bible is housed in the Houghton Library of Harvard University. See Sealts, item 65. This Bible contains one other major inscription of Melville's, which I discuss in "The Translation of Pierre Bayle's *An Historical and Critical Dictionary* Owned by Melville," *Papers of the Bibliographical Society of America*, 71 (1977), 347–51.

one of Nulli's (Calhoun's) slaves "has Oro in his eye. . . . I swear he is
a man" (M, 532). Thus, whatever difficulties the "Unitarian tragedy"
of Allan Melvill may have posed for his son's belief in a benevolent
God—and *Pierre*'s and *The Confidence-Man*'s satires of liberalism
notwithstanding—Melville seems early to have cultivated Unitarian
sentiments because a noble outlook on human nature coincided with
the emancipationist effort to combat what Melville later called "an
Anglo-American empire based upon the systematic degradation of
man."[55] Indeed, with rhetoric approaching that of the second inscription quoted above, William Ellery Channing celebrated emancipation
in the British West Indies by reminding Americans that the "infinite
worth [of] every human being" was not unrelated to Christ's "uniting
himself most intimately with our nature, manifesting himself in a human form, for the very end of making us partakers of his own perfection." Moreover, as James Freeman Clarke (the Unitarian minister who
gave Elizabeth communion on the morning of her marriage to Herman) put it, slavery was unchristian and inhumane "because it degrades
man, the image of God, into a thing." Not unexpectedly, therefore,
Melville drew upon this Unitarian precept in his 1849 denunciation of
Francis Parkman's ethnic condescension: "We are all of us—Anglo-
Saxons, Dyaks, and Indians—sprung from one head, and made in one
image. . . . And wherever we recognize the image of God, let us reverence it, though it hung from the gallows."[56]

Still, the seeds of Melville's discontent with excessive liberal optimism (such as that depicted in the Serenia chapters of *Mardi*) are evident from a trance in which Babbalanja experiences "strange sounds
. . . of gladness that seemed mixed with sadness:—a low, sweet harmony
of both" (M, 633). A spirit explains that this harmony somehow reflects
a tragic world view, in which man's essential nature is "sad, even in un-
development" (M, 636). That this sadness has at least some orthodox
ramifications seems obvious from the response Babbalanja receives

---

55. "Supplement" to *The "Battle-Pieces" of Herman Melville*, ed. Hennig Cohen
(New York: Thomas Yoseloff, 1963), p. 197. My allusion to Allan Melvill's "Unitarian
tragedy" is to Herbert, *"Moby-Dick" and Calvinism*, pp. 45–56.

56. Channing, "An Address Delivered . . . on . . . the Anniversary of Emancipation
in the British West Indies" (1842), in *Works*, p. 919; James Freeman Clarke, *A Protest
Against American Slavery, by One Hundred and Seventy-Three Unitarian Ministers*
(Boston: B. H. Greene, 1845), p. 9. On Clarke's administering communion to Elizabeth,
see Leon Howard, *Herman Melville: A Biography* (Berkeley: Univ. of California Press,
1951), p. 107. For a discussion of Unitarian support for the emancipation of slaves in
America, see Daniel Walker Howe, *The Unitarian Conscience: Harvard Moral Philosophy, 1805–1861* (Cambridge, Mass.: Harvard Univ. Press, 1970), pp. 270–305. Melville's response to Parkman is from "Mr. Parkman's Tour," *The Literary World*, 4 (31
March 1849), 29.

after asking the spirit whether the murmurings of these souls have anything to do with sin; for the spirit's answer not only challenges unthinking optimism in human nature but does so in a way consistent
with *Mardi*'s critique of both individuals and institutions seeking to embody ideal moral standards: "But as perfect wisdom can be only Oro's;
so, perfect holiness is his alone. And whoso is otherwise than perfect in
his holiness, is liable to sin" (M, 634). Moreover, by predicating God's
love for mankind upon a profound awareness of sadness, the omni-
scient spirit foreshadows what we shall explore in another chapter as
the christological drama of *The Confidence-Man:* "Great Love is sad;
and heaven is Love" (M, 636). Aptly, then, Babbalanja's penultimate
vision of the Divinity is inseparable from a tragic view of existence:
"The air was filled with fire;—deep in which, full of showers of silvery
globes, tears magnified—braiding the flame with rainbows" (M, 636).
Thus, while the Serenian chapters of *Mardi* reflect the sort of liberal defense of human nature characteristic of the inscriptions in Melville's
Bible, Babbalanja's vision at least hints at Melville's early presentiment
of that "Calvinistic sense of Innate Depravity and Original Sin, from
whose visitations, in some shape or other, no deeply thinking mind is
always and wholly free."[57] As we have seen in the correspondence between Taji's and Vivenza's criminality, and as we shall again observe
in the political implications of the way Redburn betrays Harry Bolton,
the relation in Melville's fiction between personal and national modes
of turpitude conforms to Hawthorne's belief that "the heart, the heart
...was the little yet boundless sphere wherein existed the original
wrong of which the crime and misery of this outward world were
merely types."[58]

---

57. Melville, "Hawthorne and His Mosses," *The Literary World*, 7 (17 Aug. 1850),
126. Both Dillingham (pp. 120–22) and Herbert (*"Moby-Dick" and Calvinism*, p. 79)
show Serenia to represent an inadequate outlook for Melville.

58. Hawthorne, "Earth's Holocaust," in *The Complete Works of Nathaniel Hawthorne*, ed. George P. Lathrop, 12 vols. (Boston: Riverside Press, 1883), II: 455.

C H A P T E R II

Democratic "Individualism" and the Redeemer Nation:
Redburn

"For the Melvilleian narrator," Edgar A. Dryden has observed, "memory is an imaginative act which makes the present a moment of creative understanding of a past adventure that was experienced initially as an unintelligible and frightening chaos of sensations." Precisely this phenomenon generates *Redburn's* critique of what Cushing Strout has called the "American image of the Old World." The romantic phase of the American view of Europe is expressed in Longfellow's remark, in *Outre-Mer* (1833–34), that "to my youthful imagination the Old World was a kind of Holy Land." With less religious but equally romantic rhetoric, Washington Irving proclaimed, "Europe held forth the charms of storied and poetical association.... My native country was full of youthful promise: Europe was rich in the accumulated treasures of age."[1] Of course, this romanticized view found its opposite in Andrew Jackson's contempt for European ceremony, as well as in the combined Jacksonian and Jeffersonian view of Europe as the world's moral gutter. According to one devoted Jacksonian, America had rescued the "vestal fire of liberty ... from the sickening depravity of the Stuarts, to be rekindled amid the primeval forests."[2]

1. Edgar A. Dryden, *Melville's Thematics of Form: The Great Art of Telling the Truth* (Baltimore, Md.: Johns Hopkins Univ. Press, 1968), p. 35; Longfellow, *The Complete Writings of Henry Wadsworth Longfellow*, 11 vols. (Boston and New York: Houghton Mifflin, 1904), I: 18–19; Washington Irving, *The Sketch-Book of Geoffrey Crayon, Gent.* (1819–20), in *Irving's Works*, 28 vols. (New York: G. P. Putnam and Son, 1868–69), II: 14–15. For a review of outlooks such as these, see Cushing Strout, *The American Image of the Old World* (New York: Harper and Row, 1963), pp. 74–85.

2. Henry D. Gilpin, *A Speech Delivered at the Union and Harmony Celebration ... Of the Twenty-First Anniversary of the Victory at New Orleans* (Philadelphia, 1836), pp. 6–7; quoted by John William Ward, *Andrew Jackson: Symbol for an Age* (London: Oxford Univ. Press, 1953), pp. 142–43. For earlier Jeffersonian views of this sort, see Strout, p. 28.

Indebted to still older New England traditions of seeing in England an oppressor of God's chosen people, this sentiment finds exaggerated expression in a remark by White-Jacket: "Escaped from the house of bondage, Israel of old did not follow after the ways of the Egyptians. To her was given an express dispensation; to her were given new things under the sun. And we Americans are the peculiar, chosen people—the Israel of our time" (WJ, 150–51). Of course, Melville would later dramatize the naivete of this outlook in *Israel Potter* (1854–55). Israel, an American Revolutionary patriot stranded in England, is said to be "well named—bondsman in the English Egypt." Nonetheless, in its description of America's "unprincipled, reckless, predatory, [and] boundless ambition," the narrative exposes as hyperbolic America's self-imposed identity as a New Israel or "Promised Land." Indeed, after a symbolic "forty torpid years of pauperism," Israel returns home—not, however, to any New Jerusalem, but only to an indifferent reception and a "Potter's Field" grave.[3]

The pertinence of this political context for *Redburn* becomes clear when we recognize that the story's older narrator describes the enthusiasm with which he began his journey to England and the contempt that he subsequently developed for the Old World. At the outset, for instance, young Redburn views with "romantic charm" (RB, 3) the prospect of travel, falls into "long reveries about distant voyages," and talks of Europe in a conspicuously Irvingesque spirit: "Indeed, during my early life, most of my thoughts of the sea were connected with the land; but with fine old lands, full of mossy cathedrals and churches, and long, narrow, crooked streets without sidewalks, and lined with strange houses" (RB, 5).[4] But these ideas of "wild romance" (RB, 75) dissipate after Redburn views the rather ordinary appearance of Ireland's coast (RB, 124) and after a crafty Irishman steals one of the *Highlander*'s ropes: "Here, then, was a beautiful introduction to the eastern hemisphere; fairly robbed before striking soundings" (RB, 125). Ashore, moreover, Redburn voices what could easily be taken for a direct response to *The Sketch Book:*

---

3. Quoted from Melville, *The Works of Herman Melville*, 16 vols. (London: Constable, 1922–24), XI: 209, 158, 221, 23–24, 223. For the background of ideas pertaining to America's vision of national election *vis à vis* Great Britain, see Sacvan Bercovitch, *The Puritan Origins of the American Self* (New Haven, Conn.: Yale Univ. Press, 1975), pp. 72–108. For the way such ideas function in *Israel Potter*, see Robert Zaller, "Melville and the Myth of Revolution," *Studies in Romanticism*, 15 (Fall 1976), 607–22.

4. Melville had already used this kind of rhetoric in *Mardi*. See Merrell R. Davis, *Melville's "Mardi": A Chartless Voyage* (New Haven, Conn.: Yale Univ. Press, 1952), p. 120, n. 9. For other similarities between Irving's *Sketch-Book* and *Redburn*, see Hershel Parker's "Historical Note" (RB, 327–28).

"[W]here are the old abbeys, and the York Minsters, and the lord may-
ors, and coronations, and the May-poles, and fox-hunters, . . . which,
from all my reading, I had been in the habit of associating with England?" (RB, 133). Moreover, Redburn's disillusionment becomes even
more intense when, wandering through the "pestilent lanes and alleys"
(RB, 191) of Liverpool, he suffers the physical assault of a dealer in con-
traband, thereafter shunning "these scoundrels like the leprosy" (RB,
195). Upset, too, by the starvation and death in "Launcelott's Hey" (ch.
37) and by the incessant misery of "The Dock-Wall Beggars" (ch. 38),
Redburn is amazed that "such an array of misery could be furnished by
any town in the world." Thus, Redburn learns that a romantic view of
the Old World fails to account for the centers of poverty, vice, and misery that are also *outre-mer*.

Prone to extremes, the younger Redburn retreats to clichés that
calumnize England and the rest of the Old World as standing in
wretched contrast to America's messianic and millennial youth. In
fact, Redburn expresses his greatest disenchantment with England by
subconsciously equating Liverpool with Jerusalem and by imagining
his rambles through the town to resemble Christ's agonizing proces-
sion along the Via Dolorosa. And he does so in a manner that takes
most literally something like Jonathan Edwards's belief that since the
"old continent" had "crucified Christ, they shall not have the honour
of communicating religion in its most glorious state to us, but we to
them." But however much Redburn might wish to share Edwards's
faith in the way the millennium *"is probably to begin in America,"*
and how "the most glorious renovation of the world shall originate
from the new continent,"[5] Redburn's betrayal of Harry Bolton picks
up where the Vivenza sections of *Mardi* leave off in dramatizing a
failure to live up to messianic aspirations.

Redburn's ability to walk the Via Dolorosa of the Old Continent
as a way of affirming his superior American virtues is not impaired by
Melville's lack, in 1849, of firsthand knowledge of the Levant. Nor should
Melville's use, in the creation of Redburn's jaunt, of a guidebook of
Liverpool prevent us from perceiving the mideastern texture of
Redburn's allegory. From the chapters of *Mardi* that deal with orthodox Maramma we know how Melville had already satirized aspects of
pilgrimages both to the Vatican and Palestine. Redburn presently
imposes mideastern and Scriptural significance upon many of the personalities and edifices that Melville may have seen mentioned in *The*

---

5. Jonathan Edwards, *Some Thoughts Concerning the Present Revival of Religion
in New England,* in *The Works of President Edwards,* ed. Sereno E. Dwight, 10 vols. (New
York: S. Converse, 1829–30), IV: 130, 128, 130.

Picture of Liverpool (1808).[6] For instance, Redburn compares one pious old pensioner to "the *muezzin* or cryer of prayers on the top of a Turkish mosque" (RB, 175) and describes the dilapidated brick buildings of Liverpool as "Sodom-like" (RB, 191). He also thinks of the depraved dock area as reminiscent of "notorious Corinthian haunts" (RB, 138) and even regards his room at London's Aladdin's Palace as "a bower in Babylon" (RB, 230). Prone to redefine his transatlantic experiences within biblical categories, he points out a resemblance between Liverpool's stone walls and "the old Pyramids of Egypt" (RB, 161) and experiences a "feeling somewhat akin to the Eastern traveler standing on the brink of the Dead Sea" (RB, 158). In fact, Redburn allegorically places himself in the very midst of Jerusalem when, passing a lane of beggars, he remarks that they "thronged the docks as the Hebrew cripples did the Pool of Bethesda" (RB, 188).

In associating the sound of a bell with "judgment and the resurrection, like belfry-mouthed Paul of Tarsus" (RB, 127), Redburn reveals devotional attitudes that anticipate his regard for himself as something of a persecuted emissary of the Redeemer Nation. Insofar, moreover, as Redburn refers to his bed-plank as a "crucifix" (RB, 75), and even projects the identity of Judas Iscariot (RB, 19) upon one of the pawnbrokers with whom he deals, he compares his own tribulations to those of the suffering Christ. And he seems specifically to identify with Christ's agony along the Via Dolorosa when, while tracing his father's footsteps through Liverpool, Redburn momentarily regards his guidebook as something of a Bible. In fact, Redburn commences this allegorical walk when he aptly sets out toward "Lord-street" (RB, 154) to visit the hotel where his father—whom he thinks "infinitely purer and greater" (RB, 34) than himself—once lodged. Remarking that "God is the true Father of all" (RB, 140), Redburn goes so far in his identification with Christ as to call this jaunt a "filial pilgrimage to spots which would be hallowed in my eyes" (RB, 154). And even though Redburn feels anguished by his father's "trials and troubles" (RB, 155), the syntax of this episode blurs the distinction between Redburn's concern for his father and his own self-pity.[7] Thus, in what may at some level of consciousness be a conflation of his and his father's suffering with the flagellation of Christ, Redburn says, "Yes, in this very street, thought I, nay, on this very *flagging* my father walked. Then I almost wept, when I looked down on my sorry apparel, and marked how the people regarded me;

---

6. For Melville's debt to this guidebook, see Willard Thorp, "Redburn's Prosy Old Guidebook," *PMLA*, 53 (Dec. 1938), 1146–56.

7. For commentary on this linguistic feature of Redburn's anguish, see Pearl

the men staring at so grotesque a young stranger, and the old ladies
...*crossing* the walk a little to shun me."[8] And, as if tracing the Stations of the Cross, Redburn even passes under "a cloister-like *arch of
stone*, whose *gloom* and narrowness delighted me.... There, *leaning*
against the colonnade, I took out my map, and traced my father right
across Chapel-street, and actually through the very *arch* at my back"
(RB, 154–55; emphasis added). With respect to Redburn's thoughts
about death (RB, 155) in the midst of all this, the fullest significance of
his turmoil may be gleaned from any number of travel books that
Melville consulted long before his trip to the Levant in 1857.

In "old Harris's collection of voyages" (MD, 226)—to use Ishmael's casual title—Melville could have perused *The Travels of Mon-
sieur Thevenot into the Levant* (a section of Harris's *Voyages* that
Taji mentions in *Mardi* [p. 228]), including its description of the Via
Dolorosa's "large Arch, where *Pilate* set our Lord, when he said,
Behold the Man." And in the *Pilgrimage* of "pious old Purchas" (M,
228)—as Taji refers to still another of these travelers—Melville might
have read about the *"Dolorous way*: alongst which our Saviour was
led to his Passion.... And a little beyond there is an ancient Arch that
crosseth the street, and supporteth a ruined Gallerie...where *Pilate*
presented Christ to the people."[9] Melville may even have known
George Sandys's detailed sketch of the Via Dolorosa (see Figure D),
and also Dr. Edward Robinson's skeptical thoughts about "the place
where the Saviour, fainting under his burden, *leaned* against the wall
of a house; and the impression of his shoulder remains unto this

---

Chesler Solomon, *Dickens and Melville in Their Time* (New York: Columbia Univ.
Press, 1975), p. 190. With a different emphasis, Lawrance Thompson, in *Melville's
Quarrel With God* (Princeton, N.J.: Princeton Univ. Press, 1952), pp. 82–84, first
pointed out that Redburn regarded his guidebook as a Bible. My allegorical reading of
Redburn's stroll explains why Melville refers to Riddough's, on Lord Street, instead of
the Liverpool Arms, on Castle Street, where Allan Melvill actually stayed when visit-
ing Liverpool. See William H. Gilman, *Melville's Early Life and "Redburn"* (New
York: New York Univ. Press, 1951), pp. 189, 349, n. 39.

8. Melville more obviously draws upon traditions surrounding the Flagellation of
the Savior in a chapter of *White-Jacket* that describes "Flogging Through the Fleet" as
something of a "Golgotha" (WJ, 369).

9. John Harris, *Navigantium atque Itinerantium Bibliotheca: or, a Compleat Collection of Voyages and Travels*, 2 vols. (London: Thomas Bennet, 1705), II: 436; Samuel
Purchas, *Purchas His Pilgrimage*, 2 vols. (1613; rpt. London: William Stansby, 1625),
II: 1324. Quite possibly, Purchas' account of this "ruined Gallerie" influenced Melville's description of the Via Dolorosa in a canto of *Clarel* titled "The Arch":

> With gallery which years deface,
> Its bulk athwart the alley grim,
> The arch named Ecce Homo threw;
> The same, if child-like faith be true,

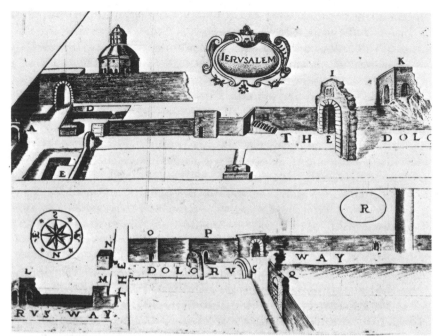

A. *The Gate of Saint Steuen.*
B. *The gate that opens into the court of the Temple.*
C. *The mofque, where once flood the Temple of Salomõ.*
D. *The poole Bethefda.*
E. *The Church of Saint Anna.*
F. *Where the Palace of Pilate flood.*
G. *Where the Court of Herod.*
H. *Where the holy Staires.*
I. *Pilats arch.*

K. *The Church oft the fwowning of the bleffed Virgin.*
L. *Where they met with Simon of Cyrene.*
M. *Where Chrift faid, Weepe not for me you daughters of Ierufalem.*
N *Where the houfe of the rich glutton flood.*
O *Where the houfe of the Pharife.*
P. *Where the houfe of Veronica.*
Q. *The Gate of Iuftice.*
R. *Mount Caluary.*

Figure D. George Sandys, *A Relation of a Journey Begun An: Dom: 1610*, 3rd ed. (London: Allot, 1632), p. 194. Courtesy of the Humanities Research Center, The University of Texas at Austin.

day."[10] Moreover, William Bartlett's *Walks About . . . Jerusalem* (1844), which Melville owned, has a succinct description of the *"gloomy street"* which leads to "an archway" where "Pilate showed Jesus to the people." Bartlett's book also features a fold-out map of Jerusalem with the Via Dolorosa traced in blue, a feature far more characteristic of Red-

---

From which the Lamb of God was shown
By Pilate to the wolfish crew. (I.xiii.22–27)
10. Edward Robinson, *Biblical Researches in Palestine, Mount Sinai and Arabia Petrae: A Journal of Travels in the Year 1838*, 3 vols. (Boston: Crocker and Brewster, 1841), I: 344; emphasis added. Some of Robinson's other research had appeared in *The Literary World* (17 March 1849). For Melville's familiarity with George Sandys's *A*

burn's guidebook than of anything in *The Picture of Liverpool.*[11] Thus, when Melville actually visited the Via Dolorosa in 1857 he would already have possessed much of the vocabulary to describe "the arch—the stone he [Christ] leaned against—the stone of Lazarus & c. City like a quarry—all stone.—Vaulted ways—buttresses (flying) Arch (ECCE HOMO)."[12]

Consistent with Redburn's imaginative excursion along the Via Dolorosa is his emergence from the "cloister-like arch of stone" into "the fine quadrangle of the Merchants' Exchange" (RB, 154). According to Bartlett, it "was *without this wall* [i.e. of the "chief seat of business"] that Jesus was crucified, and there is a near approach to probability in the monkish tradition of the 'Via Dolorosa,' along which he is said to have been led to execution, so far as the direction is concerned."[13] And suggestive of the governor's house along the Via Dolorosa (pictured on Bartlett's map) is Redburn's remark that "so vivid was now the impression of his [father's] having been here, and so narrow[14] the passage from which he had emerged, that I felt like running on, and overtaking him round the Town Hall adjoining" (RB, 155). Moreover, even Redburn's name—as well as the "red woolen shirt" (RB, 24, 153) that he dons just prior to his figurative walk along the Via Dolorosa—may dispose him to identify with the suffering Christ.[15]

Relation of a Journey Begun An: Dom: 1610, see the review by Robert Forsythe of Raymond Weaver's 1935 edition of Melville's *Journal Up the Straits,* in *American Literature,* 8 (March 1936), 93.

11. William Bartlett, *Walks About the City and Environs of Jerusalem* (London: George Virtue, n.d.), pp. 101–2. The preface to this volume is dated 1844, which, according to a footnote in the opening sentence of Bartlett's *Jerusalem Revisited* (London: T. Nelson and Sons, 1864), p. v, was the first year of *Walks'* publication. We cannot know for sure when Melville acquired this book, which he eventually gave to his wife (see Merton M. Sealts, Jr., *Melville's Reading: A Check-List of Books Owned and Borrowed* [Madison: Univ. of Wisconsin Press, 1966], item 50). Yet Dorothee Finkelstein, in *Melville's Orienda* (New Haven, Conn.: Yale Univ. Press, 1961), p. 66, has already shown that "both Clarel's and Celio's walks about Jerusalem may be traced with accuracy in Bartlett." Moreover, Redburn's claim that "traced with a pen, I discover a number of dotted lines [on the foldout map of his father's guidebook], radiating in all directions from the foot of Lord-street" (RB, 145) is more representative of Bartlett's foldout map, which traces the Via Dolorosa in blue ink (using as a color guide a segment of blue ink drawn over dotted lines), than it is of anything featured in *The Picture of Liverpool* (see Thorp, p. 1151, n. 12).

12. Melville, *Journal of a Visit to Europe and the Levant, October 11, 1856–May 6, 1857,* ed. Howard C. Horsford (Princeton, N.J.: Princeton Univ. Press, 1955), p. 150.

13. Bartlett, p. 34.

14. In *Clarel* Melville describes the Via Dolorosa as a "lane, / Narrow" (IV.xxxiv.7–8).

15. In *Figures or Types of the Old Testament,* 2nd ed. (London, 1705), Samuel

Redburn's suffering and his messianic tendencies have not only religious implications but political dimensions as well. These are best approached with reference to Emerson's "The American Scholar" (1837), which Oliver Wendell Holmes proclaimed America's "intellectual Declaration of Independence."[16] Asserting that "we have listened too long to the courtly muses of Europe," Emerson seeks to liberate America from "the mind of the Past." Attitudes of this "Young American" variety may well cast light upon Redburn's ability to change from being so dolorous about the unreliable nature of his father's guidebook to his conceding more optimistically that "the thing that had guided the father, could not guide the son"; "every age makes its own guide-books, and the old ones are used for waste paper" (RB, 157). Emerson, we should recall, had already used a similar metaphor to help unshackle America from British intellectual standards. "Books are the best type of the influence of the past," he claimed, and "each age...must write its own books.... The books of an older period will not fit this."[17] Thus, Redburn's disenchantment with his father's guidebook may at least partly reflect America's more positive effort to define a national identity by rejecting transatlantic ties.[18] We may even speculate that Redburn views the European heritage as something of a crucifying source of persecution. And he does so in a way suggestive of Jonathan Edwards's belief that the Passion of Christ was an indictment of the Old World and a promissory seal to America's glorious millennial future.

Important for this reading are factors that might incline Redburn to entertain ideas about America's moral and political superiority to Great Britain. Pertinent here is Redburn's revolutionary heritage,

---

Mather explains how redness points to "the Humane Nature of Christ, which he had from *Adam, who was made out of red Earth*, Gen. 2. 7....Thus Christ is red, and that in regard of his Sufferings." (p. 307). Familiar with Christian typology (see Ursula Brumm, *American Thought and Religious Typology*, trans. John Hoaglund [New Brunswick, N.J.: Rutgers Univ. Press, 1970], pp. 162–97), Melville writes in *Clarel*, "Restored the Second Adam stood— / Not as in Eden stood the First / All Ruddy" (I.v.84–86); and Clarel explicitly links redness with Christ's Passion by referring to "Thy white, thy red, thy fairness and thy tragedy" (I.xiii.102). Also, from *Clarel* (IV.x.6–28), we know of Melville's familiarity with traditions associating bloody wool with the suffering Christ.

16. Holmes, *The Writings of Oliver Wendell Holmes*, 14 vols. (Boston and New York: Houghton Mifflin, 1909), XI: 88.

17. Emerson, *The Complete Works of Ralph Waldo Emerson*, ed. Edward Waldo Emerson, 12 vols. (Boston and New York: Houghton Mifflin, 1903–4), I: 87, 88.

18. Sacvan Bercovitch, "Melville's Search for National Identity: Son and Father in *Redburn, Pierre* and *Billy Budd*," *College Language Association Journal*, 10 (March 1967), 217–20.

which finds expression in his very name, since it was "Senator Welling-borough, who died a member of Congress in the days of the old Consti-tution, . . . after whom I had the honor of being named" (RB, 7; cf. 67, 212). Also, Redburn takes pride in a "grandfather of mine, who had fought . . . at Bunker's Hill" (RB, 125), and he proudly remembers his childhood aspiration of "becoming a great orator like Patrick Henry," whose speeches he once performed on stage (RB, 36). Unable, however, to engage in the more militant Americanism of his ancestors, Redburn verbally expresses his rejection of British values in his encounter with Harry Bolton, their relationship dramatizing the opposition between New World democracy and Old World aristocracy. In his discussions with Harry, for instance, Redburn falls back upon his "old uncle the senator" to counter Harry's "array of dukes, lords, curricles, and count-esses" (RB, 221); and when the two visit Aladdin's Palace, a London gambling establishment, Redburn regards the vice and decadence of this ornate building in a manner reminiscent of the way Walt Whit-man contrasted "American Munificence" with "that splendid yet wretched system which has made our mother-land so full of outside grandeur and inside destitution." As one critic remarks, "[T]he Old World in *Redburn* is characterized by the social evils of Liverpool, the gilded depravities of the Palace of Aladdin, and the aristocratic deca-dence of Harry Bolton—all rather conventional ideas. The fresh New World and its spirit stand in contrast to all this, and it is not denied in the book that for the individual to survive, and hopefully to get ahead, the American Way is best."[19] This outlook, in fact, is likewise evident in Redburn's response to the poverty of Liverpool. Overlooking his own financial distress, Redburn boasts how in his country "such a be-ing as a native beggar is almost unknown; and to be a born American citizen seems a guarantee against pauperism; and this, perhaps, springs from the virtue of a vote" (RB, 202).

Given Redburn's self-assumed Christly identity, this political chauvinism recalls the messianic outlook that Melville had already satirized in *Mardi*, where Vivenza fancies itself "a young Messiah" (M,

---

19. Nicholas Canaday, Jr., "Harry Bolton and Redburn: The Old World and the New," in *Essays in Honor of Esmond Linsworth Marilla*, ed. Thomas Austin Kirby and William John Olive (Baton Rouge: Louisiana State Univ. Press, 1970), p. 298. Whitman's remark is from "American Munificence and English Pomp" (16 July 1846), in *The Gathering of the Forces by Walt Whitman: Editorials, Essays, Literary and Dramatic Reviews . . . Written by Walt Whitman as Editor of the "Brooklyn Daily Eagle" in 1846 and 1847*, ed. Cleveland Rodgers and John Black, 2 vols. (New York: G. P. Putnam's Sons, 1920), I: 38–39. For the possibility that Melville read Whitman's editorials, see my "Satiric Precedent for Melville's 'The Two Temples,'" *American Transcendental Quarterly*, 42 (Spring 1979), 137–45.

472). And in a passage that anticipates White-Jacket's exaggerated view of America as the "political Messiah" (WJ, 151), Redburn remarks, "The other world beyond this, which was longed for by the devout before Columbus' time, was found in the New." He also believes that the millennium will probably begin in America, which "shall see the estranged children of Adam restored as to the old hearth-stone in Eden.... The seed is sown, and the harvest must come; and our children's children, on the world's jubilee morning, shall all go with their sickles to the reaping" (RB, 169). Still, scholarship that addresses this aspect of Redburn's enthusiasm draws upon the guidebook chapter to demonstrate as illusory the standards by which Redburn distinguishes an Arcadian American future from the degenerate European present.[20] As we shall see, nowhere is this more evident than in the way our self-styled messiah fails to practice even a modest degree of charity toward the "prodigal," Harry Bolton, after the *Highlander* docks at New York. Having subconsciously walked the Via Dolorosa of the "Old Continent" to affirm his "New World" American identity, Redburn fails miserably in demonstrating on a personal basis the attributes that he considers characteristic of the Redeemer Nation. And that the text invites a political reading of Redburn's relationship with Harry is evident from Redburn's remark, "I stood toward [Harry] in the attitude of the prospective doer of the honors of my country; I accounted him the nation's guest" (RB, 279).

Redburn's final indifference to Harry is surprising also in light of his earlier views on charity. In the opening chapters, for example, Redburn is upset with Max, who fails to lend him any seaworthy clothes: "Like many other well-wishers, he contented him with sympathy" (RB, 79). Later, Redburn feels "amazed and shocked" (RB, 103) at Riga's indifference to a wrecked ship, and he even scolds the readers of his narrative for not showing more charity and hospitality to sailors: "Will you throw open your parlors to [them]; invite [them] to dinner?" (RB, 140). More vociferous yet is Redburn's outrage with man's inhumanity to man after he witnesses the callous response of a policeman to starvation and death in Liverpool's poverty-stricken districts: "What right had any body in the wide world to smile and be glad, when sights like this were to be seen?" (RB, 181). Nonetheless, Redburn's "sad thoughts concerning the cold charities of the world" (RB, 213) often seem artificial—and especially when viewed in the context of the way he deserts

---

20. See Michael Davitt Bell, "Melville's *Redburn*: Initiation and Authority," *New England Quarterly*, 46 (Dec. 1973), 570; cf. John Gerlach, "Messianic Nationalism in the Early Works of Herman Melville: Against Perry Miller," *Arizona Quarterly*, 28 (Spring 1972), 11.

Harry Bolton.[21] Although he knows that Harry is impoverished, "friendless," and a "stranger in the land" (RB, 304), Redburn abandons him in New York, offering no explanation other than that some letters "compelled my departure homeward" (RB, 304). At home he "plunge[s] into embraces, long and loving" (RB, 311), ignoring his earlier resolve that Harry's "prospects and plans should engage our attention, in preference to my own" (RB, 279). Resourceless and desperate, Harry signs aboard a whaler, where he eventually falls overboard to his death. Perhaps for this reason, guilt and despondency characterize Redburn-as-narrator, who at the outset of his story admits that he is not yet on his own legs (RB, 9), and who at one point even wishes himself "dead and buried" (RB, 33).[22]

Of course, some readers acquit Redburn of wrongdoing by attributing Harry's downfall both to Harry's own moral delinquency and to his failure to achieve a sense of identity.[23] Yet such responses overlook the implications of Redburn's view of Harry as a "prodigal." In reference to the way in which Harry squanders his "patrimony" (RB, 217), Redburn wonders "what was best to be done for the young prodigal's welfare" (RB, 222); for, "like many prodigals," Harry "scorn[s] to return home... and amend" (RB, 218). These remarks are obviously allusions to St. Luke's "Parable of the Prodigal Son," to which Melville had referred in an episode of *Mardi* in which Taji stumbles across "a little colored print, representing the harlots... having a fine time with the Prodigal Son" (M, 60). Presently, Harry's sexual gaming (RB, 221) and his manner of wasting his inheritance "in the company of gambling sportsmen and dandies" (RB, 217) conform to Luke 15:13, which describes how "the younger son gathered all together, and took his journey into a far country, and there wasted his substance with riotous living." In fact, Melville may mean to confer additional verbal emphasis on Harry's spiritual shortcomings by having him hide from Lord

---

21. My reading of Redburn's merely nominal concern for humanity is consistent with views expressed by Theodore L. Gross, *The Heroic Ideal in American Literature* (London: Collier-Macmillan, 1971), p. 36; Thompson, pp. 80–81; H. Bruce Franklin, "Redburn's Wicked End," *Nineteenth-Century Fiction*, 20 (Sept. 1965), 190–94; John Seelye, *Melville: The Ironic Diagram* (Evanston, Ill.: Northwestern Univ. Press, 1970), p. 52.

22. Here I concur with Dryden (p. 67), who says that Redburn "denies his brother, and the book which he writes is a confession of this fact."

23. James Schroeter, "*Redburn* and the Failure of Mythic Criticism," *American Literature*, 39 (Nov. 1967), 294; Charles Haberstroh, "*Redburn*: The Psychological Pattern," *Studies in American Fiction*, 2 (Autumn 1974), 142–43; Christopher W. Sten, "Melville's 'Gentleman Forger': The Struggle for Identity in *Redburn*," *Texas Studies in Literature and Language*, 21 (Fall 1979), 363–66.

Lovely (RB, 222), whose title transcends its merely aristocratic associations when Harry later curses as "recreant and apostate" the hand "with which I pledged Lady Blessington, and ratified my [apparently broken] bond to Lord Lovely" (RB, 281). [24]

Yet whatever Harry's immaturity and recreance, Melville would have known that Luke uses the "Parable of the Prodigal Son" to illustrate the nature of *unmerited grace*. And not inconceivably we might expect a self-proclaimed messiah such as Redburn to exercise a related charity rather than allow Harry to succumb to a nearly suicidal despair (RB, 235). In fact, in *The Anatomy of Melancholy* (1621), with which both Melville and Redburn seem familiar, Robert Burton draws upon St. Luke's "Parable" to caution against the sins of despair and suicide:

> there is no sin so hainous which is not pardonable in it selfe; no crime so great but by Gods mercy it may be forgiven.... *As a father* (saith David, Psal. 103. 13.) *hath compassion on his children, so hath the Lord compassion on them that feare him;* and will receive them again as the prodigall son was entertained, Luke 15. if they shall so come with tears in their eys [*sic*], and a penitent heart. ... *The Lord is full of compassion and mercy, slowe to anger, of great kindness,* Psal. 103. 8.[25]

In *Redburn*, Harry possesses this penitent heart, Melville making it clear that Harry has in some degree "atoned" for his past "by dwelling upon the future" (RB, 278) in America. Harry, in fact, tells Redburn that he plans "never again to return to England; and that somewhere in America he must work out his temporal felicity" (RB, 279). More-

---

24. Although Lady Blessington was an authentic London Bluestocking, her name is as open to pun as is Lord Lovely's. In any event, my reading supplements what may be a limited debt on Melville's part to a character in J. Ross Browne's *Etchings of a Whaling Cruise* (see Robert Sattelmeyer's "The Origin of Harry Bolton," *American Transcendental Quarterly*, 31 [Summer 1976], 23–25). I also seek to open up new possibilities surrounding Melville's motive in possibly having entered Harry as a late insertion in the completed manuscript of *Redburn* (see Parker, "Historical Note" [p. 332]).

25. Robert Burton, *The Anatomy of Melancholy*, 2 vols. (1621; rpt. London: Thomas Davison, 1821), II: 580. Both William Braswell and Merton M. Sealts, Jr., have shown that Redburn's knowledge of "that theory of Paracelsus and Campanella, that every man has four souls within him" (RB, 249) is derived from Burton's *Anatomy* (see Braswell's *Melville's Religious Thought: An Essay in Interpretation* [Durham, N.C.: Duke Univ. Press, 1943], pp. 86–87). Melville bought *The Anatomy* in 1847 (see Sealts, items 102–3). For his use of Burton's thoughts on religious melancholy and despair in other works, see Dryden, pp. 189–91; Nathalia Wright, "Melville and 'Old Burton,' with 'Bartleby' as an Anatomy of Melancholy," *Tennessee Studies in Literature*, 15 (1970), 1–13.

over, in describing Harry's reformation, Melville may even be suggesting the idea of Christian "grace" as Harry ponders whether he can secure a clerical job in New York: "[D]o you not think, that such a hand as *that* might dot an *i*, or cross a *t*, with a touching grace and tenderness?" (RB, 281). But while Redburn, too, speaks of proffering sympathy "with the best grace" (RB, 279), his final indifference toward this "prodigal" negates the redemptive impetus of Luke's parable, shifting the burden of sin to himself.

Thus, despite his declarations that "the whole world is the *patrimony* of the whole world" (RB, 292; emphasis added); that a foreigner would be welcome to "a dinner and a bed" (RB, 212) in his home; and, most importantly, that "inefficient, as a benefactor, as I certainly was; still, being an American, . . . I stood toward him in the attitude of the prospective doer of the honors of my country" (RB, 279)—despite all this, Redburn still abandons the "prodigal" in a relatively helpless condition, offering little more than a token gesture of goodwill by placing Harry in the indifferent care of Goodwell. Given a real opportunity to be Harry's "bosom friend" (RB, 280)—a term Melville probably knew to have originated in Christly compassion, as well as a concept that he associates in *Moby-Dick* with the fidelity entailed in one person's willingness to sacrifice himself for another[26]— Redburn fails to act in accordance with Luke's atoning injunction.

Melville even highlights the antiredemptive tendency of Redburn's neglect by having Harry succumb to the sort of melancholy and suicidal emotions described in Burton's *Anatomy* as characteristic of persons who despair of God's grace. From Harry's confessions in London, we know him to be "a desperate man," likely to take a "long jump" (RB, 238) off the dock; and Redburn is quite aware that this "friendless, penniless foreigner in New York . . . must have had the

---

26. Of course, Melville uses the term "bosom friend" in its most secular sense in both *Omoo* (p. 152) and *Mardi* (p. 384). Familiar, however, with Sir Thomas Browne's *Pseudodoxia Epidemica*, or *Vulgar Errors* (see M, 39; MD, 4), Melville would probably have known Browne's explanation of the term's origins in John 13:23: "*Erat recumbens unus ex Discipulis ejus in sinu Jesu quem diligebat; Now there was leaning on Jesus' bosom one of his Disciples whom Jesus loved*; . . . And the very same expression is to be found in Pliny, concerning the Emperour Nerva and Veiento whom he favoured; . . . and from this custom arose the word ἐπιστήθιος, that is, a near and bosom friend" (*The Works of Sir Thomas Browne*, ed. Geoffrey Keynes, 4 vols. [Chicago: Univ. of Chicago Press, 1964], II: 353). In chapter 10 of *Moby-Dick* ("A Bosom Friend"), Melville seems to exploit the Christly origins of the term when, just prior to Queequeg's division of "thirty dollars in silver" (cf. White-Jacket's allusion to "the criminality of Judas, who, for thirty pieces of silver, betrayed his Master" [p. 157]) between himself and Ishmael, Ishmael says, "henceforth we were married; meaning, in his country's phrase, that we were bosom friends; he would gladly die for me, if need should be" (MD, 53).

most terrible incitements to committing violence upon himself" (RB, 311–12). Harry, of course, never overcomes this despair, one remedy for which is an offer of companionship. As Burton says, despairing persons "must not be left solitary, or to themselves, never idle, never out of company." But in what may be an ironic reference to this passage, Redburn twice remarks that Harry seemed "left to himself," and in a "friendless condition" (RB, 304) in New York. Redburn, moreover, deludes himself into believing that, to diminish the anxieties of "solitude," he kept "constant company" with Harry.[27] Understandably, then, Harry *"grew more and more melancholy"* and committed a symbolic act of despairing suicide: *"I can not believe,"* says Goodwell, *"that his melancholy could bring him to the insanity of throwing himself away in a whaler"* (RB, 311). Ironic, indeed, is Redburn's earlier warning against the sinful tendency to which the abandonment ultimately leads: "Now, my dear friend,...while I am gone, keep up a stout heart; *never despair,* and all will be well" (RB, 310; emphasis added). Yet Harry does despair, thereby failing to achieve the rebirth in Christ which Crèvecoeur in 1782 had proclaimed the regenerative outcome of emigrating to America.[28]

Well merited, then, is a shift in Redburn's identity from Christ to Cain. In fact, Redburn, who is familiar with the literary works of Lord Byron (RB, 122, 281), may echo one of the most despairing lines in *Cain* when he admonishes Harry for being unable to climb the *Highlander*'s rigging: " 'Then, Harry,' said I, 'better you had never been born' " (RB, 255).[29] Also, in what may be an allusion to Genesis 4:9 (*"Am* I my brother's keeper?"), a sailor asks Redburn whether the deceased " 'Harry Bolton was not your brother?' " (RB, 312). Redburn even alludes to Genesis 4:15 ("And the LORD set a mark upon Cain") by associating his life's failure with "such a scar that the air of Para-

---

27. *The Anatomy,* II, 578. Cf. *Mardi,* p. 109: "He who is ready to despair in solitary peril, plucks up a heart in the presence of another. In a plurality of comrades is much countenance and consolation." In his "Historical Note" to *Redburn,* Parker notes "a discrepancy between Redburn's assertion (p. 278) that he and Harry kept 'constant company' with one another and his failure to have Harry in his company or even to mention Harry in many chapters that deal with his own experiences among the sailors and the emigrants" (RB, 331–32).

28. See Werner Sollors, "The Rebirth of *All* Americans in the Great American Melting Pot: Notes Toward the Vindication of a Rejected Popular Symbol; or: An Ethnic Variety of a Religious Experience," in *Prospects: An Annual of American Cultural Studies,* ed. Jack Salzman, vol. 5 (New York: Burt Franklin, 1980), 84–92.

29. In Byron's play, Cain offers the same despairing consolation for his child's future: " 'T were better that he never had been born." *Works of Lord Byron,* 17 vols. (London: John Murray, 1832–36), XIV: 84–85 (act III, line 136). Melville's wife acquired Byron's *Dramas* in 1847 (see Sealts, item 109).

dise might not erase it" (RB, 11). Yet insofar as Redburn accounts Harry the nation's guest, the mark extends to America's messianic visage and in a way is related to the *Highlander*'s docking "at the foot of Wall-street," where Redburn praises that "free and indepen-dent Yankee mud" (RB, 301) just prior to deserting Harry. From "Bartleby" we know that Melville thought Wall Street an apt setting for tales dramatizing the cold, futilely perverse charities of American enterprise; yet *Redburn* anticipates "Bartleby" by illustrating the anti-Christian tendencies of the Redeemer Nation's independent, individu-alistic, and laissez-faire outlooks.

The specifically monetary dimension of these concerns finds an analog in the episode in which Redburn sells his rifle. Having early and naively imagined economics to be grounded in benevolence,[30] he learns that trade is in fact governed by rules less charitable. But how-ever necessary this awakening, Redburn's perverse stance as "doer of the honors of my country" approaches the opposite extreme of self-interest as prescribed in Adam Smith's *Wealth of Nations* (1776), a major source of inspiration to Jacksonian democrats[31] and a book in which Redburn "fancied lay something like the philosopher's stone, a secret talisman, which would transmute even pitch and tar to silver and gold" (RB, 86). Often having the volume immediately accessible (RB, 118), and even using it as a pillow (RB, 87), Redburn reads at least ten chapters of this treatise, the publication date of which cor-responds to his own country's Declaration of Independence. Yet Red-burn would have had to peruse scarcely more than the text's opening pages to learn how very independent of one another people can actu-ally be. While "man has always constant occasion for the help of his brethren," says Smith, "it is in vain for him to expect it from their benevolence only. He will be more likely to prevail if he can interest their self-love in his favour." Thus, in a line which may figure in Harry's lament, "Where am I going to dine, this day week?"(RB, 304), Smith remarks, "[I]t is not from the benevolence of the butcher, the brewer, or the baker, that we expect our dinner, but from their regard to their own interest. We address ourselves, not to their humanity but to their self-love."[32] Perhaps since Harry can appeal to nothing but

---

30. "I ... knew so little of money," says Redburn, "that when I bought a stick of candy, and laid down a sixpence, I thought the confectioner returned five cents, only that I might have money to buy something else. ... How different my idea of money now!" (RB, 36).

31. See Arthur M. Schlesinger, Jr., *The Age of Jackson* (Boston: Little, Brown, 1946), pp. 314–16.

32. *An Inquiry into the Nature and Causes of the Wealth of Nations*, 8th ed., 3 vols.

charity, Redburn offers little in return, his attitude devoid of the disinterested benevolence that one might expect from a self-styled ambassador of the Redeemer Nation. Instead, Redburn's behavior recalls the sort of Vivenzan shortcoming denounced by King Media in *Mardi*: "Your nation is like a fine, florid youth, full of fiery impulses, and hard to restrain; his strong hand nobly championing his heart. . . . But years elapse, and this bold boy is transformed. His eyes open not as of yore; his heart is shut up as a vice. He yields not a groat" (M, 526).

The national analog to Redburn's negligence is perhaps most evident in the way the *Highlander*'s return voyage dramatizes America's indifference to the welfare of the poorer emigrants seeking asylum in "the promised land" (RB, 290–291). Their misery aboard the American ship represents a more institutionalized form of the Redeemer Nation's neglect for humanity. It also renders ludicrous Redburn's Crèvecoeurian habit of seeing emigration as the main vehicle for fulfilling the mandate of Pauline Christianity to substitute a universal church composed of persons from all nations for an exclusively chosen people:[33] "We are not a narrow tribe of men, with a bigoted Hebrew nationality. . . . We are the heirs of all time, and with all nations we divide our inheritance. On this Western Hemisphere all tribes and people are forming into one federated whole; and there is a future which shall see the estranged children of Adam restored as to the old hearth-stone in Eden" (RB, 169).[34] Harry Bolton finds such rhetoric

---

(London: Strahan, Cadell, Davies, 1796), I: 21–22. Redburn doubtless finds the book's first chapter "dry as crackers," and claims to receive little "profits" from reviewing other chapters. Still, in Redburn's statement that he "read on and on, about '*wages and profits of labor*,'" Melville alerts us to Redburn's having arrived at the book's tenth chapter. And though "giv[ing] it up for lost" (RB, 87), Redburn would certainly not have forgotten all he read. Worth recalling, too, is Melville's satire of the vicious tendencies of current economic theories in both the Diranda section of *Mardi* (chs. 138–40) and in his short fiction. See Davis, p. 181; Beryl Rowland, "Sitting Up with a Corpse: Malthus According to Melville in 'Poor Man's Pudding and Rich Man's Crumbs,'" *Journal of American Studies*, 6 (April 1972), 69–83.

    33. For Crèvecoeur's application of Pauline Christianity to emigration, see Sollors, p. 92. The relation between millennialism and Pauline transethnicism is discussed by Ernest Lee Tuveson, *Redeemer Nation: The Idea of America's Millennial Role* (Chicago: Univ. of Chicago Press, 1968), pp. 138–39.

    34. Redburn's outlook strikingly approaches Walt Whitman's millennialist view of emigration. See Whitman's "American Futurity" and "The New World and the Old," in *Gathering of the Forces*, I: 15–18, 27–28. Melville, however, would most likely have known how *Yankee Doodle* (27 Feb. 1847, p. 228) had already satirized the habit of seeing in the great migration of the 1840's an affirmation of America's millennial status:

    This universal starvation is only the outward sign of the steady and infallible development of the destiny of Europe. . . . The reconstructive era of human destiny must come to pass elsewhere—HERE. YANKEE DOODLE is the master-spirit, the

empty at best, for he, like so many thousands of other emigrants, receives less than a gracious reception in America. And while Harry suffers mainly from Redburn's indifference, the more bigoted response of nativists (RB, 292) toward the Irish emigrants invalidates an American messianic identity predicated upon offering asylum to the world's oppressed.[35] Moreover, related to this inquiry into American isolationism is Tocqueville's remark about the way an American "will be found engaged with some new project for the purpose of increasing what he has; talk not to him of the interests and the rights of mankind [;] this small domestic concern absorbs for the time all his thoughts." In Melville's book, this habit is best understood with reference to Redburn's encounter with the misanthrope, Jackson, whose claims about being "a near relation of General Jackson of New Orleans" (RB, 57) help clarify Redburn's concern with the sort of isolationism and self-absorption that Tocqueville thought the most lamentable feature of Jacksonian democracy and "individualism."[36]

That more than a casual tie exists between Redburn's Jackson and the hero of New Orleans is suggested by both the emaciated appearance of Melville's villain and his consumptive condition. Redburn also describes Jackson as being a "dictator" (RB, 61) and a

---

architect, who is to draw order from this chaos and to construct an eternal edifice of human happiness from these incongruous, titanic, abundant materials. He is ready for the task. Welcome, worn-out, starving, dying Europe to the freshness and abundance of Yankeedoodledom!

Tellingly, however, the anonymous author of this lampoon adds, "For the correctness of these speculations YANKEE DOODLE begs leave to refer to ... the three thousand starving emigrants in this city."

35. See Robert Ernst, "The Asylum of the Oppressed," *South Atlantic Quarterly*, 40 (Jan. 1941), 1-10; Cecil B. Eby, "America as 'Asylum': A Dual Image," *American Quarterly*, 14 (Fall 1962), 483-89. Melville had already challenged the legitimacy of America's "asylum" identity in Media's expression of exasperation with Vivenzan slavery: "Asylum for all Mardi's thralls!" (M, 532).

36. All references to *Democracy in America* (1835-40) are to the Henry Reeve translations: part I, 3rd Am. ed. (New York: George Adlard, 1839); part II (New York: J. & H. G. Langley, 1840). The passage quoted here is from part II, pp. 270-71. By 1850, Reeve's translations had been issued in eighteen American editions, most published in New York. Melville's interest in *Democracy in America* would doubtless have been aroused by "De Tocqueville," an anonymous article in the *Democratic Review*, 21 (Aug. 1847), 115-23, which devotes three pages (117-20) to a discussion of *Typee* and *Omoo*.

Little, to date, has been done with Melville's encounter with Tocqueville. Barbara Meldrum, however, in "Melville on War," *Research Studies* (Wash. State Univ.), 37 (June 1969), 130-31, suggests the influence of *Democracy in America* upon White-Jacket's belief that military officers in a democracy thrive on war. John J. Gross, in "Forward from Tocqueville," *Emerson Society Quarterly*, 35 (1964), 15-16, applies Tocqueville's critique of American "individualism" to *Pierre*.

"tyrant" (RB, 276) in his "extraordinary dominion...over twelve or fourteen strong, healthy tars" (RB, 274), who are earlier portrayed as cringing and fawning about him "like so many spaniels" (RB, 59). Suggestive, too, is Redburn's description of Jackson as having lived a life full of riotous events which "few men could have plunged into... without paying the death-penalty" (RB, 58). These descriptions caricature the notorious general whom Seba Smith's literary creation, Major Jack Downing, had already satirized as looking "like deth's hed on a mopstic" because of his many physical disorders, attributed at the time to consumption.[37] And because many of Jackson's critics charged that his recklessness in the Seminole affair—that "rat-killing war" (RB, 101), as Larry refers to it—violated nearly every standard of justice and international law, Downing pictures Jackson's mother schooling her son in "the adventurs, and fair fites, and robberies, and murders of her country." Believing, as well, that President Jackson's "unjust dictation" approached "the usages of despotic countries," Downing anticipates Melville's portrait of Jackson's extraordinary dominion over the *Highlander*'s crew. "The ignorant," says Downing, "always licks the feet of a tyrant in proportion as he is cruel." This was especially true of General Jackson's more timid associates, who "wou'd argu, defend, protect, fite for, do his biddin, and follow arter him jist like a...whipt spaniel." And that "their are spaniels enuff of this kind" Downing fully knows.[38] Perhaps for reasons related to similar dictatorial episodes aboard the *Highlander*, Redburn believes that his own "Yankee Jackson" merits a "lofty gallows in history" (RB, 276). But since Redburn is hardly prone to act tyrannically, his fear of becoming like this perverse shipmate (RB, 62) is better approached with reference to Jacksonian views about the Old World and the New, and in the context of Tocqueville's critique of Jacksonian individualism, self-help, and self-reliance.

Important in this respect is the opinion that, whatever Redburn's

---

37. Seba Smith [Major Jack Downing], *The Life of Andrew Jackson, President of the United States* (Philadelpha: T. K. Greenbank, 1834), p. 26. Although Jackson may not have had consumption, his contemporaries thought as much, since he showed every conventional symptom of that disease. For a superb overview of Andrew Jackson's physical ailments, many of which correspond to the maladies of Melville's Jackson, see Frances Tomlinson Gardner's "The Gentleman from Tennessee," *Surgery, Gynecology, and Obstetrics, with International Abstracts of Surgery*, 88 (March 1949), 405–11. For the possibility that Melville also drew upon a villain in Marryat's *Phantom Ship* to shape features of Jackson's personality, see Bernard Rosenthal's "Melville, Marryat, and the Evil-Eyed Villain," *Nineteenth-Century Fiction*, 25 (Sept. 1970), 221–24.

38. Smith, pp. 3, 143, 144, 72, 39, 169. In a related vein, Bell (p. 568) observes how "Melville is simply embodying in Jackson the insight presented for all by the rise of

legitimate motives in rejecting Old World values, and whatever the merits of his peculiarly American mode of "self-reliance," Redburn's final insensitivity toward Harry negates the possibility of a "fuller humanity" on his own side of the Atlantic.[39] Our application of Andrew Jackson's career to *Redburn* is facilitated by the way the general's victory over the British at New Orleans initiated the most cogent reaffirmation of America's independence from Old World values since the Revolution. It is clear that Jackson symbolized for many citizens the brawny American alternative to the sort of European degeneracy earlier denounced by Jefferson. Coupled, moreover, with "the ideal of self-sufficient individualism" that Jackson's rise from orphaned poverty to his country's presidency seemed to typify, such patterns of thinking underlie Redburn's democratic aversion to the Old World and his self-reliant indifference to Harry's welfare.[40]

Andrew Jackson's early poverty and adversity, moreover, led many Americans to think him "the self-made man *par excellence* because, alone in the world from the very beginning, he must have created his own future beyond any possible doubt."[41] In a similar vein, Redburn asks, "[W]hat castaway will not promise to take care of himself, when he sees that unless he himself does, no one else will?" (RB, 11). Insisting, too, that "every one in this world has his own fate intrusted to himself" (RB, 220), Redburn not surprisingly masters his difficulty in running aloft to loose the main skysail. In short, he practices "the cult of self-help" that so many Americans prior to Emerson worshipped as the Jacksonian ethic of self-reliance.[42] Redburn, however, fails to achieve a fuller humanity in the process; for when Harry finds himself unnerved at the prospect of going aloft, Redburn offers nothing but the despairing admonition, "[B]etter you had never been born" (RB, 255). Moreover, the uncharitable tendency of this remark possibly transcends a specifically Jacksonian context to reflect the

---

Napoleon and for many by the rise of Andrew Jackson—namely, that the toppling of tyrants in the name of democracy leads inevitably to the elevation of new despots in their place."

39. Canaday, p. 298.

40. For these aspects of Jacksonianism, see Ward, pp. 67–69, 149, 174.

41. Ward, p. 172.

42. Ward, pp. 167–68, 174, discusses the Jacksonian ethic of self-help. Perhaps Melville's effort to allegorize this political context accounts for his radical departure from autobiography in describing the degree of Redburn's impoverishment and despondency when he signs aboard the *Highlander*. As William H. Gilman, in "Melville's Liverpool Trip," *Modern Language Notes*, 61 (Dec. 1946), 543–47, has shown, Melville was both older than Redburn and materially better off when he set sail for Liverpool aboard the *St. Lawrence* in 1839.

more contemporary ethic of democratic "self-trust" celebrated in Emerson's essay "The American Scholar":

> Another sign of our times, also marked by an analogous political movement, is the new importance given to the single person. Every thing that tends to insulate the individual,—to surround him with barriers of natural respect, so that each man shall feel the world is his, and man shall treat with man as a sovereign state with a sovereign state,—tends to true union as well as greatness. "I learned," said the melancholy Pestalozzi, "that no man in God's wide earth is either willing or able to help any other man." Help must come from the bosom alone.[43]

Emerson, of course, was not alone in celebrating the merits of self-reliance; James Fenimore Cooper likewise thought that "all greatness of character is dependent on individuality,"[44] a position we shall explore in the chapter on *White-Jacket*. Still, both Ahab's failure to help the captain of the *Rachel* search for his lost son and *The Confidence-Man*'s satire of Transcendental "friendship" show isolation from humanity to be the most serious shortcoming of an otherwise noble democratic ethic of self-reliance.[45] And mainly this tendency Redburn fears in his attraction to Jackson: "I found myself a sort of Ishmael in the ship, *without a single friend or companion; and I began to feel a hatred growing up in me against the whole crew*—so much so, that I prayed against it, that it might not master my heart completely, and so make a fiend of me, something like Jackson" (RB, 62; emphasis added). Moreover, Melville may even dramatize the most appalling result of democratic isolationism in Jackson's habit of rejoicing in a sickness that threatens everybody but himself (RB, 273), for this approaches Fisher Ames's belief that democracy "is an illuminated hell,

---

43. Emerson, "The American Scholar," in *Works*, I: 113. For a more general discussion of Melville's response to ideas such as these, see R. E. Watters, "Melville's 'Sociality,'" *American Literature*, 17 (March 1945), 33–49.

44. James Fenimore Cooper, *The American Democrat* (1838), ed. H. L. Mencken (New York: Alfred A. Knopf, 1931), p. 174.

45. Ward, pp. 200–201, explores the Jacksonian nature of Ahab's self-reliance. For Melville's satire of Emersonian ideas about "friendship," see Egbert S. Oliver, "Melville's Picture of Emerson and Thoreau in *The Confidence-Man*," *College English*, 8 (Nov. 1946), 61–72. Also worth reviewing is Lucy Lockwood Hazard's statement, in *The Frontier in American Life* (New York: Thomas Y. Crowell, 1927), p. 155, about the isolationist nature of Transcendental self-reliance: "[E]ven the closest and dearest of personal ties, are to be subordinated to the interest of the individual, to be worn lightly while they last, and dropped unregretfully when they go. Sympathy with one's fellows is a waste of time and energy. The law of self preservation is the first and greatest commandment; let every man help himself and expect his neighbor to do the same."

that in the midst of remorse, horrour, and torture, rings with festivity; for experience shews, that one joy remains to this most malignant description of the damned, the power to make others wretched."[46]

Stressing this theme of isolation from humanity, one critic remarks that "from the beginning, . . . the only possible direction for [Redburn] is Jackson's, and the question is only how far toward Jackson's lonely fate he will be driven."[47] Also related to *Redburn*'s critique of democracy and its sometimes misanthropic tendencies is Tocqueville's remark that "in democratic communities each citizen is habitually engaged in the contemplation of a very puny object, namely, himself." Pursuing this theme in a chapter entitled "Individualism in Democratic Countries," Tocqueville also anticipates both Redburn's quandary about Harry and America's response to the Irish emigrants: "In democratic ages . . . , when the duties of each individual to the race are much more clear [than in aristocratic ages], devoted service to any one man becomes rare; the bond of human affection is extended, but it is relaxed." Also applicable to Redburn's isolationism is Tocqueville's belief that in democracies (and specifically the Jacksonian variety) people "owe nothing to any man, they expect nothing from any man; they acquire the habit of always considering themselves as standing alone, and they are apt to imagine that their whole destiny is in their own hands." Expressing an outlook that may be implicated in Redburn's abandonment of Harry, Tocqueville says that democracy "throws [the citizen] back for ever upon himself alone, and threatens in the end to confine him entirely within the solitude of his own heart"—"reduced to care for himself alone." And another passage from Tocqueville can help us account for the way that, after abandoning Harry, Redburn returns home to plunge "into embraces, long and loving" (RB, 311); the French statesman observes that "individualism . . . disposes each member of the community to sever himself from the mass of his fellow-creatures, and to draw apart with his family and his friends; so that, after he has thus formed a little circle of his own, he willingly leaves society at large to itself."[48] Of course, these are varieties of isolationism that Ishmael seeks to combat in "The Monkey-Rope" chapter of *Moby-Dick*. To prevent Queequeg and himself from being jammed between the ship and a whale while "cutting-in," he must acknowledge "that my own *individuality* was now merged in a joint stock company of

---

46. Ames, "The Dangers of American Liberty," in *Works of Fisher Ames* (Boston: T. B. Wait, 1809), p. 432.

47. Alan Lebowitz, *Progress into Silence: A Study of Melville's Heroes* (Bloomington: Indiana Univ. Press, 1970), p. 112.

48. Tocqueville, part II, pp. 82, 105, 106, 107, 104.

two" (MD, 271; emphasis added). In *Redburn*, though, Harry Bolton ends up fatally "jammed between the ship, while [his mates] were cutting the fish in" (RB, 312); and though his accidental fall differs from Queequeg's peril, the parallel still invites speculation as to whether Redburn might not have been able to compromise his own individuality to the extent of tying a spiritual monkey rope to his so-called bosom friend.

Tocquevillean categories also clarify why Redburn's democratic rejection of the Old World aristocracy typified by Harry's acquaintances (RB, 221) fails to result in a more conspicuous humanism. "As each class approximates to other classes, and intermingles with them," says Tocqueville, "its members become indifferent and as strangers to one another. Aristocracy had made a chain of all the members of the community, from peasant to the king: democracy breaks that chain, and severs every link of it." And this, in turn, possibly explains the specifically democratic nature of Redburn's interest in *The Wealth of Nations*. Indeed, his attraction to this book becomes especially acute after he learns how people are indifferent to his being the "Son-of-a-Gentleman" (RB, 67–71) and how Smith may provide "the true way to retrieve the poverty of my family, and again make them all well to do in the world" (RB, 86). In Tocqueville's words,

> When the reverence which belonged to what is old has vanished, birth, condition, and profession no longer distinguish men, or scarcely distinguish them at all: hardly anything but money remains to create strongly marked differences between them, and to raise some of them above the common level.

Moreover, precisely the sort of economy that we earlier saw to be at the basis of Adam Smith's rejection of benevolence and possibly also of Redburn's disregard for Harry seems implicit in Tocqueville's remark, "When all the members of a community are independent of or indifferent to each other, the co-operation of each of them can only be obtained by paying for it."[49] By contrast, *Redburn*'s implicit critique of such attitudes approaches what Horace Bushnell referred to in 1837 as "The True Wealth of Nations." Responding to the pervasive influence upon America of Adam Smith's economics, Bushnell maintained that a country's true wealth is "personal, not material. It includes the natural capacity, the industry, the skill, the science, the bravery, the loyalty, the moral and religious worth of the people." Insofar, then, as Redburn believes himself an ambassador of the Redeemer Nation, he

---

49. Tocqueville, part II, pp. 105, 243, 242.

might do well to heed Bushnell, who quotes Milton in an effort to stress that "a commonwealth ought to be but as one huge Christian personage, one mighty growth and stature of an honest man, as big and compact in virtue as in body; for look, what the grounds and causes are of a single happiness to one man, the same ye shall find them to a whole state."[50]

Appropriately, therefore, the subtitle of *Redburn* speaks of "confessions," for the confessional and autobiographical form used by the book's narrator subverts both the enthusiasm of the younger Redburn and the conventions of an autobiographical genre that typically mirrored the messianic and mythic dimensions of American culture.[51] Indeed, whatever the virtues of Redburn's democratic ethic of self-help, a world of difference still exists between the sort of "self-reliance" that fits a man "to steer his bark through the trackless ways of life,"[52] and the more radical self-reliance that proclaims, "[D]o not tell me...of my obligation to put all poor men in good situations. Are they *my* poor? I tell thee, thou foolish philanthropist, that I grudge the dollar, the dime, the cent I give to such men as do not belong to me and to whom I do not belong." Or, as Emerson says elsewhere in "Self-Reliance," "nature suffers nothing to remain in her kingdoms which cannot help itself."[53] To some degree, the latter expression of self-help looks backward to Adam Smith and forward to the social Darwinism of William Graham Sumner and Herbert Spencer. And insofar as Melville explores these tendencies, Redburn's *graceless* encounter with Harry—symbolic, we have seen, of the way America's more general indifference to the welfare of emigrants belies arguments for messianic nationalism—constitutes an important moment in literary and intellectual history. *Redburn* becomes the first novel to dramatize the tension between Christianity's regenerative premise and a democratic ethic of self-help cultivated in an atmosphere of laissez-faire individualism that is governed solely by laws of fitness and chance. As early as 1845 Melville could have read how "everywhere we see the arrangements for the species perfect; the individual is left, as it were, to take his chance amidst the *mêlée* of the various laws affecting him. If he be found inferiorly endowed, or ill befalls him, there was at least no par-

---

50. Horace Bushnell, *The True Wealth or Weal of Nations* (1837), in *Representative Phi Beta Kappa Orations*, ed. Clark S. Northup (1915; rpt. New York: Elisha Parmele Press, 1930), pp. 6, 12.

51. See William C. Spengemann and L. R. Lundquist, "Autobiography and the American Myth," *American Quarterly*, 17 (Fall 1965), 501–19.

52. John Truck, in Cooper's *Homeward Bound* (1838), in *The Works of James Fenimore Cooper*, Mohawk Edition, 33 vols. (New York: G. P. Putnam's Sons, n.d.), XIII: 89.

53. *Works*, II: 52, 70.

tiality against him. The system has the fairness of a lottery, in which every one has the like *chance* of drawing a prize."[54] As *Redburn* shows, some men just happen to be constitutionally more fit than others to overcome the perils of climbing the mainmast; and on this voyage, at least, Redburn "chance[s] to survive" (RB, 312). Yet his indifference to the prodigal provides a fictional enactment of what at least one critic of evolutionary thought had already lamented as the absence of a "personal God" in a system where "the individual must suffer whilst nature is grinding out some higher development."[55] Of course, from the economic decline of his own family, Redburn should have known that even the most gentlemanly classes are subject to these same laws. But this lesson would remain for Hardy and Dreiser to dramatize in the downfall of the D'Urbervilles and Hurstwoods of this world.

---

54. Robert Chambers, *Vestiges of the Natural History of Creation* [1845]—*With a Sequel* (New York: William H. Colyer, 1846), p. 194; emphasis added. For Melville's familiarity with the concerns of Chambers's book, see chapter 132 of *Mardi*, and especially Babbalanja's remark, "Nature works, at random warring, chaos a crater, and this world a shell" (M, 417). For a discussion of Melville's vast knowledge of pre-Darwinian ideas about evolution, and possibly those of Chambers, see Elizabeth S. Foster, "Melville and Geology," *American Literature*, 17 (March 1945), 50–65, esp. pp. 59, n. 6 and 63, n. 34.

55. Taylor Lewis, "Vestiges of the Natural History of Creation" (review essay), *American Whig Review*, 1 (May 1845), 538–39. Moreover, with rhetoric appropriate to our discussion of Redburn's failure to redeem the "prodigal," Lewis explicitly articulates the antagonism between Christian "grace" and evolutionary theories of "chance" and development:

> "*It may be*," [Chambers] observes, "*it may be*, that whilst we are committed to take our chance in a natural system, & c., there is a system of grace and mercy behind the screen." And this is the language of one who would repel the name of infidel, and who professes respect for the Scriptures. . . . Now, of all the sentences in the book, this one furnishes the strongest evidence that the author is what we have called him, an infidel, a disingenuous, unmanly infidel. "There *may*, perhaps, be a system of grace and mercy behind the screen of nature!" and all this said with as much simplicity, as though just such a system of grace and mercy was not the subject which occupies the whole Bible from its commencement to its close. (pp. 541–42)

I quote this passage not to suggest that Melville necessarily shared Lewis's views, but rather to demonstrate the currency of ideas that I believe are implicit in Redburn's "graceless" rejection of the "prodigal."

C H A P T E R   III

"White Enough in All Conscience": The Democratic World of *White-Jacket*

Written mainly in the summer of 1849, *White-Jacket* partly recounts the incidents of Melville's tour with the flagship *United States*, aboard which he enlisted as an ordinary seaman at Honolulu in August of 1843, primarily as a means of returning home after his South Seas excursion. He therefore served aboard the vessel until it docked at Boston in October of 1844. But in renaming the ship the *U.S.S. Neversink*, Melville initiated only the first of several changes that would transform his narrative from a record of personal experience to a fictional undertaking with political concerns that pick up where *Redburn* leaves off. Whereas *Redburn* points out the isolationist tendencies of democratic self-reliance, *White-Jacket* explores the inconsistencies among America's professed messianic identity, her man-of-war outlook, and the institution of slavery. Also central to *White-Jacket*'s political concerns is the suggestion that democracies must tolerate enough individualism and intellectualism to encourage a leveling-up instead of a leveling-down of manners and taste.[1] The present chapter will explore the way Whig and "Conscience Whig" categories not only unify these concerns, but throw new light, as well, upon social outlooks that preoccupied Melville in the months preceding his more "leviathanic" commentary on the American political scene.

Important for our inquiry into *White-Jacket*'s Whiggery is a brief

1. My biographical summary is indebted to Charles Roberts Anderson's "Introduction" to his edition of Melville's *Journal of a Cruise to the Pacific Ocean, 1842–1844, in the Frigate "United States"* (Durham, N.C.: Duke Univ. Press, 1937), pp. 3–18; Leon Howard, *Herman Melville: A Biography* (Berkeley: Univ. of California Press, 1951), pp. 73–88. For an early but still informative account of Melville's interweaving of fact and fiction in *White-Jacket*, see Charles Roberts Anderson, *Melville in the South Seas* (1939; rpt. New York: Dover Publications, 1966), pp. 361–419. A more detailed study of Melville's use of external source materials is Howard P. Vincent's *The Tailoring of Mel-*

review of the book's more conspicuous political features, including its attention to "reform." Conditions shown to be in need of reform range from the absurd hours of dining aboard a man-of-war, to the ridiculous neatness that some captains demand of their sailors, to the incompetence of officers in the American Navy, to the severity of the Articles of War, and to the criminality of excessive flogging. *White-Jacket* also challenges misconceived ideas about "reform," and especially the nineteenth-century view of war as a beneficent institution destined to extend the blessings of liberty to mankind. "Under the influence of Utopianism, nationalism, and sentimental idealism," says Edward McNall Burns, "war ceased to be regarded as an inevitable calamity and came to be thought of as a kind of rainbow of promise." Walt Whitman, for example, assumed this posture when, in an 1846 editorial, he asked, *"Will not the future effect of even this* [Mexican] *war extend the area of Peace Principles—and hasten the advent of that holy era when all swords shall be beat into plough shares and spears into pruning-hooks?"*[2] White-Jacket at one point casually mentions "the recent war with Mexico" (WJ, 149); and in a chapter with events occurring before the Mexican War, Cuticle speaks of "the war now threatening between the States and Mexico" (WJ, 257). Both allusions suggest that the book's concern with war has a timely analog in the recently concluded Mexican campaign, which extended America's borders to the Pacific coast. *Mardi,* however, had already challenged the integrity of America's idealistic and messianic justifications for hostility against Mexico. And compatible with this earlier satire is White-Jacket's remark, "[A]s the whole matter of war is a thing that smites common sense and Christianity in the face; so every thing connected with it is utterly foolish, unchristian, barbarous, brutal, and

---

ville's "White-Jacket" (Evanston, Ill.: Northwestern Univ. Press, 1970). The most important studies of *White-Jacket*'s encounter with the political contexts mentioned above are John Gerlach's "Messianic Nationalism in the Early Works of Herman Melville: Against Perry Miller," *Arizona Quarterly,* 27 (Spring 1972), 5–26; Priscilla Allen Zirker, "Evidence of the Slavery Dilemma in *White-Jacket,*" *American Quarterly,* 18 (Fall 1966), 477–92; Carolyn L. Karcher, *Shadow Over the Promised Land: Slavery, Race, and Violence in Melville's America* (Baton Rouge: Louisiana State Univ. Press, 1980), pp. 39–55; Larry J. Reynolds, "Antidemocratic Emphasis in *White-Jacket,*" *American Literature,* 48 (March 1976), 13–28.

2. Edward McNall Burns, "War as an Instrument of Mission," in *The American Idea of Mission* (New Brunswick, N.J.: Rutgers Univ. Press, 1957), p. 239; Whitman, "'The Most Bloodless' War Ever Known" (16 Dec. 1846), in *The Gathering of the Forces by Walt Whitman: Editorials, Essays, Literary and Dramatic Reviews... Written by Walt Whitman as Editor of the "Brooklyn Daily Eagle" in 1846 and 1847,* ed. Cleveland Rodgers and John Black, 2 vols. (New York: G. P. Putnam's Sons, 1920), I: 253–54.

savoring of the Feejee Islands, cannibalism, saltpetre, and the devil"
(WJ, 315). Indeed, war belies America's messianic identity. "Those
maxims," says White-Jacket, "which, in the hope of bringing about a
Millennium, we busily teach to the heathen, we Christians ourselves
disregard" (WJ, 324). The means, therefore, not only fail to justify the
end; they actually negate it.

John Bernstein shows *White-Jacket*'s pacifistic appeal to be
"based on both religious *and* democratic values, on both the Bible
and the Declaration of Independence." Still, critics seem erroneously
to conflate *White-Jacket*'s sometimes ultra-democratic narrator with
Melville and to assert that "Melville gives White-Jacket none of Taji's
obnoxious arrogance or Redburn's foolish conceit."[3] Opinions such
as these overlook the subtle but still pervasive contradiction between
White-Jacket's transcendent faith in a peculiarly American millennium and his suspect political and racial outlooks. For even though
White-Jacket points out the antimessianic tendencies of war, he still
flaunts the precise Jacksonian rhetoric that had already helped America justify her Mexican aggressions:

> And we Americans are the peculiar, chosen people—the Israel of
> our time; we bear the ark of the liberties of the world. Seventy
> years ago we escaped from thrall; and, besides our first birth-
> right—embracing one continent of earth—*God has given to us,
> for a future inheritance, the broad domains of the political pa-
> gans,* that shall yet come and lie down under the shade of our
> ark, without bloody hands being lifted.... We are the pioneers of
> the world; the advance-guard, sent on through the wilderness of
> untried things, to break a new path in the New World that is
> ours.... Long enough have we been skeptics with regard to our-
> selves, and doubted whether, indeed, the political Messiah had
> come. But he has come in *us*, if we would but give utterance to
> his promptings. (WJ, 151; emphasis added)[4]

One might with less difficulty attribute the conscious exaggera-

---

3. Quotations are from John Bernstein, *Pacifism and Rebellion in the Writings of
Herman Melville* (The Hague: Mouton, 1964), p. 79; Reynolds, p. 19.

4. Gerlach (p. 12) says that this statement "is a calculated exaggeration which exposes its own foolishness. Taken literally it recasts the present expansionistic policy as
part of the divine plan for an apocalypse, replacing the Second Coming of Christ with
the ascendency of the American nation." Nonetheless, some ideas in the passage coincide with the outlook advanced by Andrew Jackson in his "Farewell Address" of 4
March 1837. See James D. Richardson, ed., *A Compilation of the Messages and Papers
of the Presidents, 1789–1897*, 11 vols. (Washington, D.C.: Government Printing Office,
1896–1908), III: 308.

tion of this passage to White-Jacket were he not the author of still other remarks tending to negate his millennial vision. Whatever White-Jacket's professions about "the genius of the American Constitution" (WJ, 143) and the "broad principles of political liberty and equality" (WJ, 144), he is still racially condescending in speaking about barbarous Feejee Islanders (WJ, 315) and in describing how the *Neversink*'s "jolly Africans thus [make] gleeful their toil by their cheering songs" (WJ, 58). In the latter case White-Jacket engages in the sort of racism that Frederick Douglass thought characteristic of northerners who erroneously mistook the singing of Negroes for "evidence of their contentment and happiness." Indeed, White-Jacket little suspects that beneath these "St. Domingo melodies" (WJ, 58) rests the potential for violence, which had already occurred in the bloody slave revolt in Santo Domingo and which finds parodic reenactment aboard the *San Dominick* in "Benito Cereno."[5] Not yet possessing Benito Cereno's wisdom that is woe, White-Jacket perpetrates racial stereotypes by describing Guinea's "ebon face fairly polished with content; ever gay and hilarious; ever ready to laugh and joke" (WJ, 379). Thus, even though White-Jacket protests the "head-bumping" exercises in which May-Day and Rose-Water engage to provide "Fun in a Man-of-War" (ch. 66), he fails to fathom the injustice of Captain Claret's so-called "impartial" whipping of both Negroes after they begin to fight in earnest because one calls the other a "nigger" (WJ, 275). With an obtuseness rivaling that of Amasa Delano, White-Jacket simply says, "Justice commands that the fact of the Captain's not showing any leniency to May-Day—a decided favorite of his, at least

---

5. Douglass, *Narrative of the Life of Frederick Douglass: An American Slave* (1845), ed. Benjamin Quarles (Cambridge, Mass.: Harvard Univ. Press, 1960), p. 38. (Melville could have had access to Douglass's *Narrative* in Duyckinck's library. See "Duyckinck Collection," *Lenox Library Short-Title Lists*, 8 [1887], 18.) That Melville would have been aware of the racially condescending nature of White-Jacket's response is suggested both by Babbalanja's inquiry into the state of the slaves' alleged happiness in "the extreme South of Vivenza" (M, 532–33) and by Melville's even earlier investigation of this stereotype in *Omoo*. See Edward S. Grejda, *The Common Continent of Men: Racial Equality in the Writings of Herman Melville* (Port Washington, N.Y.: Kennikat Press, 1974), pp. 35–66. Melville's use of the Santo Domingo revolt in "Benito Cereno" is discussed by H. Bruce Franklin, *The Wake of the Gods: Melville's Mythology* (Stanford, Cal.: Stanford Univ. Press, 1963), p. 145. In using the term "racism" I have in mind not overtly slanderous prejudice so much as more subtle—but equally reprehensible—modes of ingrained condescension and stereotypes. As Glenn C. Altschuler shows, Melville was ahead of his time in recognizing a distinction between the two types of intolerance. See Altschuler's "Whose Foot on Whose Throat? A Reexamination of Melville's 'Benito Cereno,'" *College Language Association Journal*, 18 (March 1975), 383–92.

while in the ring—should not be passed over." Completely overlooking the racial and moral issues that set the blacks at one another's
throats, White-Jacket feels satisfied that Captain Claret "flogged both
culprits in the most impartial manner" (WJ, 276).[6]

Moreover, something of a stereotype involving the virility of
black males may function in White-Jacket's encounter with the
Neversink's cannon; for he likens "the long twenty-four pounders"
and their "ebon hue" to a "stud of sable chargers in their stalls" (WJ,
42). We might here evade the suggestion of racial innuendo were it
not for the way still another of White-Jacket's encounters with the
ship's cannon reveals his subliminal urge to exploit black women:

> The carronade at which I was stationed was known as "Gun No.
> 5," on the First Lieutenant's quarter-bill. Among our gun's crew,
> however, it was known as *Black Bet*. This name was bestowed by
> the captain of the gun—a fine negro—in honor of his sweet-heart,
> a colored lady of Philadelphia. Of Black Bet I was rammer-and-
> sponger; and ram and sponge I did, like a good fellow. (WJ, 66)

As William Ellery Channing had already said, slavery "robs the colored female of protection against licentiousness. Still worse, it robs
her of self-respect. It dooms her class to prostitution.... Undoubtedly
a smile will be provoked by expressions of concern for the delicacy of
a colored woman. But is this a conventional, arbitrary accomplishment, appropriate only to a white skin?" *White-Jacket*, I suggest,
shows this question to apply not merely to the conduct of slave-
holders, but—and here the book anticipates "Benito Cereno"—to the
condescending attitudes and stereotypes of northern liberals as well.
White-Jacket may admit that "we snatch at a chance to deceive ourselves into a fancied superiority to others, whom we suppose lower in
the scale than ourselves" (WJ, 277), but this is a lesson that he has yet
entirely to grasp himself.[7]

Fittingly, therefore, Melville has White-Jacket come to appreciate
more emotively the injustices of racial inequality; for example, White-

---

6. I differ here, and below, from Grejda (pp. 71–72), who would acquit White-
Jacket of indulging in racial condescension.

7. Channing, "Remarks on the Slavery Question," in *The Works of William E.
Channing, D.D.* (Boston: American Unitarian Assoc., 1895), p. 810. The implications
that I assign to White-Jacket's ramming and sponging seem to be supported by the
parallels established in *Typee* between conventionally energetic forms of exertion and
sexual activity. See James L. Babin's account of Kory-Kory's fire-lighting activities, in
"Melville and the Deformation of Being: From *Typee* to Leviathan," *Southern Review*,
7 (Jan. 1971), 97–98. For Melville's concern in other works with the sexual exploitation

Jacket speaks about military service as if it were a form of slavery (WJ, 378), and he protests the punishment of flogging by appealing to egalitarian logic, the abolitionist implications of which have been amply demonstrated by Priscilla Allen Zirker. Also, to impress upon both White-Jacket and his readers the indignity of flogging, Melville creates a scene in which Captain Claret threatens White-Jacket with a whipping as unjustified as those recorded by Frederick Douglass, who had already described how "to be accused was to be convicted, and to be convicted was to be punished."[8] Although Jack Chase and Colbrook manage to save White-Jacket from both the lash and a retributive murder-suicide (WJ, 280–81), White-Jacket, along with his literary audience, must nonetheless acknowledge with real anguish the prospect of being whipped. Thus, it little matters that nineteenth-century readers seem not to have understood *White-Jacket*'s antislavery allegory; of greater importance is the empathy that the book arouses for *any* person threatened with flogging. Indeed, more influential than propaganda in legislating social reform is the literary artist's ability to impart the *perspective* that first sensitizes people to the plight of individuals who are the object of social injustice. *White-Jacket* compels readers to imagine how it feels to be rejected solely because of something as arbitrary as the "pigment" (WJ, 121) and "complexion" (WJ, 78) of an external covering. By inverting traditional color stereotypes, the narrative forces white readers to share White-Jacket's frustration at being "black-ball[ed]" (WJ, 62) merely because his mates "nourished a *prejudice* against my white jacket" (WJ, 61; emphasis added). And to dramatize the sort of identity crisis experienced by victims of racial prejudice, Melville even has the book's largely Caucasian audience imagine what it is like for a person to feel so persecuted because of color as always to wish to rub or paint his jacket *black* (WJ, 24, 78, 88, 201)—or "tawny" (WJ, 121), a word otherwise used to denominate an "old negro" (WJ, 311) aboard ship. Thus, *perspective*, the unacknowledged legislator of social attitude, becomes the book's main vehicle of social reform. As Shelley says,

---

of slaves, see Karcher, pp. 243–44, and her thoughts about Amasa Delano's "projection of the white man's tabooed sexuality" (p. 134) upon the Negro. I differ, however, from Karcher (p. 53) in attributing less than self-conscious parody to all of White-Jacket's racist attitudes.

8. Douglass, p. 46. My emphasis on the way *White-Jacket* seeks to sensitize white readers to racial concerns is compatible with Wai-Chee S. Dimok's more general observation that, for Melville, the reader of *White-Jacket* becomes "an external source of anxiety..., an unrespected arbiter whom Melville bows to but also resents." See Dimok's informative study, "*White-Jacket*: Authors and Audiences," *Nineteenth-Century Fiction*, 36 (Dec. 1981), 296–317, esp. 317.

"[A] man, to be greatly good, must imagine intensely and comprehensively; he must put himself in the place of another and of many others; the pains and pleasures of his species must become his own."[9]

The more obvious "reform" emphases in *White-Jacket* have not gone unnoticed. Two rear admirals, Livingston Hunt and Thomas O. Selfridge, separately denounced the book's narrator, whom they took for Melville, as a leveling and radical democrat.[10] White-Jacket, after all, does champion "the spirit of our democratic institutions" almost to the point of committing murder to prevent persons in authority from violating "the essential dignity of man" (WJ, 146). Also, White-Jacket resorts to liberal Christian logic in maintaining, "It is to no purpose that you apologetically appeal to the general depravity of the man-of-war's man. Depravity in the oppressed is no apology for the oppressor; but rather an additional stigma to him, as being, in a large degree, the effect, and not the cause and justification of oppression" (WJ, 142). Since regenerate assessments of human nature are consistent with egalitarian protests against submission to any tyrannical power,[11] Rear Admirals Hunt and Selfridge were partly correct in pointing out *White-Jacket*'s latent radicalism.

Still, anybody familiar with either the antidemocratic nature of

---

9. "A Defence of Poetry," in *Shelley's Prose, or the Trumpet of A Prophecy*, ed. David Lee Clark (Albuquerque: Univ. of New Mexico Press, 1954), p. 283. My sense of the compatibility of *imagination* and *legislation* in *White-Jacket* finds an analog in the strategy that Melville would later use in pleading with northern legislators to exercise restraint in dealing with the conquered Confederacy: "In our natural solicitude to confirm the benefit of liberty to the blacks, let us forbear from measures of dubious constitutional rightfulness toward our white countrymen.... *In imagination let us place ourselves in the unprecedented position of the Southerners...*" (from "Supplement" to *The "Battle-Pieces" of Herman Melville*, ed. Hennig Cohen [New York: Thomas Yoseloff, 1963], p. 200; emphasis added).

10. Livingston Hunt, "Herman Melville as a Naval Historian," *Harvard Graduates' Magazine*, 39 (Sept. 1930), 22; Charles Roberts Anderson, ed., "A Reply to Herman Melville's *White-Jacket* by Rear-Admiral Thomas O. Selfridge, Sr.," *American Literature*, 7 (May 1935), 139.

11. See Jonathan Mayhew's *A Discourse Concerning Unlimited Submission and Non-Resistance to the Higher Powers* (1750). Joseph Haroutunian, in *Piety Versus Moralism: The Passing of the New England Theology* (New York: Henry Holt, 1932), p. 12, explains the tie between theological liberalism and political radicalism: "It is only natural that this champion of the rights of men should have entertained humane and exalted ideas concerning them; that he should have had their natural and moral capacities in full view."

Media's anonymous scroll or with the external sources that Melville consulted in creating White-Jacket's radicalism knows that the two admirals probably erred in conflating the book's author and narrator. Less than accurate, too, is their belief that "an apostle of leveling and democracy . . . writes the story of White-Jacket,"[12] since to regard White-Jacket as an *uncompromising* egalitarian and democrat is to overlook his narrative's challenge to religious and political liberalism. This challenge, in fact, is foreshadowed in *Typee*, for just after praising the virtue and benevolence of the natives—and then using this factor as a means of speculating optimistically about "human nature" generally—Tommo says, "[S]ince then I have been one of the crew of a man-of-war, and the pent up wickedness of five hundred men has nearly overturned all my previous theories" (T, 203). White-Jacket, too, admits that his "liberal" reveries were "sorely jarred, now and then, by events that took our philosophy aback" (WJ, 186). Bland, for example, turns out to be "an organic and irreclaimable scoundrel" (WJ, 188); and only five chapters later, White-Jacket alludes to things that are "tyrannical and repelling in human nature" (WJ, 208). In fact, at one point White-Jacket speaks of the navy as a place where "the children of calamity meet the offspring of sin" (WJ, 74), perhaps accounting for the way he associates chiefly with the aristocracy of intellect and character aboard ship. Also, he balances his enthusiasm for "the political equality of all social conditions" (WJ, 114) with less flattering allusions to the "rabble rout" of personalities that poses such a huge threat to man's true "dignity" (WJ, 51). Thus, while Charles Roberts Anderson may have been too biographical in believing "Melville sets himself apart as a sheep among goats, securely cloaked in the aristocratic tatters of his White Jacket," he anticipated more recent scholarly concern for the double vision of White-Jacket's democratic outlook. In the words of another critic,

> When he views them [the "people"] in the ideal he sees and values their dignity and equality and willingly acknowledges a democratic brotherhood with them; when he views them realistically, however, he sees their depravity, vulgarity, and ignorance and feels a sense of superiority toward them. In theory White-Jacket accepts and embraces the common sailors as equals; in

---

12. Hunt, p. 22. For Melville's alteration of autobiographical facts and for his use of external sources to create much of White-Jacket's radicalism, see Anderson, *Melville in the South Seas*, p. 361; Page S. Procter, Jr., "A Source for the Flogging Incident in *White-Jacket*," *American Literature*, 22 (May 1950), 176–77; Thomas L. Philbrick, "Another Source for *White-Jacket*," *American Literature*, 29 (Jan. 1958), 431–39.

practice he disdains them and aligns himself with a few select individuals of social and intellectual distinction.[13]

Far from being a leveling democrat, White-Jacket entertains sentiments echoing Redburn's belief that "hell is a democracy of devils, where all are equals" (RB, 276). In addition, White-Jacket's outlook approaches both Tocqueville's and Cooper's concern for the threat posed by mediocre and often tyrannical majorities to individual creativity and integrity. Indeed, of ultimate value in White-Jacket's double vision are the qualities embodied in Jack Chase's status as a complete "gentleman" (WJ, 14).

This quasi-aristocratic outlook, however, is hardly "antidemocratic," for Edwin H. Cady has shown that "a man concerned for the overt realization of the ideal of democracy has nothing to fear from the gentleman in America. From Jefferson forward some of the best of American thought has been employed in the assimilation of the doctrine of the 'true' gentleman to that of democracy." Indeed, Jefferson, whom Tocqueville thought "the most powerful advocate democracy has ever sent forth," asked John Adams whether "that form of government is the best, which provides the most effectually for a pure selection of these natural aristoi [of virtue and talent] into the offices of government." And, though wary of how American aristocracy might rise to a previously oppressive European status, Adams nonetheless proposed a social system modeled upon "natural aristocracy."[14] Of the same persuasion was Henry Hugh Brackenridge, whose *Modern Chivalry* (1792) dramatized the necessity of electing an aristocracy of virtue and talent. Washington Irving, too, lamented the "all-pervading commonplace" at a time when Emerson celebrated the virtues of "Manners" and "Aristocracy"—and when Emerson and Thoreau rejoiced in the resurrection of hero worship, seeing in Carlyle "a discriminator of kingly qualities in these republican and democratic days." But Dr. Oliver Wendell Holmes best summarized the compatibility of democ-

---

13. Quotations are from Anderson, *Melville in the South Seas*, p. 418; Reynolds, pp. 14–15. Cf. William B. Dillingham's observations about White-Jacket's solitariness, in *An Artist in the Rigging: The Early Works of Herman Melville* (Athens: Univ. of Georgia Press, 1972), pp. 65–66; and Rowland A. Sherrill's chapter on "Democracy and Identity in *White-Jacket*," in *The Prophetic Melville: Experience, Transcendence, and Tragedy* (Athens: Univ. of Georgia Press, 1979), pp. 62–81.

14. Edwin H. Cady, *The Gentleman in America: A Literary Study in American Culture* (Syracuse, N. Y.: Syracuse Univ. Press, 1949), p. 26; Alexis de Tocqueville, *Democracy in America* (1835–40), trans. Henry Reeve, part I, 3rd American ed. (New York: George Adlard, 1839), p. 268. Jefferson and Adams are quoted by Cady, pp. 94, 74.

racy and aristocracy in his remark, "I go politically for *equality* ... and socially for *the* quality."[15]

Less attractive, as Cooper had already shown in both *Home as Found* (1838) and *The American Democrat* (1838), was the sort of coarse-minded democracy that, in *White-Jacket,* finds expression in that "fierce ... republican," Jonathan, whose name Melville would have known to be symbolic of America generally.[16] When a Brazilian emperor visits the *Neversink,* White-Jacket feels embarrassed to hear Jonathan exclaim, "Look you, Don Pedro II., ... how do you come to be Emperor? Tell me that. You cannot pull as many pounds as I on the main-topsail-halyards; you are not as tall as I" (WJ, 235). Unable to appreciate or respect natural aristocracy, Jonathan is a caricature of those Americans whom Cooper had earlier shown to "mistake a vulgar audacity for independence. ... [T]hey are not what their idle vanity would give reason to suppose they fancy themselves, the equals of those whom they insult by their coarseness." Moreover, Cooper might well have lauded Jack Chase's delicacy in choosing "to humor" (WJ, 236) Jonathan into silence, for "the whole embarrassment on this point exists in the difficulty of making men comprehend qualities they do not themselves possess."[17] Willing, therefore, to admire Jack Chase as "a little bit of a dictator" in "mending our manners and improving our taste" (WJ, 15), White-Jacket gladly bows to a variety of coercion that counters the most vulgar tendencies of Brother Jonathan. Hardly antidemocratic, this bias corresponds to Cooper's belief that "he is the purest democrat who best maintains his rights, and no rights can be dearer to a man of cultivation, than exemptions from unseasonable invasions of his time, by the coarse-minded and ignorant."[18]

---

15. Holmes is quoted by Cady, p. 158; Irving, by Van Wyck Brooks, *The World of Washington Irving* (New York: E. P. Dutton, 1944), p. 401. Thoreau's sentiments are from his *Graham's Magazine* article on "Thomas Carlyle and His Works" (1847), in *The Writings of Henry D. Thoreau: Early Essays and Miscellanies,* ed. Joseph J. Moldenhauer *et al.* (Princeton, N.J.: Princeton Univ. Press, 1975), p. 243. For Emerson's essays on "Manners" and "Aristocracy," see *The Complete Works of Ralph Waldo Emerson,* ed. Edward Waldo Emerson, 12 vols. (Boston and New York: Houghton Mifflin, 1903–04), III: 119–55; X: 31–66.

16. See Ishmael's allusion to "John Bull" and "Brother Jonathan" (MD, 333), names for England and America derived from James K. Paulding's *The Diverting History of John Bull and Brother Jonathan* (1812).

17. James Fenimore Cooper, *The American Democrat,* ed. H. L. Mencken (New York: Alfred A. Knopf, 1931), pp. 145, 89. Also applicable to Jonathan is Cooper's discussion of decorum and rudeness (pp. 146–48). Melville remarked of Cooper, "[H]is works are among the earliest I remember, as in my boyhood producing a vivid, and awakening power upon my mind" (L, 145).

18. Cooper, *American Democrat,* p. 91.

From this angle, the more serious dictatorial threat in *White-Jacket* rests in the tyranny of the majority (or, to use Cooper's phrase, the tyranny of "the people"—characterized by "prejudices, provincialisms, ignorance and passions")[19] over those who would aspire to manly independence of thought. In fact, White-Jacket's largest conflict with "the people" of the *Neversink* may be compared to the section of *Home as Found* in which John Effingham takes on "the public" to defend his rights. Effingham is warned that "the public is an awful power," and that its constituents have "openly libelled you, by passing a resolution declaring you to be odious." Yet he maintains his individuality by declaring, "[O]f all tyranny, a vulgar tyranny is to me the most odious."[20] Concession to the public, Cooper recognized, was just another form of slavery: "No Asiatic slave stood more in terror of a vindictive master," says Cooper's narrator, "than Mr. Dodge stood in fear and trembling before the reproof... of every man ... who happened to belong to the political party that just that moment was in power." Insofar, then, as a main concern of *White-Jacket* is its defense of manhood and human dignity, the narrative's antislavery allegory is consistent with White-Jacket's aversion to the tyrannical "people." As Tocqueville remarked, "In democratic States..., the authority of the majority is so absolute and so irresistible, that a man must give up his rights as a citizen, and almost abjure his quality as a human being, if he intends to stray from the track which it lays down."[21] Quite possibly, then, unconditional democracy is antithetical to human dignity. Thus, whereas *Redburn* examines the isolationist and uncharitable tendencies of democratic self-reliance, *White-Jacket* considers the opposite concern of how best to preserve and encourage whatever individual talents and endowments enhance a republican government. And in this respect, at least one facet of White-Jacket's shifting political outlook is distinctly Whiggish.

Indeed, the *American Whig Review* is a good source of political contexts appropriate to this more conservative dimension of White-

19. Cooper, *American Democrat*, pp. 140, 141.

20. Cooper, *Home as Found*, in the Mohawk Edition of *The Works of James Fenimore Cooper*, 33 vols. (New York: G. P. Putnam's Sons, n.d.), XIV: 219, 226. Quotations below from Cooper's *Homeward Bound* will be to volume XIII of *The Works*. Existing scholarship suggests Melville's familiarity with both of these novels. See Nathalia Wright, "The Confidence Men of Melville and Cooper: An American Indictment," *American Quarterly*, 4 (Fall 1952), 266–68; Morton L. Ross, "Captain Truck and Captain Boomer," *American Literature*, 37 (Nov. 1965), 316.

21. Cooper, *Homeward Bound*, p. 88; Tocqueville, *Democracy in America* (1835–40), trans. Henry Reeve, part II (New York: J. & H. G. Langley, 1840), p. 263.

Jacket's world view. As we have seen, White-Jacket sometimes regards "the people" as a tyrannical and ill-educated "mob and rabble" (WJ, 192), and he not surprisingly respects the cultured mannerisms of Jack Chase, who "almost redeemed all the rest" (WJ, 385). These positions are consistent with the *Whig*'s disgust for "*ochlocracy*, or the dominion of the rabble." Similarly, the *Whig* remarks how "the people [are prone to]...manifest their weakness, blindness, and folly, in their political as much as in their other relations....[W]e will not flatter and fawn upon the people, and endeavor to blind them to their own deficiencies, and need of better guidance." The *Whig* also prescribes something like White-Jacket's nearly sacred homage to Jack Chase: "What is now needed more than anything, is for the good and great men...[to] place themselves where they belong, at the head of the masses, to guide, teach and save them."[22] And consistent with what we have explored as *White-Jacket*'s concern for independent thought is the way the *Whig*'s opening issue compares Locofoco majoritarianism with conservative respect for the rights of a citizen "to abide by what he [feels], to express an opinion of his own." A "slave at heart," says the *Whig*, is any person "who thus adores the popular deeds whatever they may be, exalts all they think, sanctifies their very mistakes,...and forever finds all that pleases them 'Wisest, virtuousest, discreetest, best.'" Echoing Tocqueville and foreshadowing the concerns of *White-Jacket*, the *Whig* posits as oppressively autocratic "the Will of the Majority." "Advocates of this new tyranny declare that law is the decree of 'the People,' as by courtesy it is now customary to name the majority."[23]

Far better, claims the *Whig*, is the effort of conservative republicanism to allow any "individual to free himself, in his own personality and independently of all others, from the oppressions of party, the fear of society, and the terror of one or of a number." Conservatism "goes with the *individual* into all the relations of life, confirms him in his rights, defends him in his cause,...and by a silent influence, develops all the better qualities of his soul." Anticipating White-

---

22. "Ancient Greece," *American Whig Review*, 7 (Mar. 1848), 296–97; "Responsibility of the Ballot Box; With an Illustration," *American Whig Review*, 4 (Nov. 1846), 442. Cf. the *Whig*'s discussion of "Civilization: American and European," 4 (July 1846), 32: "The people may be supreme, yet not infallible. Their voice may be the fiat of destiny, yet not the sentence of truth or right"; for "who shouted against the Son of God, 'Crucify him! crucify him!' And can men still without shuddering echo back 'Vox populi, vox Dei?'"

23. From the *American Whig Review*: "The Position of the Parties," 1 (Jan. 1845), 15; "The Progress and the Disorganization," 2 (July 1845), 96; J. D. W., "The Spirit of Liberty," 2 (Dec. 1845), 618.

Jacket's respect for an aristocracy of talent, the *Whig* celebrates the right of "Nature's nobleman . . . to mount, each according to his proper powers."[24] Whereas, in *Typee*, Mehevi is "one of Nature's noblemen" (T, 78), in *White-Jacket* the example of Jack Chase, "our noble First Captain of the Top" (WJ, 13), suggests to White-Jacket that all men are not necessarily equal. Indeed, the eloquence with which Jack Chase convinces the *Neversink*'s commodore to grant the crew "liberty" (WJ, 215) dramatizes the Whig contention that each individual "has a right to an influence, not in the arithmetical ratio of one of the whole mass, but in the moral ratio of his intelligence and virtue—i.e. in proportion as those elements which . . . have a legitimate claim to authority predominate in his character."[25] Quite possibly, then, *White-Jacket*'s emphasis on both an aristocracy of intellect and the necessity of freeing individuals from the tyranny of the majority conforms to Whiggish attitudes that Melville may have harbored when he told Hawthorne, "[I]t is true that there have been those who, while earnest in behalf of political equality, still accept the intellectual estates" (L, 126).

Still, whatever Melville's respect for this intellectually liberating feature of political conservatism, he could probably not have tolerated the failure of the Whig party to protest southern slavery with the same fervor it invoked to censure enslavement to public opinion. Afraid that a too-vigorous outcry against slavery would lead to civil war, the *Whig* would have its readers regard Negro servitude as "a local affection and not a general disease. It is doubtless a curse where it is, but only there. . . . [I]t is a chronic only to a limb, not to the main body."[26] Although this opinion appeared in the *Whig* shortly after

---

24. "A Word to Southern Democrats, from a Northern Conservative," *American Whig Review*, 10 (Aug. 1849), 193 (Melville's *Typee* is advertised on p. 218 of this issue); "Political Bigotry—Conservatism—Radicalism," *American Whig Review*, 6 (Sept. 1847), 245; "The Progress and the Disorganization," p. 93. Whiggish outlooks such as this could have helped to shape what scholarship defines as Melville's more general respect for the idea of "Nature's nobleman" in a natural political hierarchy. See Thomas Scorza's "Tragedy in the State of Nature: Melville's *Typee*," *Interpretation: A Journal of Political Philosophy*, 8 (Jan. 1979), 114.

25. "Civilization: American and European," p. 29. Whig respect for a governing aristocracy of intellect and talent is compatible with Platonic ideas known to Melville about "government of the state by its best and wisest." See Merton M. Sealts, Jr., "Melville and the Platonic Tradition," in *Pursuing Melville: 1940–1980* (Madison: Univ. of Wisconsin Press, 1982), p. 289.

26. "Dangers and Safeguards of the Union," *American Whig Review*, 9 (Feb. 1849), 118. For other instances of the *Whig*'s complacency in regard to slavery, see "The Oregon Bill," 9 (Aug. 1848), 115; "The Hon. Robert Charles Winthrop," 7 (March 1848), 278.

the publication of *Mardi*, Melville satirized such complacency in his novel. In response to Babbalanja's belief that Britain errs in stigmatizing "all Vivenza, as a unity" for slavery, Media wryly says, "Babbalanja, you yourself are made up of members:—then, if you be sick of a lumbago,—'tis not *you* that are unwell; but your spine" (M, 537). Media also remarks that "if... *conscience* be the awarder of its own doom; then, of these tribes, many shall be found exempted from the least penalty of this sin [of slavery]" (M, 534; emphasis added). Melville here anticipates the "Conscience Whig" context of *White-Jacket*, the opening sentence of which—"It was not a *very* white jacket, but white enough in all conscience" (WJ, 3)—foreshadows the abolitionist allegory implicit in White-Jacket's belief that flogging is "religiously, morally, and immutably *wrong*." Insofar as White-Jacket calls for "its abolition" on the grounds that "it is not a dollar-and-cent question of expediency; it is a matter of *right and wrong*" (WJ, 146), his narrative reflects the split that developed in the Whig party over the issue of slavery.

This emphasis is best approached by recalling that such conservative "Cotton Whigs" as Abbott Lawrence, Robert C. Winthrop, and Leverett Saltonstall, who had financial interests in the cotton mills of Lowell and Lawrence, pleaded for the status quo in relation to slavery. Yet the "Conscience Whigs," whose ranks included Charles Francis Adams, John Gorham Palfrey, and Charles Sumner, argued the priority of conscience over profit in their advocacy of emancipation. Thus, when in 1848 the Whig Party nominated Zachary Taylor, a slaveholder, for the Presidency, the Conscience Whigs abandoned Whig affiliation to help form the Free Soil Party, and eventually the Republican Party.[27] Since Melville actually knew Sumner prior to the publication of *White-Jacket*, the book's debt to Conscience Whig sentiment may be significant. In fact, by writing *White Slavery in the Barbary States* (1847), Sumner had already forced Americans to lend out their imaginations to the anguish of southern blacks by pondering the enslavement of whites in Algiers. Since White-Jacket com-

---

27. See Kinley J. Brauer, *Cotton Versus Conscience: Massachusetts Whig Politics and Southwestern Expansionism, 1843–1848* (Lexington: Univ. of Kentucky Press, 1967). Worth noting is William Norris's suggestion, in "Abbott Lawrence in *The Confidence-Man*," *American Studies*, 17 (Spring 1976), 25–38, that both Lawrence and many issues surrounding the split between Cotton and Conscience Whigs figure in that book's chapter titled "A Gentleman with Gold Sleeve-Buttons." Interestingly, White-Jacket compares his outlook aboard the *Neversink* to the frame of mind experienced by the "tenders of power-looms in cotton factories" (WJ, 46). As Brauer (pp. 8–10) remarks, Lawrence and his Cotton Whig associates were principally responsible for the introduction of the power loom into the American cotton industry.

pares service aboard the *Neversink* to white slavery (WJ, 378), and since he tells us of his reading about "corsairs [and] captives" in *"Morgan's History of Algiers"* (WJ, 168), we should review at least one passage from Sumner's essay that anticipates the Conscience Whig allegory of *White-Jacket*. Sumner invoked Royall Tyler's *Algerine Captive* (1797)—a book to which Melville could have had access in Duyckinck's library—to emphasize the abolitionist tendencies resulting from a white man's suffering the indignities that, in America, were reserved for blacks:

> And when he is at length made captive himself by the Algerines, he records his meditations and resolves. "Grant me," he says, from the depths of his own misfortune, "once more to taste the freedom of my native country, and every moment of my life shall be dedicated to preaching against this detestable commerce. I will fly to our fellow-citizens in the Southern States; I will, on my knees, conjure them, in the name of humanity, to abolish a traffic which causes it to bleed in every pore.

As Sumner says elsewhere in *White Slavery*, "Forgetful of the brotherhood of the race, Christian powers have regarded the slavery of blacks as just and proper, while the slavery of whites has been branded as unjust and sinful."[28] Obviously, only a small conceptual leap exists from this insight to *White-Jacket*'s suggestion that an appeal before the Congress protesting exclusively "the bleeding wounds of the lacerated backs of white citizens"[29] was insufficient.

ppropriate to *White-Jacket*'s political outlook is its disjunctive and spasmodic form,[30] which aptly coincides with the narrator's shifting and sometimes contradictory sentiments on the nature of democracy. White-Jacket, we have seen,

28. Charles Sumner, *White Slavery in the Barbary States* (Boston: William D. Ticknor, 1847), pp. 38, 59. In 1847 Melville and Sumner attended the same party, and in 1849 Lemuel Shaw requested of Sumner a letter of introduction in England for Melville. See Jay Leyda, ed., *The Melville Log*, 2 vols. (New York: Harcourt, Brace, 1951), I: 254, 312. For Duyckinck's ownership of Tyler's *Algerine Captive*, see "Duyckinck Collection," VIII: 62.

29. The words are those of Senator John Parker Hale, speaking on "Flogging in the Navy," *Congressional Globe*, 21st Cong., 1st sess. (28 Sept. 1850), p. 2058. Although Hale was noted for his antislavery posture, in this case he seems not to have transferred his sentiments from one issue to the other.

30. Vincent aptly notes that "Written rapidly, *White-Jacket* was clearly not planned

wavers among positions espoused by such diverse groups as Democrats, Whigs, and Conscience Whigs. Similarly, White-Jacket balances his defense of natural rights with descriptions of the disorder resulting from too much liberty. And here Melville invites readers to consider the slim line separating abstract egalitarianism from social chaos.

Consider, for instance, White-Jacket's description of Fourth of July festivities aboard the *Neversink*. Since the Fourth was never celebrated aboard the *United States* during Melville's tour, *White-Jacket*'s departure from autobiography invites speculation about the tie between the nearly fatal disorder that occurs during the performance of a drama titled "The Old Wagon Paid Off" and the democratic ideology that the event aims to celebrate. This is the same ideology, in fact, that Walt Whitman applauded as "Stark Democracy's Destructiveness," with its "'end and aim' of rooting out all that interferes with man's native-born and rational freedom." Also worthwhile recalling is Whitman's claim that "all that is good and grand in any political organization... is the result of... turbulence and destructiveness; and controlled by the intelligence and common sense of such a people as the Americans, it never has brought harm, and never can."[31] But this is hardly the implication of White-Jacket's description of the uproar occurring after Jack Chase valorously acts out the rescue of fifteen · oppressed sailors from the watchhouse. In what possibly comprises an instance of the "indeterminateness" that Whitman considered "no part of Democracy,"[32] the riotous "people" become oblivious to the

---

in detail but was written *ad hoc*. It grew almost at random.... *White-Jacket*, then, is disjunctive, spasmodic, but this disturbs only when the reader demands or expects what Melville never intended to write—a novel" (pp. 107–8). Some small measure of unity is, however, inferable from what Scott Giantvalley and Christina C. Stough, in "'Precedents Are Against It': An Examination of *White-Jacket* as a Corrective for the 'Two Moby-Dicks' Theory," *Studies in American Fiction*, 8 (Autumn 1980), 165–81, discuss as the way "references to previous chapters and foreshadowings of future incidents function integrally within the bodies of many chapters" (pp. 179–80).

31. Whitman, "Stark Democracy's Destructiveness" (16 Apr. 1847); "American Democracy" (20 Apr. 1847), in *Gathering of the Forces*, II: 13; I: 3. (For the possibility that Melville read Whitman's editorials, see my "Satiric Precedent for Melville's 'The Two Temples,'" *American Transcendental Quarterly*, 42 [Spring 1979], 137–45.) Anderson, in *Melville in the South Seas*, p. 399, shows that "the Fourth of July was celebrated in port at Calloa, just before sailing for home, merely by the firing of a national salute." Anderson also remarks that Harrison Robertson, one of Melville's shipmates aboard the *United States*, annotated this section of *White-Jacket* as being "fiction."

32. Responding to the New York *Evening Star*'s query whether "Democracy's indeterminateness and unquestionable destructiveness" are "also beautiful," Whitman says, "Yes: to us the 'destructiveness' of Democracy is very beautiful; because, without it, all the accumulated tyranny and the hoary abuses and abominations of the past would continue. 'Indeterminateness' is no part of Democracy—which has the definite... 'end

officer-of-the-deck's command to take in the top-gallant sails to prevent the ship from capsizing in an approaching squall. Only the measured forms of a drumbeat to quarters counteract the potentially fatal antinomianism of "the people," allowing them to lower the sails: "The sailors pricked their ears at it [the bass drum], as horses at the sound of a cracking whip, and confusedly stumbled up the ladders to their stations. The next moment all was silent but the wind, howling like a thousand devils in the cordage" (WJ, 94). Failing, however, to understand the conservative implications of what he describes, White Jacket mentions the "pleasurable feelings [with which] I witnessed the temporary rupture of the ship's discipline. . . . I thought to myself, this now is as it should be. It is good to shake off, now and then, this iron yoke round our necks" (WJ, 95).

But White-Jacket's is a shifting outlook, and elsewhere Melville provides his narrator with the perception to recognize the woeful significance of those "thousand devils in the cordage." For instance, White-Jacket regrets "the lamentable effects of suddenly and completely releasing *the people'* of a man-of-war from arbitrary discipline. It shows that . . . 'liberty,' at first, must be administered in small and moderate quantities, increasing with the patient's capacity to make a good use of it" (WJ, 227). Also, in a line that could easily have issued from the lips of Captain Vere, White-Jacket early hints at the real significance of the incident involving the squall: "Were it not for . . . regulations a man-of-war's crew would be nothing but a mob, more ungovernable stripping the canvass in a gale than Lord George Gordon's tearing down the lofty house of Lord Mansfield" (WJ, 9).[33] Thus, the *Neversink's* Fourth of July theatricals challenge the opti-

---

and aim' of rooting out all that interferes with man's native-born and rational freedom" (*Gathering of the Forces*, II: 13).

Although without reference to Whitman, Steven E. Kemper, in "*Omoo:* Germinal Melville," *Studies in the Novel*, 10 (Winter 1978), 426, anticipates the most general significance that I assign to the Fourth of July theatricals aboard the *Neversink*. Also, the context that I believe to inform *White-Jacket*'s encounter with the Fourth is best summarized by John F. Berens, in *Providence and Patriotism in Early America, 1640–1815* (Charlottesville: Univ. Press of Virginia, 1978), p. 115:

The Fourth of July was explicitly termed "the political Sabbath of freedom." Clear evidence of the sanctification of American nationalism, the Fourth of July became literally the holy day of obligation for American patriots. This concept survived the triumph of a secular American culture as a central component of America's civil religion, so that well after the passing of providential thought the Fourth of July remained for public spokesmen the prescribed time for ritualized pronouncements on the character and consequences of the American experience.

33. In an editorial note to this reference, A. R. Humphreys remarks, "Lord George Gordon (1751–93) led the 'No Popery' demonstrations of 1780 provoked by the cancella-

mistic view of human nature inherent in the Declaration of Independence; the crew's riotous tendencies comprise something like "The grimy slur on the Republic's faith implied, / Which holds that Man is naturally good, / And—more—is Nature's Roman, never to be scourged."[34] Indeed, when Rear Admiral Selfridge remarked how "the laws [aboard a man-of-war]... protect [a sailor] against his own depraved inclinations"—insisting, as well, that "without the certainty of immediate punishment, anarchy & insubordination would prevail"[35]—he failed to understand how *White-Jacket* conservatively dramatizes the tendency of "inborn and inalienable" (WJ, 280) rights toward anarchy; how the book explores the incompatibility of absolute liberty and the "measured forms" of society; and how, through its dialectical political outlook, White-Jacket's narrative investigates the opposition between *natural* and *civil* liberty. In Melville's time Tocqueville had already resurrected this distinction by quoting John Winthrop's skeptical assessment of human liberty:

> There is a liberty of corrupt nature, which is affected both by men and beasts to do what they list; and this liberty is inconsistent with authority, impatient of all restraint; by this liberty, *"sumus omnes deteriores"*: 'tis the grand enemy of truth and peace, and all the ordinances of God are bent against it. But there is a civil, a moral, a federal liberty, which is the proper end and object of authority; it is a liberty for that only which is just and good:... This liberty is maintained in a way of subjection to authority; and the authority... will... be quietly submitted unto by all but such as have a disposition to shake off the yoke and lose their true liberty, by their murmuring at the honor and power of authority.[36]

---

tion of certain disabilities of the Roman Catholics. Rioting broke out and London lived for a fortnight under a reign of terror, during which the house of Lord Chief Justice Mansfield was sacked and burnt" (*White-Jacket, or the World in a Man-of-War* [London: Oxford Univ. Press, 1966], p. 8, n. 1).

34. Quoted from "The House Top" (1863), in *The "Battle-Pieces" of Herman Melville*, p. 90. The theological and political point of the segment of poetry just quoted obviously challenges the merely rhetorical nature of White-Jacket's question, "Is it lawful for you to scourge a man that is a Roman? asks the intrepid Apostle, well knowing, as a Roman citizen, that it was not. And now, eighteen hundred years after, is it lawful ... to scourge a man that is an American?" (WJ, 142).

35. Selfridge, pp. 134–35, 138.

36. Tocqueville, part I, pp. 38–39. Tocqueville excerpts this passage from Cotton Mather's *Magnalia Christi Americana*. For the historical context of Winthrop's sentiment, see Perry Miller's introductory remarks to "Speech to the General Court," in *The American Puritans: Their Prose and Poetry* (New York: Anchor, 1956), pp. 89–90. Perhaps Winthrop's distinction between *natural* and *civil* liberty also informs Fleece's

The last line of this passage may link White-Jacket's wish "to shake off, now and then, this iron yoke [of discipline] round our necks" (WJ, 95) to the ungovernable liberty that Winthrop sees as the singular tendency of human depravity. But insofar as White-Jacket's outlook shifts back and forth between noble and denigrating views of "the people," his corresponding political views on *authority* neither completely affirm nor deny the tenets of any one political party. Instead, they dramatize the pervasive tension in the American democratic system that had earlier caused Madison, Hamilton, and Jay to insist upon a constitutional division of powers to provide checks and balances to offset the worst tendencies of human nature.[37] Thus, far from being inconsistent, White-Jacket's disjunctive narrative captures the full range of aspirations and limitations implicit in republican notions of liberty and democracy.

Crucial, moreover, to this dialectical inquiry is *White-Jacket's* concern with anticipatory versus antipathetic modes of democracy.[38] The first derives from Paul's injunction (Gal. 3:28), "There is neither Jew nor Greek,...bond nor free,...male nor female: for you are all one in Christ Jesus." As the Dominican remarks in *Clarel*, "Before the Church our human race / Stands equal" (II.xxv.89–90). According to Tocqueville, American egalitarianism owed much to this religious outlook, since "Christianity, which has declared that all men are equal in the sight of God, will not refuse to acknowledge that all citizens are equal in the eye of the law." The currency of this idea in the nineteenth century is evident in the way an 1838 issue of the *Boston Quarterly Review* asserts that "Christianity has a social and political character" and that "all men [are] equal before God, and consequently equal among themselves." Moreover, during the same month that Melville probably began writing *White-Jacket*, the *American Whig Review* advertised the publication of E. L. Magoon's *Republican Christianity: or True Liberty, as Exhibited in the Life, Precepts, and Early Disciples of the Great Redeemer* (Boston, 1849).[39] Melville, of course, knew how

---

views, in *Moby-Dick*, about "natur[al]" sharkishness and "cibil" [sic] self-government (MD, 251).

37. See Benjamin Fletcher Wright's discussion of "Human Nature, Motives, and Factions," in his introduction to *The Federalist (By Alexander Hamilton, James Madison, and John Jay)*, ed. Benjamin Fletcher Wright (Cambridge, Mass.: Harvard Univ. Press, 1961), pp. 26–41.

38. I am indebted in my use of these terms to Sanford A. Lakoff's "Christianity and Equality," in *Equality* (Yearbook of the American Society for Political and Legal Philosophy), IX, ed. J. Roland Pennock and John W. Chapman (New York: Atherton Press, 1967), pp. 115–33.

39. Tocqueville, part I, p. 9; "Democracy of Christianity," *Boston Quarterly*

Americans reverenced "that unshackled, democratic spirit of Christianity in all things."[40] White-Jacket, for example, speaks pleasurably about "the temporary equality of the Church," for it permits him, his shipmates, and the *Neversink*'s officers to "unite in acknowledging Almighty God" (WJ, 290). Anticipatory assumptions also lead White-Jacket to protest how inequalities resulting from divisions of rank "tend to beget in most armed ships a general social condition which is the precise reverse of what any Christian could desire" (WJ, 375). Transcending, therefore, a merely anthropomorphic egalitarianism, White-Jacket's assault upon autocratic tyranny sometimes approaches the sort of anticipatory assumptions that find exaggerated expression in Ishmael's claim, "[T]his august dignity I treat of, is not the dignity of kings and robes, but. . . . that democratic dignity which . . . radiates without end from God; Himself! . . . The centre and circumference of all democracy! His omnipresence, our divine equality" (MD, 104).

White-Jacket, nonetheless, wavers between this sort of exuberancy and a more sober authoritarianism, the latter echoing the antipathetic assumption that Christianity sponsors no social ideals corresponding to the equality of all souls before God. Saint Augustine had already spoken of social inequality as a "desert of sin"; and American Congregationalists had early derived from Calvin's doctrine of "equal depravity" the duty of a theocracy of saints to protect the populace from its own natural liberty.[41] Thus, to the degree that White-Jacket speaks disparagingly of "what human nature is, and what it must forever continue to be" (WJ, 218), and to the extent that he knows, "[S]o long as a man-of-war exists, it must ever remain a picture of much that is tyrannical and repelling in human nature" (WJ, 208), an antipathetic skepticism undercuts his anticipatory fervor. Invoking the spirit of the "blessed Redeemer [who] came down to redeem our whole man-of-war world; to that end, mixing with sailors and sinners as equals" (WJ, 229), White-Jacket may finally see that while all men are equal before God, their equality extends to the allotment of depravity each possesses.[42]

For all this, however, a conspicuous anticipatory tenor character-

Review, 1 (Oct. 1838), 445, 447; "Critical Notices," *American Whig Review*, 10 (July 1849), 108. The *Whig* mentions that Magoon "believes that Jesus Christ, eighteen centuries ago, gave our race a perfect model of republicanism."

40. Melville, "Hawthorne and His Mosses," *Literary World*, 7 (24 Aug. 1850), 146.

41. Lakoff, pp. 126–27, 129–30.

42. My thoughts on the connection between depravity and democracy in *White-Jacket* are consistent with what Gene Bluestein, in "The Brotherhood of Sinners: Literary Calvinism," *New England Quarterly*, 50 (June 1977), 206, defines as Melville's more general conclusions about egalitarianism.

izes Ishmael's paean to "divine equality," suggesting Melville's continued attention in his next, and greatest, work to still other aspects of
the discontinuities between democratic ideals and practice. Indeed,
whereas *White-Jacket* comprises a sort of jeremiad, lamenting the gap
between America's potential greatness and the obstacles posed by
racism and man-of-war attitudes to its achievement, *Moby-Dick*, as we
shall see presently, locates the inspiration for America's bellicosity
and much of her racial tensions in both the jeremiad tradition itself
and in the covenant psychology implicit in anticipatory modes of
democratic thought.

C H A P T E R IV
Nationalism and Providence in Ishmael's White World

Thus far we have explored Melville's fictional encounter with the imperialist, racist, and man-of-war tendencies of "civilization"; his dramatization of the self-serving nature of seemingly benevolent rhetoric about Manifest Destiny; his skepticism about anticipatory and millennial outlooks on democracy and republicanism; and his distress with the institution of slavery. As observed, such concerns reflect the immediate political climate of 1845–50, during which years Melville wrote his first five books. By the time he began *Moby-Dick,* America had settled its dispute with Great Britain over Oregon, had annexed Texas, and had engaged in a war with Mexico that extended the boundaries of the Union to the Pacific. Celebration, however, was short, since the lands ceded to the United States by the Treaty of Guadalupe Hidalgo (1848) had the potential of upsetting the delicate balance between "slave" and "free" states temporarily secured by the Missouri Compromise of 1820–21. Thus, the Union found itself confronting the specter of nullification because southerners were fearful of David Wilmot's 1846 proviso calling for the prohibition of slavery in lands acquired from Mexico. A period of calm, however, ensued after Henry Clay's "Compromise of 1850." This abolished the slave trade in the District of Columbia; admitted California to the Union as a free state; divided the rest of the Mexican cession into two territories (New Mexico and Utah) that would decide for themselves whether to apply for membership into the Union as free or slave states; and appeased southern slave owners by devising a fugitive slave law, which, together with the Fugitive Slave Act of 1793, was vigorously enforced by judges no less eminent than Melville's father-in-law, Lemuel Shaw, Chief Justice of the Massachusetts Supreme Court.[1]

1: For an overview of the Compromise, see Joseph G. Rayback, *Free Soil: The Election of 1848* (Lexington, Ky.: Univ. Press of Kentucky, 1970), p. 308; Robert

Since Ishmael composes his narrative between 1850 and 1851 (MD, 310, 172), it not surprisingly echoes many of these political issues. As scholarship shows, parallels exist between the *Pequod*'s pursuit of the White Whale and America's westward strivings; between Ahab's monomania and the expansionist and democratic outlooks of Andrew Jackson and James K. Polk; and between Ahab's defiance of "God's Law Supreme" and John C. Calhoun's uncompromising insistence that slavery be extended into the new territories acquired from Mexico.[2]

Still, whatever Ahab's importance to the book's political allegory, Ishmael provides the informing consciousness of *Moby-Dick*'s narrative,[3] which he writes several years after the *Pequod*'s catastrophe with the purpose, at least in part, of reaffirming his faith in a caring God. Conspicuous, too, is Ishmael's willingness to correlate his seemingly special salvation with the divine wrath visited upon Ahab and his crew, whose fate Ishmael sees as foreshadowing the punishment in store for a bellicose, proslavery, and unrepentant republic. Thus, Ishmael salvages a sense of optimism by advancing his abolitionist rendition of the *Pequod*'s demise within the penultimately affirmative outlook of a jeremiad, positing his own survival as an example of God's promissory grace for a reformed America. Melville's abhorrence of slavery, however, should not elicit unqualified praise for the jeremiad *form* that Ishmael imposes on his abolitionist narrative. In truth, the covenant assumption implicit in the American jeremiad had already fostered exclusive racial outlooks by encouraging pioneers to view the

McNutt McElroy, *The Winning of the Far West* (New York: G. P. Putnam's Sons, 1914), pp. 313–48, esp. 345. For Shaw's support of the Fugitive Slave Act, and for possibilities surrounding Melville's imaginative response to this controversy, see Leonard W. Levy, *The Law of the Commonwealth and Chief Justice Shaw* (Cambridge, Mass.: Harvard Univ. Press, 1957), pp. 73–108; Charles H. Foster, "Something in Emblems: A Reinterpretation of *Moby-Dick*," *New England Quarterly*, 34 (March 1961), 3–35.

2. See Edwin S. Fussell, *Frontier: American Literature and the American West* (Princeton, N.J.: Princeton Univ. Press, 1965), pp. 256–79; Charles Olson, *Call Me Ishmael* (New York: Reynal & Hitchcock, 1947), pp. 113–19; John William Ward, *Andrew Jackson: Symbol for an Age* (London: Oxford Univ. Press, 1953), pp. 201–2; Alan Heimert, "*Moby-Dick* and American Political Symbolism," *American Quarterly*, 15 (Winter 1963), 507–11, 524–26.

3. For the centrality of Ishmael's consciousness to the narrative of *Moby-Dick*, see Walter E. Bezanson, "*Moby-Dick*: Work of Art," in "*Moby-Dick*" *Centennial Essays*, ed. Tyrus Hillway and Luther S. Mansfield (Dallas, Tex.: Southern Methodist Univ. Press, 1953), pp. 30–58; Paul Brodtkorb, Jr., *Ishmael's White World: A Phenomenological Reading of "Moby-Dick"* (New Haven: Yale Univ. Press, 1965), pp. 102–48; Warwick Wadlington, *The Confidence Game in American Literature* (Princeton, N.J.: Princeton Univ. Press, 1975), pp. 73–103; Bainard Cowan, *Exiled Waters: "Moby-Dick" and the Crisis of Allegory* (Baton Rouge: Louisiana State Univ. Press, 1982), esp. pp. 60–77, 119–25, 157–58.

Great West as a New Canaan, or promised land, for God's mainly white chosen people.[4] Thus, I challenge Carolyn Karcher's thesis that Ishmael is a cultural hero who transcends the "ethnocentrism and color consciousness" of his countrymen. Karcher shows that Melville could not believe—like the Abolitionists—in a millennium that would result from the eradication of slavery. Nevertheless, like an even more recent commentator on the "war in Melville's imagination," she fails to detail how Ishmael imbues his abolitionist narrative with millennial assumptions having an exclusive "covenant" premise that shadows forth the race hatred and violence he nominally repudiates.[5]

From the outset, however, we should distinguish between the transient and the permanent in *Moby-Dick*, the greatest concerns of which relate to unbounded pride, the conquest of nature, and disregard for human limitations. Every era witnesses unique manifestations of these transgressions, which in eighteenth- and nineteenth-century America surfaced in the issues raised by the Declaration of Independence: America had a destiny to implement and spread a republican form of government, but *how* was it to do so, and how would the institution of slavery figure in this continental enterprise? By addressing these questions, *Moby-Dick* ultimately transcends its emphasis on specific parallels between Ahab and mid-century America to confront the more enduring issue of emancipated self-interest, the Tocquevillean features of which Melville had already explored in *Redburn*.

Nonetheless, the precise strategy with which Melville structures a response to these concerns hinges on the form of Ishmael's narrative. This we shall see to be structured upon Bishop Butler's *Analogy of*

---

4. See, for example, Ernest Lee Tuveson, "Chosen Race ... Chosen People," in *Redeemer Nation: The Idea of America's Millennial Role* (Chicago: Univ. of Chicago Press, 1968), pp. 150–53; Lawrence J. Friedman, *Inventors of the Promised Land* (New York: Alfred A. Knopf, 1975), pp. 217–18; Klaus J. Hansen, "The Millennium, the West, and Race in the Antebellum American Mind," *Western Historical Quarterly*, 3 (Oct. 1972), 373–90, esp. 389.

5. I here take issue with Carolyn L. Karcher's reading of Ishmael, in *Shadow Over the Promised Land: Slavery, Race and Violence in Melville's America* (Baton Rouge: Louisiana State Univ. Press, 1980), pp. 63–72 (p. 69 is quoted), 15, 17. I also question Joyce Sparer Adler's thesis, in *War in Melville's Imagination* (New York: New York Univ. Press, 1981), pp. 73–76, about Ishmael's destiny to effect an order opposite from that of his captain. Ishmael is neither the cultural relativist described by Karcher nor Adler's "new, more human, being" (p. 75). Rather, he is a distant relative of Judge Hall, a historian whom Adler (pp. 111–12) rightly indicts as an accessory to Indian genocide. My reading, therefore, also stands opposed to Cowan's assertion (pp. 70, 179, 180) that Ishmael's retrospective narration and allegorical outlook provide a basis for participating in "community." I concur that Ishmael longs for a sense of community but hold that the jeremiad format of his narrative will forever keep him in exiled waters.

Religion (1743) as well as to resemble a Puritan jeremiad. Yet to understand the connection between narrative form and politics in *Moby-Dick*, we must first review Ishmael's portrait of Ahab, which is intimately linked to the elusive connection among such factors as expansionism, slavery, and whaling.

Nobody, of course, would wish to deny that Melville's experiences aboard whaling ships provided intellectual grist for *Moby-Dick*. However, so commonplace were associations between the valor of whalemen and the fortitude of pioneers that this analogy almost certainly contributed, along with Melville's practical experience, to the political texture of Ishmael's narrative. Consider, for instance, the almost Ishmaelian conflation of whaling and pioneering in Sergeant S. Prentiss's "Address on the Landing of the Pilgrims" (1845):

> It is upon the unstable element the sons of New England have achieved their greatest triumphs. Their adventurous prows vex the waters of every sea. Bold and restless as the old Northern Vikings, they go forth to seek their fortunes in the mighty deep. The ocean is their pasture, and over its wide prairies they follow the monstrous herds that feed upon its azure fields. As the hunter casts his lasso upon the wild horse, so they throw their lines upon the tumbling whale. They "draw out Leviathan with a hook." They "fill his skin with barbed irons," and in spite of his terrible strength they "part him among the merchants." To them there are no pillars of Hercules. They seek with avidity new regions, and fear not to be "the first that ever burst into unknown sea." Had they been companions of Columbus, the great mariner would not have been urged to return, though he had sailed westward to his dying day.

As a resident of New York in 1846, Melville may have seen the issue of the *New York Morning News* in which John L. O'Sullivan quotes this passage.[6] In any event, its informing sentiment shows Ishmael

---

6. *New York Morning News* (2 Jan. 1846). For the full text, see *A Memoir of S. S. Prentiss*, ed. George Lewis Prentiss, 2 vols. (New York: Charles Scribner, 1855), II: 397–408. Worth recalling are the ties that existed between the *New York Morning News* and the Duyckinck circle, which included Melville. See John Stafford, *The Literary Criticism of "Young America,"* English Studies, no. 3 (Berkeley: Univ. of California Press, 1952), p. 25; Johannes D. Bergmann, "The *New York Morning News* and *Typee*," *Melville Society Extracts*, 31 (Sept. 1977), 1–4.

not to be alone in believing "for many years past the whale-ship has been *the pioneer* in ferreting out the remotest and least known part of the earth" (MD, 99; emphasis added). And Ishmael's boast is also compatible with the views of William Gilpin, who bragged that America's "pioneer army" consisted both of overland adventurers and a marine whaling fleet: "Upon the Atlantic coast the pioneer force has thrown itself into ships, and found in the ocean-fisheries food for its creative genius. The whaling fleet is the *marine* force of the pioneer army." Suggestive, too, for *Moby-Dick*'s expansionist concerns is Gilpin's proclamation:

> The men of these two great enterprises of which we have spoken may not be thwarted. The ambition of the one incarcerates him in the womb of a ship, to pursue over the boundless ocean and through exciting dangers the capture of the salt sea-monster; his spoil is blubber; oil illumes the long night of his home, ivory rolls over the billiard table, and whalebone bends to the fancies of female taste. The other rescues the wilderness from savage masters and idle nature.... In both burns the glorious genius of enterprise, commingled of virtue and valor.... Together, side by side, linked in the freshness of the bridal hour, let them tread onward their wedded and indissoluble career.[7]

Elsewhere evident in Gilpin's treatise is his effort to convince the northeastern business community—which by 1846 had millions of dollars tied up in whaling—that westward expansion was in its best interest. Several United States Presidents also used this tactic: Andrew Jackson, for example, hoped to see the Republic of Texas—then petitioning for statehood—conquer sections of California, the harbors of which would appeal to the whaling industry. As William H. Wharton, representative from Texas, wrote in 1837, "General Jackson says that Texas must claim the Californias on the Pacific in order to paralyze the opposition of the North and East to Annexation; that the fishing interest [whaling] of the North and East wish a harbor on the Pacific; that this claim of the Californias will give it to them, and will diminish their opposition to annexation." Looking westward in 1842, President Tyler likewise remarked that "the acquisition of so good a port on the Pacific as St. Francisco.... would be useful to Whale

---

7. 29th Cong., 1st sess., *Senate Documents* (ser. 474), no. 306 (20 April 1846): Report of the Committee on the Post Office and Post Roads, pp. 23, 45. Recall that this is the same document that contains a discussion of the isothermal zodiac, the expansionist implications of which are compatible with Taji's zodiacal wanderings through Mardi. See chapter I above.

Ships and trading vessels of the United States." And Waddy Thompson, Tyler's Minister to Mexico, claimed that possession of San Francisco and Monterey "would secure the only places of refuge & rest for our numerous fishing vessels, and would no doubt...secure the trade of India and the whole Pacific Ocean." In 1845, moreover, James Buchanan, Secretary of State under James K. Polk, justified America's expansionist designs with reference to "the interests of our commerce and our whale fisheries on the Pacific Ocean"—as did President Polk, who, in the midst of war with Mexico, reassured Americans that

> Upper California is bounded on the north by our Oregon possessions; and if held by the United States, would soon be settled by a hardy, enterprising, and intelligent portion of our population. The bay of San Francisco, and other harbors along the California Coast, would afford shelter for our navy, for our numerous whale ships, and other merchant vessels employed in the Pacific ocean, and would in a short time become the marts of an extensive and profitable commerce with China, and other countries of the East.[8]

The exact source, if any, of Melville's parallel between whaling and expansionism, is, then, less important than the currency of an idea that provides ample precedent for Ishmael's Prentiss-like decree that Nantucket whalers have "overrun and conquered the watery world like so many Alexanders; parcelling out among them the Atlantic, Pacific, and Indian oceans.... Let America add Mexico to Texas, and pile Cuba upon Canada;...two thirds of this terraqueous globe are the Nantucketer's. For the sea is his; he owns it, as Emperors own empires" (MD, 63). Here, though, Ishmael exhibits enthusiasm of the sort that led the *Democratic Review* to advise that "we may...be taking a great deal for granted, in discussing the consequences of extending our territorial limits further to the westward than the boundaries of Texas, and to be unmindful of Mrs. Glass's instructions in cooking a fish—first catch it." Suggestive for its related political emphasis is an article in the *American Whig Review* titled "Our Adventures in Search of a Cat Fish—with...Directions how Not to Cook One when

---

8. Wharton's remark is quoted by Frederick Merk, *The Monroe Doctrine and American Expansionism: 1843–1849* (New York: Alfred A. Knopf, 1966), p. 107. The statements of Tyler and Thompson are quoted by Norman A. Graebner, *Empire on the Pacific: A Study in American Continental Expansion* (New York: Ronald, 1955), p. 71. For the remarks of Buchanan and Polk, see *The Works of James Buchanan*, ed. John Bassett Moore, 12 vols. (Philadelphia: J. B. Lippincott, 1908–11), VI: 275; "Message of the President," *Congressional Globe*, 30th Cong., 1st sess. (7 Dec. 1847), Appendix, p. 3.

Caught." Catching and cooking Texas was not all that difficult; but barbecuing Mexico in its aftermath proved more exhausting: "Waste not your precious time in taking cats, but *if* taken, dream not of barbecuing them, but return them unsinged to the stream, and so shall a great waste of time and patience be spared."[9]

Melville's Ahab stands to learn much the same lesson insofar as his career echoes that of the biblical King Ahab, whose criminality in stealing Naboth's Vineyard (1 Kings 21) was, as Alan Heimert shows, often cited in the nineteenth century to denounce American expansionism in the Southwest. "Arguments... addressed to our national cupidity and pride," warned one congressman debating the annexation of Texas, "are the arguments with which Ahab reconciled to himself the seizing of Naboth's Vineyard."[10] Granted, the seemingly unrelated exasperation of losing a limb instigates the mischief of Melville's Ahab. Melville, however, may have known how President Polk legitimized America's claims upon Texas by arguing that the Louisiana Purchase (1803) had given the United States absolute title to this land but that John Quincy Adams had foolishly "dismembered" the territory from the Union by ceding it to Spain as part of the Florida Treaty of 1819. Polk, therefore, often spoke less in terms of "annexation" than he did of "reannexation." Several U.S. senators even supported a resolution stating that "the country dismembered from the United States by the treaty of 1819... OUGHT TO BE reunited to the United States." But in a rebuttal that possibly imbues with political overtones Ahab's vow to "dismember my dismemberer" (MD, 147), Senator Thomas Hart Benton presented a lengthy review of the Texas issue, finally lauding the prudence of Andrew Jackson, who, "in seeking to recover the dismembered part of our own country... did not undertake to dismember the empire of a neighbor." And Melville

---

9. "Territoral Aggrandizement," *Democratic Review*, 17 (Oct. 1845), 247; "Angling," *American Whig Review*, 11 (Jan. 1850), 39. The latter's explicitly political context is evident from its opening paragraph, which places the story's events "in the first youth of one of the last born sisters of our Union, who, after a misalliance with a Mexican,... terminated the affair by scratching his eyes out, taking forcible possession of ... [his] property,... and then ... coming home again, and getting her friends to fight out the battle for her" (pp. 33–34).

10. The remark is that of Kenneth Rayner, of North Carolina, as recorded in *Cong. Globe*, 28th Cong., 2nd sess. (26 Feb. 1845), Appendix, 360. It was made shortly after Jacob Collamer's nearly identical warning in *Cong. Globe*, 28th Cong., 2nd sess. (23 Jan. 1845), Appendix, 404. See also David Lee Child's *The Taking of Naboth's Vineyard; or, History of the Texas Conspiracy* (New York: S. W. Benedict, 1845), p. 29. Heimert, p. 503, offers an overview of these and other political references to King Ahab. Of course, still pertinent to any consideration of Ahab's name is Nathalia Wright's *Melville's Use of the Bible* (Durham, N.C.: Duke Univ. Press, 1949), pp. 61–72.

may well have consulted the 1844 volume of the *Congressional Globe* that includes this passage, for it also contains an account of the stump speech in which Melville's brother, Gansevoort, coined the name "Young Hickory" for James K. Polk.[11]

The expansionist nature of Ahab's quest also gives added significance to both "the sleeplessness of his vow" (MD, 173) and to the fact that "even when wearied nature seemed demanding repose he would not seek that repose in his hammock" (MD, 202). Ahab either paces the deck, "always wakeful" (MD, 112) and mindful of his purpose, or he reclines at his charts with his head thrown back, as if he were reading the telltale, which, suspended from the ceiling, helps guide him to Moby-Dick. As Starbuck says, "[S]leeping in this gale, still thou steadfastly eyest thy purpose" (MD, 202). Ahab's, in short, is an "unsleeping, ever-pacing thought" (MD, 140), which finds an analog in the *Foreign Quarterly Review*'s criticism of both the "restless and reckless race" of American pioneers and "the American passion for going a-head, and keeping in perpetual motion." To this charge the New York *Herald* responded, insisting that Europe was merely intimidated by America's crusade to widen the area of liberty: "[I]t is this very 'restlessness' that alarms the despotisms of the ancient world—a 'restlessness' to which steam, the railroad, the electric telegraph... give such vastly increased impetus and power...." And Ahab's restlessness approaches this precise variety of continentalism: "The path to my fixed purpose is laid with iron rails" (MD, 147).[12]

---

11. For Polk's use of the terms "dismemberment" and "reannexation" in relation to the loss of Texas, see John S. Jenkins, *James Knox Polk and a History of His Administration* (Auburn and Buffalo, N.Y.: John E. Beardsley, 1850), pp. 120–23 (quoted in Merk, *Monroe Doctrine*, pp. 135–36). The Senate resolution concerning the 1819 dismemberment of Texas is cited in the opening column of Thomas Hart Benton's speech on the "Annexation of Texas," *Cong. Globe*, 28th Cong., 1st sess. (16–20 May 1844), Appendix, 474, which also contains (pp. 483–84) the remark of Benton quoted above. As Heimert (pp. 507–8) shows, Gansevoort's 1844 speech about "Young Hickory" is in *Cong. Globe*, 28th Cong., 1st sess., Appendix, 662. Moreover, Polk's "dismemberment" of Mexico was criticized in the *American Whig Review*, 7 (Jan. 1848), 13, as was the earlier annexation of Texas, which the *Whig* called "the consummation of a scheme of treachery without a parallel in the history of the intercourse of civilized nations, unless we except that most atrocious of national crimes, the dismemberment of Poland" (2 [Nov. 1845], 457). And that Melville was fully aware of the political use of "dismemberment" is evident from his allusion in *Clarel* to "dismembered Poland" (IV.xii.30). Of course, beyond the specifically political connotations of Ahab's dismemberment exist what one critic describes as the crises of "identity" and "meaning" in Ahab's "disembodiment." In this vein, see Sharon Cameron, *The Corporeal Self: Allegories of the Body in Melville and Hawthorne* (Baltimore, Md.: Johns Hopkins Univ. Press, 1981), pp. 15–75, esp. 62–63, 66–71.

12. "The Oregon Territory," *Foreign Quarterly Review*, 35 (July 1845), 492; New

Consistent with this expansionist outlook is Ahab's messianic fervor. To begin with, Ahab imitates Christ by lying "like dead for three days and nights" (MD, 87) after first encountering Moby-Dick. Also, he fancies this creature the dragon of iniquity and upon its white hump piles "the sum of all the general rage and hate felt by his whole race from Adam down" (MD, 160). And nominally redemptive are both the *Pequod*'s departure on Christmas Day (ch. 22) and Ahab's wearing a "crucifixion in his face" (MD, 111). In short, Ahab fancies himself a champion of afflicted humanity, protesting "the world's grievances before that bar from which not very many . . . ever came back" (MD, 108). He may, as one critic suggests, even fancy himself "entrusted with the fate of the national Israel, and . . . representative of the chosen people, having wandered for 'forty years on the pitiless sea.'"[13] Moreover, Melville seems to imbue Ahab's restlessly messianic outlook with some degree of Jacksonian enthusiasm.[14] To the extent that he does so, we may explore Ahab's nominally democratic—if actually demagogical—quest within the specifically Jacksonian context of "extending the area of freedom." As we know from *Mardi*, Melville would have recognized the expansion of freedom as the idea most often used by Americans to justify territorial expropriation from neighboring, and sometimes distant, nations. "In 1825," says John William Ward, "Americans were to save the world by example; in 1845, Americans were to save the world by absorbing it."[15] Precisely these two impulses find expression in Ahab's expansionist voyage, purportedly a mission of redemption: "Ho, ho! all ye nations before my prow, I bring the sun to ye! Yoke on the further billows; hallo! a tandem" (MD, 423). And Ahab makes much the same

York *Herald* (13 Sept. 1845). The excerpt from the *Herald* (a paper that Melville mentions in *White-Jacket*, p. 244, and to which he is said to have subscribed [see chapter I, note 45]) is quoted by Merk, *Monroe Doctrine*, p. 157. For the expansionist import of Ahab's allusion to "iron rails," see Leo Marx, *The Machine in the Garden: Technology and the Pastoral Ideal in America* (London: Oxford Univ. Press, 1964), p. 196.

13. Michael T. Gilmore, "Melville's Apocalypse: American Millennialism and *Moby-Dick*," *ESQ: A Journal of the American Renaissance*, 21 (1975), 155. Cf. Milton R. Stern, "*Moby-Dick*, Millennial Attitudes, and Politics," *Emerson Society Quarterly*, 54 (1969), 51–60. Still important for any discussion of Ahab's nominally messianic status is Richard Chase's *Herman Melville: A Critical Study* (New York: Macmillan, 1949), pp. 44–45.

14. See Ward, pp. 201–2; Edward Stone, "Ahab and Old Hickory," in Jack Salzman, ed., *Prospects: An Annual of American Cultural Studies*, 4 (New York: Burt Franklin, 1979), 185–95.

15. Ward, p. 136. The concept of extending the area of freedom is discussed at greater length by Albert K. Weinberg, in *Manifest Destiny: A Study in Nationalist Expansion in American History* (Baltimore, Md.: Johns Hopkins Univ. Press, 1935), pp. 100–29.

point by vowing "to raise [lightning] rods on the Himmalehs and Andes, that all the world may be secured" (MD, 415).

Compatible with this emphasis on messianic expansionism is Ahab's conviction, "This whole act's immutably decreed.... I am the Fates' lieutenant; I act under orders" (MD, 459). As early as *Mardi* this premise informed the expansionist and imperialist policies of King Uhia, who believes that a manifest "destiny" (M, 275) has "foreordained [him] to the dominion of the entire Archipelago" (M, 276). From a nationalist outlook, therefore, significance rests in Ahab's belief that "the future, as purpose, has determined the present."[16] The American experiment has always relied on a sense of "cosmic determinism," like that which led the *American Literary Magazine* to declare "the destiny of California ... fixed. It will soon be part of our Republican Confederacy"—or that which inspired the *Democratic Review* to speak of annexation as "inevitable and irrevocable": "*Che sarà, sarà*— what must be, must be.... That Texas is to be, sooner or later, included in the Union, we have long ... regarded as an event already indelibly inscribed in the book of future fate and necessity."[17] This frame of mind also throws new light on Ahab's belief that "all visible objects ... are but as pasteboard masks. But in each event ... some unknown but still reasoning thing puts forth the mouldings of its features from behind the unreasoning mask" (MD, 144). Little difference exists between this position and the expansionist premise that

> [b]ehind the series of outward events we are made to see the Supreme Disposer touching the springs of human action, permitting or thwarting the outward results of men's free determinations, and swaying with absolute grasp the agencies of nature....

> Invisibly, in and behind the visible procession of events, the Supreme Disposer has presided over the course of events which have made the last year [1848] memorable in the annals of the old world and the new.[18]

In *Mardi* Media's scroll had already challenged this type of outlook by warning how Vivenza's "grand error ... seems this:—The conceit that

---

16. Brodtkorb, p. 68.

17. For America's "cosmic determinism," see Ward, p. 10. The periodical citations are from "California," *American Literary Magazine*, 3 (Dec. 1848), 341; "Annexation," *Democratic Review*, 17 (July 1845), 5; "The Texas Question," *Democratic Review*, 14 (April 1844), 423.

18. "California," *American Whig Review*, 9 (April 1849), 334, 335. A close reading suggests that this article may parody Locofoco enthusiasm.

Mardi is now in the last scene of the last act of her drama; and that all preceding events were ordained, to bring about...a universal and permanent Republic" (M, 525). *Moby-Dick* examines the fatalistic premises behind this assumption, dramatizing in Ahab's despairing career the less glamorous tendencies of a wholesale abdication of free will. As Alexis de Tocqueville had remarked, the American historical mentality tended to "deprive the people themselves of the power of modifying their own condition, and [to] subject them either to an inflexible Providence, or to some blind necessity."[19]

Appropriate, therefore, is Ahab's association with Macbeth, and Fedallah's resemblance to the "weird sisters" who assure Macbeth that "none of woman born / Shall harm [thee]" and that "Macbeth shall never vanquished be until / Great Birnam Wood to high Dunsinane Hill / Shall come against him." Similarly, Fedallah promises Ahab that "neither hearse nor coffin can be thine"; that "ere thou couldst die...two hearses must verily be seen by thee on the sea; the first not made by mortal hands; and the visible wood of the last one must be grown in America"; that "though it come to the last, I shall still go before thee thy pilot"; and that "hemp only can kill thee" (MD, 410–11). The momentous political significance of these correspondences between *Macbeth* and *Moby-Dick* may be understood through reference to the *American Whig Review,* which regularly protested the idea "that it is the inevitable destiny of the Anglo-Saxon race to overrun and ruin its neighbors." Moreover, with rhetoric appropriate to Ahab's expansionist inclinations, the *Whig* drew upon Shakespeare to characterize the self-aggrandizing fatalism involved in America's so-called Manifest Destiny:

> The accurate historian, commenting upon this remarkable argument, will have to class it among the worst of those speculative delusions which have infested modern nations. The crime of our ambition finds an argument in destiny; the sorcerers of the press have foretold it, and like the mad Macbeth we hasten to realize a dream of glory, by the perpetration of a crime.[20] (See Figure E)

---

19. Alexis de Tocqueville, *Democracy in America,* trans. Henry Reeve, part II (New York: J. & H. G. Langley, 1840), p. 92.

20. "The Late Negotiations for Peace," *American Whig Review,* 6 (Nov. 1847), 451. Without reference to political contexts, Olson (pp. 53–54) first noticed the analog between Ahab and Macbeth. My citations of *Macbeth* (IV.i.80–81, 92–93) are from *Shakespeare: The Complete Works,* ed. G. B. Harrison (New York: Harcourt, Brace, and World, 1952), p. 1208.

THE NEW BANQUO.

*POLK.—THOU CANS'T NOT SAY I DID IT; NEVER SHAKE
THY GORY LOCKS AT ME.*

Figure E. Silas Wright, noted for his opposition to the extension of slavery into America's new states and territories, haunts President Polk (America's new Macbeth) at the height of the Mexican War (*Yankee Doodle*, 13 February 1847, p. 209). Courtesy of the Newberry Library, Chicago.

Timely, indeed, was such advice for a people who believed that "[o]ur national progress seems to be mysteriously ordered: even our sins seem to be overruled for the ultimate good of the world."[21] In Ahab, then, Melville dramatizes this tendency, within a Shakespearian context current among well-read opponents of President Polk's expansionist designs upon Mexico.

In fact, the importance of the Mexican War to *Moby-Dick* is suggested by Ishmael's two allusions to the "All of Mexico" campaign

---

21. "California," *American Literary Magazine*, p. 343.

(MD, 62, 334); by the *Pequod*'s similarity to an enraged elephant (MD, 95; 201; see Figure A); by Ishmael's comparing the excitement of a chase to the feelings of a "raw recruit, marching ... into the fever heat of his first battle" (MD, 193); and by his reference to Starbuck, Stubb, and Flask as "captains of companies" who, as if "by universal prescription" (MD, 106), lead their platoons into battle. Thus, Ishmael's description of the *Pequod* as a "cannibal of a craft, tricking herself forth in the chased bones of her enemies" (MD, 67) may bring to mind the *American Whig Review*'s satire of Lewis Cass's "All of Mexico" enthusiasm:

> Gen. Cass was in favor of our Executive War of conquest and spoliation..., and thought our digestive powers would carry us safely through, even if *'we should swallow the whole of Mexico.'* He seems to look upon the United States as if the country were some monster reptile, that must subsist and swell its huge, unsightly bulk, by gorging itself with every living thing, small and great, that comes in its way.

And in a passage that may help to explain Ahab's thoughts about "cannibal old me" (MD, 444), the *Whig* elsewhere says, "Mr. Polk has made us the cannibal of nations, and at his bidding we devour our sister republic."[22] Moreover, as early as *Mardi*, Media's scroll had complained about the Polk administration's having "gone to war without declaring intentions." (M, 528), a charge presently allegorized in the way Ahab continues for some time upon the "nominal purpose of the Pequod's voyage" (MD, 184) before letting the crew know his actual designs. Ishmael, however, advises that "had any of his old acquaintances on shore but half dreamed of what was lurking in him then, how soon would their aghast and righteous souls have wrenched the ship from such a fiendish man!" (MD, 162). This opinion corresponds to accusations about President Polk's having begun the Mexican War as

> a secret, selfish plan, which he dared not disclose to the American people; since he well knew how sternly the faces of all considerate and disinterested persons would be set against it, and how surely a project of that sort, if known in time, would be

---

22. "The Whigs and Their Candidate," *American Whig Review*, 8 (Sept. 1848), 225; "Executive Usurpation," *American Whig Review*, 5 (Mar. 1847), 229. For the possibilities surrounding Melville's association of elephant imagery with the Mexican War, see Donald Yannella, " 'Seeing the Elephant' in *Mardi*," in *Artful Thunder*, ed. Robert J. DeMott and Sanford E. Marovitz (Kent, Ohio: Kent State Univ. Press, 1975), p. 114.

repudiated, scouted, disclaimed and discarded by the whole sober sense of the country.[23]

Like Ahab, moreover, Polk justified his aggression as "indemnity for acknowledged acts of outrage and wrong," though much to the grief of prominent Whigs, who, like Starbuck reflecting upon Ahab, blamed the President for "shift[ing] the responsibility of the war, in its inception, from himself, and fasten[ing] it upon Mexico." This, insisted the Whigs, was "purely an Executive war—a war of the President's own *seeking*, or if not specifically *sought* by him, a war into which he was precipitated by acts of his own, of the most unjustifiable and the most reprehensible character." Indeed, as Starbuck tells Ahab, "See! Moby Dick seeks thee not. It is thou, thou, that madly seekest him" (MD, 465).[24]

Not surprisingly, Melville rounds off *Moby-Dick*'s encounter with the Mexican War by probing the relation between expansionism and the extension of slavery. And he does so in a manner consistent with David Lee Child's strategy of exposing the motives that guided latter-day Ahabs in the stealing of Naboth's Vineyard. "It is openly avowed and officially proclaimed," said Child, "that the object of [Texas's] annexation is the security and aggrandizement of human slavery." Subject to similar criticism was the Mexican War, which Charles Sumner labeled "an enormity born of Slavery."[25] Thus, Ahab's "intense bigotry of purpose" (MD, 141), his "Guinea-coast slavery of solitary command" (MD, 443), and the Parsee's status as Ahab's "slave" (MD, 439) are consistent with the book's larger attention to expansionism. Fedallah and his four companions, as one critic argues, may even bring to

23. "The President and His Administration," *American Whig Review*, 7 (May 1848), 443. For an informative account of Polk's initial secrecy, see John H. Schroeder, *Mr. Polk's War: American Opposition and Dissent, 1846–1848* (Madison: Univ. of Wisconsin Press, 1973), pp. 52–53.

24. For Polk's emphasis on indemnity, see "Message of the President," *Cong. Globe*, 29th Cong., 2nd sess. (8 Dec. 1846), Appendix, 2; Frederick Merk, *Manifest Destiny and Mission in American History: A Reinterpretation* (New York: Alfred A. Knopf, 1963), pp. 112–19. The quotations about Polk's shifting of responsibility and his seeking a war are from "The President's Message: The War," *American Whig Review*, 5 (Jan. 1847), 11; "Our Relations with Mexico," *American Whig Review*, 4 (July 1846), 1; emphasis added. For a study that elaborates upon Starbuck's Whig-like response to Ahab, see my "'A Pantomime of Action': Starbuck and American Whig Dissidence," *New England Quarterly*, 55 (Sept. 1982), pp. 432-39.

25. Child, p. 9; Sumner, "Speech Against the Mexican War" (1846), in *Orations and Speeches by Charles Sumner*, 2 vols. (Boston: Ticknor, Reed, & Fields, 1850), II: 148. For the tie between expansionism and the extension of slavery, see Frederick Merk, *Slavery and the Annexation of Texas* (New York: Alfred A. Knopf, 1972); Merk, *Monroe Doctrine*, pp. x, 9–10, 14–18.

mind the controversy surrounding the Constitution's "three-fifths rule" for calculating the congressional representation of slave states, an issue everywhere evident in the annexationist debates of the 1840's.[26] Aptly, then, Fedallah is funereally invested in a "black cotton" jacket (MD, 187), and Ishmael compares the rowing style of the Parsee and his comrades to the mechanism of a "Mississippi steamer" (MD, 190). Allusions to slavery also surface in Stubb's remark that "a whale would sell for thirty times what you would, Pip, in Alabama" (MD, 346) and in Ishmael's comparison of sharks feeding on a whale carcass to those that follow "slave ships crossing the Atlantic" (MD, 249). And this context may even figure in Ahab's failure to linger at a *gam* beyond whatever time he needs to inquire about the White Whale; for, "as touching Slave-ships meeting," says Ishmael, "they are in such a prodigious hurry, they run away from each other as soon as possible" (MD, 206). Indeed, Ahab is no "Conscience Whig" intent upon abolitionism; as he himself confesses, "[M]y conscience is in this ship's keel" (MD, 393). Thus, Heimert aptly compares Ahab to John C. Calhoun, whose "unsurrenderable...will...seemed to defy mortality itself in his efforts to defeat the Compromise of 1850" (see Figure F).[27]

Ahab's identification with John C. Calhoun helps, in fact, to

---

26. Heimert, p. 512. For the relation of the three-fifths rule (Article I, Section 2, paragraph 3, of the Constitution) to the debate surrounding annexationist policies, see Merk, *Slavery and the Annexation of Texas*, pp. 126–27; "Mr. J. R. Ingersol's Report," in *House Documents*, 28th Cong., 1st sess. (ser. 446), no. 404 (4 April 1844), pp. 45–77.

27. Heimert, p. 524. More recently, T. Walter Herbert, Jr., in *"Moby-Dick" and Calvinism: A World Dismantled* (New Brunswick, N.J.: Rutgers Univ. Press, 1977), p. 147, attributes Ahab's defiance to the nineteenth-century debate between Calvinists and Unitarians over the nature of God, and even more specifically to William Ellery Channing's belief in "a principle within us, which forbids us to prostrate ourselves before mere power." But by ignoring *Moby-Dick*'s political context, Herbert fails to account for the way Ahab's Calhoun-like effort to extend the area of slavery violates Unitarian respect for human dignity. As Channing says in *Slavery* (1835), "Self-respect, founded on a consciousness of our moral nature and immortal destiny, is, indeed, a noble principle; but this sentiment includes, as a part of itself, respect for all who partake our nature. A consciousness of dignity, founded on the subjection of others to our absolute will, is inhuman and unjust." Also, the possibility of viewing Ahab as existing strictly within the Unitarian context of rectitude grows more remote when we recall Channing's denunciation of the slave trade in terms suggestive of Ahab's behavior: "[T]he natural tendency of bringing others into subjection of our absolute will, is to quicken into fearful activity the imperious, haughty, proud, self-seeking propensities of our nature.... It is a *usurpation of the divine dominion*, and its natural influence is to produce a spirit of superiority to divine as well as to human laws" (*The Works of William E. Channing, D.D.* [Boston: American Unitarian Assoc., 1895], p. 715; emphasis added). Melville's wife owned an 1848 edition of Channing's complete *Works*. See Merton M. Sealts, Jr., *Melville's Reading: A Check-List of Books Owned and Borrowed* (Madison: Univ. of Wisconsin Press, 1966), item 130.

Figure F. The *American Whig Review* (August 1850) commemorates the death of Calhoun.

clarify Pip's lunacy, as well as Ahab's resemblances to both Prometheus and King Lear. As early as *Mardi*, Melville had satirized Calhoun's threats of nullification, in the ravings of Vivenza's Nulli. Also lampooned was the myth of the Negro's happiness in bondage: "These serfs are happier than [thy Northern ones]; though thine, no collars wear; more happy as they are, than if free" (M, 533). This represents the theory of "stewardship," the most exaggerated statement of which was Calhoun's insistence that slaves would go insane if abandoned to their own fate. Thus, the important metaphysical issues of "The Castaway" (ch. 93) notwithstanding, precisely this theme finds articulation in Melville's portrait of Ahab and Pip. Deceptive, indeed, is Ahab's compassion for Pip (MD, 428), which existing scholarship explains in terms of Lear's sympathetic attitude toward his fool. For Pip's status as a freeman from Connecticut (MD, 345, 363) who goes insane after Stubb "abandoned [the] poor little negro to his fate" (MD, 347) echoes John C. Calhoun's belief that

> in all instances in which the States have changed the former relation between the two races, the condition of the African, instead of being improved, has become worse. They have been invariably sunk into vice and pauperism, accompanied by the bodily and mental inflictions incident thereto—deafness, blindness, insanity, and idiocy—to a degree without example; while, in all other States which have retained the ancient relation between them, they have improved greatly in every respect.[28]

Similarly, after his abandonment, Ahab's "little negro went about deck an idiot; such, at least, they said he was" (MD, 347). Ahab's compassion, therefore, is less a gesture of benevolence than a parody of southern arguments about the necessity of "stewardship" for slaves: "Oh, ye frozen heavens! look down here. Ye did beget this luckless child, and have abandoned him, ye creative libertines. Here, boy; Ahab's cabin shall be Pip's home henceforth while Ahab lives. Thou touchest my inmost centre, boy; thou art tied to me by cords woven of my heart-strings" (MD, 428).[29] Indeed, Ahab's affection for Pip dra-

---

28. John C. Calhoun, "Letter to Pakenham" (18 April 1844), in *Senate Documents*, 28th Cong., 1st sess. (ser. 435), no. 341, p. 52. For a superb discussion of the controversy linking Negro insanity to abolitionism, see Merk, *Slavery and the Annexation of Texas*, pp. 59–67, 89, 91, 119.

29. As Drew Gilpin Faust, in "A Southern Stewardship: The Intellectual and Proslavery Argument, " *American Quarterly*, 31 (Spring 1979), 74, says,

> The Southern system institutionalized the Christian duties of charity in the master and humility in the slave. But at the same time [as] it justified the Southern way of life, stewardship legitimated the thinkers' claims to authority. It was, after all, the "intellectual Caucasian," who, as Tucker observed, "bore the characteristics of his race in the highest perfection," who served as the most natural steward over both whites and blacks. As Simms proclaimed, "the true business of genius" was "to lift and guide" the lesser members of the human race.

My political emphasis seems compatible with Sharon Cameron's more interpersonal reading of Ahab and Pip: "*Moby-Dick* is a tragedy not of the relations between persons, but rather of persons who keep themselves from relationship because relationship is not equivalence" (p. 32).

matizes the condescending paternalism of the white man's burden: "Come! I feel prouder leading thee by thy black hand, than though I grasped an Emperor's!" (MD, 428); and Pip, unfortunately, resigns himself to Ahab's stewardship: "Oh master! master! I am indeed downhearted when you walk over me. But here I'll stay, though this stern strikes rocks" (MD, 437).

Ahab, moreover, counteracts Pip's momentary dream of equality, in which Pip fancies himself "host to white men with gold lace upon their coats!" (MD, 437), by telling him, "[T]hou shalt sit here in my own screwed chair; another screw to it" (M, 436). And this racist suppression of human development and talent may give added meaning both to Ahab's transformation into King Lear and Pip's identity as Lear's fool. Indeed, with Calhoun-like oratory, an article in the *American Whig Review* had already argued that "neither slaves, . . . nor idiots, . . . nor persons subject to guardianship . . . are qualified for the exercise of free opinion." The author of these views illustrates his case for guardianship by pointing out:

> In the dreadful tragedy of Lear, the rebellion of the bastard Edmund against the authority of the good Gloster [*sic*], begins a series of bloody catastrophies ending in the ruin of a noble house. Equal in wickedness to the foul ambition of the bastard, is that bloody philanthropy which excites the uneducated and dependent slave against his master.

Although Pip has more in common with Lear's fool than with Edmund, Ahab still refers to Pip as the "abandoned" bastard of "creative libertines." Thus, by fusing elements of both Edmund and Lear's fool in Pip, Melville dramatizes in Ahab the worst racial assumptions of both John C. Calhoun and of educated northern conservatives who flaunted Shakespeare in their defense of proslavery "stewardship."[30]

For Ahab, then, the White Whale represents what D. H. Lawrence called "the deepest blood-being of the white race. He is our deepest blood-nature. And he is hunted, hunted, hunted by the maniacal fanaticism of our white mental consciousness."[31] Moreover, this obsession accounts for Ahab's change in identity from Lear to Prometheus; as Ishmael says, "[T]hy thoughts have created a creature in thee; and he

---

30. The quotation about Edmund and misguided abolitionism is from "Freedom of Opinion," *American Whig Review*, 9 (June 1849), 557. Melville may have consulted this issue of the *Whig* (p. 565) for its comic allusion to *Omoo*. For a more compassionate analysis of the Ahab-Lear correspondence, see Olson, pp. 60–63.

31. D. H. Lawrence, *Studies in Classic American Literature* (New York: Thomas Seltzer, 1923), p. 238.

whose intense thinking thus makes him a Prometheus; a vulture feeds upon that heart for ever; that vulture the very creature he creates" (MD, 175). Suggestive here is one critic's observation about the importance to this comparison of Robert Burton's remarks about "the true Prometheus, which is bound to Caucasus; the true Tityus, whose bowels are still by a vulture devoured." Yet the potentially ethnological importance of Ahab's Promethean identity rests in the way Burton defines the vulture as a narcissistic projection of one's "anxieties" and "griping cares,"[32] for the racial cares that devour Ahab originate upon the *Caucasian* rock from which he, like proslavery apologists obsessed with the supremacy of the so-called "intellectual Caucasian," refuses to liberate himself. In fact, the Caucasus mountain range, located between the Black Sea and the Caspian, was actually the area to which the nineteenth-century anthropologist, Johann Friedrich Blumenbach (1752–1840), traced the origins of the white race.[33] Melville presumably knew the origin of the word "Caucasian," since he mentions the "cliffs of Caucasus" in *Mardi* (p. 553), and in *White-Jacket* (p. 379) compares Black Guinea to the *Neversink*'s "Caucasian crew." And that Ahab's Promethean anxiety is Caucasian in both origin and tendency is apparent from Ahab's bigoted recollection of the myth: "I do deem it now a most meaning thing, that the old Greek, Prometheus, who made men, they say, should have been a blacksmith, and animated them with fire. ... How the soot flies! This must be the remainder the Greek made the Africans of" (MD, 390).

The vulture of racial supremacy hovers, as well, over the book's concern with American expansionism. David Jaffé long ago showed that Ahab is partly modeled upon Charles Wilkes, who sailed in search of Antarctica, "the mysterious white continent."[34] And we may now speculate that Melville posited a similar quest among politicians who sought to define the limits of the newly expanded American continent in related terms: "I know ... that we have never dreamt of incorporating into our Union any but the Caucasian race," claimed Calhoun, "the free white race."[35] This opinion was also echoed on the

---

32. Burton's *Anatomy of Melancholy* is quoted by Gerard M. Sweeney in a discussion of Ahab's Promethean nature: see Sweeney, *Melville's Use of Classical Mythology* (Amsterdam: Rodopi N. V., 1975), p. 58.

33. See "Caucasian," in the *Oxford English Dictionary* (1933; rpt. Oxford: Oxford Univ. Press, 1966), II: 191.

34. David Jaffé, "The Captain Who Sat for the Portrait of Ahab," *Boston University Studies in English*, 4 (Spring 1960), 8.

35. "Calhoun's Speech Against the Conquest of Mexico," *American Whig Review*, 7 (March 1848), 222. For a discussion of Calhoun's use of racism to protest the "All of Mexico" frenzy, see Merk, *Manifest Destiny*, pp. 161–63.

floor of the U.S. Senate when William H. Seward declared that the population of the United States should consist mainly of Caucasians: "The African race,... being incapable of...assimilation and absorption, remain[s] distinct, and owing to their peculiar condition, they constitute inferior masses, and may be regarded as accidental, if not disturbing political forces." Quoted in an issue of the *American Whig Review* that Melville may have read, Seward's views are introduced to corroborate the position that "the empire of freedom has now within its geographical boundaries every element of power; a hardy and enlightened *ruling race*, of the best blood of the human family." This attitude may surface in what C. L. R. James early identified as Ahab's "master race" mentality, which we have seen to be enslaved narcissistically to its own reflection.[36] Perhaps James Fenimore Cooper best anticipated Melville's point by having one of the Indians in *The Prairie* correct a similar misconception among white settlers: "Your warriors think the Master of Life has made the whole earth white. They are mistaken. They are pale, and it is their own faces that they see."[37] As Ishmael says early in *Moby-Dick*, narcissism "is the key to it all" (MD, 14).

A bove, we have reassessed and supplemented existing theories about *Moby-Dick* and American political symbolism by rethinking the place of whaling in the history of American expansionism and by proffering several new suggestions about the relation of Macbeth, Lear, Prometheus, and Narcissus to *Moby-Dick*'s encounter with the Mexican War and the attendant implications for the institution of slavery. Still to be addressed, though, is the connection between Ishmael's western and abolitionist outlooks, as well as the regrettable cultural implications of the covenant psychology that makes him an accessory to Ahab's belligerency and race hatred. Ishmael may write a putatively abolitionist narrative, but the Christian apologetical strategies that he uses to convince us of the *Pequod*'s miraculous demise have an opposing

36. For both Seward's remark and the *Whig*'s advocacy of a "ruling race," see "Review of the Report of Hon. Thomas Butler King of California," *American Whig Review*, 11 (May 1850), 443, 444. (Melville may have consulted this issue of the *Whig* for its comparison [p. 495] of *Gargantua* to *Mardi*). Ahab's "master race" outlook is discussed by C. L. R. James, *Mariners, Renegades, and Castaways: The Story of Herman Melville and the World We Live In* (New York: C. L. R. James, 1953), p. 11.

37. Cooper, *The Prairie* (1827), in the Mohawk Edition of *The Works of James Fenimore Cooper*, 33 vols. (New York: G. P. Putnam's Sons, n.d.), V: 228.

tendency: They link his "jeremiad" both to the Puritans' accounts of their massacre of the Pequot Indians in 1637 and to common nineteenth-century beliefs that providential sanctions upheld America's aggressive territorialism and the institution of slavery. And here rests the most crucial connection between historical context and literary form in *Moby-Dick,* for the narrative form that Ishmael uses to describe the *Pequod*'s demise ultimately subverts his largest humanistic and crosscultural aspirations. This interpretation rests partly on an awareness of Alan Heimert's political reading of "The *Town-Ho*'s Story," which itself mandates a review of the events and personalities that gave rise to the Free Soil Convention of 1848.

In considering the Free Soil Convention, the factions deserving mention include the Liberty Party—which, though ready to work for constitutional abolition of slavery, shunned traditional party affiliation—and the more radical Abolitionists, who, unlike the Liberty men, were willing to abandon third-party politics, the electoral process, and even the Union itself to achieve emancipation. Then there were the Democrats, the majority of whom came to be called Hunkers (after the Dutch, "hanker," or *greedy*) for remaining silent on the issue of slavery. This group of Democrats, in turn, libeled as "Barnburners" (after the fable about the farmer who burned down his barn—in this case the Union—to rid it of rats) the radical Democrats who supported the Wilmot Proviso. Likewise split on the issue of slavery were the Whigs. Owning most of the textile industries of the Northeast, their leaders were too dependent on southern slavery to risk disunion over abolitionism. Included in the ranks of such "Cotton Whigs" were Nathan Appleton, Robert C. Winthrop, Leverett Saltonstall, and their "most leading man," Abbott Lawrence, whom Melville possibly satirizes in *The Confidence-Man*'s portrait of "A Gentleman with Gold Sleeve-Buttons" (ch. 7).[38] As one historian remarks, "Lawrence and his associates tried to make [the] policy of si-

---

38. My summary of party positions and divisions is derived from Rayback, pp. 61, n. 15, 72, 116, 119–20, 160–61; Kinley J. Brauer, *Cotton versus Conscience: Massachusetts Whig Politics and Southwestern Expansion, 1843–1848* (Lexington: Univ. Press of Kentucky, 1967), pp. 21–24; Merk, *Manifest Destiny,* pp. 100–101; Sumner, "Address ... Explaining ... the Free Soil Movement ... " (1849), in *Orations and Speeches,* II: 292–331; William Lloyd Garrison, preface to the *Narrative of the Life of Frederick Douglass: An American Slave—Written by Himself* (1845), ed. Benjamin Quarles (Cambridge, Mass.: Harvard Univ. Press, 1960), p. 15; Lawrence J. Friedman, "Confidence and Pertinacity in Evangelical Abolitionism: Lewis Tappan's Circle," *American Quarterly,* 31 (Spring 1979), 102–6. For Melville's satire of Lawrence, see William Norris, "Abbott Lawrence in *The Confidence-Man*: American Success or American Failure?" *American Studies,* 17 (Spring 1976), 25–38.

lence on slavery 'official' Whig policy."[39] This movement, however, greatly distressed such "Conscience Whigs" as Charles Sumner, Charles Francis Adams, Henry Wilson, and John Gorham Palfrey, who, as we have already seen in our discussion of *White-Jacket*, championed "conscience" over economic expediency and avidly supported the Wilmot Proviso. Thus, when in 1848 the Whigs nominated Zachary Taylor, a slaveowner, as their standard-bearer, the Conscience Whigs bolted the party—as did the Barnburners, in response to the Democratic Party's nomination in Baltimore of Lewis Cass, a Hunker. Within a month, the Barnburners met independently in their famous Utica Convention and nominated Martin Van Buren for President, a prelude to his subsequent acceptance by the coalition of Barnburners, Conscience Whigs, and Liberty men who created the Free Soil Party that August at Buffalo, New York. And "the Buffalo convention," we are told, "marked the moment when men of vastly different and hostile political principles . . . were able to submerge their differences . . . to pursue a common goal—prevention of the extension of slavery into the territories."[40]

The issue of slavery, as Alan Heimert shows, surfaces in Ishmael's narration of "The *Town Ho*'s Story," in which Steelkilt's mutiny, precipitated by Radney's failure to proffer him "that common decency of human recognition which is the meanest slave's right" (MD, 210), has reference both to James K. Polk's earlier victory over Martin Van Buren at the Democratic Party's Baltimore Convention of 1844 and to subsequent events leading to the formation of the Free Soil Party:

> Free-Soil Democracy had its origin in the Baltimore Convention of 1844, where the South, rejecting Van Buren, strove to tighten its grip on the party by adopting the two-thirds rule. The consequent Barnburner revolt seemed—especially as the insurgency presented itself as a movement by younger Democrats against their experienced elders—as a "mutiny" by "fresh water lads." This crisis is strikingly parallelled in the *Town-Ho* section of *Moby-Dick*. The abortive mutiny of ten crewmen out of thirty, the early defection of seven of Steelkilt's associates, the ultimate capitulation of the others and the successful commandeering of another ship, follow closely the sequence of historical events from 1844, through the state-by-state bolts from the Party, to the Utica Convention of 1848 and the formation of the Free-Soil Party at Buffalo. Moreover, the geographical center of the new party was the very canal and lake region from which Steelkilt and his supporters came. . . . The tyran-

---

39. Brauer, p. 24.
40. Rayback, p. 230.

nical Radney, finally, has southern characteristics.... The account of Steelkilt's long being "retained harmless and docile" by the "inflexible firmness" of Radney, "only tempered by that common decency of human recognition which is the meanest slave's right," could well stand as a paraphrase of the grievances with which David Wilmot introduced his Proviso. The Free-Soil revolt flourished on the refusal of northern Democrats like Wilmot to remain the "white slaves" of the South."[41]

In addition, Steelkilt's remarks about various "improvements" (MD, 212) may bring to mind the support provided the Free Soil Party by political factions concerned with the "internal improvements" of the Great Lakes and Western waterways.[42] Moreover, since Steelkilt refuses to surrender for fear of being flogged (MD, 219)—an act upon which Melville had already constructed the antislavery allegory of *White-Jacket*—his five-day holdout and ultimate flogging from Radney may resemble the plight of a fugitive slave returned for punishment. In fact, this interpretation possibly explains why Steelkilt's last two comrades turn upon him in a manner that recalls the betrayal of Christ by Peter and Judas,[43] and why he is placed for punishment between two renegades who "lifelessly hung their heads sideways, as the two crucified thieves are drawn" (MD, 219). This entire scenario may, I propose, echo John Pierpont's *Discourse on the Covenant with Judas* (1842), which denounced Melville's father-in-law, Chief Justice Shaw, for detaining in prison George Latimer, a runaway slave:

> [H]owever it may appear to the moral vision of other men, to mine, the morality that requires and compels me to deliver up a fellow man to chains and torture—to hopeless slavery, if not to death, because others have covenanted for me that I shall do so ... is ... the morality of a Judas, who would deliver up the Son of Man to be scourged and crucified.[44]

41. Heimert, pp. 529–30.

42. Angered by President Polk's veto of several "improvements" bills, many Democrats from areas around the snag-filled rivers near Chicago and the Great Lakes joined ranks with the Barnburners at Utica and even managed to have demands for internal improvements included in the "Resolutions" of the Barnburner Convention. See "Utica Barnburner's Convention," *Niles National Resister*, 74 (20 Dec. 1848), 387; Rayback, pp. 219–20, 263–64, 306.

43. For the betrayal and crucifixion motifs in "The *Town-Ho*'s Story," see Don Geiger, "Melville's Black God: Contrary Evidence in 'The *Town-Ho*'s Story,'" *American Literature*, 25 (Jan. 1954), 468; Wright, p. 127. My suggestion concerning Steelkilt's resemblance to a fugitive slave finds support in Karcher's remarks (*Shadow*, pp. 56–58) about Steelkilt's instigating a mutiny that serves as "a paradigm of slave insurrection."

44. John Pierpont, *A Discourse on the Covenant with Judas* (Boston: Charles C.

Quite possibly, then, Ishmael rounds out the Free Soil dimension of "The Town-Ho's Story" with a biblical metaphor of betrayal having particular reference to Judge Shaw's stance on fugitive slaves. As we shall see, moreover, the most outspoken defense of Shaw came from Peleg Chandler, whose name provides still another clue to the complex puzzle of Ishmael's political allegory.

For the moment, suffice it to say that "The Town-Ho's Story" contains a concise allegory of the issues and parties surrounding the Free Soil Convention of 1848, a fact crucial to Ishmael's larger narrative technique in depicting the White Whale as the providential agent of a God intent upon the demise of proslavery advocates. This is evident in the way Ishmael characterizes Radney's fatal encounter with Moby-Dick as "a certain wondrous, inverted visitation of one of those so called judgments of God which at times are said to overtake some men" (MD, 208). In fact, just as Steelkilt is about to murder Radney for having previously administered the lash of punishment, "by a mysterious fatality, Heaven itself seemed to step in to take out of his hands into its own the damning thing he would have done" (MD, 221). Thus, to Ishmael's mind, Moby-Dick here acts as a vehicle of God's justice, dispensing "predestinated" (MD, 213) punishment to sinners who perpetrate various modes of slavery. And this theo-political assumption also informs Ishmael's jeremiad recounting the Pequod's catastrophe. Indeed, insofar as Ahab embodies the proslavery ideology of John C. Calhoun, Ishmael may well feel justified in viewing the Pequod's demise as still another instance of the divine punishment in store for those who stand opposed to "God's law supreme" concerning the abolition of slavery.[45]

Inseparable, however, from Ishmael's motives in constructing this jeremiad is his initial uncertainty, after surviving the Pequod's wreck, whether existence is divinely ordered. In fact, Ishmael's tendency toward psychological nihilism is evident in his narration of "The Castaway" (ch. 93), the horrors of which are probably not as much Pip's as

---

Little & James Brown, 1842), pp. 32–33. For an overview of Shaw's judicial stance in the Latimer case, see Leonard W. Levy, The Law of the Commonwealth and Chief Justice Shaw (Cambridge, Mass.: Harvard Univ. Press, 1957), pp. 78–85.

45. See Heimert's comparison (p. 509) of Ahab's relentless will with the sort of proslavery obstinacy denounced in James Marsh's God's Law Supreme: A Sermon Aiming to Point Out the Duty of a Christian People in Relation to the Fugitive Slave Law (Worcester, Mass.: Henry J. Howland, 1850). Ishmael may even play upon Marsh's title in remarking that Ahab "yield[ed] up all his thoughts and fancies to his one supreme purpose; that purpose, by its own sheer inveteracy of will, forced itself against gods and devils into a kind of self-assumed, independent being of its own" (MD, 175; emphasis added).

they are apprehensions that Ishmael ascribes to Pip by way of articulating anxieties occasioned by his own "like abandonment" atop Queequeg's coffin:

> Pip saw the multitudinous, God-omnipresent, coral insects that out of the firmament of waters heaved the colossal orbs. He saw God's foot upon the treadle of the loom, and spoke it.... So ... man comes at last to the celestial thought, which, to reason, is absurd and frantic; and weal or woe, feels then, uncompromised, *indifferent as his God*. (MD, 347; emphasis added)

Here, Richard Slotkin remarks, Ishmael expresses fear at the prospect of a God whose method is "blind process, not purpose." Thus, the mere recollection of Pip's madness becomes an awful reminder to Ishmael of his own apprehensions about God's indifference: "This way comes Pip—poor boy! would he had died, or I; he's half horrible to me" (MD, 362). A related fear surfaces in Ishmael's discourse on "The Whiteness of the Whale" (ch. 42), where, as Millicent Bell says, "[T]his atheistical surmise that there is 'nothing beyond' ... has seized the heart of Ishmael more strongly than it has that of his vengeance-bent captain." More skeptical yet are Ishmael's apprehensions about the cenotaphs at the Whaleman's Chapel, which likewise suggest a universe potentially devoid of a guiding spiritual principle.[46]

Still, Ishmael finally affirms that "some certain significance lurks in all things, else all things are little worth, and the round world itself but an empty cipher" (MD, 358). Ishmael overcomes his despair by ultimately positing Moby-Dick's annihilation of the *Pequod* as divinely decreed; and he emphasizes this understanding by quoting the words of Father Mapple's hymn, which provides reassuring precedent for God's using leviathan as both the agent of retribution and as the vehicle of His even greater love and concern for despairing humanity (MD, 44). Ishmael also combats the notion of a universe devoid of a caring God by claiming that "Faith, like a jackal, feeds among the tombs, and even from these dread doubts she gathers her most vital hope" (MD, 41). Precisely this belief that faith provides its own inspiration allows Ishmael to attribute to Queequeg features that betray his own *will to believe*: "There, then, he sat, holding up that imbecile candle in the heart of that almighty forlornness. There, then, he sat, the sign and symbol

---

46. For Ishmael's near-crisis of faith in these episodes, see Richard Slotkin, *Regeneration Through Violence: The Mythology of the American Frontier, 1600–1860* (Middletown, Conn.: Wesleyan Univ. Press, 1973), p. 542; Millicent Bell, "Pierre Bayle and *Moby-Dick*," *PMLA*, 66 (Sept. 1951), 646; Robert Zoellner, *The Salt-Sea Mastodon, A Reading of "Moby-Dick"* (Berkeley: Univ. of California Press, 1973), p. 135.

of a man without faith, hopelessly holding up hope in the midst of despair" (MD, 195). And consistent with this "faithful" narration of events is Ishmael's use of Father Mapple's hymn about Jonah, which finally sets the largely optimistic tone of Ishmael's narrative, itself a form of spiritual autobiography that will document his own special salvation:

> My song for ever shall record
>   That terrible, that joyful hour
> I give the glory to my God,
>   His all the mercy and the power. (MD, 44)[47]

Worth recalling here is the remark of one critic who sees in Ishmael's narrative a form of "self-interested exegesis." Whereas Ahab disowns Queequeg's coffin as a symbol of faith (MD, 433), Ishmael retrospectively views both this vehicle of his own salvation and the benign sharks of the "Epilogue" as manifestations of God's providence. Not only, therefore, does he compare himself to Lazarus in having "survived myself" (MD, 197); he may, as Nathalia Wright argues, even adopt the name "Ishmael" ("God shall hear") because of its associations in Genesis with miraculous deliverance.[48] Moreover, by concluding (or actually, by commencing) his book with the refrain of Job's four messengers—"AND I ONLY AM ESCAPED ALONE TO TELL THEE" (MD, 470)—Ishmael imbues his narrative with a sense of divine intent behind the seeming chaos of what follows. Like the Jonah of Father Mapple's sermon, Ishmael then fancies himself something of a prophet, saved to preach the word of God to his audience of Hunker Ninevites.[49] Since, however, the biblical Ishmael was an outcast, and not a prophet, we may question the propriety of Ishmael's perception about his mandate. Also, we shall see that even Ishmael's tendency to fancy himself a prophet is

---

47. Appropriately, "Deliverance from Despair" is the subtitle of the actual hymn that Melville modified to suit Father Mapple's theme. See David H. Battenfeld, "The Source for the Hymn in *Moby-Dick*," *American Literature,* 27 (Nov. 1955), 393–96. For studies emphasizing Ishmael's journey from despair to psychological stability and religious faith, see Zoellner, p. 120; Thomas Werge, "*Moby-Dick* and the Calvinist Tradition," *Studies in the Novel,* 1 (Winter 1969), 484–506, esp. 489; Rowland A. Sherrill, *The Prophetic Melville: Experience, Transcendence, and Tragedy* (Athens: Univ. of Georgia Press, 1979), pp. 85–188.

48. Wright, pp. 48, 50–51. For Ishmael's "self-interested exegesis," see Brodtkorb, p. 124. Ishmael's belief in his own providential salvation is discussed by Henry Nash Smith, "The Image of Society in *Moby-Dick*," in Hillway and Mansfield, eds., "*Moby-Dick*" *Centennial Essays,* pp. 73, 75; James Baird, *Ishmael* (Baltimore, Md.: Johns Hopkins Press, 1956), p. 270.

49. See, in this respect, Nicholas Canaday, Jr., *Melville and Authority,* University of Florida Monographs: Humanities, no. 28 (Gainesville: Univ. of Florida Press, 1968), pp. 51–52; Karcher, *Shadow,* pp. 78–79.

not necessarily positive, subject as it is to *Moby-Dick*'s revisionist consideration of the sublunary forces that shape seemingly "inspired" and "prophetic" interpretations of American history and destiny.

To this end, recall how Ishmael's attempt to impose form and fixity upon the chaos of events parallels his effort, in *Moby-Dick*'s cetological chapters, at the "classification of the constituents of a chaos" (MD, 117); for "what is classification," asked Emerson, "but the perceiving that . . . objects are not chaotic, . . . but have a law which is also a law of the human mind?" Thus, Ishmael finally "classifies" his adventure as a fatalistic and providential event that punishes the *Pequod* and at the same time preserves him to record this *Magnalia Dei*. Further, the political dimension of Ishmael's allegory is enhanced if we apply Emerson's remark that "classification" also reflects the mind's tendency "to join two things and see in them one nature; . . . discovering roots running under ground whereby contrary and remote things cohere and flower out from one stem."[50] Ishmael does precisely this by attributing both providential *and* abolitionist significance to the otherwise random and arbitrary incidents of "The *Town-Ho*'s Story." And implicit in this conflation is the tie between historical context and narrative form in *Moby-Dick*: by classifying his experiences with the aid of political and theological fabrications, Ishmael indulges in providential historiography. Yet this genre's dual emphases on politics and religion place Ishmael's record of events within a jeremiad tradition conspicuous in certain colonial histories. Works in this tradition typically reaffirm America's corporate faith and covenanted status with reference either to special "deliverances" or to the annihilation of such enemies of the New World Israel as the Pequot Indians. The Puritans, it will be recalled, expropriated the Pequots' land after acknowledging God's providential assistance in that tribe's eradication. Of course, by 1846 the enemy had shifted from the Northeast to the Southwest, but the logic of territorial aggrandizement perpetuated in the theological premise of Ishmael's narrative remained the same. As will become evident, moreover, the *exclusive* tendencies of the covenant psychology undergirding all jeremiads lead Ishmael to betray the abolitionist egalitarianism he purports to champion.

In this connection, it is relevant to review the at least nominally abolitionist overtones conveyed in Ishmael's description of Father Mapple, whose respect for *higher law* Charles H. Foster has shown to

---

50. Emerson, "The American Scholar," in the Centenary Edition of *The Complete Works of Ralph Waldo Emerson*, ed. Edward Waldo Emerson (Boston and New York: Houghton Mifflin, 1903–04), I: 85, 86. For the possibility that Melville drew upon this essay as early as *Redburn* (1849), see chapter II.

conform to the doctrine of radical abolitionism.[51] Thus, to the degree that Ishmael imagines Ahab to persist in a Calhoun-like disobedience to "God's law supreme," Ahab resembles the unrepentant Jonah of Father Mapple's sermon. In fact, precedent for this comparison exists in *The Biglow Papers*, which describes how

> no ship of state was ever freighted with a more veritable Jonah than this same domestic institution of ours. Mephistopheles himself could not feign so bitterly, so satirically sad a sight as this of three millions of human beings crushed beyond help or hope by this one mighty argument,—*Our fathers knew no better!* Nevertheless, it is the unavoidable destiny of Jonahs to be cast overboard sooner or later.[52]

Potentially abolitionist, as well, is Father Mapple's insistence that man should both "disobey [himself]" (MD, 45) and also stand "forth his own inexorable self" (MD, 51) to preach Truth to the face of Falsehood. One critic interprets Mapple as suggesting that "mere humility and repentance may suffice for ordinary persons, but for the exceptional man they are not enough: he must embrace a militant evangelism—a prophetic defiance of all within culture which ignores or rejects God." This interpretation is consistent with ideas about "evangelicalism and immediate emancipation," or the regard for abolitionism as a stance common among people ready to stand forth and reform social abuses antagonistic to God's supreme law.[53] Also, Mapple's emphasis on the preeminence of "Gospel duty" (MD, 50) in a world of potentially corrupt "Senators and Judges" (MD, 51) may bring to mind the sentiment of Charles Sumner, who held that "Amidst the shifts and changes of party our DUTIES remain, pointing the way to action. By no subtle compromise or adjustment can men suspend the commandments of

---

51. Foster, pp. 17-20.

52. Lowell, *The Biglow Papers* (1846-48), in *The Writings of James Russell Lowell*, 10 vols. (Boston: Houghton Mifflin, 1890), VIII: 96. Melville and Lowell encountered one another prior to the publication of *Moby-Dick*. See Jay Leyda, ed., *The Melville Log*, 2 vols. (New York: Harcourt, Brace, 1951), I: 392. Moreover, Melville would most likely have seen the first collected edition of *The Biglow Papers* reviewed in the *Literary World*, 3 (2 Dec. 1848), 872-73.

53. On Mapple, see Albert McLean, "Spouter Inn and Whaleman's Chapel: The Cultural Matrices of *Moby-Dick*," in *Melville and Hawthorne in the Berkshires: A Symposium*, ed. Howard P. Vincent (Kent, Ohio: Kent State Univ. Press, 1968), pp. 106-7. Also see Anne C. Loveland, "Evangelicalism and 'Immediate Emancipation' in American Antislavery Thought," *Journal of Southern History*, 32 (May 1966), 172-88, esp. pp. 178, 180; Donald M. Scott, "Abolitionism as a Sacred Vocation," in *Antislavery Reconsidered: New Perspectives on the Abolitionists*, ed. Lewis Perry and Michael Fellman (Baton Rouge: Louisiana State Univ. Press, 1979), pp. 51-74.

God. . . . By no . . . hocus-pocus of politicians . . . can we be released from this obedience."[54] In many respects, then, Father Mapple's sermon indirectly challenges the Whig Party's homage to civil *law;* and Judge Shaw, we know, "remained an old-line Whig" with "a love for law and order" in his various rulings that upheld the fugitive slave law.[55]

Significant, therefore, is the degree to which Father Mapple's sermon appeals to Ishmael, who reproduces it in its entirety and then allies himself with the Barnburner and Free Soil Parties by referring to greedy Bildad as an "incorrigible old hunks" (MD, 72). Of course, Melville could have had firsthand knowledge of the opposition between Barnburners and Old Hunkers, or he may have read, in the *American Whig Review* or elsewhere, about their differences on the issue of slavery.[56] In any event, Ishmael seems familiar with the political meaning of "hunks" or "hunkers," since at the beginning of his narrative he uses the term in a way that foreshadows the "Free Soil" revolt aboard the *Town-Ho.* This event is precipitated by Radney's command that Steelkilt "get a broom and sweep down the planks" (MD, 212). Ishmael foreshadows both the rhetoric and abolitionist significance of this episode by asking, "What . . . if some old hunks of a sea-captain orders me to get a broom and sweep down the decks? . . . Do you think the archangel Gabriel thinks anything the less of me, because I promptly and respectfully obey that *old hunks . . . ? Who aint a slave?*" (MD, 15; emphasis added). Thus, in calling Bildad an "old hunks," Ishmael may well reveal his bias against the proslavery overtones of the *Pequod's* voyage. And this reading becomes even more plausible because of Peleg's partnership in the venture.

The name Peleg is hardly relevant solely for its biblical context (Gen. 10:25: "And unto Eber were born two sons: the name of one *was* Peleg; for in his days was the earth divided."). It assumes potentially immediate significance, however, as a reference to Peleg Chandler, who, as editor of the conservative *Monthly Law Reporter,* in 1843 zealously defended Chief Justice Shaw's decision to return the runaway slave George Latimer to the custody of his master. In an emotional apologia

---

54. Sumner, "Speech on Our Present Anti-Salvery Duties, at the Free Soil State Convention in Boston, Oct. 3, 1850," in *Orations and Speeches,* II: 410.

55. Levy, p. 91. For a classic statement of Whig allegiance to law, see "The Fugitive Slave Law," *American Whig Review,* 13 (May 1851), 393–94.

56. See Heimert (pp. 528–29) on Ishmael's use of the term "old hunks." Also, see "Origin of the Two Parties," *American Whig Review,* 9 (Jan. 1849), 6, 10; also, "The Whig Victory in New York," *American Whig Review,* 10 (Dec. 1849), 648–49, which explains that "the Old Hunker division . . . were disposed to hold to the doctrine that Congress had no right to interfere to prevent the extension of slavery over the national territory." The term eventually came to signify anybody opposed to abolitionism.

for the behavior of both Shaw and Mr. Justice Story, Chandler lauded the two judges for preventing personal conscience from overriding constitutional responsibilities involved in the extradition of fugitive slaves. In fact, Chandler was especially upset by the Mapple-like oratory of John Pierpont's *Discourse on the Covenant with Judas.* Advocating assumptions like those denounced by Father Mapple, Chandler disclaims the right of any judge to stand forth his own inexorable self against either codified law or an oath of office:

> Does not this preacher know, that a judge has nothing to do with the moral character of laws which society chooses to make, and which, when made, it places him upon the bench to apply to the facts before him?... Does he not know, that the very object of the oath of office, is to prevent the judge from exercising his discretion, in declaring or not declaring what the law is, according to his opinion or feeling of its moral character?

Chandler, then, holds that Pierpont's *Discourse* represents the most sophistical "argument as has yet been devised, in the pulpit, to undermine the moral sense of the people in the obligations of [a constitutional] oath."[57] Still, Ishmael's aversion to the Hunkerism of all such Pelegs is evident from his Pierpont- or Mapple-like respect for the pulpit as "this earth's foremost part; all the rest comes in the rear; the pulpit leads the world" (MD, 43). Not surprisingly, therefore, abolitionist overtones characterize Ishmael's relationship with "dark complexioned" (MD, 22) Queequeg. Indeed, Ishmael finds it regrettable that their companionship invites ridicule, especially since a white man seems to Ishmael nothing more than "a white-washed negro" (MD, 60).[58]

Not surprisingly, Ishmael celebrates that "just Spirit of Equality, which has spread one royal mantle of humanity over all my kind!" (MD, 105). He even claims that this "democratic dignity... radiates without end from God; Himself!... The centre and circumference of all

---

57. "The Latimer Case," *Law Reporter,* ed. Peleg W. Chandler, 5 (March 1843), 492–94. Chandler may have known Shaw personally, since the *Law Reporter* was published in Boston and since Chandler speaks with a tone of privileged familiarity (see p. 483, n. 1, and p. 494, lines 34–36). Levy (pp. 82–84) discusses Chandler's defense of Shaw. Cf. William M. Wiecek, "Latimer, Lawyers, Abolitionists, and the Problem of Unjust Laws," in Perry and Fellman, eds., *Antislavery Reconsidered,* pp. 219–37.

58. For abolitionist readings of the Ishmael-Queequeg relationship, see Eleanor E. Simpson, "Melville and the Negro: From *Typee* to 'Benito Cereno,'" *American Literature,* 41 (March 1969), 28; Edward S. Grejda, *The Common Continent of Men: Racial Equality in the Writings of Herman Melville* (Port Washington, N.Y.: Kennikat Press, 1974), pp. 93–96; Willie T. Weathers, "*Moby-Dick* and the Nineteenth-Century Scene," *Texas Studies in Literature and Language,* 4 (Winter 1960), 496; Karcher, p. 64.

democracy! His omnipresence, our divine equality!" (MD, 104). As
shown above, *White-Jacket* explores the ambiguities of such "anticipatory" political mandates. Yet the abolitionist context of Ishmael's narrative lends itself to this outlook. In fact, in 1849 Charles Sumner
pleaded in very similar terms, before Chief Justice Shaw, against the
constitutionality of "Separate Colored Schools." A schoolteacher by
profession (MD, 14), Ishmael conceivably could have had more than a
passing interest in Sumner's belief that "when the Saviour taught the
Lord's prayer, he taught the sublime doctrine of the Brotherhood of
Mankind, infolding the Equality of men." Compatible, as well, with
Ishmael's outlook is Sumner's ultimate anticipatory appeal to the court:
"Where this [Christian spirit] prevails, there is neither Jew nor Gentile,
Greek, nor barbarian, bond nor free; but all are alike. From this we de-
rive new and solemn assurances of the Equality of mankind, as an or-
dinance of God." Perhaps correspondences such as these inspired
Richard Henry Dana to have the Boston Committee of Vigilance name
its Underground Railroad schooner the *Moby-Dick*.[59]

In any event, Ishmael clearly believes in a God who sanctions
egalitarian principles. This belief is evident in his attribution of providential and political significance to Moby-Dick's destruction of
Hunkerish Radney, as well as in the "leviathanic" jeremiad that he
pens to commemorate the retributive destruction of the iniquitous
Pequod and its slave-driving captain. Thus, Ishmael's narrative
allows him to identify with the "converted" Jonah, since Father
Mapple's sermon offers "a two-stranded lesson; a lesson to us all as
sinful men, and a lesson to me as *a pilot of the living God*" (MD, 45;
emphasis added). According to Mapple, Jonah's sinfulness lay in his
effort to escape the "Gospel duty" of preaching "unwelcome truths"
to the wicked population of Nineveh (MD, 50). And this lesson is not
lost on Ishmael, who seeks to impose a sense of divine order on an
otherwise chaotic experience by assuming a Jonah-like responsibility
to be a pilot of the living God and by preaching in allegorical terms
about the doom in store for a ship of state that harbors the curse of
slavery. In fact, this mission to report the miraculous displays of
God's wrath against the Hunkerism of Radney and the Calhoun-like
thinking of Ahab becomes the raison d'être—or, to Ishmael's mind,
the *merit*—of his survival. Thus, while Melville may have written

---

59. Sumner, "Argument Against the Constitutionality of Separate Colored Schools,
Before the Supreme Court of Massachusetts, in the Case of Sarah C. Roberts vs. The
City of Boston, Dec. 4, 1849," in *Orations and Speeches*, II: 335, 376–77. (Levy, pp.
109–17, discusses Shaw's conservative ruling.) For Dana's use of Melville's title, see
Sidney Kaplan, "The *Moby-Dick* in the Service of the Underground Railroad," *Phylon*,
12 (1951), 173–76. Dana, it is worth recalling, argued before Chief Justice Shaw in

Father Mapple's sermon with something less than personal commitment to its strictures, Ishmael certainly takes it seriously enough to use it as a device upon which to structure the incidents and assumptions of his own political jeremiad. And while one might wonder why Melville did not actually name his narrator "Jonah" or "Jeremiah," subsequent discussion about the dire implications of the jeremiad's covenant assumptions will reveal as appropriate Ishmael's use of a name that has associations with territorial expropriation and proslavery sentiment.

The "Ishmaelian" dimension of these political concerns is best approached by our recalling that jeremiads presuppose a belief in the miracles that God uses to manifest either His love or wrath toward humanity. Perhaps to suppress in his own mind that suggestion of God's indifference and to prepare us for Moby-Dick's miraculous destruction of the *Pequod*, Ishmael fills his narrative with allusions to scriptural miracles. In his account of "The Monkey-Rope," for instance, he calls the maneuver "a sort of interregnum in Providence; for its even handed equity never could have sanctioned so gross an injustice" (MD, 271). However casually Ishmael makes this remark, its premise informs his allusions elsewhere to such benevolent miracles as God's concern for Jonah; the miracle of the Ahaz dial (MD, 122; cf. Isa. 38:8); and God's redemption of Shadrach, Meshach, and Abednego from Nebuchadnezzar's fiery furnace (MD, 356; cf. Daniel 3). Still, as Father Mapple warns, and as Ishmael's experience aboard the *Pequod* seems to corroborate, God is more "chiefly known" through his "rod" of chastisement (MD, 51), a fact that Ishmael finds confirmed in the retributive miracle of Noah's flood: "The first boat we read of, floated on an ocean that with Portuguese vengeance had whelmed a whole world without leaving so much as a widow" (MD, 235). And perhaps to prepare us for the providential conclusion of his narrative—in which he describes how "the great shroud of the sea rolled on as it rolled five thousand years ago" [i.e., at the time of Noah's flood, according to nineteenth-century biblical chronology]—Ishmael remarks that "that same ocean rolls now; that same ocean destroyed the wrecked ships of last year." Ishmael also reminds us that "preternatural terrors rested upon the Hebrews, when under the feet of Korah and his company the live ground opened and swallowed them up for ever." And to stress again the plausibility of his narrative's miraculous conclusion, Ishmael says that "not a modern sun ever sets, but in precisely the same manner the live sea swallows up ships and crews." Aptly, therefore, Ishmael asks, "Wherein differ the

February of 1851 to secure the freedom of the runaway slave Frederick Wilkins (alias Shadrach) and later protested Shaw's Hunkerism (see Levy, pp. 87–91).

sea and the land, that a miracle upon one is not a miracle upon the other?" (MD, 235).[60]

To bring us typologically to the threshold of Ishmael's abolitionist jeremiad we have one critic's thesis that the *Pequod*'s fate is directly connected to God's judgment on Babylon, "the ancient empire that *enslaved* the Jews," and that "it can hardly have escaped Melville's notice that the judgment on the mystical Babylon corresponds exactly to the fall which Jeremiah foresaw for the Babylon of old."[61] Ishmael would not be the first author to have linked jeremiad and abolitionist assumptions. James Montgomery's "The Witnesses"—and recall that Ishmael has been reading Montgomery (MD, 7)—prophesies how one day all the slaves who ever died in transit to hellish bondage "Shall rise in judgment from their gloomy beds, / To call down vengeance on the murderers' heads." Of course, a conservative journal like the *American Whig Review* dismissed such poetry as "silly jeremiading," a choice of terms that echoes the warnings of abolitionists who cautioned, "Surely the curse of God and the reproach of man is against us. Worse than the seven plagues of Egypt will befall us. If Algiers shall be punished sevenfold, truly America seventy and sevenfold."[62] This same retributive premise is evident in Marsh's *God's Law Supreme*, which warns that whoever "retreat[s] from this moral battlefield, shall run upon the sword of divine retribution"; indeed, almost foreshadowing Ishmael's worst fears about Elijah, Marsh confirms that "faithful voices have long warned us of judgments to come." And in a remark that might bring to mind Gabriel's apocalyptical threats against Ahab (ch. 71), Marsh cautions, "if we twine our arms about this evil, and make common cause with it, we cannot escape the vials of wrath that God will yet pour out upon it without mixture or stint."[63]

Appropriately, therefore, Ishmael recalls how the "judgment claps" (MD, 446) of the Negro, Daggoo, raise the sleeping crew on the

---

60. With related emphasis, Herbert (p. 112) shows how Ishmael's perception of the whale's malice owes something to a clerical tradition identifying the Leviathan of Job as "a manifestation of divine power aroused by human impudence. Calvin published sixty-five sermons on the Book of Job, and in the tradition that he established, the Leviathan was typically identified as the whale, and was invoked to terrify impudent sinners."

61. Gilmore, p. 160; emphasis added.

62. Montgomery's "The Witnesses" is quoted in a review titled "Longfellow's Poems," *American Whig Review*, 13 (April 1851), 367, the author of which also speaks of Montgomery's "silly jeremiading." The apocalyptical remark about Algiers and America is from a pamphlet titled *Tyrannical Libertymen, a Discourse on Negro Slavery* (1795), quoted in Sumner's "White Slavery ... " (1847), in *Orations and Speeches*, I: 262.

63. Marsh, pp. 10, 24, 26.

morning of "The Chase—First Day," perhaps dramatizing the jeremiad's function of awakening sinners from their sinful complacency.
Melville, in fact, may have known how John Greenleaf Whittier had
already adapted this convention of the jeremiad to his abolitionist
poem "Follen" (1834):

> Oh! rouse ye, ere the storm comes forth,
>   The gathered wrath of God and man,
> Like that which wasted Egypt's earth,
>   When hail and fire above it ran.
> Hear ye no warnings in the air?
>   Feel ye no earthquake underneath?
> Up, up! why will ye slumber where
>   The sleeper only wakes in death?[64]

Melville was obviously familiar with such abolitionist rhetoric. In "the
extreme South of Vivenza" (*Mardi,* ch. 162), it will be recalled, Yoomy
cries, "Just Oro! ... do no thunders roll,—no lightnings flash in this ac-
cursed land!" (M, 532). For reasons germane to the tie between covenant psychology and socially exclusive politics (a tie we shall explore
shortly), Melville would most likely have responded in the negative to
Yoomy. Nevertheless, he endows the narrator of *Moby-Dick* with the
conviction that God will indeed chastise the unrighteous. In recounting, for instance, how "God's burning finger has been laid on the [*Pequod*]," and how His " 'Mene, Mene, Tekel, Upharsin' has been woven
into the shrouds and the cordage" (MD, 415),[65] Ishmael clearly believes
that God has a retributive end in mind for a ship of state "plunging
into that blackness of darkness" (MD, 354). The latter phrase, as Nathalia Wright has shown, is an allusion to Jude 13, which describes the
abode of the eternally damned and which precedes directly the prophecy that God will come "to execute judgment upon all, and to con-

---

64. Whittier, *The Writings of John Greenleaf Whittier,* 7 vols. (Cambridge, Mass.:
Houghton Mifflin, 1888), III: 28. "Follen" originally appeared under the title "Expos-
tulation" in the *Liberator* (20 Sept. 1834). With a slightly different emphasis, Karcher
(*Shadow,* p. 88) anticipates the significance I assign Daggoo's "judgment claps." As for
Melville's familiarity with the writings of Whittier: In a line that Evert Duyckinck
deleted from the original draft of Melville's review of "Hawthorne and His Mosses,"
Whittier is referred to as one of the eight leading American writers. Hershel Parker has
restored this line to the text of "Hawthorne and His Mosses," in *The Norton Anthol-
ogy of American Literature,* ed. Ronald Gottesman *et al.,* 2 vols. (New York: W. W.
Norton, 1979), I: 2063.

65. See Dan. 5:25–28, where this event prophesies God's judgment against Belshazzar, and "Belschazzar, a Poem," *Knickerbocker,* 33 (June 1849), 516–17: "Thus a lesson
shall be taught thee, an example to all / Who, possessed of large dominion, deem it
difficult to fall."

vince all that are ungodly among them of all their ungodly deeds
which they have ungodly committed, and of all their hard *speeches*
which ungodly sinners have spoken against him." Such a punishment
Ishmael might well deem appropriate for that "ungodly, god-like man,
Captain Ahab" (MD, 76).[66]

Thus, having already suggested that in the sperm whale's brow
"you feel the Deity and the dread powers more forcibly than in behold-
ing any other object in living nature" (MD, 292), Ishmael ultimately
compares the battered *Pequod* to Satan and his fallen angels after their
defiant rebellion (MD, 469). Regarding the White Whale as the vehicle
of a retributive miracle, he records that "Retribution, swift vengeance,
eternal malice were in his whole aspect . . . [as] the solid white buttress
of his forehead smote the ship's starboard bow, till men and timbers
reeled" (MD, 468). As will become evident below, Ishmael here repeats
Ahab's epistemological error of attributing designing intelligence to
Moby-Dick. For the present, we need only recognize that Ishmael, far
from perceiving Moby-Dick as uniformly evil, posits the White Whale's
apparent vengeance as a form of the retribution foretold by Whittier,
Sumner, and Marsh in relation to slavery. And insofar as Moby-Dick is
the same whale that Ishmael has previously represented as providentially punishing the Hunkerism of Radney, Ahab's demise allows Ishmael both to deliver an even more momentous jeremiad against slavery
and to reaffirm his faith in a designing God whose retributive acts are
cause for celebration. In fact, he does this in a way that conforms to
Whittier's outlook in "The Sentence of John L. Brown" (1844), a poem
in which antislavery sentiment is converted into a profession of faith:

But ye who own that Higher Law
  Whose tablets in the heart are set,
Speak out in words of power and awe
  That God is living yet!

Breathe forth once more those tones sublime
  Which thrilled the burdened prophet's lyre,
And in a dark and evil time
  Smote down on Israel's fast of crime
And gift of blood, a rain of fire![67]

As suggested in our discussion of Yoomy's abolitionism, Melville's reservations about the socially exclusive tendencies perpetuated by related
modes of jeremiad logic might also leave him with something less than

66. See Wright, p. 30.
67. Whittier, *Writings*, III: 92–93.

Ishmael's enthusiasm about the seemingly miraculous conclusion of the story of the White Whale. We may best prepare ourselves for Melville's ultimate *reductio ad absurdum* of Ishmael's jeremiad logic—and by implication, of the justification that its covenant assumptions often provided for slavery and Manifest Destiny—by briefly reviewing the apologetical strategies that Ishmael uses to bolster the credibility of his account of the *Pequod*'s miraculous demise.

I shmael confesses his apprehension that his readers will doubt the *"reasonableness* of the whole story of the White Whale, more especially the [*Pequod*'s] catastrophe," and worries that they may even "scout at Moby Dick as a monstrous *fable,* or still worse ..., a hideous and intolerable *allegory*" (MD, 177; emphasis added). In short, he fears that they will react with the skepticism that such Deists as Thomas Woolston, Peter Annet, and Tom Paine directed toward the "reasonableness" of scriptural miracles, which in the Deist view were "fabulous" and merely "allegorical." Accordingly, Ishmael incorporates into his narrative the "testimonial" and analogical strategies espoused by such Christian apologists as William Paley, Bishop Butler, and Thomas Hartwell Horne to defend the historical credibility of scriptural miracles.[68] From "Jonah Historically Regarded" (ch. 83) and from "Monstrous Pictures of Whales" (ch. 55) we know of Ishmael's familiarity with debates between Deists and apologists.[69] Having, therefore, already offered to swear on a copy of the Holy Evangelists (MD,

---

68. For Deist inquiries into both the "reasonableness" of Scripture and its solely "allegorical" credibility, see Hans J. Hillerbrand, "The Historicity of Miracles: The Early Eighteenth-Century Debate Among Woolston, Annet, Sherlock, and West," *Studies in Religion / Sciences Religieuses,* 3, no. 2 (1972), 132–36, 141; John Toland, *Christianity Not Mysterious,* 2nd ed. (London, 1696), p. 115. Recourse to "fabulous" readings of Scripture are evident in Lord Henry Bolingbroke's uncertainty whether there was "not time more than enough between MOSES and DAVID to make fabulous traditions pass for authentic history?" ("A Letter Occasioned by one of Archbishop Tillotson's Sermons," in *The Works of the late ... Henry St. John, Lord Viscount Bolingbroke,* 5 vols. (London, 1754), III: 277). Even the subtitle of Paine's *The Age of Reason* speaks of "an Investigation of True and Fabulous Theology." Thus, Paine several times compares Scripture to "fable," most notably "Aesop's 'Fables'" (*The Life and Works of Thomas Paine,* ed. W. M. Van der Weyde, 10 vols. [New York: Thomas Paine National Historical Assoc., 1925], VIII: 20, 142, 153, 163). Ishmael uses the word "fable" in this context when he mentions "those fabled undulations of the Ephesian sod over the buried Evangelist St. John" (MD, 399). Moreover, in *Clarel* Melville exploits the word's skeptical connotations (IV.1.17) and details the Deist challenge to historical Christianity (I.xvii.116–50; II.xvi.38–41; III.xxiii.38; IV.xvii.71–72).

69. See H. Bruce Franklin, *The Wake of the Gods: Melville's Mythology* (Stanford,

224) to the authenticity of Moby-Dick's miraculous intervention in "the *Town-Ho*'s Story," Ishmael proceeds in "The Affidavit" (ch. 45) to draw upon *affidavits, testimonies,* and *evidence* of the whale's seemingly supernatural capacities for destruction to support the verity of his narrative's astounding conclusion. While such legalistic rhetoric has obvious secular importance, Hawthorne's "Rappaccini's Daughter" (1844) and "Mr. Higginbotham's Catastrophe" (1834)—both of which Melville knew—indicate that, in a religious tale, none of these terms can be considered in isolation from debates between Deists and Christian apologists (and later, between Transcendentalists and Unitarians) over the authenticity of miracles or their importance to the act of faith.[70] Since, by the time he wrote *Moby-Dick*, Melville had already adapted this legalistic rhetoric to discussions of miracles in both *Mardi* and his private correspondence,[71] we should briefly pause over "The Affidavit," in which Ishmael draws upon apologetical jargon and logic to add credibility to his impressions of the providential punishment visited upon the *Pequod*.

In "The Affidavit" Ishmael advises, "[Y]ou will not fail to see, that not only is the most marvellous event in this book [i.e., the *Pequod*'s destruction] corroborated by plain facts of the present day, but that these marvels (like all marvels) are mere repetitions of the ages" (MD, 181). His use of the term "marvel" is especially suggestive since "the original meaning of *miraculum* is that of a wonder or marvel, and

---

Calif.: Stanford Univ. Press, 1963), p. 66–70.

70. On "Rappaccini's Daughter," see Michael J. Colacurcio, "A Better Mode of Evidence—The Transcendental Problem of Faith and Spirit," *Emerson Society Quarterly*, 54 (1969), 12–22. Also see my "Sceptical Context of Hawthorne's 'Mr. Higginbotham's Catastrophe,'" *American Literature*, 48 (Nov. 1976), 292–301. Since "Rappaccini's Daughter" is included in *Mosses From an Old Manse*, we can assume Melville's familiarity with that story—as we can his awareness of "Mr. Higginbotham's Catastrophe," which appeared in *Twice-Told Tales*, which Melville claimed to have read and enjoyed (L, 121).

71. See Babbalanja's skepticism about "additional authority" (M, 278) brought to bear upon "the truth of [a] miracle" (M, 277), and his later reservations about Mohi's "account of Alma [i.e., Christ]" because "what you relate rests not upon testimony of your own;... I never was so thorough a disbeliever as now" (M, 349). Moreover, when John Murray demanded "documentary evidence" to verify the truth of facts related in *Typee*, Melville responded by referring to the phrase in a way that reveals his more general association of evidential rhetoric with miraculous Gospel history and Christian apologetics:

—By the way, you ask again for "documentary evidence" of my having been in the South Seas, wherewithall to convince *the unbelievers*—Bless my soul, Sir, will you Britons not credit that an American can be a gentleman, & have read the Waverly Novels, tho' every digit may have been in a tar bucket? You make *miracles* of what are common-places to us. I will give no evidence—Truth is mighty & will prevail.... (L, 72; emphasis added)

is the word employed in the Vulgate to translate a variety of Hebrew and Greek expressions used to refer to the works of God and Jesus Christ in the Old and New Testaments."[72] And that Ishmael thinks the most marvelous event in his narrative to be miraculous is evident from his remark in "The Affidavit" about recording history no less true than the Mosaic miracles:

> People ashore have indeed some indefinite idea that a whale is an enormous creature of enormous power; but I have ever found that when narrating to them some specific example of this two-fold enormousness, they have significantly complimented me upon my facetiousness; when, I declare upon my soul, I had no more idea of being facetious than Moses, when he wrote the history of the plagues of Egypt. (MD, 178)

Having elsewhere dealt with old Sag Harbor's "want of faith" (MD, 307) in "the general miracle" (MD, 308) of Jonah, Ishmael presently defends his narrative from a more public declaration of skepticism by describing the fate of Commodore J__, who "was pleased to be sceptical touching the amazing strength ascribed to [whales]." Ishmael, though, imbues with miraculous significance the destructive assault of a whale upon J__'s ship: "I consider the Commodore's interview with that whale as providential. Was not Saul of Tarsus converted from unbelief by a similar fright?" (MD, 179). Earlier in *Moby-Dick* Ishmael speaks of "gospel cetology" (MD, 2) and warns of "more special leviathanic *revelations* . . . to follow" (MD, 116; emphasis added). Commodore J__'s and Radney's "providential" encounters with leviathan are two such events; the *Pequod*'s destruction will be still another.

Ishmael also fancies himself an Evangelist of miraculous events. Note, for instance, how in recounting the miraculous events associated with the *Town-Ho*, he swears, "So help me Heaven, . . . the story I have told . . . is in substance and its great items true. I know it to be true; . . . I knew the crew; I have seen and talked with Steelkilt since the death of Radney" (MD, 224). Appropriately, Ishmael uses what critics perceive as a basically *artless* and confiding tone throughout his narrative; for Christian apologists habitually pointed to this feature of the Gospels in arguing the improbability of the Evangelists' having wished to deceive their readers.[73] Not surprisingly, then, Ish-

---

72. J. M. Cameron, "Miracles," *Month,* 22 (Nov. 1959), 291. In *Clarel* Melville refers to Elisha's miraculous "healing of the spring" (II.xv.3; cf. 2 Kings 2:19–22) as a "marvel done" (xv. 2). He also uses the words "marvel" and "miracle" interchangeably in a passage of *Pierre* that explains how the heavens "surcharge the heart with all rapturous marvellings . . . only because we ourselves are greater miracles" (p. 51).

73. For the artless and truthful tone of Ishmael's narrative, see Wadlington, p. 95;

mael proceeds in "The Affidavit" to become his own apologist by offering "testimony entirely independent of my own" (MD, 178) to "take
away any incredulity[74] which a profound ignorance of the entire subject may induce in some minds, as to the natural verity" (MD, 175) of
his narrative's conclusion. And this strategy of proffering concurrent
testimonies in support of sacred truths conforms to William Paley's belief, in *A View of the Evidences of Christianity*, that "there is in the
evangelic history a cumulation of testimony which belongs hardly to
any other history"[75] and that the probable truth of a scriptural account
is proportional to the number of witnesses or historians, *sacred* or *profane*, who either attest to its credibility or who mention scriptural
events as if there were no reason to doubt their truth.[76] Similarly, the

---

Warner Berthoff, *The Example of Melville* (Princeton, N.J.: Princeton Univ. Press,
1962), pp. 128–32. Cf. Thomas Hartwell Horne's belief, in *An Introduction to the Critical Study and Knowledge of the Holy Scriptures*, 4 vols., 5th ed. (London: A. & R.
Spottiswoode, 1825), I: 138–41, that "the authors of the Bible. . . . narrate their story
unambitiously and without art. . . . They relate facts with utmost simplicity"—proof,
thinks Horne, that no person "can suppose that men of such a character would wish to
deceive their readers."

74. Worth recalling, again, is Babbalanja's specifically theological use of this term:
"I wholly reject your Alma; . . . every thing . . . strengthens my incredulity; I never was
so thorough a disbeliever as now" (M, 349).

75. Paley, *A View of the Evidences of Christianity* (1794), in *The Works of William
Paley, D.D.*, 6 vols. (Cambridge, Mass.: Hilliard and Brown, 1830), II: 71. Also, Ishmael
quotes from *Natural Theology*—another of Paley's responses to the Deists—in
"Extracts" (MD, 7), and Franklin (pp. 147–48, 215–16) believes that a scene in "Benito
Cereno" echoes a line of Paley's *Evidences*. Moreover, William H. Gilman suggests
that, at the Albany Academy, Melville was probably exposed to Alexander Archibald's
*Evidences of the Authenticity, Inspiration, and Canonical Authority of the Holy Scrip-
tures*. See *Melville's Early Life and "Redburn"* (New York: New York Univ. Press,
1951), pp. 53–54.

76. This context informs *Moby-Dick*'s opening paragraph on "EXTRACTS (Sup-
plied by a Sub-Sub-Librarian)":

It will be seen that this . . . poor devil of a Sub-Sub appears to have gone through
the long Vaticans and street stalls of the earth, picking up whatever random allusions to whales he could anyways find in any book whatsoever, *sacred* or *profane*.
Therefore you must not, in every case at least, take the higgledy-piggledy whale
statements, however *authentic*, in these extracts, for veritable *gospel* cetology. (MD,
2; emphasis added)

The italicized words parody the rhetoric of Christian apologists, such as Archibald (see
preceding note) and Horne, whose *Introduction to the Critical Study . . . of the Holy
Scriptures* explores the "Genuiness and Authenticity of the New Testament" (I: 68) and
"the apparent contradictions . . . between sacred and profane writers" (I: vii). Also, see
his thoughts "On the Critical Use . . . of Profane Authors": "We have . . . seen that the
heathen writings, substantiate, by independent and collateral report, many of the
events, and the accomplishment of many of the prophecies recorded by the inspired
writers . . . " (II: 312).

more testimonies Ishmael gathers from different sources concerning the maliciousness of whales (providential or otherwise), the more credible will be his final description of Moby-Dick staving the *Pequod*.[77] Such is Ishmael's motive for introducing testimony in a chapter that describes events while comparing them to miraculous scriptural history, the main point of which is so marvelous as to induce disbelief as severe as St. Paul's prior to conversion.

Indeed, as Ishmael says, "A fact... set down in substantial history cannot easily be gainsaid" (MD, 182). Nonetheless, Ishmael knows that, however well documented the miracles of either the Old or New Testaments, or whatever the recorded instances of whales seemingly acting as providential agents of God's wrath, landsmen ignorant of leviathan's most basic physiological design will still be skeptical about the whale's ability to accomplish the sort of miraculous feat described at the conclusion of his narrative. To understand how Ishmael deals with this problem, let us first note how Bishop Butler sought to dismiss Deist charges that "no one, except... a divine, will presume to say, that the histories of the Old Testament are conformable to the ... natural course of things";[78] he did so by maintaining that scriptural miracles were just as believable as any equally incredible, but still actual, event in nature: "[U]pon Supposition of a Revelation, it is highly credible beforehand, we should be incompetent Judges of it,... and that it would contain many things appearing to us liable to great Objections: in case we judge of it otherwise, than by the Analogy of Nature."[79] The classic example of this logic rests in

---

77. Worth noting in this respect are correspondences in tone and rhetoric between Paley's *Evidences* and Ishmael's documentation in "The Affidavit." For instance, in the concluding testimony of chapter IX, Paley closes

> the series of testimonies with that of Eusebius, bishop of Caesarea, who flourished in the year 315.... This voluminous writer, and most diligent collector of the writings of others, beside a variety of large works, composed a history of the affairs of Christianity from its origin to his own time. His testimony to the scriptures is the testimony of a man much conversant in the works of Christian authors, written during the first three centuries of its era.... (II: 100)

To establish the whale's incredible destructiveness, Ishmael likewise concludes his testimonies by calling upon a historian, and by similarly praising his credentials:

> In the sixth Christian century lived Procopius, a Christian magistrate of Constantinople, in the days when Justinian was Emperor and Belisarius general. As many know, he wrote the history of his own times, a work every way of uncommon value. By the best authorities, he has always been considered a most trustworthy and unexaggerating historian, except in some one or two particulars, not at all affecting the matter to be mentioned. (MD, 181)

78. Bolingbroke, *Works*, III: 280. Cf. Annet's thoughts about miracles' running counter to the "Nature of Things," in Hillerbrand, p. 139.

79. Bishop Butler, *The Analogy of Religion, Natural and Revealed, to the Consti-*

Butler's opening argument for the miracle of an afterlife by way of analogy to the transformation of worms into flies—a strategy that Babbalanja refutes in *Mardi*.[80] But when Ishmael remarks how the try-works "smells like the left wing of the day of judgment; it is an argument for the pit" (MD, 353), he parodies Butler's effort, by way of analogy to nature, to support the truths of Revelation. So does Ahab, who says, " [I]f I feel the smart of my crushed leg, though it be now so long dissolved; then, why mayst not thou, carpenter, feel the fiery pains of hell for ever, and without a body?" (MD, 391). Also, insofar as Ishmael regards the "leviathanic revelations" of his narrative as nothing short of miraculous, he seeks to disarm us of incredulity, in such chapters as "The Nut," "The Prairie," "The Tail," and "The Battering Ram," by showing how, naturalistically and physiologically—in short, how by analogy to nature—the whale is structured in a way that renders it capable of performing the apparently miraculous destruction of the *Pequod*:

> Ere quitting, for the nonce, the Sperm Whale's head, I would have you, as a sensible physiologist, simply—particularly remark its front aspect, in all its compacted collectedness. I would have you investigate it now with a sole view of forming to yourself some unexaggerated, intelligent estimate of whatever battering-ram power may be lodged there. Here is a vital point; for you must either satisfactorily settle this matter with yourself, *or for ever remain an infidel* as to one of the most appalling, but not the less true events, perhaps anywhere to be found in all recorded history. (MD, 284; emphasis added)

Thus, to counteract any such infidel responses to his description of the *Pequod*'s miraculous demise, Ishmael asserts in the same chapter, "[W]hen I shall hereafter detail to you all the specialities and con-

---

tution and Course of Nature (London, 1736), p. 170.

80. As William Braswell, in *Melville's Religious Thought* (Durham, N.C.: Duke Univ. Press, 1943), pp. 29–30, has shown, "An idea advanced in Bishop Butler's *Analogy* is indicted in one of the arguments in *Mardi*. When Babbalanja is asked whether he considers the transformation of larva into the butterfly 'a fit illustration of the miraculous change to be wrought in man after death,' he answers":

> No; for the analogy has an unsatisfactory end. From its chrysalis state, the silkworm but becomes a moth, that very quickly expires. Its longest existence is as a worm. All vanity, vanity ... to seek in nature for positive warranty to these aspirations of ours. Through all her provinces, nature seems to promise immortality to life, but destruction to beings. (M, 210)

Perhaps Melville availed himself of one of Evert Duyckinck's two pre-1844 editions of Butler's *Analogy*. See "Duyckinck Collection," *Lenox Library Short-Title Lists*, 8 (1887), 9.

centrations of potency everywhere lurking in this expansive monster[,] ... I trust you will have renounced all ignorant incredulity" (MD, 285). For similar reasons, he describes the physiological "indomitableness" of the whale's brow, again by way of preparation for his narrative's miraculous conclusion: "And that the great monster is indomitable, you will yet have reason to know" (MD, 294).[81] Thus, for reasons which we shall see to bear upon Melville's *reductio ad absurdum* of providential historiography, the main point to remember is that, in seeking to support the "natural verity" (MD, 175) of a miraculous or providential occurrence, Ishmael structures his narrative in a manner consistent with Butler's argumentative strategy in *The Analogy of Religion*.

Of course, given the way Ishmael perceives the *Pequod*'s destruction as a retributive miracle—and himself as both an Evangelist and an apologist for this divine sign against the iniquity of American slavery—readers might follow him in thinking that he merits a salvation consistent with the fervor of his "leviathanic" jeremiad. But this would be to overlook how Ishmael's expansionist mentality actually typifies the enthusiasm that fostered both the abuses of Manifest Destiny (too often justified with appeals to the sort of providential assumptions inherent in Ishmael's point of view) and the issue of whether to extend slavery into the territories acquired as a result of the Mexican War. In fact, Ishmael's outlook and historiography make him an unwitting post facto accomplice to his captain's worst nationalistic transgressions, the racial overtones of which are everywhere evident.

Worth recalling in this respect is the opinion that "in Ishmael's New Bedford experiences, which begin on a stormy night, the expensive inns of the Crossed Harpoons and the Sword-Fish that he passes by, and the Negro Church that he stumbles into and dubs the 'Trap,' are reminders of the materialistically inspired Mexican War, and the slavery dilemma it created."[82] Although we cannot know if Melville used these symbols with exactly such intent, the reminder of the relation between expansionism and the extension of slavery is accurate. Moreover, I would suggest that Ishmael, like Walt Whitman before him, actually helps create this trap. A staunch advocate of both westward expansionism and the Mexican War, Whitman was eventually forced from his editorship of the *Brooklyn Daily Eagle* because he protested the ex-

---

81. Howard P. Vincent has shown that Ishmael's preoccupation with leviathan's physiology is directed toward the evidence of the whale's ability to accomplish the destructive acts recorded at the end of *Moby-Dick*. See *The Trying-Out of "Moby-Dick"* (Boston: Houghton Mifflin, 1949), pp. 371 (esp.), 123, 166, 186, 192, 250, 260, 387.

82. Weathers, p. 486.

tension of slavery into territory to be acquired from Mexico.[83] His predicament embodied the paradox of an American generation whose President—ignoring the sentiments of persons like John Quincy Adams, William Ellery Channing, and David Lee Child—labeled as "mischievous [and] wicked" any effort to link expansionism and the extension of slavery, effectively laying the "trap" for the Civil War.[84] Indeed, the Berrien-Stephens proposal of 1847 to disavow territorial gain as a result of the Mexican War found little support among either northern legislators intent upon expansionism or among northern Democratic journals that regarded such legislation as a plot to keep free states from entering the Union.[85] Yet even the champions of "free soil" were often more preoccupied with free soil for free white settlers than with the immorality of slavery—to such a degree, in fact, that some "even tried to shift the main goal of the party by centering their campaigns on the dangers involved in land monopoly rather than on the wrongs of Negro slavery."[86] But because the issue of slavery was inevitably bound up with territorial expansion, northeastern hunger for new land and states helped precipitate the national crisis over disunion that Henry Clay tried unsuccessfully to stave off in the Compromise of 1850; as the *American Whig Review* said, "[Calhoun] opposed the war of invasion against Mexico; he opposed the acquisition of territory; but, once acquired, he wished it to be slave territory."[87] Thus, whatever Ishmael's

---

83. See *The Gathering of the Forces by Walt Whitman: Editorials, Essays, Literary and Dramatic Reviews ... Written by Walt Whitman as Editor of the "Brooklyn Daily Eagle" in 1846 and 1847*, ed. Cleveland Rodgers and John Black, 2 vols. (New York: G. P. Putnam's Sons, 1920), I: xxvii–xxxvi.

84. As Schroeder (p. 4) says, Polk "refused to concede that the slavery question was closely related to expansion in the Southwest, and throughout the war with Mexico he adamantly maintained that the two issues were not legitimately related. Rather Polk labeled the extension of slavery an 'abstract question,' which when considered in connection with territorial expansion was 'not only mischievous but wicked.' " The Whigs, too, as Brauer (p. 114) shows, "insisted that the distinction between ... antiannexationism and abolitionism be kept clear." Nonetheless, Merk (*Slavery and the Annexation of Texas*, p. 181) describes how the roots of the Civil War "lay deep in the soil of Texas."

85. Rayback, pp. 121–23.

86. Rayback, p. 265. (Also see pp. 60, 211, 222–23 for the tie between "Free Soil" and the well-being of free white labor.) The connection is equally conspicuous in *Niles National Register*, 74 (20 Dec. 1848), 387, and the *American Whig Review*, 8 (Aug. 1848), 115.

87. "A Word to Southern Democrats by a Northern Conservative," *American Whig Review*, 10 (Aug. 1849), 195. Cf. *American Whig Review*, 12 (Aug. 1850), 212. As Calhoun explained in *Cong. Globe*, 31st. Cong., 1st sess. (4 March 1850), 451–55, the South could not afford to make concessions because the influx of free states into the Union had already disrupted the balance both of "slave" and "free" territory and of congressional representation based upon population. Merk (*Manifest Destiny*, p. 214) succinctly puts it thus: "In 1860 pressures, past, present, and future, blasted the Union

Free Soil leanings—which we have seen to find notable expression in both his jeremiad against the mania of a slave-driving Captain and in his meticulous apologetical effort to convince us of God's providential destruction of such sinners—we may now explore how he espouses the very northeastern enthusiasm for expansionism which helped calcify southern resistance to "God's law supreme." Also to be addressed is the way that, in believing both the *Pequod*'s destruction and his own salvation miraculous, Ishmael finally indulges in a mode of covenant psychology having isolationist and exclusive tendencies that belie his apparent liberalism.

"Chief among [the] motives" that send Ishmael to sea is "the overwhelming idea of the great whale himself." And in his remark that "such a portentous and mysterious monster roused all my *curiosity*. . . . I am tormented with an everlasting itch for things remote. I love to sail forbidden seas, and land on barbarous coasts" (MD, 16; emphasis added), Ishmael adopts an attitude compatible with the *American Whig Review*'s description of the pioneering spirit:

> A period of every age of the world has been marked for its spirit of adventure; either for the discovery and exploration of unknown countries, or for the colonization and settlement of countries previously known. *Curiosity* is, doubtless, the first principle which directs human footsteps to penetrate where they had not before trodden; to scan the broad ocean in quest of new lands; or to explore the depths of the African continent, and amid her burning sands, and her pestilential climate, to trace the sources of her mysterious rivers.[88]

Consistent with this pioneering spirit is Ishmael's dislike for city life, in which men are "tied to counters, nailed to benches, clinched to desks" (MD, 12–13). This disposition brings to mind travel narratives

---

apart. Not least were past, present, and future expansionist pressures. . . . The doctrine of Manifest Destiny, which in the 1840's had seemed Heaven-sent, proved to have been a bomb wrapped up in idealism."

88. "Sir John Franklin and the Arctic Expeditions," *American Whig Review*, 11 (June 1850), 572; emphasis added. Although Fussell (pp. 256–79) details the pervasiveness of western imagery and metaphors in *Moby-Dick*, he does so without seriously considering what I here seek to establish as the significance of Ishmael's western point of view. Closer to the mark, I think, are Chase (pp. 67–69), who early compared Ishmael to Davy Crockett, and Slotkin (p. 540), who notes a correspondence between Ishmael's temperament and that of Daniel Boone.

that cited a desire to escape "monotonous" city existence as one of the key attractions of the American West. And an entire generation of Americans well knew that ample precedent existed in the career of Sam Houston for young schoolmasters such as Ishmael periodically to flee to the wilderness for adventure.[89] Not surprisingly, therefore, Ishmael refers to "that unfallen, western world, which to the eyes of the old trappers and hunters revived the glories of those primeval times when Adam walked majestic as a god" (MD, 165). He also romantically compares the sea to the prairie and the *Pequod* to an emigrant's horse (MD, 405). Moreover, in "The Mast-Head" (ch. 35) he indulges in Transcendental reveries consistent with his pioneering spirit.[90] Indeed, this "western" dimension of Transcendental fervor is earlier conspicuous in Ishmael's celebration of "the serene Pacific," the "new-built Californian towns," and the prospect of trade with Japan—all under the more general rubric of "Pan[theism]" (MD, 399–400).

Also related to Ishmael's western temperament is the figure of an expanding circle. "Since the Americans have acquired Louisiana," said Félix de Beaujour in his *Sketch of the United States of North America* (1814), "they appear unable to bear any barriers round them." During the Mexican War a similar geographical and geometrical image characterized Walt Whitman's remark, "The daring, burrowing energies of the Nation will never rest till the whole of this northern section of the Great West World is circled in the mighty Republic."[91] Ishmael, in

---

89. For pioneers' disenchantment with "monotonous" city life, see George F. Ruxton, *Adventures in Mexico and the Rocky Mountains* (1848), quoted in the *American Whig Review*, 7 (March 1848), 315. For Sam Houston's inclination to shift back and forth between the woods and the classroom, see Charles Edwards Lester, *Sam Houston and His Republic* (New York: Burgess, Stringer, 1846), p. 15. This tendency of Houston's is also mentioned in the *American Whig Review*'s review of Lester's book ("Sam Houston and His Republic," 5 [June 1847], 578). Worth noting in this context is what Laurence M. Hauptman shows to be the way nineteenth-century schoolbooks "mirrored and rationalized society-at-large's view about continental expansion." See Hauptman's "Mythologizing Westward Expansion: Schoolbooks and the Image of the American Frontier before Turner," *Western Historical Quarterly*, 8 (July 1977), 269–82.

90. Lucy Lockwood Hazard, in *The Frontier in American Literature* (New York: Thomas Y. Crowell, 1927), p. 153, remarks that "constant contact of man with nature, accompanied by a never-failing belief in the supremacy of man over nature is a basic condition of both transcendental philosophy and frontier life." Cf. Marx, p. 236, and James Freeman Clarke's "First Crossing the Alleghanies," which, published in a journal no less Transcendental than the *Dial* (1 [Oct. 1840], 159–60), stresses man's spiritual correspondence with the Great West: "When soul stimulates soul, pulses together beat. / He has a world within to match thine, beautiful mother!"

91. De Beaujour is quoted in the *North American Review*, 2 (Nov. 1815), 99. Whitman's remark is from "A Visit to a Camp, etc.," *Brooklyn Daily Eagle* (29 Aug. 1846), in *Gathering of the Forces*, II: 122.

turn, celebrates a similar expansionist vision in the "Nantucket" chapter of *Moby-Dick*:

> What wonder, then, these Nantucketers, born on a beach, should take to the sea for a livelihood! They first caught crabs and quohogs in the sand; grown bolder, they waded out with nets for mackerel; more experienced, they pushed off in boats and captured cod; and at last, launching a navy of great ships on the sea, explored this watery world; *put an incessant belt of circumnavigations round it;* ...and in all...oceans *declared everlasting war* with the mightiest mass that has ever survived the flood.... (MD, 62; emphasis added)

Here, then, Melville hints that his narrator's expansionist temperament is precisely the sort that culminated in the Mexican War and its policies of territorial aggrandizement; indeed, in the very next paragraph Ishmael voices a grand hosanna to conquest and imperialism: "Let America add Mexico to Texas, and pile Cuba upon Canada; let the English overswarm all India, and hang out their blazing banner from the sun; two thirds of this terraqueous globe are the Nantucketer's. For the sea is his; he owns it, as Emperors own empires" (MD, 62–63).

Thus, more than a casual compatibility exists between Ishmael's political outlook and Ahab's. Ahab's furious rape of nature, moreover, finds an analog in Ishmael's refusal to concede that the whale will ever be over-hunted; instead, Ishmael holds that leviathan's seemingly boundless "pasture" will result in the whale's remaining "immortal in his species, however perishable in his individuality" (MD, 384). Yet insofar as Ishmael uses this argument to disown any comparison between the plight of hunted whales and the nearly extinct American buffalo (MD, 383), his shortsightedness perpetuates what one historian has called the "myth of super-abundance," or the eighteenth- and early nineteenth-century "belief in the inexhaustibility of western resources."[92] Also, by romanticizing the way "the Nantucketer...alone resides and riots on the sea; he alone, in Bible language, goes down to it in ships, to and fro ploughing it as his own special plantation" (MD, 63), Ishmael echoes the argument for a "destined use of the soil" to which Americans from John Winthrop through James K. Polk appealed in justifying territorial expropriation.[93] And Melville would

---

92. See Harlan Hague, "Eden Ravished: The Land, Pioneer Attitudes, and Conservation," *American West*, 14 (May/June 1977), 30–33, 65–69. Media's scroll had earlier cautioned America about what historians of the Frederick Jackson Turner school later called the "safety valve theory" of the frontier. See *Mardi*, p. 526. Also see *Clarel* (IV.xxi.90–100) and Bezanson's note to this passage (p. 639) for Melville's cynicism about the West's supposedly unlimited "vast reserves" (IV.xxi.94).

93. For the backgrounds of this concept, see Weinberg, pp. 72–99. As late as 1846,

have known that Washington Irving had already exposed the more lamentable political tendencies of this logic in Diedrich Knickerbocker's reflections that

> Heaven intended the earth should be ploughed and sown, and manured, and laid out into cities, and towns, and farms, . . . all which the Indians knew nothing about—therefore, they did not improve the talents Providence had bestowed on them—therefore, they were careless stewards—therefore, they had no right to the soil—therefore, they deserved to be exterminated.[94]

As we shall see, Ishmael's description of the *Pequod*'s providential destruction places him closer to such exterminationist policies than he would care to admit.

There are, indeed, some earlier indications that Ishmael may be disposed to sympathize with ideas of America's covenanted right to the New Canaan of the Great West. For instance, Ishmael pleasurably recalls a stanza of Bildad's hymn that describes the Children of Israel standing on the threshold of their enemy's land, which they deem promised them by divine covenant:

> Sweet fields beyond the swelling flood,
>   Stand dressed in living green.
> So to the Jews old Canaan stood,
>   While Jordan rolled between. (MD, 95)

Timothy Dwight had already shown that the American experiment was from the beginning modeled upon the "conquest of Canaan."[95] And since Ishmael mentions "Anak" (MD, 238), father of the giants who inhabited Canaan prior to its occupation by the Israelites (Numbers 13:32–33), he apparently understands the biblical referent of Bildad's hymn. In typical Yankee fashion, Ishmael thinks the hymn "full of hope and fruition" (MD, 95)—a confession that allies him with the sort

John Quincy Adams justified America's claims to Oregon with an argument for the destined use of the soil derived from the Book of Genesis. See *Cong. Globe*, 29th Cong., 1st sess. (9 Feb. 1846), 340.

94. Irving, *A History of New York* (1809), in *The Works of Washington Irving*, 28 vols. (New York: G. P. Putnam and Son, 1868–69), I: 70–71. For evidence of Melville's familiarity with *A History of New York*, see my "Melville's Use of Irving's *Knickerbocker History* in *White-Jacket*," *Melville Society Extracts*, 46 (May 1981), 1, 4–6.

95. Timothy Dwight, *The Conquest of Canaan: A Poem* (1788). Cf. Diedrich Knickerbocker's remark, in *A History of New York*, p. 412, that "As their prototypes of yore went forth into the land of Canaan ... to settle themselves down in the land and possess it; so these chosen people of modern days [i.e., the Yankees] would progress through the country."

of covenant logic used to justify territorial encroachment and, as will become evident, the extermination of Indians and Mexicans.[96]

Americans, however, prided themselves on their covenanted sense of mission because of its nominal mandate to "extend the area of freedom." Ishmael possibly thinks in similar terms when he compares the *Pequod*'s crew of thirty (MD, 422, 431, 455; i.e., one crewman for each state in the Union) to an "Anacharsis Clootz deputation" (MD, 108). As Milton R. Stern remarks, the French National Assembly granted Clootz the right "to confederate the entire human race into one vast democratic whole."[97] Also, Ishmael explicitly links whaling with an extended area of freedom by saying that "if space permitted, it might be distinctly shown how from those whalemen at last eventuated the liberation of Peru, Chili, and Bolivia from the yoke of Old Spain, and the establishment of the eternal democracy in those parts." Moreover, that Ishmael here adopts a messianic tone distinct from the sentiments of Melville is evident from his satisfaction with the manner in which "uncounted isles of all Polynesia . . . do commercial homage to the whaleship, that cleared the way for the missionary and the merchant, and in many cases carried the primitive missionaries to their first destinations" (MD, 100). One suspects that the author of *Typee* and *Omoo* would, in his own character, hardly have subscribed to such a view.

Perhaps we may see in Ishmael a reflection of the zeal with which some of his Presbyterian brethren, because of the Mexican War, "awaited the hour when vast new areas would be opened to the true Gospel of the Protestant missionary."[98] Indeed, claiming "Possession" to be "half the law: that is, regardless of how the thing came into possession," Ishmael perceives Mexico as a "Loose Fish" and asks, "What to that apostolic lancer, brother Jonathan [i.e., America] is Texas but a Fast Fish?" (MD, 333–34). Harrison Hayford seems best to explain the implications of attitudes such as these: "[Ishmael] does not care to be a superior to inflict the physical hurt, but once it has been, as it were, legally and duly done he accepts and respects the result." Also, Ishmael's use of the term "apostolic lancer" makes his sympathies as culpable as those assailed by James Russell Lowell in a

---

96. For a related reading of the political import of Bildad's hymn—but one that does not stress Ishmael's accessory role in exterminationist and racially oppressive tendencies—see Viola Sachs, *The Myth of America: Essays in the Structures of Literary Imagination* (Paris: Mouton, 1973), pp. 48–56.

97. I here quote Stern's editorial note concerning the Clootz reference in *Billy Budd, Sailor: An Inside Narrative* (Indianapolis, Ind.: Bobbs-Merrill, 1975), p. 4, n. 5.

98. Schroeder, p. 109. Cf. Clayton Sumner Ellsworth, "The American Churches and the Mexican War," *American Historical Review*, 45 (Jan. 1940), 307. Ishmael "was . . . born and bred in the bosom of the infallible Presbyterian Church" (MD, 54).

section of *The Biglow Papers* that exposes the hypocritical and self-serving use of "conversion" rhetoric to justify the invasion of Mexico:

> Those have not been wanting...who have maintained that òur late inroad upon Mexico was undertaken not so much for the avenging of any national quarrel, as for the spreading of free institutions and of Protestantism.... Verily I admire that no pious sergeant among these new Crusaders beheld Martin Luther riding at the front of the host upon a tamed pontifical bull, as, in that former invasion of Mexico, the zealous Gomara...was favored with a vision of St. James of Compostella, skewering the infidels upon his *apostolical lance.*[99]

The point is that political romanticism such as that espoused by Ishmael, and exposed by Lowell, sanctioned the Polk administration's less than benevolent drive toward both the Rio Grande and the Pacific. Ishmael, after all, *chooses* to ship aboard the *Pequod*, fully knowing it to be "a cannibal of a craft, tricking herself forth in the chased bones of her enemies" (MD, 67).[100]

Even Ishmael's adopted name may implicate him in his captain's belligerently expropriationist quest. As early as 1644 John Winthrop capitalized upon the description of the biblical Ishmael as a "wild man; his hand *will be* against every man, and every man's hand against him" (Gen. 16:12) to slander Anne Hutchinson and her followers as latter-day instances of *"Cain, Hagar,* and *Ishmael,* [who] were expelled as troublers of the families, (which were then as commonwealths)." Moreover, even in the nineteenth century Diedrich Knickerbocker perceived the Yankees as a group of "notorious squatters" who possessed

> a certain rambling propensity, with which, like the sons of Ishmael, they seem to have been gifted by heaven, and which continually goads them on, to shift their residence from place to place, so that a Yankee farmer is in a constant state of migration; *tarrying* occasionally here and there; clearing lands for other people to enjoy, building houses for others to inhabit, and... may be considered the wandering Arab of America.

Perhaps James Fenimore Cooper had this passage in mind when he named the land-mongering "squatter" of *The Prairie* Ishmael Bush.

---

99. Harrison Hayford, "'Loomings': Yarns and Figures in the Fabric," in DeMott and Marovitz, eds., *Artful Thunder*, p. 127 (emphasis added); Lowell, *Writings*, VIII: 61 (emphasis added).

100. For the temperamental similarities between Ishmael and Ahab, see Hayford, pp. 121–25, 134.

Constantly taking "possession [of land]... without much deference to forms of law," Bush clearly anticipates the Ishmael of "Fast Fish and Loose Fish," who justifies America's claim to Texas by asking, "[I]s not Possession the whole of the law?" (MD, 333).[101]

Ahab, I would argue, embodies a furiously restless form of these Ishmaelian attitudes, though Ishmael finally steps back to deliver a jeremiad against the slave-driving mentality of a captain whose identity shifts from James K. Polk, who coveted Naboth's vineyard, to John C. Calhoun, who defied "God's law supreme" in seeking to extend the area of slavery over it. What Ishmael fails to realize, though, is that his own expansionist outlook implicates him in what we have explored as the tie between America's territorial imperative and the extension of slavery. And remaining to be addressed is Ishmael's inability to comprehend that his covenant assumptions render hypocritical his desire for a society predicated upon the inherent equality of all souls before a "great democratic God."

Covenant psychology brings us to the largest political and racial concerns raised by Ishmael's jeremiad, for his narrative is a testimonial of hope and faith in a retributive—but just—God who insures the protection and destiny of His "chosen." In fact, Ishmael retrospectively compares himself atop Queequeg's coffin to one of the children for whom Rachel weeps (MD, 470), probably knowing the promissory dimension of this otherwise somber allusion to Jeremiah 31:15:

---

101. John Winthrop, *A Short Story of the Rise, reign, and ruine of the Antinomians, Familists & Libertines* (1644), in *The Antinomian Controversy, 1636–1638: A Documentary History*, ed. David D. Hall (Middletown, Conn.: Wesleyan Univ. Press, 1968), p. 254 (cf. p. 261); Irving, *A History of New York*, p. 194; Cooper, *The Prairie*, p. 325 (cf. pp. 64, 103). Perhaps the pioneering facet of Ishmael's identity caused Melville to imbue his Ishmaelian narrator with both harsh memories of his stepmother (MD, 32; cf. Brodtkorb's remark [p. 104] that "Ishmael left home because, where there is no love, one is already emotionally homeless") and a persistent feeling of being orphaned (MD, 406, 470). Indeed, consistent with Ishmael's western enthusiasm, his loneliness as an orphan, and Winthrop's antinomian explanation of the name "Ishmael" is what Lucy Lockwood Hazard (pp. 154–55) describes as the essential "rootlessness of the pioneer":

> Pioneering involved a break with the past.... The story of the Puritan frontier is a story of constantly strengthening Separatist tendencies in church and state until the frail ties that bound the colonies to the mother country were snapped in a moment of exaggerated resentment. The story of the typical frontiersman begins with "When a boy, he ran away from home." The frontier is born in the throes of schisms within schisms, insurrections within insurrections.

In this respect, Melville's portrait of Ishmael anticipates what more recent historical scholarship discusses as the tie between the western territorial imperative and a sense of being orphaned. See Louie W. Attebery, "The American West and the Archetypal Orphan," *Western American Literature*, 5 (Fall 1970), 205–17, esp. 215–17.

> Thus saith the LORD; A voice was heard in Ramah, lamentation *and* bitter weeping; Rachel weeping for her children refused to be comforted for her children, because they *were* not.
>
> Thus said the LORD; Refrain thy voice from weeping, and thine eyes from tears: for thy work shall be rewarded, saith the LORD; and they shall come again from the land of the enemy.

Thus, whatever the retributive emphasis of his narrative, Ishmael's application of the more redemptive dimension of Jeremiah to his own salvation conforms to the fundamentally optimistic nature of "the American Jeremiad," which Sacvan Bercovitch has shown to feature God's restoration of his "elect" after a period of probation and tribulation. Despite God's readiness to punish apostasy, His elect people remain "chosen nonetheless, still the keepers of the ancient promise to Abraham. And Jeremiah asserts the fulfillment of the promise as the very telos of history." Aptly, then, as Nathalia Wright has shown, this paradox between chastisement and restoration is the distinguishing feature of Father Mapple's sermon, upon which Ishmael models both his own account of the *Pequod*'s retributive demise and the apostolical mandate implied by his salvation: "As sinful men, it is a lesson to us all, because it is a story of the sin, hard-heartedness, suddenly awakened fears, the swift punishment, repentance, prayers, and finally the deliverance and joy of Jonah" (MD, 45).[102]

Melville's use of the term "jeremiade" in *The Confidence Man* (p. 189) suggests his knowledge of the general convention that, I believe, underlies the expression of Ishmael's outlook; moreover, from any number of sources, including the *American Whig Review*, Melville could have come to understand the jeremiad's Janus-like nature:

> To the old Puritan, every event was under the superintending Providence of an all-seeing God. . . . Nothing to him was the result of chance, and scarcely anything the effect of natural causes. His religion was of a character which *admitted neither of despair under reverses, nor doubt of ultimate success.* Obstacles in his pathway he counted as trials of his faith, and bravely surmounted them; . . . tempest upon the ocean, famine upon the land, destruction to human life, were each *the rods of discipline, which a heavenly Father used in love for his ultimate good.*[103]

---

102. Sacvan Bercovitch, *The American Jeremiad* (Madison: Univ. of Wisconsin Press, 1978), p. 31; Wright, pp. 87–93, 147–48. Bercovitch also addresses the paradox between divine chastisement and the ultimate promise of redemption (pp. 8, 26, 55, 102, 120, 121, 130). For the covenant assumptions of Jeremiah's logic, see Bercovitch, "Horologicals to Chronometricals: The Rhetoric of the Jeremiad," *Literary Monographs*, no. 3, ed. Eric Rothstein (Madison: Univ. of Wisconsin Press, 1970), p. 7.

103. "Colonel Seth Pomeroy (Part Second)," *American Whig Review*, 7 (June

From such ideas prevalent during his time, Melville could have developed an artistic strategy: a jeremiad format would allow his narrator to evade despair by learning to regard the *Pequod*'s demise as an instance of God's correcting rod of discipline. Ishmael, in fact, probably appropriates the significance of the "swift punishment" (MD, 45) visited upon Jonah to the "swift vengeance" (MD, 468) that he finds in Moby-Dick's destruction of the *Pequod*. Also, Ishmael retrospectively views the *Pequod*'s fate with a feeling of the "eternal delight and deliciousness" that Father Mapple attributes to persons who can say, "O Father!—chiefly known to me by Thy rod" (MD, 51). Feeling this kinship with the redeemed Jonah of Father Mapple's sermon, Ishmael, too, becomes a "pilot of the living God" by preaching a "leviathanic" jeremiad, the practical function of which is to warn the Ship of State from its disastrous racial course. Quite possibly, then, "the shipwreck in *Moby-Dick*, followed as it is by Ishmael's salvation, emerges as a symbol of hope to the faithful disciples of democracy."[104] Moreover, to the degree that the *Pequod*'s destruction reveals God's displeasure with slavery, Ishmael's outlook borders on the millennialist optimism of antislavery jeremiads such as that of Whittier:

> And, from her dark iniquities,
>   Methinks I see my country rise:
> Not challenging the nations round
>   To note her tardy justice done;
> Her captives from their chains unbound. . . .
> O, then to Faith's annointed eyes
>   The promised token shall be given;
> And on a nation's sacrifice,
> Atoning for the sin of years,
> And wet with penitential tears,
>   The fire shall fall from Heaven![105]

Here and in several other abolitionist poems, Whittier concludes his jeremiad by affirming God's covenant with his reformed and *still chosen people*, which is the precise assumption that one critic shows to function in Ishmael's millennialist perception of his own survival.[106] As suggested earlier, however, Ishmael's most laudable humanistic as-

---

1848), 599; emphasis added.

104. Heimert, p. 527.

105. Whittier, "The World's Convention" (1840), in *Writings*, III: 79–80. For other instances of Whittier's optimistic use of jeremiad logic in poems dealing with slavery, see "A Summons" (1836) and "The Pastoral Letter" (1837), in *Writings*, III: 42–43, 54.

106. Gilmore, p. 159, remarks that

the covenant forsaken by the nation at large survives in the person of Melville's

pirations become ensnared by the socially exclusive and bellicose tendencies of covenant psychology. Insofar as the typical colonial jeremiad seeks "to recast the country's adversities into a confirmation of its mission," and to the extent that God's wrath under such circumstances becomes a sign of national election, Ishmael commits himself to a world view that effects a transcendence of cosmic despair by generating belief in an exclusively "chosen" people. Yet beliefs such as this, historians argue, comprise the conceptual foundation of theories linking Manifest Destiny to the racial superiority of white, Anglo-Saxon Protestants.[107]

I do not mean to suggest that Melville would have regarded racism as a *necessary* feature of covenant psychology; in fact, Melville's treatment of orthodox Judaism in *Clarel,* and especially in the persons of Ruth and Agar, is sensitive, warm, and sometimes inspiring. Rather, in juxtaposing Ahab's and Ishmael's messianic outlooks with spectres of the Mexican War and the Pequot Massacre of 1637, Melville dramatizes the disparity between the "Model of Christian Charity" that people such as John Winthrop regarded as the identifying feature of a nation in covenant with God,[108] and the enslavingly selfish tendencies of such logic once it succumbs to a lust for Naboth's Vineyard.

Exploitation of covenant psychology for political gain surfaces in the same article of the *American Whig Review* that describes the "rods of discipline" with which God guides His chosen people. Included in its account of the colonists' campaign against the French at Louisburg in 1755 are passages from the journal of Colonel Seth Pomeroy declaring that "God hath gone out of his common providence in a remarkable and almost miraculous manner" to assure New Englanders of victory, and that all this is part of a grand design for His children in covenant:

> It is plain to anybody... that the Lord of hosts and God of armies hath both begun, carried on, and finished this great design, and de-

---

fictional hero.... Ishmael watches the "unharming sharks" glide by "as if with padlocks on their mouths; the savage sea-hawks sailed with sheathed beaks" (p. 470). It is a common theme in the Old Testament, as well as in the millennial writings of divines such as Edwards, that in the kingdom to come the beasts of prey wll be transformed into peaceable creatures. By virtue of his redemption, in short, Ishmael figures as the saving remnant, a concept that the emigrant Puritans were wont to apply to themselves.

107. The quotation concerning the confirmation of mission is from Bercovitch, "Horologicals to Chronometricals," p. 26 (cf. 86). For the ties between covenant psychology, Manifest Destiny, and racial superiority, see Tuveson, pp. 150–53, Friedman, *Inventors of the Promised Land,* pp. 217–18, Hansen, p. 389.

108. See John Winthrop, "A Model of Christian Charity," in Perry Miller, ed., *The American Puritans: Their Prose and Poetry* (New York: Anchor, 1956), pp. 78–84.

livered this strong city into our hands. My hearty desire and prayer is, that as long as I have a being, I may give the great name of God the praise of it, that he has written salvation for New England.[109]

Obviously, theories of Manifest Destiny incorporated nominally "pacific" versions of such logic. For example, in claiming that "a wise and merciful Providence has guided our course, nourished our growth, increased our vigor, and each day poured new blessings upon our head," John L. O'Sullivan brought to its nineteenth-century fruition the jubilant and promissory dimension of the jeremiad. Yet these same assumptions had earlier allowed both the Puritans and the colonists to see in their ever-expanding territory (however obtained) and ever-increasing population evidence of their elect status. "The frontier movement," says Bercovitch, "came to provide a sort of serial enactment of the ritual of the jeremiad. It was the moving stage for the quintessentially American drama of destined progress...."[110] Thus, however Ishmael may try to dissociate himself from Ahab's mad enthusiasm, their political compatibility is all too evident in the expropriationist tendencies of the jeremiad outlook upon which Ishmael draws to structure the narrative of *Moby-Dick*. Aptly, then, *Ishmael* narrates the history—a *Magnalia Dei Americana*, as it were—of a ship named after the decimated Pequot Indians.

To appreciate the extent of Ishmael's culpability, recall Bercovitch's explanation that "the significance of 'holy land' depends on other lands not being holy; the chosenness of the chosen people implies their antagonism to the *goyim*, the profane 'nations of the earth.' Moreover, sacred history means the gradual conquest of the profane by the sacred."[111] And precisely this habit of thought was satirized by the *American Whig Review* in its parody of oratory used by supporters of Polk's war against Mexico: "We were Anglo-Saxon Americans; it was our 'destiny' to possess and to rule this continent—we were *bound* to do it! We were a chosen people, and this was our allotted inheritance, and we must drive out all other nations before us!"[112] Yet this assumption is likewise an implication of the stanza in Bildad's hymn with which Ishmael becomes enamored—as well of expansionist ends to

---

109. "Colonel Seth Pomeroy (Part Second)," p. 602.

110. John L. O'Sullivan, "European Dominion in America," New York *Morning News* (1 Dec. 1845); Bercovitch, *American Jeremiad*, p. 164; cf. Bercovitch's observations in "Horologicals to Chronometricals," pp. 80–81, about the relation between the jeremiad and Manifest Destiny.

111. Bercovitch, *American Jeremiad*, p. 178.

112. "Our Relations with Mexico," *American Whig Review*, 4 (July 1846), 14 (really p. 16).

which the Puritans applied Psalm 2:8 (in which God promises to give His chosen people "the heathen *for* thine inheritance, and the uttermost parts of the earth *for* thine inheritance, and the uttermost parts of the earth *for* thy possession") in justifying expropriation of Indian lands: "[T]he Lord was pleased to smite [the Pequots] in the hinder parts, and to give us their land for an inheritance."[113] Melville had already shown related expropriationist attitudes to be a product of jeremiad mentality; for White-Jacket (whose effort to catalog America's iniquities while celebrating her potential greatness is a jeremiad writ large) clearly states that "we Americans are the peculiar, chosen people— the Israel of our time. . . . God has given to us, for a future inheritance, the broad domains of the political pagans . . ." (WJ, 151).

Whatever the chance that White-Jacket self-consciously parodies such ideas, Ishmael's more calculated imposition of jeremiad logic upon the significance of the *Pequod*'s demise makes him a conceptual accessory to his country's ruthless expansionism. Not surprisingly, Ishmael compares the whale hunt to a search for murderous Indian savages (MD, 177), knowing that "*Pequod* . . . was the name of a celebrated tribe of Massachusetts Indians, now extinct as the ancient Medes" (MD, 67). They became extinct when, out of lust for land, the Puritans massacred somewhere between five and six hundred Pequots in a blazing fire and then justified their act with claims of God's miraculous intercession on behalf of His chosen people: "[T]he Conquest obtained [*sic*] over the *pequots* was wonderfully the Lords doing," declared Increase Mather, who also recorded its being a "Divine providence" that "deserve[s] to be mentioned amongst the *Magnalia Dei*, which he hath wrought for his *New England-People*."[114] And this is the very sense in which Melville resurrects the Pequod issue when, in *Clarel*, Nathan makes a bigoted comparison between Arabs and American Indians:

> Himself and honest servants three
> Armed husbandmen became, as erst
> His sires in Pequod wilds immersed.
> Hittites—foes pestilent to God

---

113. John Allyn, *A Brief History of the War with the Pequot Indians in New England; Anno 1637*, in Increase Mather's *A Relation of the Troubles which have hapned [sic] in New-England, By reason of the Indians there. . . . Wherein . . . the wonderful providence of God in disappointing their devices, is declared* (Boston: John Foster, 1677), p. 41.

114. Mather, *Relation of the Troubles*, pp. 51, 55. Although Herbert (p. 106) links the name of Ahab's ship to the New Israel massacre of the Pequots, he does not consider how covenant psychology and a jeremiad format implicate Ishmael in a recognizably American mode of aggressiveness.

His fathers old those Indians deemed:
Nathan the Arabs here esteemed
The same—slaves meriting the rod;
And out he spake it; which bred hate
The more imperiling his state. (I.xvii.305–13)

Thus, even though Ishmael expresses aversion to Ahab's violence, his narrative reenactment of God's ability to destroy the *Pequod*—a ship that Ishmael aptly describes as iniquitously "freighted with savages" (MD, 354)—perpetuates the logic used from his country's inception to justify its policies of ethnic extermination and territorial aggrandizement. In fact, Ishmael concludes his narrative of the *Pequod*'s demise by quoting a line from the Book of Job ("AND I ONLY AM ESCAPED ALONE TO TELL THEE" [MD, 470]) that Melville probably knew to be parodied in the providential finale of Thomas Shepard's rendition of the Pequot massacre: "And 'tis verily thought, scarce one man escaped, unless one or two to carry forth tidings of the lamentable end of their fellows."[115]

Ishmael, then, is the American child who trips over his own conceptual shoestrings while seeking to flee the brutality of his nation's past. In believing "God's burning finger" (MD, 415) to have marked the *Pequod* for destruction, Ishmael espouses the sort of assumption evident in the *Democratic Review*'s 1844 defense of American rights to "the magnificent region allotted already by the unequivocal finger of Providence, for the main centre and home of the great republican confederated empire of the West." And this mode of thought also allowed U.S. senators to justify western expansionism by citing America's earlier extermination of Indians: "We were a feeble band of pilgrims on Plymouth rock," announced Senator Andrew Kennedy in 1846, and

[f]rom this small beginning, and in a short time, we have gone on, step by step, multiplying and advancing towards the Pacific, till the aborigines of the country had disappeared before us.... *Was not the hand of destiny in that? He who did not see it must be an infidel*, or stone blind. To the Pacific ocean it is our destiny to

---

115. *Thomas Shepard's Memoir of His Own Life*, in Alexander Young, ed., *Chronicles of the First Planters of the Colony of Massachusetts Bay, from 1623–1636* (Boston: Charles C. Little and James Brown, 1846), p. 550. As Luther Stearns Mansfield and Howard P. Vincent show in "Explanatory Notes" to their edition of *Moby-Dick* (New York: Hendricks House, 1952), p. 631, Melville would almost surely have known about this book. Alexander Young was the minister who officiated at Melville's wedding, and he had dedicated the *Chronicles* to Lemuel Shaw, Melville's father-in-law; Shaw would certainly have owned a copy.

go. The hand of Providence pointed us onward.[116]

Melville's use of the Pequot massacre, therefore, is appropriate in a novel having as its immediate political concern the patriotic fervor with which America descended upon Mexico from 1846 to 1848. The *New York Evening Post* actually identified "the Mexicans" as *"Aboriginal Indians"* who "must share the destiny of their race"—and in a similar vein the *Democratic Review* proclaimed that "the Mexican race now see, in the fate of the aborigines of the north, their own inevitable destiny." Lamenting that the Spanish had failed to display the same competence in purging Mexico of Mexicans as Anglo-Saxons had shown in ridding North America of Indians, the *Review* regretted that all significant acts of international conscience fall upon American shoulders: "[T]he process, which has been gone through at the north, of driving back the Indians, or annihilating them as a race, has yet to be gone through at the south."[117] Conceptually, then, it is a small step from the Puritans' use of jeremiad logic to justify the Pequot massacre, to Walt Whitman's belief that the Mexican War signified "the vengeance of a retributive God," to Orestes Brownson's explanation of how "Mexico has offended God.... Almighty God is angry with her, and uses us as his instruments for her chastisement, that he may one day remember her in mercy."[118] As early as his "Authentic Anecdotes of Old Zack," Melville had characterized American soldiers as feeling "called by Divine Providence to perform their martial functions" in Mexico. In this respect the guiding providential assumption of Ishmael's narrative perpetuates a political outlook that, as William Ellery Channing had already lamented in a passage detailing the Puritan origins of American expansionism, "sacrificed justice and humanity" in the execution of "atrocities at which communities grown gray in corruption might blush."[119]

In *Mardi*, however, Babbalanja questions logic such as Brownson's:

---

116. "The Texas Question," *Democratic Review*, 14 (April 1844), 424; Andrew Kennedy, *Cong. Globe*, 29th Cong., 1st sess. (14 Jan. 1846), 180; emphasis added.

117. *New York Evening Post* (24 Dec. 1847), quoted in Merk, *Manifest Destiny*, p. 158; "The War," *Democratic Review*, 20 (Feb. 1847), 100.

118. Whitman's remark is from "The Mexican War Justified," *Brooklyn Daily Eagle* (11 May 1846), in *Gathering of the Forces*, I: 241. Brownson's statement is from his review of Fletcher Webster's "Oration," in *Brownson's Quarterly Review*, o.s. 3 (Oct. 1846), 518. The heritage of such ideas is the subject of John F. Berens's *Providence and Patriotism in Early America, 1640–1815* (Charlottesville: Univ. Press of Virginia, 1978).

119. For the quotation from Melville's "Old Zack" sketch, see *Yankee Doodle*, 7 Aug. 1847, p. 172. Channing's remark is from "A Letter to the Hon. Henry Clay on the Annexation of Texas," in *Works*, p. 761.

"Where our warrant, with Oro's sign-manual, to justify the killing, burning, . . . or far worse, the social persecutions we institute in his behalf?" (M, 428). Moreover, in response to Yoomy's abolitionist belief that "Oro will van the right," Babbalanja offers an even more compelling challenge to the jeremiad assumptions that we have seen to shape Ishmael's outlook as well: "Oro champions none. In all things, man's own battles, man himself must fight" (M, 533). Surprisingly, even White-Jacket at one point speaks out against the habit of believing that God intercedes on behalf of any nation or cause. White-Jacket regrets that "in relating the story of the Battle of Navarino, [Jack Chase] plainly . . . held the God of the blessed Bible to have been the British Commodore in the Levant, on the bloody 20th of October, A.D. 1827." What we deem "Divine Providence," says White-Jacket, is actually "Fate," and "Fate everlastingly sustains an armed neutrality"; hence, White-Jacket's *reductio ad absurdum* of providential historiography:

> Admiral Codrington's victory undoubtedly achieved the emancipation of Greece, and terminated the Turkish atrocities in that tomahawked state, yet who shall lift his hand and swear that a Divine Providence led the van of the combined fleets of England, France, and Russia at the battle of Navarino? For if this be so, then it led the van against the Church's own elect—the persecuted Waldenses in Switzerland. (WJ, 320)[120]

More compelling yet in its challenge to providential historiography is *Moby-Dick,* since the analogical premise of Ishmael's apologetical strategy, together with the book's emphasis on comparative mythology and religion, renders absurd the idea of either an intervening Providence or of a specially "chosen" master race for the North American continent.

The long-standing interpretations of the White Whale as a natural force, the only evil of which rests in Ahab's narcissistic projection, are

---

120. By extension, I question the accuracy of Adler's belief that in *Battle-Pieces* Melville "makes clear . . . *his* moral stand on the basic issue of war. In poem after poem God is the image standing for the 'Right' that the Union upholds, Satan the image signifying the 'Wrong' for which the South is fighting" (p. 134; emphasis added). As Melville says in the "Supplement" to *Battle-Pieces,* his poems record "though but dramatically and by way of a poetic record, the passions and epithets of civil war" (quoted from Hennig Cohen, ed., *"The Battle-Pieces" of Herman Melville* [New York: Thomas Yoseloff, 1963], p. 198). Among prevalent attitudes relating to the war, northern belief in God's providential aid to a righteous Union cause was commonplace (see Tuveson, pp. 187–202). In "The Fall of Richmond" (1865) and in "The Battle for the Mississippi" (1862), Melville shows that typological readings of northern victory resulted from "impassioned" (p. 125) fervor and "victory's roar" (p. 72).

compatible with this thesis. And as Richard Slotkin has shown, a similarly "innocent" stance is one of the informing premises of the expropriationist mentality: "By conceiving of themselves as being purely victims of the Indians, rather than the agents of their own troubles, the Puritans put the onus of their morally questionable acts on the Indians and justified their extermination of them."[121] The point to be stressed here is that, in narrating and then defending apologetically his account of the *Pequod*'s miraculous destruction, Ishmael is as disposed as Ahab to project designing intelligence upon the neutral face of events. And the significance of this is momentous for the analogy it suggests between Ahab's "pathetic fallacy" (in attributing premeditative malice to Moby-Dick) and the psychological projections that sustain such providential readings of history as those of both Ishmael and Increase Mather in their respective accounts of the Pequots' annihilation.

Implicated in Ishmael's providential historiography is the way he regularly fabricates and then superimposes meaning upon nature: "Nor when expandingly lifted by your subject," he says, "can you fail to trace out great whales in the starry heavens, and boats in pursuit of them" (MD, 233). Moreover, Ishmael indulges in the "pathetic fallacy" by speaking of the sea's "subtleness" and "Portuguese vengeance" (MD, 235), and by describing how the *Pequod* rushes "through the water with a vindictive sort of leaping and melancholy rapidity" (MD, 109). In ascribing presumptive qualities to unthinking objects, Ishmael is predisposed to an outlook that, leavened by a narration of events recollected in tranquillity, posits divine sanction for Moby-Dick's destruction of both Radney and Ahab. Thus, while Ishmael admittedly chides Ahab for failing to see "the demoniac indifference with which the white whale tore his hunters" (MD, 437), he fails to understand how the same observation applies to the way Moby-Dick splinters the *Pequod*. Instead, Ishmael affirms his belief in God by imagining the wreck to be a retributive miracle, which he then defends with argumentative strategies derived from such Christian apologists as William Paley and Bishop Butler. But as somebody like James Russell Lowell might have known, miraculous interpretations of history too easily lent respectability to nationalist crimes committed under the banner of Manifest Destiny.[122] Ishmael, then, fails to realize how the epistemological "moral" of his own narrative suggests that it is no more legitimate to discern

---

121. Slotkin, p. 514.
122. In Lowell's *Biglow Papers* (p. 62) Homer Wilbur says, "While so many miracles ... vouched by eyewitnesses, have encouraged the arms of Papists..., it is strange that our first American crusade was not in some such wise also signalized. Yet it is said that the Lord hath manifestly prospered our armies."

the finger of God in history than to mistake animal instinct for designing malice. And here rests the largest irony of *Moby-Dick*'s use of
Bishop Butler's *Analogy*: instead of demonstrating the "analogy of religion, natural and revealed, to the constitution and course of nature,"
Ishmael's providential description and defense of the "retribution, swift
vengeance, [and] eternal malice" with which the White Whale sinks the
Pequod suggest a more appropriate analogy between American history,
providentially and miraculously conceived, and the constitution and
course of the pathetic fallacy. Thus, Ishmael unwittingly calls into
question the certitude of knowing *any* event to be miraculous, let alone
miraculously disposed for any nation's benefit or harm. His narrative
casts into a limbo of skepticism the assumptions which undergird all
providential, millennial, and messianic readings of American history
and aggression. As Hawthorne had already suggested in *The Scarlet
Letter*, providential world views were often initiated by some extraordinary event in nature, the significance of which too often "rested on
the faith of some lonely eye-witness, who beheld the wonder through
the colored, magnifying, and distorting medium of his imagination,
and shaped it more distinctly in his afterthought." Finally, Ishmael's
providential outlook is just another instance of a mode of narcissistic
historiography that, like the tormenting view of the heavens held by
Hawthorne's character Dimmesdale, extends "his egotism over the
whole expanse of nature, until the firmament itself should appear no
more than a fitting page for his soul's history and fate!"[123]

Still, thinking himself "miraculously buoyed up by Queequeg's
coffin...to warn his compatriots away from the vortex toward which
their ship of state is heading,"[124] Ishmael overlooks the significance of
his own remark that *"It so chanced"* (MD, 470) that he ended up at the
margin of the vortex that yields up Queequeg's coffin. And here we
would do well to recall how, in *Mardi*, Taji says of his escape from
the doomed *Arcturion*, "We hear of providential deliverances. Was
this one?" (M, 25)—but that the narrator of *Timoleon* asks of still
another incident, "Is that high Providence, or Chance?"[125] Forever
ready to affirm that "some certain significance lurks in all things,"

123. Hawthorne, *The Scarlet Letter* (1850), in *The Complete Works of Nathaniel
Hawthorne*, ed. George Parsons Lathrop, 12 vols. (Cambridge, Mass.: Riverside Press,
1883), V: 188. That Melville was familiar with *The Scarlet Letter* prior to publishing
Moby-Dick is suggested by a reference to it as an "excellent" book in his review of
"Hawthorne and His Mosses," *Literary World*, 7 (24 Aug. 1850), 146.

124. Karcher, "Melville and Racial Prejudice: A Re-evaluation," *Southern Review*,
12 (Apr. 1976), 296; cf. Karcher's *Shadow*, pp. 89–90.

125. *Collected Poems of Herman Melville*, ed. Howard P. Vincent (Chicago: Packard, 1947), p. 209.

Ishmael chooses a providential interpretation of his survival, ignoring the arbitrariness of chance and fate by imbuing his narrative with jeremiad and covenant assumptions antagonistic to his aspirations of human brotherhood and democratic equality. Unlike his narrator, Melville understood how the concept of a "divine Providence guarding the sacred heritage conferred on one people"[126] was potentially more *exclusive* than redemptive. Indeed, to some degree this concern had earlier informed Redburn's effort to disown any connection between Americanism and the "bigoted" tendencies of those who fancy themselves in special covenant with God:

> Settled by the people of all nations, all nations claim her for their own.... We are not a narrow tribe, with a bigoted Hebrew nationality—whose blood has been debased in an attempt to ennoble it, by maintaining an exclusive succession among ourselves. No: our blood is as the flood of the Amazon, made up of a thousand noble currents all pouring into one. (RB, 169)

Of course, this tolerant posture was belied by Americans who justified expansionism with appeals to extending the area of freedom, but who then occupied essentially vacant lands to avoid amalgamation with that "sickening mixture" of "Negroes, and Rancheros, Mestizoes, and Indians...." As Lewis Cass put it, "We do not want the people of Mexico, either as citizens or subjects. All we want is a portion of territory, ... generally uninhabited."[127] Thus, Redburn's universalism notwithstanding, the "virtual disappearance of continentalism from American thought after 1848" has been traced by one scholar to "a national reluctance to add peoples of mixed blood to a blood that was pure, and an unwillingness in some parts of the population to have unfree blood added as well." God, it seemed, had a special plan for the "American race"; and in this respect, the covenant mentality behind Manifest Destiny was ultimately just that—a racial issue with serious exclusive implications.[128]

---

126. "The Anglo-Saxon Race," *American Whig Review*, 7 (Jan. 1848), 46.

127. The quotation about Negroes and Rancheros is from the *Augusta Chronicle and Sentinel* (31 July 1846), quoted by Schroeder, p. 53. Cass's statement is from *Cong. Globe*, 29th Cong., 2nd sess. (10 Feb. 1847), 369. For commentary on America's hypocrisy in "extending the area of freedom" to unoccupied territories, see Weinberg, p. 164.

128. Merk, *Manifest Destiny*, p. 227. The quoted phrase "American race" is from Edward D. Baker's praise of Manifest Destiny in *Cong. Globe*, 20th Cong., 1st sess. (3 Jan. 1846), 136. As Tuveson (p. 153) remarks, Theodore Parker listed among the five leading "peculiarities of the Anglo-Saxon tribe" its "exclusive nationality" and "hostility to other tribes of men." Also worth noting for the ties between covenant, or jeremiad, mentality and racial exclusiveness is Bercovitch, *American Jeremiad*, p. 154.

Mardi, in fact, had already illustrated the tie between covenant psychology and racially exclusive politics. The Vivenzans acknowledge as free and equal everybody except the tribe of "Hamo" (M, 513)— presumably because in Genesis 9:22–26, just after receiving God's covenant, Noah condemns Ham and his descendants forever to be the servants of Shem. Also, Melville may have known that the story of Hagar and Ishmael provided proslavery apologists with an intriguing precedent for justifying involuntary servitude through appeals to covenant psychology. In fact, one of *Moby-Dick*'s great ironies may rest in the way its temperamentally abolitionist narrator espouses the sort of covenant assumptions that excluded the biblical Ishmael from his inheritance because he was the son of a bondwoman. Early in 1851 the *Southern Literary Messenger* exploited this context in denouncing abolitionism as a perverse Ishmaelian usurpation of Isaac's rights, a deplorable breach of "God's covenant blessings" to white America: "[T]his putting away of the bondwoman and her child accorded with the serene purposes of the Ruler of the world," who "looked on Isaac ... as the future patriarch of his chosen nation, with whom his covenant was to be established, and by whom his truth was to be kept for the world—the nation that should take possession of Canaan." And in a paragraph that even more clearly shows the compatibility of covenant psychology with both Manifest Destiny and slavery, the author asks,

> And shall any inferior nation stop us in our heaven-marked course? Can any nation do it? Did the red men arrest us? And who removed them from before our fathers, but the God who planted our fathers here—the same God that has made us increase by the same manifest destiny by which he has made them wane and fade away. And shall the black man stop us? If one must yield, are we not right in saying—the son of the bondwoman shall not be heir with the son of the free?[129]

Thus, while Ishmael's symbolic "marriage" to Queequeg quite possibly implies that "salvation for America lies in consecrating the marriage of her white and colored citizens," the exclusive and isolationist tendencies of Ishmael's covenant psychology will forever render this union barren.[130]

---

129. S. L. C., "Isaac and Ishmael," *Southern Literary Messenger*, 17 (Jan. 1851), 24, 23. My stress on this article's use of covenant psychology to assert white supremacy supplements Heimert's demonstration (p. 529) that the author employs the name *Ishmael* to signify an abolitionist.

130. The quotation is from Karcher's "Melville and Racial Prejudice," p. 295 (cf. *Shadow*, pp. 77, 89). My sense of the hollowness of Ishmael's encounter with Queequeg

Not surprisingly, therefore, Ishmael mentions that "in the Vision of St. John, white robes are given to the redeemed" (MD, 164), almost immediately after he has remarked that the "preeminence" of whiteness applies "to the human race itself, giving the white man ideal mastership over every dusky tribe" (MD, 163). In fact, Ishmael even echoes the Puritan conflation between darkness and demonism: "To look at the tawny brown of [Tashtego's] lithe snaky limbs, you would almost have credited the superstitions of the earlier Puritans, and half believed this wild Indian to be a son of the Prince of the Powers of the Air" (MD, 107).[131] Although Daggoo elsewhere responds violently to such stereotypes (MD, 153–54), the habit of attributing satanic qualities to dark skin still dominates Ishmael's outlook when he early stumbles into a Negro church and, even as he writes retrospectively—in his allegedly regenerate state—compares its congregation to "the great Black Parliament sitting in Tophet," presided over by "the black Angel of Doom" (MD, 18). Thus, whatever his apparent liberalism in suggesting that white persons are merely whitewashed Negroes (MD, 60), Ishmael reveals an egregiously racist streak when he asserts that "the blood of a Polar whale is warmer than that of a Borneo negro in summer" (MD, 261), for the remark implies that Negroes might have a predictably higher blood temperature than that of Caucasians. And this assumption gains added importance in the context of nineteenth-century debates about whether Negroes were a separate species, because an affirmative answer to that question would have devastating implications for the egalitarian values nominally championed by Ishmael.[132]

---

is consistent with readings by Lawrence, p. 219, and William B. Dillingham, "The Narrator of *Moby-Dick*," *English Studies*, 49 (Feb. 1968), 23–24.

131. Although Edward Stone, in "The Whiteness of 'The Whale,'" *College Language Association Journal*, 18 (March 1975), 354–55, anticipates several of my observations about Ishmael's ingrained racism, he errs, I think, in often (esp. pp. 349, 352, 359, 361) attributing Ishmael's racial condescension to Melville. The author of "Benito Cereno" surely could have imbued a narrator such as Ishmael with racist attitudes to which he himself did not subscribe. As Jane H. Pease and William H. Pease, in "Antislavery Ambivalence: Immediatism, Expediency, Race," *American Quarterly*, 77 (Spring 1965), 682–95, have shown, abolitionists often retained ingrained assumptions about the racial inferiority of blacks, while professing to champion their rights. We may credit Melville with having successfully dramatized this ambivalence in the nominal radicalism of his narrator. For a corroborating statement about Ishmael's being "trapped by a limited religious and cultural outlook," see Herbert, p. 105.

132. See, for example, "The Unity of the Human Race," *American Whig Review*, 12 (Dec. 1850), 567–86 (esp. 580); and "Critical Notices," *American Whig Review*, 10 (Oct. 1849), 439–40, advertising Josiah C. Nott's *Two Lectures on the Connection between the Biblical and Physical History of Man* (New York, 1849), which takes the position "that the negro, and other varieties of the human race, are distinct species." For a more comprehensive discussion of the "species" argument, which also informs

Ishmael's racial condescension has earlier been revealed in his remark about loving to "land on barbarous coasts" (MD, 16). The term "barbarian," invented by the Greeks to apply to outsiders, has always been used by self-consciously "civilized" people both to compare themselves favorably with their neighbors and to help rationalize exploitation and aggression.[133] In *Mardi* King Bello's and Vivenza's "brigand" expropriation of so-called "barbarous" (M, 468) lands and countries features this use of the term. With particular reference to Mexico, however, Albert Gallatin recognized the central problem to be an American sense of "hereditary superiority" that violates democracy's egalitarian premise: "Is it compatible with the principles of democracy, which rejects every hereditary claim of individuals, to admit an hereditary superiority of races?"[134] Whatever the question's rhetorical tone, our discussion of the *Southern Literary Messenger*'s thoughts about "Isaac and Ishmael" has shown covenant psychology to be the theological analog of this genetic postulate. In Ishmael's case the "separatist" assumptions of his jeremiad mentality will forever expatriate him—and, by implication, others who espouse ideas about either national or racial modes of "special election"—from the common continent of men. This complex barrier to human fraternity is, I propose, assailed by *Moby-Dick*'s mythological concerns, which highlight the essential similarities among the world's past and present civilizations and religions.

Worth recalling in this respect is Francis Parkman's belief that "a civilized white man can discover but very few points of sympathy between his own nature and that of an Indian. . . . [A]n impassable gulf lies between [them]." To this, Melville responded, "We are all of us— Anglo-Saxons, Dyaks, and Indians—sprung from one head, and made in one image."[135] This sentiment corresponds to the basically cross-cultural nature of Ahab's and Ishmael's *Nekyia*, which one critic defines as "the universal, archetypal theme of the night sea journey, or descent to the underworld. *The theme has no national or racial boundaries.*"[136]

---

the racial condescension of Amasa Delano in "Benito Cereno," see Karcher, *Shadow*, pp. 21–27, 130.

133. See Francis Jennings, *The Invasion of America: Indians, Colonialism, and the Cant of Conquest* (Chapel Hill: Univ. of North Carolina Press), pp. 6–7; W. R. Jones, "The Image of the Barbarian in Medieval Europe," *Comparative Studies in Society and History*, 13 (Oct. 1971), 376–407, esp. 377.

134. "Peace with Mexico" (1847), in *The Writings of Albert Gallatin*, ed. Henry Adams, 3 vols. (Philadelphia: J. B. Lippincott, 1879), III: 585.

135. Francis Parkman, *The California and Oregon Trail* (New York: G. P. Putnam, 1849), pp. 316–17; Melville, "Mr. Parkman's Tour," *Literary World*, 4 (31 March 1849), 291.

136. Edward F. Edinger, *Melville's "Moby-Dick": A Jungian Commentary ("An*

Although the Jungian vocabulary of a "collective unconscious" was obviously unavailable to Melville, he might still have read about a "world-consciousness" which tied nineteenth-century America to many previous races.[137] Moreover, the currency of such ideas while Melville was writing *Moby-Dick* is evident from the publication in April 1851 of Ephraim G. Squier's *The Serpent Symbol... in America.* This book explains that "there... exist[s] among nations of men the most widely separated a wonderful unity of elementary beliefs and conceptions." Foremost among these, Squier lists such religious symbols as the serpent, the generative sun, and the phallus. Whether or not Melville knew of Squier's book, H. Bruce Franklin long ago showed that phallicism in "The Cassock" chapter "implies that the modern Western priests have their phallic progenitors." Hence, Franklin compares Ahab to Osiris, the Egyptian God whose seasonal dismemberment and regeneration caused Melville to wonder in *Clarel* (I.xxxi.211–28) whether Christian belief in Resurrection is merely the outgrowth of an earlier Egyptian myth. Here, as in Pierre Bayle's *Historical and Critical Dictionary,* comparative mythology and theology suggest skepticism concerning the supremacy of the Judaeo-Christian heritage over cultures with analogous ritualistic customs.[138]

The fallacy of ethnocentrism seems also to be an implication of Squier's "Manabozho and the Great Serpent" (1848), an essay that describes the belief of American Indians in an incarnate god who achieves the redemption of his people by slaying an odious creature. Squier also recounts how the Mexicans (or, more precisely, the southern Californians) once worshipped Quaagagp, a savior whose similarities to Christ are striking.[139] The resemblance between this name and Queequeg's

---

American Nekyia") (New York: New Directions, 1978), p. 21; emphasis added. Cf. Baird, pp. 101–3.

137. For example, "Civilization: American and European," *American Whig Review,* 3 (June 1846), 616:

A man truly civilized is distinguished for breadth and comprehension of view. He has what the Germans call a world-consciousness. He carries about with him the familiar feeling that he is here in a world where there are not only New Englanders, with their peculiar prejudices and institutions—not only Americans and Europeans, but Hindoos also, and Turks, and Tartars, and Chinese and Japanese, who, like his own neighbors, are all proud of their several countries, creeds and characters;... in short, his mind is to a certain degree a geographical and historical omnipresence.... He is not a mere isolated individual.

138. Ephraim G. Squier, *The Serpent Symbol, and the Worship of the Reciprocal Principles of Nature in America* (New York: George P. Putnam, 1851), p. 18 (the preface is dated April 1851); Franklin, pp. 71–98 (esp. p. 91). On Bayle and comparative mythology, see Bell, pp. 631–33, 636–37.

139. Squier's article entitled "Manabozho and the Great Serpent" (*American Whig*

may be coincidental, but Queequeg's most generally redemptive features are not: he suggestively divides thirty pieces of silver with Ishmael just prior to vowing that he will die for his "bosom friend" (MD, 53), a term with origins that Melville would have known to be explicitly Christian.[140] Also, insofar as Ishmael survives atop Queequeg's coffin, and later compares himself to Lazarus (MD, 197), the concept of a magnanimous savior seems once again to transcend the bounds of 54°-40'. Thus, whereas in *Typee* and *Omoo* Melville draws upon the ideas of Edwards and Hopkins to show how Polynesians already possess the virtue thought to be reserved for converted Christians (see chapter I, above), in *Moby-Dick* he goes a step further in suggesting that Christianity is possibly derived from the same collective unconscious that spawned the beliefs and cultural traits of nations and races whose general inferiority and *barbarism* are presupposed in theories of Manifest Destiny and messianic nationalism. "Recognizing," as Charles Sumner put it, "that God 'hath made of one blood all nations of men,' and that all his children are brethren, the distinctions of country disappear, and ALL WAR BECOMES FRATRICIDAL."[141] Ahab, then, aptly bears the scar of Cain (MD, 110), a symbol that again emerges when the Spanish sailor taunts Daggoo about the devilishness of his black skin color. The crew calls for "[a] ring, a ring!" in which the two can fight; but the old Manx Sailor responds, "Ready formed. There! the ringed horizon. In that ring Cain struck Abel" (MD, 154).

For all this, however, Ishmael's jeremiad perpetuates the sort of exclusive religious and racial assumptions that find exaggerated expression in a ruthless Ahabian quest, the covenant psychology of which ought to have taught Ishmael that true salvation rests in the abandonment of covenants.[142] But failing to realize this, Ishmael "classifies" his

---

Review, 8 [Oct. 1848], 392–98) offers the following account of Quaagagp (later included in *Serpent Symbol*, p. 191):

> The southern *edues* (priests or "medicine men") of the Californians ... taught that there was a supreme Creator, *Niparaga*, who had three sons, one of whom, *Quaagagp*, came upon the earth and taught the Indians the arts, and instructed them in religion. Finally, through hatred, the Indians killed him; but although dead, he is incorruptible and beautiful.... To him they pay adoration, as the mediatory power between earth and the supreme Niparaga. (pp. 393–94)

140. For Melville's familiarity with the Christly association of the term "bosom friend," see chapter II, note 26, above. For previous readings that stress Queequeg's Christ-like attributes, see William Rosenfeld, "Uncertain Faith: Queequeg's Coffin and Melville's Use of the Bible," *Texas Studies in Literature and Language*, 7 (Winter 1966), 321–22; Carl F. Strauch, "Ishmael: Time and Personality in *Moby-Dick*," *Studies in the Novel*, 1 (Winter 1969), 480.

141. Sumner, "Fame and Glory ... " (1847), in *Orations and Speeches*, I: 339.

142. For a more general account of Ishmael's misguided allegiance to covenanted

previous turmoil within an allegory of divine retribution and personal election. And despite the abolitionist overtones of his jeremiad, its covenant premise will forever exclude him from truly appreciating the dignity of a transpersonal psyche. At best, for example, his tolerance of Queequeg's worship of Yojo is a patronizing prelude to the condescending views he holds about his friend's "ridiculous Ramadan" (MD, 81–82).[143] Thus, while Ishmael may pay nominal homage to "the great and everlasting First Congregation of this whole worshipping world" (MD, 83)—and while his observations in "The Honor and Glory of Whaling" (ch. 82) and "Of Whales in Paint, in Teeth, & c." (ch. 57) imply his sentimental attraction for the brotherhood of man—the more regrettably exclusive tendencies of his outlook find expression in "Monstrous Pictures of Whales" (ch. 55). Because in this chapter Ishmael sounds like a Christian apologist intent upon discrediting the integrity of mythological and cross-cultural analogs to Christian Revelation,[144] his outlook comprises a portrait in miniature of the sometimes inhumane implications of covenant psychology. In fact, as long as Ishmael narrates the events of the *Pequod*'s catastrophe and his own salvation within the confines of jeremiad logic—and he is, of course, doomed to do so eternally—he will remain adrift from the common continent of men. Ixion-like (MD, 470), Ishmael will shift endlessly between the extremes of human compassion and isolation, bound as egoistically to the exclusive tendencies of his jeremiad as Ahab is to the desolate mountains of Caucasus.[145]

---

outlooks, see Gregory H. Singleton, "Ishmael and the Covenant," *Discourse,* 12 (Winter 1969), 54–67, esp. 61–62.

143. As Vincent (p. 80) shows, "Ishmael's efforts to persuade Queequeg are ... a parody of the activities of missionaries in Polynesia, who pretended tolerance, but tried to impose their ways on the natives, only with incongruous and lamentable results."

144. Franklin (pp. 66–68) discusses Ishmael's use of apologetic strategies in "Monstrous Pictures of Whales." For a rather precise correspondence to Ishmael's efforts, see Horne's ridicule (I: 158–61) of the "impertinent, ridiculous, and absurd relations ... often introduced" into cross-cultural myths that resemble Christian Revelation. Indeed, "Monstrous Pictures of Whales" even anticipates Clarel's apologetic disdain for "monstrous figments blabbed of Jove, / Or Worse, rank lies of Islam's herd" (*Clarel,* I.vi.18–23). Perhaps Melville had read Channing's remark, in "Evidences of Christianity," that "there have been ages when men believed any thing and every thing; and the more monstrous the story, the more eagerly was it received by the credulous multitude" (*Works,* p. 210).

145. As Edinger (p. 139) explains, "The wheel is a mandala, a symbol of the Self. Ixion, by presuming to seduce a goddess, was acting out of an inflated attitude. He was identified with the Self and hence behaved as though he were a deity. In such a state, the self becomes a fiery torture wheel to the ego. The individual is bound to it by his own identification."

C H . A P T E R V

Subjective Transcendentalism: *Pierre*

Perhaps the best introduction to *Pierre* (1852), appearing as it did such a short time after *Moby-Dick*, is Ishmael's belief that God has etched his "Mene, Mene, Tekel, Upharsin" (MD, 415) upon the *Pequod*. Although in *Pierre* Melville's emphasis shifts from expansionism and metaphysics to the profound depths of the human mind, a preoccupation with prophecy is still evident: Isabel's face, we are told, is "vaguely historic and prophetic; backward, hinting of some irrevocable sin; forward, pointing to some inevitable ill" (P, 43). Indeed, like Ishmael fancying the *Pequod's* blazing shrouds as something like God's dire warning on the wall of Belshazzar's feast, Pierre imagines that "against the wall of the thick darkness of the mystery of Isabel, recorded as by some phosphoric finger was the burning fact, that Isabel was his sister" (P, 170). Still, Pierre's homage to "Memory, and Prophecy, and Intuition" (P, 112) is inspired by a sexual impulse that Pierre misconceives as a heavenly mandate to champion Isabel. In both books, therefore, Melville makes a similar point: "Silence is the only Voice of [a] God" (P, 204) whose seemingly prophetic finger is all too often fashioned from the greed, insecurities, and inner passions of those who would read in the heavens the dictates of their own minds and hearts.[1]

Whereas *Moby-Dick's* prophetic dimension has reference to Puritan historiography and western territorialism, the failure of prophecy in *Pierre* is connected with Transcendentalism. Indeed, while the Polk administration espoused prophecy as a concept implicit in America's destiny to extend the area of freedom to the Southwest, New England Transcendentalists labored, by means of a corresponding theory of prophecy, to liberate Boston from the shackles of Unitarian material-

---

1. For an informative study in this vein, see Robert A. Kelly, "The Failure of Prophecy in Melville's *Pierre*," *Christianity and Literature*, 27 (Spring 1978), 18–27.

ism, formalism, and historical apologetics. Insofar as Pierre wishes to do "something transcendently great" (P, 284), his allegiance to "Prophecy" and "Intuition" may conform to any number of Transcendental mandates encouraging young Americans to become their own prophets. "Would God, that all the Lord's children were prophets" (Num. 11:29), reiterated Jonathan Ashley Saxton in his essay "Prophecy—Transcendentalism—Progress." "If I have succeeded in the attempt to show the true significance of prophecy," he continues, "I may be permitted to say, that it is... the utterance of what is called in a modern system of philosophy, the Spontaneous Reason, the intuitions, the instincts of the soul."[2] And since Transcendental prophecy entailed "the contemplation of eternal verities" and "the power of intellectual intuition... to discover absolute truth,"[3] outlooks of this variety mandated the sort of "correspondence" between the chronometrical and horological (i.e., heavenly and terrestrial) worlds described by a contributor to Elizabeth P. Peabody's *Aesthetic Papers* (1849):

> [O]ur action can never be perfectly harmonious, until it is regulated by the universals of correspondence; until humanity is the transparent medium and directing rein of Providence; or, in other words, until the modifying principle [man] coincides with the creative [God]. This is the attachment of correspondence to God, or its inauguration into religion.[4]

Pierre, we are told, defies this Transcendental assumption by showing that "the only way God's truth and man's truth correspond is

---

2. Jonathan Ashley Saxton, "Prophecy—Transcendentalism—Progress," *Dial*, 2 (July 1841), 83, 86. Here and below, all authorial attributions to the *Dial* have been verified in Joel Myerson's "An Annotated List of Contributions to the Boston *Dial*," in *Studies in Bibliography: Papers of the Bibliographical Society of the University of Virginia*, ed. Fredson Bowers (Charlottesville: Univ. Press of Virginia, 1973), pp. 133–66. For the "prophetic" dimension of Transcendental thought, also see Orestes A. Brownson, "American Literature," *Boston Quarterly Review*, 2 (Jan. 1839), 6 (here and below, all attributions to Brownson in the *Boston Quarterly Review* have been verified in *The Works of Orestes A. Brownson*, ed. Henry F. Brownson, 20 vols. [Detroit: Thorndike, Nourse, 1882–87]); Emerson, "Politics" (in *Essays, Second Series*), in *The Complete Works of Ralph Waldo Emerson*, ed. Edward Waldo Emerson, 12 vols. (Boston and New York: Houghton Mifflin, 1903–04), III: 216; Amos Bronson Alcott, "Orphic Sayings," *Dial*, 1 (July 1840), 91; Newton Dillaway, *Prophet of America: Emerson and the Problems of To-day* (Boston: Little, Brown, 1936), pp. 111–23.

3. "Emerson's Essays, by a Disciple," *Democratic Review*, 16 (June 1845), 592; Saxton, p. 87.

4. J. J. G. Wilkinson, "Correspondence," in *Aesthetic Papers*, ed. Elizabeth P. Peabody (New York: G. P. Putnam, 1849), p. 122.

through their contradictions.''[5] Previous studies also suggest that *Pierre* responds to Emersonian notions of "Self-Reliance," "Heroism," and the conjunction of intuition and virtue that constitutes the "moral sentiment.''[6] Remaining to be addressed, however, are the ways in which these issues emanated from the Miracles Controversy of 1836–45 and the compatibility of this context with the book's critique of uncompromising virtue.[7] We shall see that *Pierre* plays both ends of the Miracles Controversy against the middle by undercutting perfectionist modes of morality implicit in Transcendental ideas about intuition and by challenging the naïveté of Unitarian assumptions about historical certainty. Also to be explored is the way *Pierre* details the anarchical tendencies of Transcendental intuition, which Melville finally shows to originate in self-serving impulses disguised under the garb of benevolent militancy. Finally, we shall consider the relation of Pierre's decision to become an author to the book's early emphasis on Transcendentalism and incest—and we shall do so mainly in response to scholarship that views the "author" chapters of *Pierre* as either intrusive autobiography or as the self-conscious debasement of art with which Melville highlights fiction's inability to convey absolute "truth.''[8] Such scholarship overlooks the connection between Transcendental prophecy and the idea of authorship ("[W]herever and however any one is filled to overflowing with this grand idea of God in the soul of man, he will utter it. . . . He will be an American Author''[9]), as well as the relationship of such "Young American" self-sufficiency to *Pierre*'s preoccupation with incest. Pierre Glendinning is the product of a Transcendental heritage

---

5. F. O. Matthiessen, *American Renaissance: Art and Expression in the Age of Emerson and Whitman* (New York: Oxford Univ. Press, 1941), p. 471.

6. The most comprehensive account of Melville's encounter with such ideas is Barbara N. Blansett's "Melville and Emersonian Transcendentalism," Diss., Univ. of Texas, 1963, esp. pp. 40, 49, 80, 94–95, 102, 105, 110, 137, 142, 147–48, 161, 175–76, 181–82. Worth noting for its more specific attention to *Pierre*'s encounter with the Divinity School Address is Joseph P. Alaimo's "A Natural History of American Virtue: Melville's Critique of the Transcendental Hero," Diss., Univ. of Minnesota, 1974, pp. 327–62.

7. In stressing the relation of the Miracles Controversy to uncompromising virtue, I use as a point of departure Michael J. Colacurcio's discussion of *Pierre* in "A Better Mode of Evidence—The Transcendental Problem of Faith and Spirit," *Emerson Society Quarterly*, 54 (1969), 20–22.

8. See Hershel Parker, "Why *Pierre* Went Wrong," *Studies in the Novel*, 8 (Spring 1976), 7–23; Hershel Parker and Brian Higgins, "The Flawed Grandeur of Melville's *Pierre*," in *New Perspectives on Melville*, ed. Faith Pullin (Edinburgh: Univ. of Edinburgh Press, 1978), pp. 162–96; Nina Baym, "Melville's Quarrel with Fiction," *PMLA*, 94 (Oct. 1979), 918–20.

9. "American Authors" (a review of Emerson's "American Scholar"), *Boston Quarterly Review*, 1 (Jan. 1838), 115.

that contemporary Whig criticism was quick to define as narcissistic and that Herman Melville dramatized as being "incestuous" in its displacement of history and external values with the mind's somewhat "novel" and hermaphroditic utterances.

Melville claimed not to have read Emerson prior to 1849. In that year he attended one of Emerson's Boston lectures, and while visiting the Hawthornes in 1850, "one morning he shut himself in the boudoir & read Mr. Emerson's essays."[10] At least part of what he studied seems echoed in *Pierre*, which a reviewer for the *Athenaeum* mistook for "one of the most diffuse doses of transcendentalism offered for a long time to the public."[11] *Pierre* more obviously satirizes "*the Transcendental Flesh-Brush Philosophy*" (P, 295) and those "amiable philosophers of either the 'Compensation,' or the 'Optimist' school" (P, 277), among whom Emerson—who, in "Compensation," says, "the soul refuses limits, and always affirms an Optimism, never a Pessimism"[12]—must surely be numbered. *Pierre*, moreover, advances that the horological world

---

10. For Melville's assertion that he had not read Emerson prior to 1849, and for his attendance at Emerson's lecture, see *Letters*, pp. 78–79. Melville's use of Hawthorne's library is recorded in Sophia Hawthorne's letter (Autumn 1850) to her mother, first published by Eleanor Melville Metcalf, *Herman Melville: Cycle and Epicycle* (Cambridge, Mass.: Harvard Univ. Press, 1953), p. 91. Christopher W. Sten, in "Bartleby the Transcendentalist: Melville's Dead Letter to Emerson," *Modern Language Quarterly*, 35 (March 1974), 31–32, argues that Melville could have read a copy of *Nature, Addresses, and Lectures* ([1849], in *Works*, I: 3–77) that Emerson had sent Hawthorne in September of the year previous to Sophia's letter. More recently, Merton M. Sealts, Jr., in "Melville and Emerson's Rainbow," *ESQ: A Journal of the American Renaissance*, 26 (1980), 67–68, labels Melville's familiarity with this volume inconclusive, though he entertains the possibility that a reference to "superior chronometers" in "The Transcendentalist" (included in *Nature, Addresses, and Lectures*) may have inspired some of Melville's thoughts about "chronometricals and horologicals." All of this is relevant to my argument below, which centers around the compatibility of Emerson's "American Scholar" (also in *Nature, Addresses, and Lectures*) with the "author" chapters of *Pierre*. As I suggest above (chapter II), Melville seems to borrow directly from "The American Scholar" in *Redburn* (late spring and early summer, 1849), though necessarily from a printing prior to the September publication of *Nature, Addresses, and Lectures*. Therefore my discussion will stress the *currency* of Emerson's ideas in contemporary literary journals. I shall, however, follow Sealts ("Melville and Emerson's Rainbow," pp. 63–64, 70–71) in assuming Melville's familiarity, by 1850, with Emerson's *Essays, First Series* (1841) and *Essays, Second Series* (1844).

11. Quoted by Jay Leyda, ed., *The Melville Log*, 2 vols. (New York: Harcourt, Brace, 1951), I:464.

12. *Essays, First Series*, in *Works*, II: 122. As William Braswell, in "Melville as a Critic of Emerson," *American Literature*, 9 (Nov. 1937), 330, shows, Melville later wrote of Emerson, "He still bethinks himself of his optimism—he must make that good somehow against the eternal hell itself."

generally scorns "absurd and all-displacing transcendentals" (P, 262), and particularly the sort of idealistic absolutism that, "challenging [Pierre] in his deepest moral being" (P, 49), causes him to assume a "Christ-like" posture, and to vow to "square myself by the inflexible rule of holy right" (P, 106). Transcending the mere "Imitableness of Christ's Character" described by William Ellery Channing, Pierre seeks, as existing scholarship argues, to participate in the universal incarnation mandated by Emerson's Divinity School Address: "Jesus Christ... estimated the greatness of man. One man was true to what is in you and me. He saw that God incarnates himself in man, and evermore goes forth anew to take possession of his World." But despite Emerson's demands for "a bold benevolence" and the need to "resist for truth's sake the freest flow of kindness, and to appeal to sympathies far in advance," Melville's narrator aptly shows "those advanced minds, ... in spite of advance, ... to remain ... ill-regulated" (P, 166).[13] This is certainly true of Pierre, who, after ruining both his own and several other lives, betrays a still-lingering allegiance to Emersonian metaphysics. For instance, when he receives letters of rebuke from both his publishers and his enemies, Pierre folds the documents, places one under each shoe, and proclaims, "These are most small *circumstances*; but happening just now to me, become indices to all immensities.... On these I will *skate* to my acquittal!" (P, 357; emphasis added). Emerson, too, believed that

> we live amid surfaces, and the true art of life is to *skate well on them*.... [W]e should not postpone and refer and wish, but do broad justice where we are, by whomsoever we deal with, accepting our actual companions and *circumstances*, however humble or odious, as the mystic officials to whom the universe has delegated its whole pleasure for us.[14]

Yet, whatever these topical allusions to his Emersonian persuasions, Pierre's enthusiasm in championing the moral sentiment in behalf of Isabel cannot be understood in isolation from Transcendental

---

13. Emerson, Divinity School Address, *Works*, I: 128–29, 148. Cf. Blansett; Alaimo. Other informative readings of *Pierre*'s moral absolutism include Newton Arvin, *Herman Melville* (New York: Sloane, 1950), 219–32; Milton R. Stern, *The Fine Hammered Steel of Herman Melville* (Urbana: Univ. of Illinois Press, 1957), pp. 150–205; Mary E. Dichmann, "Abolutism in Melville's *Pierre*," *PMLA*, 67 (Sept. 1952), 702–15. For the way that *Pierre*'s subversion of metaphysical and ethical idealism also targets the Platonic tradition that informs Transcendental thought, see the chapter titled "Melville and the Platonic Tradition," in Merton M. Sealts, Jr., *Pursuing Melville, 1940–1980* (Madison: Univ. of Wisconsin Press, 1982), pp. 278–336, esp. 317–25.

14. "Experience" (*Essays, Second Series*), in *Works*, III: 59, 60–61; emphasis added.

discourses such as George Ripley's, which spoke of "moral relations...intuitively perceived." Nor can we ignore the connection between this intuitive moral faculty and the Transcendental quarrel with Unitarian historiography: for in the same paragraph where Emerson discourses upon intuitive perception of the Spirit and the perfectibility of "virtue," he says, "to aim to convert a man by miracles is a profanation of the soul."[15] In response, perhaps, to postulates like these, Plinlimmon takes issue with the chronometrical soul's "so-called intuitions of right and wrong" (P, 211). And against his intuitive certainty of Isabel's claim, Pierre persists in weighing historical evidence reminiscent of the Unitarian apologetics to which Emerson objected when debating Andrews Norton over the place of miracles in religion. But neither the tie between intuition and virtue nor the relation of this to Emerson's quarrel with Unitarian historiography—nor, finally, the way these matters figure in *Pierre*—can be understood without a brief review of the "Miracles Controversy."

The issue had its inception when, in the late eighteenth and early nineteenth centuries, Calvinists sought to counter Arminian and—subsequently—Unitarian disavowals of both human depravity and the Trinity. The strategy developed by the Calvinists was to equate the liberal religionists' glorification of human rational faculties with mere Deist rationalism. The liberals, as Conrad Wright has shown, found shelter within the fortress of *historical apologetics*, from which they stressed the proofs of revealed religion to the Deists, while at the same time denying to the Calvinists an absolute scriptural basis for their beliefs. In England, Unitarians such as Watson, Priestley, Clarke, and Lardner enumerated the "Evidences of Christianity"; in America, a similar office was performed by Buckminster, Ware, Channing, and Norton.[16] Challenged in the nineteenth century by the "romanticism," "rationalism," and "higher criticism" of Schleiermacher, Paulus, De

---

15. George Ripley, review of James Mackintosh's *General View of the Progress of Ethical Philosophy*, in the *Christian Examiner*, 13 (Jan. 1833), 325 (misnumbered 225); Emerson, Divinity School Address, *Works*, I: 132. Both here and below, all attributions to the *Christian Examiner* have been verified using William Cushing's author and subject indices, reproduced in *Research Keys to the American Renaissance*, ed. Kenneth Walter Cameron (Hartford, Conn.: Transcendental Books, 1967). For the largely intuitive, though sometimes "intellectual" perception of the moral sentiment in Transcendental thought, see John Q. Anderson, "Emerson and 'The Moral Sentiment,'" *Emerson Society Quarterly*, 19 (1960), 13–15; Alfred J. Kloeckner, "Intellect and Moral Sentiment in Emerson's Opinions of 'The Meaner Kinds' of Men," *American Literature*, 30 (Nov. 1958), 322–38.

16. See Conrad Wright, *The Beginnings of Unitarianism in America* (Boston: Starr King Press, 1955), pp. 150–60, and "Rational Religion in Eighteenth-Century America," in *The Liberal Christians: Essays on American Unitarian History* (Boston: Beacon

Wette, and Strauss, Unitarians remained constant in their belief that Christianity's "evidences are to be sought in history." Indeed, Channing stressed the "proofs" of revealed religion, its general "authority" and supporting "testimonies," and—most importantly for our consideration of *Pierre*—the fact that "its truth was attested by miracles. . . . A religion so attested must be true."[17] From his Dexter Chair of Sacred Literature at Harvard, Andrews Norton likewise pontificated upon the authenticity of Christianity, giving special emphasis to its historical records of God's "miraculous" powers:

> Our belief in those truths, the evidence of which we cannot fully examine for ourselves, is founded . . . on the testimony of others, who have examined their evidence, and whom we regard as intelligent and trustworthy. . . . This reliance on the knowledge of others may be called *belief on trust,* or *belief on authority;* but perhaps a more proper name for it would be *belief on testimony.* . . .[18]

Although this statement specifically takes issue with "The Modern German School of Infidelity," it also targets those Concord Transcendentalists whose more temperamental rejection of historical Christianity moved them to denounce Unitarian scholarship as "too cold, too lifeless, [and] too mechanical." Or, as Emerson stated in the opening lines of *Nature*, "Our age is retrospective. It builds the sepulchres of the fathers. It writes biographies, histories, and criticism. The foregoing generations beheld God and nature face to face; we, through their eyes."[19] In 1838, as we have seen, Emerson argued that "to aim to convert a man by miracles is a profanation of the soul," and in 1841 he denounced all persons who, in matters of the Spirit, are "spectators merely, or perhaps . . . acquainted with the fact on the evidence of third persons. It is of no use to preach to me from without."[20] Of course, the antimaterialist and antihistorical bias of all such utterances typifies the sentiments of a generation schooled in the distinction made by both the Germans and Coleridge between intuitive "reason" and Lockean

---

Press, 1970), pp. 1–21; Jerry W. Brown, *The Rise of Biblical Criticism in America, 1800–1870* (Middletown, Conn.: Wesleyan Univ. Press, 1969), pp. 10–26.

17. Channing, "Evidences of Christianity," in *The Works of William E. Channing, D.D.* (Boston: American Unitarian Assoc., 1895), pp. 188–220, esp. 196, 210.

18. Andrews Norton, *A Discourse on the Latest Form of Infidelity* (Cambridge, Mass.: John Owen, 1839), pp. 5, 57–58.

19. George Ripley, *"The Latest Form of Infidelity" Examined* (Boston: James Munroe, 1839), p. 12; Emerson, *Nature* (1836) (*Nature, Addresses, and Lectures*), in *Works*, I: 3.

20. Emerson, Divinity School Address, *Works*, I: 132; "The Oversoul" (*Essays, First Series*), in *Works*, II: 287.

(or sensational) "understanding." Moreover, as Octavius Brooks Frothingham long ago made clear, the *a priori* categories of Kant, along with the idealistic tenets of his disciples, created an atmosphere conducive to the belief that "religion was not a system of dogmas, but an inward experience;... its primal verities rested not on miracle,... but on the soul's own sense of things divine."[21]

Crucial for our discussion of *Pierre* is the way these issues finally crystallized in America in the debate between Unitarians and Transcendentalists concerning the place of miracles—the wax and seal of historical Christianity—in the act of faith. Andrews Norton and Francis Bowen insisted upon the inestimable value of miracles; Ripley, Parker, Brownson, and Emerson, upon their cumbersome, secondary status in proving the truth of a Revelation in which spiritually minded persons already believed intuitively. As Ripley remarked,

> A miracle may direct attention to the doctrine, it may clothe the person of the teacher with outward consideration, it may even give him external credibility, according to the notions of the age; but the truth of the doctrine, it can never prove; and this was acknowledged by Christ himself. His words were spirit and life; he presented living waters for the refreshment and sustenance of the soul. He announced truth, which should make the heart of man alive and free. And the proof of this, he placed in the experience of every individual. To this, outward miracles could contribute nothing.

"Jesus speaks always from within," claimed Emerson, "and in a degree that transcends all others. In that is the miracle. *I believe beforehand* that it ought so to be."[22]

By the time he wrote *Pierre*, Melville was aware of the transatlantic heritage that had helped to foster American Transcendentalism,[23] as well as of the quarrel between Unitarians and Transcendentalists over the place of miracles in religion. In *Mardi*, it will be recalled, Babbalanja advances Bardianna's maxim that "the soul needs no mentor,

---

21. Octavius Brooks Frothingham, *Transcendentalism in New England* (1876; rpt. Philadelphia: Univ. of Pennsylvania Press, 1972), pp. 49–50.

22. George Ripley, "Herder's Theological Opinions and Services," *Christian Examiner*, 19 (Nov. 1835), 195; Emerson, "The Oversoul" (*Essays, First Series*), *Works*, II: 287; emphasis added. The best overview of the Miracles Controversy is William R. Hutchison's *The Transcendental Ministers: Church Reform in the New England Renaissance* (New Haven: Yale Univ. Press, 1959), pp. 52–97.

23. The narrator of Melville's *White-Jacket* (1850) points out the *Neversink*'s "transcendental divine," whose "head had been turned by the Germans," and who has been seen "with Coleridge's Biographia Literaria in his hand" (WJ, 155).

but Oro [God]; and Oro without proxy" (M, 576); and the Old Man of
Serenia actually echoes the precise debate between Norton and the Transcendentalists by remarking how, even though Alma [Christ] "came
from Oro" and "did miracles, . . . not for these things alone do we thus
love him. We love him from an instinct in us" (M, 628). Recognizing
the difference between the transient and the permanent in religion, the
Old Man also takes pride in Serenia's lack of institutionalized worship and formal apologetics: "We have no priests, but one; and he is
Alma's self. We have his precepts: we seek no comments but our
hearts" (M, 628). Little wonder, then, that when John Murray demanded "documentary evidence" from Melville to verify the truth of
Typee, Melville responded with a remark corresponding to Emerson's
belief that, in matters of faith, "No inspired man ever . . . condescends
to . . . evidences":

> —By the way, you ask again for "documentary evidence" of my
> having been in the South Seas, wherewithall to convince the un-
> believers—Bless my soul, Sir, . . . *You make miracles of what are*
> common-places to us.—I will give no evidence—Truth is mighty
> & will prevail. . . . [24]

Existing scholarship exploring Hawthorne's encounter with the
Miracles Controversy in "Rappaccini's Daughter" (1844) also suggests
that *Pierre,* "with certain differences of emphasis, takes up the question
of faith and evidence exactly where 'Rappaccini's Daughter' had left
it."[25] Indeed, Pierre finds certain aspects of his encounter with Isabel
"most miraculous" (P, 49) and even ponders, in two consecutive sen-
tences, Isabel's "vague revelation" and the "almost miraculousness" of
her story (P, 128). Constantly weighing his "irresistible intuitions"
(P, 85) and "transcendental persuasions" against the "downright presumptive evidence," Pierre falls somewhat short of epistemological certitude: "[C]oming to the plain, palpable facts,—how did he *know* that
Isabel was his sister?" (P, 353). As Colacurcio shows, Pierre seeks to
resolve his dilemma by believing *beforehand* Isabel's claims, and by
regarding historical evidence as after-the-fact corroboration of his *a
priori* conviction: "I feel already I know the pith of all; . . . whatever
remains for thee to tell me, can but corroborate and confirm" (P, 145).
Moreover, by juxtaposing the "oaths" demanded by the "dull head"
with the untestifed evidence found in "the warm halls of the heart"
(P, 71), *Pierre* recalls the Transcendental conviction that "the testi-

---

24. Emerson, "The Oversoul," *Works,* II: 284; Melville, *Letters,* p. 72; emphasis
added.
25. Colacurcio, p. 20.

mony of the heart is as legitimate as that of the head.''[26] And Isabel mandates such heartfelt, Transcendental trust: "Do not put such impetuous questions to me, Pierre;...Oh,...far sweeter are mysteries than surmises: though the mystery be unfathomable, it is still the unfathomableness of fullness; but the surmise, that is but shallow and unmeaning emptiness" (P, 153). Aptly, then , "MYSTERY" (P, 150) is Isabel's predominating feature; for as Mark Winsome, Melville's explicitly Emersonian persona in *The Confidence-Man*, says, "Mystery is in the morning, and mystery in the night, and the beauty of mystery is everywhere" (CM, 170). Still, nineteenth-century critics of Transcendentalism cautioned that its "ranks ... are recruited, not by the earnest-minded, the thinking, but by those who are curious to dive into things shrouded in mystery"; "mystification," warned the *American Whig Review*, takes the place of "reasoning."[27]

The Transcendental quality of Isabel's "MYSTERY" is also conspicuous in the way she transfers to the chords of a guitar the emotions surrounding her past history: "All the wonders that are unimaginable and unspeakable; all these wonders are translated in the mysterious melodiousness of the guitar." Claiming how, from the first, she knew "intuitively" that the "strange humming in my heart ... seemed to prophesy of the hummings of the guitar" (P, 125), Isabel continuously stresses her "heart's deepest melodies" (P, 113), which indeed touch "the secret monochord within [Pierre's] breast" (P, 173). This conflation of music and Transcendental intuition is highly appropriate. Christopher Pearse Cranch had previously remarked that the "echoes" of Transcendental truths "are not ... unmeaning, barren responses or repetitions, but are turned into new modulations, into rich variations as of some mountain melody, and constantly growing richer and more varied, as they spread circling round the world." Of the same persuasion was Emerson, whose Divinity School Address defined the intuitive apprehension of the moral sentiment as a melodious apprehension of the spirit: when a man says " 'I ought;' when love warns him; when he chooses, warned from on high, the good and great deed; then, deep melodies wander through his soul from Supreme Wisdom."[28] Moreover, the tie between music and Transcenden-

---

26. Orestes A. Brownson, "Benjamin Constant on Religion," *Christian Examiner*, 17 (Sept. 1834), 71.

27. "Mr. Emerson and Transcendentalism," *American Whig Review*, 1 (March 1845), 237. For Winsome's identity as Emerson, see Egbert S. Oliver, "Melville's Picture of Emerson and Thoreau in *The Confidence-Man*," *College English*, 8 (Nov. 1946), 61–72.

28. Christopher Pearse Cranch, "Transcendentalism," *Western Messenger*, 8 (Jan. 1841), 406; Emerson, *Works*, I, 125.

tal intuition would have been commonplace after John Sullivan Dwight explained in 1849 that "music is religious and prophetic" and that "the soul that is truly receptive to music learns angelic wisdom." Pierre, though, is finally unable to share Dwight's confidence that "music cannot narrow or cloak the message which it bears; it cannot lie; it cannot raise questions in the mind, or excite any other than a pure enthusiasm."[29]

To the contrary, at least one dimension of Pierre's ambiguous situation arises from his inability to evade questions and uncertainties surrounding Isabel's claims. Whatever his occasional feelings about the "intuitively certain, however literally unproven fact of Isabel's sisterhood" (P, 139), Pierre can rest secure neither in Transcendental intuition nor in the kind of historical and rational evidences that Unitarians might have brought to bear upon such a dilemma. In fact, this dimension of his ambiguity is best understood as a futile effort to rationalize his otherwise intuitive apprehension. By "reasoning and expostulating," for example, he seeks to "reassure his own spontaneous impulses" (P, 53). And while "the strongest and fieriest emotions of life defy analytical insight" (P, 67), Pierre "strove to condense [Isabel's] mysterious haze into some definite and comprehensible shape" (P, 136). Moreover, though Isabel's narrative seems one of "clew-defying mysteriousness," Pierre seeks "a coinciding proof or elucidation" (P, 137) of her testimony. Also, "intuitively certain" of Isabel's story, Pierre nevertheless finds himself "alive . . . to all these searching argumentative itemizings of the minutest known facts" (P, 139). Of course, behind the Unitarian/Transcendentalist dialect of Pierre's dilemma rests the age-old effort to reconcile reason and faith; and were he to consult Pierre Bayle's *Historical and Critical Dictionary* Pierre might concur that "Human Reason falls into . . . strange Ambiguities" when it seeks to do so.[30]

---

29. John Sullivan Dwight, "Music," in Peabody, ed., *Aesthetic Papers*, pp. 30–31. One would assume that, as both a contributor (of the sketch "Main Street") to this sole issue of *Aesthetic Papers*, and as a brother-in-law of the editor (Elizabeth P. Peabody), Hawthorne would have received a copy and that Melville might have perused its contents when he availed himself of Hawthorne's library in 1850. Melville could also have learned about the volume in a rather lengthy review published in *Literary World*, 5 (29 Sept. 1849), 269–71.

30. Pierre Bayle, "Concerning the Manichees," in *An Historical and Critical Dictionary*, trans. Jacob Tonson, 4 vols. (London: Harper, 1710), IV, App., lxi. Bayle here quotes Jean Louis Guez Balzac in support of fideism. For the suggestions that Melville consulted both this essay and Tonson's translation, see Millicent Bell, "Pierre Bayle and *Moby-Dick*," *PMLA*, 66 (Sept. 1951), 643; and my "Translation of Pierre Bayle's *An Historical and Critical Dictionary* Owned by Melville," *Papers of the Bibliographical Society of America*, 71 (1977), 347–51.

Beyond dramatizing the ambiguities that arise from seeking to straddle both sides of the Norton-Ripley debate, *Pierre* offers a telling critique of the assumptions underlying both schools of thought. A subsequent section of this chapter will detail the narcissistic foundations of Emerson's so-called intuitions of the moral sentiment; presently, we shall explore the way that Pierre's more historical probings belie the informing premise of Andrews Norton's monumental study of the *Evidences of the Genuineness of the Gospels* (1837–44), which Perry Miller has called the "perfect summation of Unitarian scholarship," and which Melville seems to have read prior to writing *Pierre*.[31]

To understand Melville's strategy vis à vis Norton, recall that nineteenth century Unitarians advanced primarily two sorts of evidences—external and internal—to defend the authenticity of the Scriptures. As we know from our examination of the chapter in *Moby-Dick* entitled "The Affidavit" (chapter IV, above), external evidences are simply the cumulation of eyewitness accounts of Gospel events and their subsequent documentation in the writings of both sacred and profane historians who supposedly possess no wish or motive to misrepresent commonly accepted facts of history. But in determining the *genuineness* of the Gospels—by which Norton means "I. That the Gospels remain essentially the same as they were [when] originally composed," and "II. That they have been ascribed to their true authors"—Unitarians had recourse to a variety of "internal evidences." These were evidences gathered from such intertextual facts as that the Gospels contain nothing to indicate the authors belonged to another age; that the Gospels lack affected styles that might suggest the authors' inventiveness; that the content of the Gospels transcends the realm of uninspired forgery; and—most importantly for our discussion of *Pierre*—that the Gospels correspond, coincide, and "harmonize" with each other in their accounts of Christ's life, death, and resurrection.[32] Important in this context is Pierre's regret that "in the sweetly writ manuscript" of his life, a "sister had been omitted from the text" (P, 7). Inasmuch as Pierre first apprehends Isabel as "some fearful gospel" (P, 43), the frustration he experiences in confirming her story suggests the potential ambiguities

---

31. Perry Miller, ed., *The Transcendentalists: An Anthology* (Cambridge, Mass.: Harvard Univ. Press, 1950), p. 205. With different emphases, both Lawrance Thompson, in *Melville's Quarrel With God* (Princeton, N.J.: Princeton Univ. Press, 1952), pp. 430–31, and Thomas Vargish, in "Gnostic *Mythos* in *Moby-Dick*," *PMLA*, 81 (June 1966), 272–77, argue Melville's familiarity with Norton's *Evidences*.

32. The quotations are from Andrews Norton, *The Evidences of the Genuineness of the Gospels*, vol. 1 (Boston: John B. Russell, 1837), 18. The general summary of "internal evidences" is from Channing's "Evidences of Christianity" and "Evidences of Revealed Religion," in *Works*, pp. 202–4, 226.

in liberal Christian claims about the genuineness—or, to use Norton's alternate phrase, "the lineage"—of the Gospels.[33]

In *The Confidence-Man*, Melville refers more explicitly to internal evidences of the Scriptures, though with something less than gravity. "Old Plain Talk" is charged with the "authorship" of China Aster's epitaph, the people "alleging that the internal evidence showed that none but that veteran old croaker could have penned such a jeremiade" (CM, 189). In *Pierre*, an allusion to a crucial variety of internal evidence occurs in "The Journey and the Pamphlet" (Book XIV), where the narrator refers to the Sermon on the Mount as "that greatest real miracle of all religions" and then defends its divine origin: "Such emotions as the Sermon raises in the enthusiastic heart; such emotions all youthful hearts refuse to ascribe to humanity as their origin. This is God! cries the heart..." (P, 207-8). Here *Pierre* echoes the foremost internal evidence for the genuineness of the Gospels: the belief that "we claim for our religion a divine original, because no adequate cause for it can be found in the powers or passions of human nature,... because it can only be accounted for by the interposition of that Being to whom its first preachers universally ascribed it, and with whose nature it perfectly agrees."[34] Still another variety of internal evidence seems evident in Pierre's attraction to the "entirely artless, so almost peasant-like simplicity" (P, 142) of Isabel's narrative. In fact, in his wife's copy of Channing's *Works* Melville could have read how the Gospels "were written with the *simplicity*... and ease which are the natural tones of truth.... It is a striking circumstance... that whilst the life and character which [the Gospels] portray are the most extraordinary in history, the style is the most *artless*."[35] Yet these minor instances of internal evidence are subordinate in Pierre's mind to the largest question surrounding Isabel's genuineness, specifically (to modify Norton's definition), whether this "fearful gospel" has ascribed herself to her true father, and—presuming that Pierre's father had a daughter—whether Isabel is that daughter. Even though Melville appears to have drawn upon an actual incident of illegitimacy to create

33. Norton, *Evidences*, I: 35, 83. Applicable to my concern is what, from a more secular vantage, Edgar Dryden has shown to be the "intertextual" bases of "human relations" in *Pierre* ("The Entangled Text: Melville's *Pierre* and the Problem of Reading," *Boundary 2*, 7 [Spring 1979], 163). Yet only in the context of Norton's and Melville's attention to the genuineness (or "lineage") of the Gospels can we appreciate the full value of Dryden's remark that "Isabel as a reader may be said to be the author of her own parentage"—"a genealogical order that is partially discovered, partially invented" (p. 170).

34. Channing, "Evidences of Revealed Religion," *Works*, p. 226; emphasis added.

35. Channing "Evidences of Christianity," *Works*, p. 203; emphasis added.

Pierre's dilemma,[36] Pierre still judges Isabel's claims within categories of internal "correspondences" that have crucial implications both for Norton's argumentative strategy and for Pierre's encounter with the painting entitled *"A stranger's head, by an unknown hand."*

Melville's challenge to Norton is best apprehended by recalling that even while *"A stranger's head"* reminds Pierre of his father's indicting chair-portrait, he knows it could not possibly have had his father as its original. Yet for Isabel—who sees features of her eyes and brow (P, 351) in *"A stranger's head"*—the painting evokes thoughts of the father she remembers from her childhood, causing her to wonder whether the portrait may actually be his representation. Since Pierre had earlier based part of his belief in Isabel's identity upon her re-semblance to the chair-portrait—and *not* upon Isabel's likeness to his best recollections of his living father (P, 197)—and since, moreover, Isabel knows nothing about the chair-portrait that Pierre has de-stroyed (P, 352), Pierre is quick to perceive the potentially specious quality of the internal evidence upon which he based part of his deci-sion to champion Isabel:

> The [correspondence between Isabel's face and the] Chair-portrait, *that* was the entire sum and substance of all possible, rakable, downright presumptive evidence, which peculiarly appealed to his own separate self. Yet here was another portrait of a complete stran-ger—a European; a portrait imported from across the seas, and to be sold at public auction, which was just as strong an evidence as the other. Then, the original of this second portrait was just as much the father of Isabel as the original of the chair-portrait. But perhaps there was no original at all to this second portrait; it might have been a pure fancy-piece. (P, 353)

It is particularly appropriate, then, to view Isabel as a "fearful gos-pel," who finally provides no convincing evidence that she was known to her ascribed creator. And highly pertinent to this issue is Norton's summary of the heresy that his arguments for the Gospels' genuine-ness seek to combat. Having in mind Johann Gottfried Eichhorn (1752–1827), Norton remarks,

> an objector may say, "You have little or rather no evidence for the

---

36. Amy Puett Emmers shows that Melville's father actually had an illegitimate daughter who, along with her mother, made claims upon the Melville estate. See "Mel-ville's Closet Skeleton: A New Letter About the Illegitimacy Incident in *Pierre*," in *Studies in the American Renaissance, 1977*, ed. Joel Myerson (Boston: Twayne, 1978), 339–43.

genuineness of the Gospels, which reaches back beyond the close of the second century.... You have, in fact, no proof of their existence, *in their present form*, previous to that period. All that can be rendered probable is, that some works were in existence, which served as a basis for the Gospels you now possess."[37]

This concern with proof, I take it, corresponds to Pierre's reservations about Isabel; for "the grand point now with Pierre was, not ... whether his father had had a daughter, but whether, assuming he had had, *Isabel*, rather than any other living being, *was that daughter*" (P, 353).

Just as revealing is the use of the word "original" three times in the paragraph quoted above on the similarity between *"A stranger's head"* and the chair-portrait: In emphasizing this word, Melville is very likely responding to still another dimension of Norton's *Evidences*, which advanced the theory of a *Protevangelium*, an *"Original Gospel*, antecedent to our present Gospels, and the common source from which they have all drawn."[38] In arguing the case for such an "Ur-Gospel," Norton cites the "agreement between our present manuscript copies of the Gospels ... in whatever form these copies appear.... These were written in different countries, and at different periods, probably from the fifth century, downwards. They have been found in places widely remote from each other, in Asia, in Africa, and from one extremity of Europe to the other." The agreement among the Gospels might be considered analogous to the similarity between the chair-portrait and *"A stranger's head,"* created at different extremities of the earth, but still strikingly alike. Yet the question for both Pierre and Norton is whether such similarity necessarily indicates evolution from the same original. Melville's skepticism would appear to be directed in particular against Norton's belief that

all these different copies of the Gospels, or parts of the Gospels, so numerous, so various in their character, so unconnected, offer-

---

37. Norton, *Evidences*, I: 17.

38. This concise summary is that of Moses Stuart, "Genuineness of the Gospels" (a review of volume I of Norton's *Evidences*), *American Biblical Repository*, 11 (April 1838), 289. Stuart offers an excellent overview and critique of Norton's theory of a *Protevangelium*. This theory was derived in large part from Eichhorn (who, while advancing the existence of an *original* Gospel, doubted the *genuineness* of latter-day Gospels) and Bishop Herbert Marsh, who composed *A Dissertation on the Origin and Composition of Our Three First Canonical Gospels* (Cambridge, England: John Burges, 1801). "Several years before any of our canonical Gospels were composed," says Marsh, "a short narrative was drawn up containing the principal transactions of Jesus Christ from his baptism to his death.... It was written ... in the native language of the Jews of Jerusalem, that is, in Chaldee intermixed with ancient Hebrew words" (p. 196). Marsh argues

ing themselves to notice in parts of the world so remote from each other, concur in giving us essentially the same text.... [T]hey are all copies more or less remote, of the same original.... In respect to each of the Gospels, the copies which we possess must all be referred, for their source, to one *original* Gospel, one *original* text, one *original* manuscript.

By way of analogy, the correspondence between the chair-portrait and *"A stranger's head"* challenges both the case for a *Protevangelium* and, by implication, Norton's certainty that "the Gospels remain essentially the same, as they were originally composed."[39] Despite the two portraits' pictorial resemblance, their random similarity hardly argues a common original; instead, it denies Norton's central premise that "this agreement among different copies could not have existed, unless some archetype had been faithfully followed; and this archetype, it has been shown, could have been no other than the original text." And Melville's use of corresponding portraits to address this subject is quite appropriate, given the way Gospel "Harmonies" and "Correspondences" depend upon visual appeal (see Figure G).[40]

Aptly, then Melville rounds off his critique of such "internal evidences" with a pun on two meanings of the word *"coincidence,"* just after the paragraph that relates the different thoughts passing through the minds of Isabel and Pierre as they study *"A stranger's head"*:

> Pierre was thinking of the chair-portrait: Isabel, of the living face. Yet Isabel's fervid exclamations having reference to the living face, were now, as it were, mechanically responded to by Pierre, in syllables having reference to the chair-portrait....
> "Is it? is it? can it be?" was the intense whisper of Isabel.
> "No, it can not be, it is not," replied Pierre; "one of the wonderful *coincidences*, nothing more." (P, 352; emphasis added)

The emphasized word is especially significant because, in *Evidences of the Genuineness of the Gospels*, "Mr. Norton designs...to lay before his readers the general nature of the *coincidences* between the first three Gospels." Or, as another nineteenth-century apologist put the case, the *"undesigned coincidence* or correspondency" of the Gospels

---

that Matthew, Mark, and Luke based their Gospels on this document and its Greek translation, intermixing facts known peculiarly to themselves (pp. 195, 243).

39. Norton, *Evidences*, I: 27–30, 18; emphasis added.

40. Norton, *Evidences*, I: 107–8. Marsh, pp. 2–3, actually clarifies his argument with reference to corresponding portraits. Recall, too, that Melville refers to a "portrait" of Pierre's grandfather as "a glorious gospel framed and hung upon the wall" (P, 30).

CORRESPONDENCES OF THE GOSPELS.   cxxiii

Matthew.	Mark.	Luke.
	his mouth. And Jesus questioned his father; How long has it been thus with him? And he answered; From a child. And often it casts him into fire and into water, to destroy him. But, if thou canst do any thing, have pity upon us and help us. Then Jesus said to him; What means this, ' If thou canst '? All things may be done for him who has faith. And, immediately, the father of the child, crying out with tears, said; I have faith; help thou my want of faith. Then Jesus, seeing that the multitude was running together to	
And Jesus rebuked the demon, so that it came out of him, and the boy was well from that hour.	the spot, rebuked the unclean spirit, saying to it; Thou dumb and deaf spirit, I command thee, come out of him and enter him no more. And uttering a cry, and convulsing him much, it came out of him. And he was	But Jesus rebuked the unclean spirit, and healed the child, and delivered him to his father.

Figure G. Andrews Norton, *The Evidences of the Genuineness of the Gospels* (Boston: John B. Russell, 1837), I: cxxiii.

would seem to prove "that they have not been produced by meditation, or by any fraudulent contrivance."[41] Thus, despite the Gospels'
coinciding (corresponding) features, Melville's juxtaposition of "*A
stranger's head*" with Pierre's recollection of the chair-portrait suggests that this mode of internal evidence may conceivably reflect little
more than *mere coincidence*: "[I]t might have been a pure fancy-
piece" (P, 353). On grounds such as this, therefore, no good reason
exists for believing Isabel to be the offspring of her ascribed father.

Whatever the ambiguities surrounding Pierre's encounter with the "internal evidences" of Isabel's genuineness, this "Unitarian" dimension of his dilemma is
far less puzzling to Pierre than the "Transcendental"
phenomenon of intuition—which has its origin, Melville suggests, in
such internal drives as sexual instinct and impulse. In *Pierre*, intuition
is shown as arising from the mind's fabrications of mandates that it
projects onto the outside world and then reencounters as the "primitive and sublime sentiment of Duty, engraved by the finger of God on
the heart of man."[42] The relation, then, between Pierre's moral absolutism and his periodically intuitive encounters with that "phosphoric
finger" prophetically recording the "burning fact, that Isabel was his
sister" (P, 170) calls for a brief review of the way Transcendentalists
argued that the sentiment of virtue was contingent upon an intuitive
grasp of objective moral impulses emanating from God. Ripley, for instance, remarked how the sense of obligation depends upon "con-
formity to our moral relations, as intuitively perceived... by the
moral faculty."[43] By implication, persons who disclaimed the mind's
intuitive powers could be charged with sneaking Calvinistic depravity
in through the back door of liberal theology: "[N]one but they who

---

41. The first quotation is from Stuart, p. 319; the second, from Thomas Hartwell
Horne, *An Introduction to the Critical Study and Knowledge of the Holy Scriptures*, 4
vols., 5th ed. (London: A & R. Spottiswoode, 1825), I: 107. That Melville has in mind
categories similar to Norton's may be inferred from Pierre's earlier reflections about the
way Aunt Dorothea's account of his father "correspond[s]" with other facts—as well as
from Pierre's search for a "coinciding proof" (P, 137) of Isabel's genuineness. Note, too,
how the rhetoric of "internal evidence" surfaces in the following passage: "[A]ll that
had been inexplicably mysterious to him in the portrait, and all that had been inexplicably familiar in the face, most magically these now *coincided*; the merriness of the
one not in*harmonious* with the mournfulness of the other..." (P, 85; emphasis
added).
42. Ripley, "Review," p. 331.
43. Ripley, "Review," p. 325 (misnumbered 225).

were lost to their better nature, could fail [intuitively] to perceive . . . the revelation of God."[44] This assumption that intuition is a prerequisite for apprehending the moral sentiment helps explain why Emerson begins the Divinity School Address by extolling virtue; why he then insists that, like the religious sentiment, the moral sentiment is apprehended exclusively as an intuition of the soul; and why finally he attacks Unitarian historiography for its denigration of human nature: "To aim to convert a man by miracles is a profanation of the soul." From this angle, the essay's twofold emphasis on the moral sentiment and the defects of the historical approach to Christianity is strategically unified—as is Melville's emphasis in *Pierre* on both moral perfection and Pierre's private "miracles" controversy. Thus, Emerson holds that "the intuition of the moral sentiment is an insight of the perfection of the laws of the soul"; and Pierre's "sublime intuitiveness also paints to him the sun-like glories of god-like truth and virtue" (P, 111). Indeed, few, if any, better apprehended the relation between intuition and virtue than Melville, and nowhere are its potentially hazardous tendencies better dramatized than in Pierre's chronometrical extravagancies.[45]

The Transcendentalists insisted, further, upon a correspondence between the object of intuition and objective truth. "I speak," said Christopher Pearse Cranch,

> of that fresh, earnest, truth-loving and truth-seeking SPIRIT, which is abroad;—of that heart's-thirst, not of the fever-dream, but of the sober, waking vision of soundest health, after something *always* new and lovely and true. . . . The true Transcendentalism is that living and always new *spirit* of truth, . . . which is thus in the only sense *transcendental*, when it labors to *transcend* itself, and soar ever higher and nearer the great source of Truth, Himself.[46]

Pierre, too, vows to know "nothing but Truth; glad Truth, or sad

---

44. Ripley, *"The Latest Form of Infidelity" Examined,* p. 87. Miller, *Transcendentalists,* pp. 129–30, explains how Transcendental emphasis on intuition had reference primarily to the outer boundaries of human regeneracy.

45. Emerson, Divinity School Address, *Works,* I: 132, 122. For other writings in which Transcendentalists stress the tie between intuition and regeneracy, see Ripley, "Herder's Theological Opinions and Services," pp. 181–82; *The Works of Theodore Parker,* ed. G. W. Cooke, 15 vols. (Boston: American Unitarian Assoc., 1907–13), I: 184.

46. Cranch, p. 407. For similar Transcendental paeans to Truth, see Orestes A. Brownson, "No Error Can Be Useful; No Truth Can Be Injurious," *Boston Quarterly Review,* 3 (April 1840), 171, 180–81; Theodore Parker, "Truth Against the World: A Parable of Paul," *Dial,* 1 (Oct. 1840), 218–19.

Truth" (P, 65). Yet the point to be stressed is *Pierre*'s response to Transcendental ideas about the objective status of truth, and especially truths about the moral sentiment. Melville may have been familiar with a passage from "Self-Reliance" in which Emerson expresses a version of the general Transcendental enthusiasm for truth that disregards the full complexity of man's inner motives—including impulses that in Pierre's case help shape the contours of supposedly objective moral mandates: "Henceforward," writes Emerson, "*I am the truth's*. Be it known unto you that henceforward I obey no law less than eternal law.... I shall endeavor to nourish my parents, to support my family, *to be the chaste husband of one wife*,—but these relations I must fill after *a new and unprecedented way*."[47] In his "Unprecedented Final Resolution" (P, 172) of feigning marriage to Isabel, Pierre may well try to act out his own peculiar version of Emerson's mandate. Failing, however, to comprehend that his supposed intuitions of the moral sentiment are actually subjective, Pierre strays somewhat wide of chastity.[48]

Pierre's proneness to mistake passion for righteous love entails a criticism of Emerson's definition of love as the objective correlative—so to speak—of the intuitions of the moral sentiment: when a man says " 'I ought;' when love warns him; when he chooses, warned from on high, the good and great deed; then, deep melodies wander through his soul from Supreme Wisdom.... In the sublimest flights of the soul, rectitude is never surmounted, love is never outgrown."[49] Moreover, Emerson's ideas about "love" help to explain why, Hamlet-like, Pierre had "not only to endure a signal grief, but immediately to act upon it" (P, 87); for, says the narrator, if "the pregnant tragedy of Hamlet convey any one...moral..., it is this:—that all meditation is worthless, unless it prompt to action" (P, 169). This

---

47. Emerson, "Self-Reliance," in *Works*, II: 72–73; emphasis added.

48. As I argue elsewhere, Melville may compound Pierre's difficulty in being the chaste husband of one wife by having him base his decision to abandon Lucy and to feign wedlock with Isabel on the precise mode of infidelity of which, in *The Faerie Queene* (I.xii), Duessa accuses Redcross when he is about to wed Una. See my "Spenserian Maze of Melville's *Pierre*," *ESQ: A Journal of the American Renaissance*, 23 (1977), 220–21.

49. Emerson, Divinity School Address, *Works*, I: 125. As Dillaway (p. 361) remarks, "Accompanying or following the influx of divinity into the mind comes the birth of a sublime emotion which we designate as love. With the arrival of this emotion comes the development of what Emerson calls the 'moral sentiment.' This moral sentiment has its roots in the love which now floods the ascending man." The next few paragraphs of this chapter will explore the specifically Edwardsian dimension of Melville's encounter with Emerson's "Love." But for a more general reading of this essay's influence upon *Pierre*, see Blansett, pp. 142–43.

position is compatible with Emerson's peculiar application of "love" in condemning the "too intellectual tendency" paralyzing reformers:

> [T]he criticism which is levelled at the laws and manners, ends in thought, without causing a new method of life. The genius of the day does not incline to a deed, but to a beholding. It is not that men do not wish to act; they pine to be employed, but are paralyzed by the uncertainty of what they should do.

And the reason for this hesitation? "Their fault is that they have stopped at the intellectual perception; that their will is not yet inspired from the Fountain of Love."[50]

Inspired by love, Pierre acts precipitously and hazardously to correct the social injustices suffered by Isabel. But rather than appreciating the degree to which his decision is influenced by passion, he subscribes, instead, to the Emersonian tenet that "there can be no excess to love...in the purest sense."[51] Indeed, for Pierre, "Isabel wholly soared out of the realms of mortalness, and...became transfigured in the highest heaven of uncorrupted Love" (P, 142); and his belief in their mutual purity finds confirmation in Isabel's utterance, "I am called woman, and thou, man, Pierre; but there is neither man nor woman about it.... There is no sex in our immaculateness" (P, 149). Like Amos Bronson Alcott, who seems also to have thought that "the pure, unfallen soul.... finds no lust in her members warring against conscience," or, like E. T. Clapp, who celebrated in verse the Transcendental prospects of man's spiritual purity, Pierre believes that he and Isabel "will love with pure and perfect love of angel to an angel" (P, 154).[52]

Pierre's self-deception can perhaps best be explained by locating

---

50. Emerson, "Lecture on the Times" (*Nature, Addresses, Lectures*), in *Works*, I: 282–83, 286.

51. Emerson, "Compensation" (*Essays, First Series*), in *Works*, II: 122.

52. Amos Bronson Alcott, "Orphic Sayings," *Dial*, 1 (July 1840), 88; E. T. Clapp, "The Future Is Better than the Past," *Dial*, 2 (July 1841), 57. Worth quoting are two stanzas from the latter:

In the spirit's perfect air,
    In the passions tame and kind,
Innocence from selfish care
    The real Eden we shall find....

When all error is worked out,
    From the heart and from the life;
When the Sensuous is laid low,
    Through the Spirit's holy strife.

Emerson's essay "Love" in its context of the ideas of Jonathan Edwards. Melville was familiar, as we have seen (chapter I, above), with Edwards's definition of "true virtue" as a "benevolence to being in general"—or what the adherents of Samuel Hopkins would later call "disinterested benevolence."[53] Thus, Melville may have recognized something distinctly Edwardsian in Emerson's definition of "Love":

> Every promise of the soul has innumerable fulfillments; each of its joys ripens into a new want. Nature, uncontainable, flowing, forelooking, in the first sentiment of kindness, anticipates already a *benevolence* which shall lose all particular regards in its *general light*. The introduction of this felicity is in a private and tender relation of one to one, which is the enchantment of human life; which, like a certain divine rage and enthusiasm, seizes on man at one period and works a revolution in his mind and body; unites him to his race, ... carries him with new sympathy into nature. ...

Evident here is a strategy that, by enlarging the object of "love" from a private to a general sphere, approaches Edwards's definition of "true virtue." Says Emerson, love "is a fire that kindling its first embers in the narrow nook of a private bosom, caught from a wandering spark out of another private heart, glows and enlarges until it warms and beams upon multitudes of men and women, upon the universal heart of all, and so lights up the whole world and all nature with its generous flames." For good reason, then, Emerson finally defines the product of this sexless, generous love as *virtue*, or the moral sentiment: "Thus are we put in training for a love which knows not sex, nor person, nor partiality, but which seeks virtue and wisdom everywhere, to the end of increasing virtue and wisdom."[54]

Of course, Emerson is hardly faithful to the Calvinist spirit and application of Edwards's discourse, which limits authentic benevolence to the repertoire of regenerate Christians and which explains away the seemingly virtuous behavior of others by pointing to its origin in such self-serving "natural appetites" as "the mutual inclinations between the sexes."[55] Self-interest of this sort, as we have seen, is involved in

---

53. Jonathan Edwards, *The Nature of True Virtue*, in *The Works of President Edwards*, ed. Sereno E. Dwight, 10 vols. (New York: S. Converse, 1829-30), III: 94-95. On Hopkins, see Joseph A. Conforti, "Samuel Hopkins and the New Divinity: Theology, Ethics, and Social Reform in Eighteenth-Century New England," *William and Mary Quarterly*, 34 (Oct. 1977), 572-89.

54. Emerson, "Love" (*Essays, First Series*), in *Works*, II: 169-70 (emphasis added), 188.

55. Edwards, *Works*, III: 136.

Mardi with Taji's effort to extend the area of freedom to Yillah, as it is with Pierre's Transcendental "love" for Isabel. Despite the fact that physical impulses inspire Pierre to champion Isabel, he fancies himself a "self-renouncing victim" in quest of "enthusiastic virtue" (P, 173). And in the execution of this seemingly "virtuous cause" (P, 176), Pierre believes that he can "insure . . . against the insidious inroads of self-interest" (P, 106). Moreover, in true Augustinian and Edwardsian form, Pierre falls "dabbling in the vomit of his loathed identity" (P, 171) before announcing to Isabel the apparently self-sacrificing resolution that will unite him with the object of his lust, though under the benevolent pretense of sparing his father's reputation and his mother's feelings. Still, after remarking that he "hath consulted heaven itself" in determining how he and Isabel will remain together in a "strange way, but most pure," Pierre imprints "burning kisses upon her" (P, 192), an apt gesture of the self-interested motives that have all along inspired him. Pierre, we might speculate, would now find some difficulty in adhering to the Transcendental assumption that "[i]t is enough to know that the ground of disinterested, self-sacrificing love is placed within the heart of man, and we have at once an element, by which he may be made a partaker of the divine nature. And that this germ does exist in the human soul, who can deny?"[56] Edwards would obviously have denied the point—as does *Pierre*'s response to "Love."

In rejecting the Transcendental concepts of intuition and love in *Pierre*, Melville was probably stimulated in part by the journalistic furor that followed the American publication (in 1845) of Philip James Bailey's *Festus: A Poem* (1839). To be sure, Melville most likely had in mind the Festus of the New Testament (Acts 26:24–25) when in 1851 he wrote, "My dear Hawthorne, the atmospheric skepticisms steal into me now, and make me doubtful of my sanity in writing you thus. But believe me, I am not mad, most noble Festus!" (L, 142–43). Still, the timeliness of this allusion may be related to the wide popularity of Bailey's *Festus* in the Duyckinck circle. In fact, in Duyckinck's personal library Melville could have had access to the 1845 second London edition, of which the first American edition of *Festus* was a stereotype reproduction.[57] But not all Americans received the

---

56. George Ripley, *Discourses on the Philosophy of Religion, Addressed to Doubters Who Wish to Believe* (Boston: James Munroe, 1836), p. 38.

57. I quote below from Philip James Bailey, *Festus: A Poem*, 2nd ed. (London: William Pickering, 1845). Page references to the poem will be cited parenthetically. For the popularity of *Festus* in the Duyckinck circle, see the "Explanatory Notes" to Luther Stearns Mansfield and Howard P. Vincent, eds., *Moby-Dick, or the Whale* (New York: Hendricks House, 1952), p. 647. For Duyckinck's ownership of the edition of *Festus* that

poem favorably. Termed by *Graham's Magazine* "the strangest, most daring, most arrogant piece of composition produced in the nineteenth century,"[58] *Festus* was subjected to particular attack in the pages of the *American Whig Review* by Henry Norman Hudson, who used it as a rallying point in his campaign against Transcendentalism. Hudson's critique, as we shall see, appears to have some relevance for the major thematic concerns of *Pierre*.

Philip James Bailey (1816–1902) was an English lawyer who cared more for poetry than for the practice of law. His *Festus*—the events of which occur partly in nineteenth-century England and more generally in the imaginary realms of Heaven, Hell, interplanetary space, and the Millennial Earth—is, as Morse Peckham remarks, an attempt "to reconcile a generalized romanticism in the Byronic tradition with the Universalist doctrine of salvation for all mankind."[59] A plot summary presents something of a challenge, since this poem itself admits to having "a plan, but no plot" (p. 249) and to being a "mysterious, allegorical, / Mythical, theological, odd story" (p. 251). The poem has a recognizable affinity, however, with Goethe's *Faust* and with the Book of Job. In Bailey's poem, God allows Lucifer to tempt Festus with infinite knowledge (pp. 15–22) but does so only to prove Himself capable of infinitive forgiveness, redemption, and love (pp. 7–9). For conservative American critics, however, the trouble lay in Festus's self-imposed chronometrical mandate to accommodate divine love to sublunary human intercourse:

> Nothing will stand whose staple is not love;
> The love of God, or man, or lovely woman;
> The first is scarcely touched, the next scarce felt,

I quote in this chapter, see "Duyckinck Collection," *Lenox Library Short-Title Lists*, 8 (1887), 4. Morse Peckham, in "American Editions of *Festus:* A Preliminary Survey," *Princeton University Library Chronicle*, 8 (June 1947), 178, shows that the first American edition of *Festus* (Boston: Benjamin B. Musey, 1845) was a stereotype reproduction of the second English edition. The renown of *Festus* is evidenced by its several American editions and by its reviews (in addition to those quoted here) in such periodicals as the *Broadway Journal*, 2 (6 Sept. 1845), 136–37; the *Harbinger*, 2 (20 Dec. 1845), 25–27; the *Southern Literary Messenger*, 12 (July 1846), 426–34; the *Knickerbocker*, 26 (July 1845), 72–74; and the *Southern Quarterly Review*, 11 (Jan. 1847), 106–11.

58. *Graham's Magazine*, 28 (Nov. 1845), 238.

59. Morse Peckham, "A Bailey Collection," *Princeton University Library Chronicle*, 7 (June 1846), 149. Peckham details the biographical highlights of Bailey's life. Born April 22, 1816, he was the son of Thomas Bailey, a wealthy wine merchant. As a child, Philip was tutored by a Unitarian minister, and he later briefly attended the University of Glasgow. After studying law at Lincoln's Inn, he was admitted to the bar in 1840 but subsequently devoted most of his time to writing poetry. (Cf. James Ward's *Philip James Bailey, Author of "Festus"* [Nottingham Press, 1905].) Between 1839 and

> The third is desecrated; lift it up;
> Redeem it, hallow it, blend the three in one
> Great holy work. It shall be read in Heaven
> By all the saved of sinners of all time. (pp. 270-71)

Repeatedly, though, Festus falls short of this ideal by shifting from an ethereal love for women (pp. 30-34, 154) to a more passionate attraction to those with whom he hopes to "set [his] soul in love's ripe riot" (p. 183)—and with antinomian certainty of final salvation:

> But go and tell our God, from me,
> He must forgive what He hath given;
> And, if we be by passion driven
> To love, and all its natural madness,
> Tell Him that man by love hath thriven,
> And that by love he shall be shriven;
> For God is love where love is gladness. (p. 184)

Indeed, seventeenth-century Familism might have seemed mild stuff in comparison to Bailey's thoughts about man's resemblance to God: "The nearest point wherein we come towards Thee, / Is loving—making love—and being happy" (p. 370). Yet despite these utterances, as well as Festus's act of near rape (p. 338) and his arrogant demand to view God "face to face" (p. 196), Festus is still redeemed by the God of Love (pp. 198, 204), who initiates the Millennium and even forgives Satan and his fallen angels (pp. 362-394) to confirm the poem's pervading doctrine that "the truth of truths is love" (p. 150).

William H. Channing's reservations about the poem's "lawlessness" were understandable. Margaret Fuller, however, overlooked its flaws, among which she numbered an unfortunate adherence to "the orthodox scheme of redemption," to celebrate the "aspiration" and intensity of a human spirit that would view God directly, without "the intervention of reflective intellect."[60] Yet potentially more important for its bearing on *Pierre* is the fervor with which the *Democratic Review* and the *American Whig Review* discussed Bailey's treatment of "love." The former admired the way Festus scorns social advancement "in comparison to love and truth" and heaped lavish praise upon the poem's successful dramatization of this divine mandate: "The true and deep music of Festus breathes in its love-passages. . . . Life and love are

---

1889 Bailey expanded *Festus* in ten different editions from 8,100 lines to 39,160 lines. The 1845 edition that I quote contains 12,800 lines.

60. Channing, "Festus," *Christian Examiner*, 39 (Nov. 1845), 372; Margaret Fuller, "Festus," *Dial*, 2 (Oct. 1841), 244, 250, 236.

to [Bailey] identical, or, rather, the former derives all its interest from the latter."[61] Henry Norman Hudson, however, was of a different mind. In two consecutive issues of the *American Whig Review* that Melville may have read, Hudson anathematized *Festus* as being perverse "enough to suit the most fastidious epicure of lawlessness and deformity." Especially offensive was Bailey's "transcendental" homage to *love*: "He has a certain transcendental theory, according to which, God has made all things holy, by making them; and all men are full of the unattainable who have fallen in love with a beautiful woman, or had certain sensations so very exquisite as to seem a special visiting from heaven; and every man may be a priest and a church unto himself." Hudson, moreover, observes how the nominal disinterestedness of Transcendental "love" too easily becomes a "generosity of heart" which "cannot choose but embrace every beauty [Festus] meets." Thus, Hudson speculates that the so-called intuitions of Transcendentalists are nothing more than every man's encounter with his own inner lusts: "It is well known that authors of [Bailey's] class are ... constantly putting forth their 'glad animal movements' as divine imbreathings [*sic*]; and the result is, any quantity of revelations ... fresh from the limbo of sensual emotion."[62]

Hudson, moreover, discourses upon the precise Transcendental tenet responsible not only for the delusions of Festus but perhaps as well for the enthusiasm of Pierre, who proclaims, "The heart! the heart! 'tis God's anointed; let me pursue the heart!" (P, 91):

> Such a representation of love is really but an apotheosis of lust.... Let it be once settled, indeed, that our hearts are paramount objects of trust, our proper guides to truth and wisdom, and there is no end to the delusions and deviltries that will have possession of us; reason itself will be bribed to support the wrongs of passion; and "the candle of the Lord within us," instead of being lighted by truth, will melt away in the enthusiasm of self-conceit.[63]

---

61. "Festus," *Democratic Review*, 17 (Dec. 1845), 458.

62. Henry Norman Hudson, "Festus," *American Whig Review*, 5 (Jan. 1847), 45, 59, 54; 5 (Feb. 1847), 137. Melville's familiarity with the *Whig*'s January review of *Festus* is suggested by the fact that its opening paragraphs share a page with the last two stanzas of H. W. Parker's "Loom of Life," which may well have inspired the imagery used by Melville to express the philosophical concerns of "The Mat-Maker" chapter of *Moby-Dick*. Moreover, the February issue of the *Whig*, in which the second part of Hudson's review appears, could have interested Melville, among other reasons, because it predicts "wide popularity" (p. 210) for his forthcoming "South Seas" (*Omoo*).

63. Hudson, "Festus," *American Whig Review*, 5 (Feb. 1847), 141. The *Whig* reiterates this charge in "Hudson's Lectures on Shakespeare," 8 (July 1848), 39–53, esp. 43.

This statement is, of course, applicable to Pierre, as is Hudson's response to the notion that "The nearest point wherein we come towards [God], / Is loving—making love—and being happy." Hudson counters this credo from *Festus* by again showing how Transcendentalists mistake inner passion for divine mandates. In terms highly suggestive for Pierre's private "miracles" controversy, he does so this time by parodying the debates between Norton and the Transcendentalists over the place of miracles and "internal evidence" in the act of faith:

> Probably the prophets and apostles of old were either ignorant of these facts, or did not see fit to announce them. To be sure, the author works no miracles to accredit his revelations, unless the reception his book has met with be a miracle; but it is to be hoped men have now got sufficiently enlightened to recognize the truth without any such endorsement. Of course Heaven would not reveal anything that should transcend the reason of a transcendentalist. Assuredly, such a man needs no miracles, for he will not be caught accepting a revelation on any other than internal evidence; that is, its conformity to his "reason."[64]

From such sources, Melville could have become familiar with arguments refuting the credibility of what Hudson labels "subjective transcendentalism." Failing to acknowledge objective standards of "truth, beauty, [and] good," it "substitute[s] its own notions and feelings for them," ultimately "deifying...passions and conceptions" by "attributing a divine origin and sanction to...instincts and impulses." To this subjectivism, then, Hudson ascribes the "peculiarly vicious and vitiating tendency of [*Festus*]; the sensuality of its love,...the licentiousness of its morals."[65] As Festus himself puts it, and as Pierre might concur after confronting his less than disinterested attraction to Isabel,

> Oh! I wish I was a pure child again,
> As ere the clear could trouble me: when life
> Was sweet and calm as is a sister's kiss;
> And not the wild and whirlwind touch of passion,
> Which though it hardly light upon the lip,
> With breathless swiftness sucks the soul out of sight,
> So that we lose it, and all thought of it. (p. 59)

---

64. Hudson, "Festus," *American Whig Review*, 5 (Jan. 1847), 49.

65. Hudson, "Festus," *American Whig Review*, 5 (Feb. 1847), 138–41. Similarly disturbed by Festus's "lust and foul thoughts," the reviewer for *Graham's Magazine* (p. 238) attributed the poem "to that state of mind, often observed in fanatics, where impulses of appetite are mistaken for the impulses of the religious sentiment."

Although the *Whig* had provided a forum for Hudson's comments on the sexual and impulsive origins of Transcendental "Reason," it failed, after the publication of *Pierre*, to recognize in Melville's novel a dramatization of Hudson's position. Pierre, claimed one of its reviewers, "entertains towards this weird sister feelings which Mr. Melville endeavors to gloss over with a veil of purity, but which even in their best phase can never be any thing but repulsive to a well constituted mind."[66] Yet by showing Pierre's "transcendental persuasions" to have been "originally born... purely of an intense *procreative* enthusiasm" (P, 353; emphasis added), Melville clearly details the prurient nature of Pierre's inspiration. And to illustrate Pierre's *projection of guilt*, Melville fashions Pierre's indictment of his father out of the same sexual anxieties which, in *The Faerie Queene*, cause the Redcross Knight to indict Una, his One True Faith, for impurity.[67] However private, even this literary gloss contributes to an overall critique of Pierre that is consistent with Hudson's ideas about "subjective transcendentalism." For with rhetoric appropriate both to Pierre's guilty projection and the next phase of our discussion, in which we shall explore the implications of Ludwig Feuerbach's *The Essence of Christianity* for *Pierre*, Hudson says,

> When a man's father is dead and gone, of course he can only see him in his mind's eye, where it is not so easy for another to test his perceptions. Where there are no *objects* to be seen, a man can locate his own conceptions with all imaginable facility.... But really all this is not submitting ourselves to the written word, but substituting ourselves for it; not so much consenting to receive, as claiming to originate a religion.[68]

Even though George Eliot did not translate *Das Wesen des Christenthums* (*The Essence of Christianity*; 1841) until 1853, its seminal idea that "God is only man's intuition of his own nature"[69] was already current by the time Melville wrote

---

66. "Pierre, or the Ambiguities," *American Whig Review*, 16 (Nov. 1852), 449.

67. See my "Spenserian Maze of Melville's *Pierre*," pp. 218–19. For discussions—Oedipal and otherwise—of the way Pierre projects his own turpitude upon his father, see Henry A. Murray, "Introduction," *Pierre; or the Ambiguities* (New York: Hendricks House, 1949), p. xciii; R. Scott Kellner, "Sex, Toads, and Scorpions: A Study of the Psychological Themes in Melville's *Pierre*," *Arizona Quarterly*, 31 (Spring 1975), 7–8; Parker and Higgins, p. 178.

68. Hudson, "Festus," *American Whig Review*, 5 (Feb. 1847), 145–46.

69. Ludwig Feuerbach, *The Essence of Christianity*, trans. Marian Evans [sic;

Pierre. In fact, Feuerbach's book, in its third German edition, had achieved enough notoriety to occasion a rebuttal by Hasbrouck Davis in an 1850 issue of the *Christian Examiner*. Davis's profuse use of translated excerpts from Feuerbach made accessible to nineteenth-century Americans a mode of theological skepticism that has major implications for Melville's critique of subjective Transcendentalism in *Pierre*.

Davis traces Feuerbach's roots in Kant's "subjective" response to Humean materialism, to "the idealism of Fichte"—in which "the mind is already all in all, and the objective world practically annihilated"—to the Hegelian "final discovery" that "subject and object are *identical*," and, finally, to the culmination of all this in Feuerbach's thesis that "God has no such existence as we have usually assigned him—an objective existence." Instead, the Deity is recognized to be a projection of *"self-consciousness*," and religion "'a dream of the human soul,' because, in worshipping God, man worships himself." And while Davis clearly takes issue with this variety of "anthropomorphism," he faithfully summarizes Feuerbach's position in terms that constitute an apt commentary on both Pierre's and Emerson's Transcendental intuitions of the moral sentiment: "What you imagine the gift of a superior wisdom springs spontaneously from your own desires, and you are the victim of a miserable self-deceit." Also, in a passage that we may apply to Pierre's nearly religious encounter with Isabel, Davis quotes Feuerbach's belief that "God is man's revealed inner nature," and "religion" the "disclosure of its secret thoughts, the confession of its dearest secrets." This last phrase George Eliot would later translate as "the open confession of... love-secrets."[70]

Pierre was not the first publication in which Feuerbach's ideas were applied to a critique of Transcendentalism. In 1847 the *American Whig Review* charged that "From the nature of man, that is from himself, Mr. [William H.] Channing infers and unfolds the nature of God, which is probably the same thing that a certain German philosopher meant when he spoke of 'creating God.'" And this statement is consistent with the *Whig*'s earlier challenge to the validity of Transcendental intuition: "[I]ntellect is unable to see the image that enlightens her from above; but looking on the ground beneath her, which is nature, she perceives there her own shadow, and the shadows of the loves and

(George Eliot)] (London: John Chapman, 1854), p. 152. A note of recognition is here due Robin Kash, of the Westminster Presbyterian Church, St. Joseph, Missouri, who several years ago suggested that an inquiry into the ideas of Feuerbach might yield results compatible with my interests in *Pierre*.

70. Hasbrouck Davis, "Feuerbach's Essence of Christianity," *Christian Examiner*, 49 (Sept. 1850), 229–30, 232, 237, 231–32; Eliot, trans., in Feuerbach, p. 12.

passions. Cogitating upon these, she originates an idea of their invisible Lord.''[71]

Particularly suggestive for Pierre's almost religious early deference toward his mother is Feuerbach's contention that "the belief in the love of God is the belief in the feminine principle as divine." In fact, with respect to Pierre's initial "lover-like" adoration of a mother named *Mary* and his subsequent identification of Isabel with God,[72] Feuerbach's explanation of the formative stages of such a psychological process sheds light upon the subconscious tensions that may well affect Pierre:

> The love of the son to the mother is the first love of the masculine being for the feminine. The love of man to woman, the love of the youth for the maiden, receives its religious—its sole truly religious consecration in the love of the son to the mother; the son's love for his mother is the first yearning of man towards woman—his first humbling of himself before her.[73]

Beyond illuminating *Pierre*'s Oedipal motif, this logic can account for the way Pierre's "courteous lover-like adoration" of Mary Glendinning "seemed almost to realize here below the sweet dreams of... religious enthusiasts" (P, 16)—and can also explain why Pierre later prostrates himself before Isabel with the certainty that his "heart and soul are now full of deepest reverence," a reverence, in fact, that he defines as "the real sacrament of the supper" (P, 162). And this identification conforms, though by way of parody, to Feuerbach's most general thesis that such mysteries as communion and incarnation have an emotional basis.[74]

---

71. "Religious Union of Associationists," *American Whig Review*, 5 (May 1847), 499; "The Idealist: A Socratic Dialogue" [in which *"Socrates ... unfolds the Idealist, or Transcendental Doctrine"*], *American Whig Review*, 3 (March 1846), 268.

72. Feuerbach, p. 71. As Murray ("Introduction," p. liv) says, "Melville ... identifies God with Isabel. Pierre's final query is—'Lucy or God?' [P, 181]." Cf. Pierre's belief that Isabel's anguish "proceeded from no base, vain, or ordinary motive whatever; but was the unsuppressible and unmistakable cry of the godhead through her soul" (P, 174).

73. Feuerbach, p. 70. Melville investigates the Madonna's origin in man's yearnings for a maternal figure, in *Clarel* I.xxxix.17–26. He compares Isabel to the Madonna on p. 48 of *Pierre*.

74. See Feuerbach, pp. 49–57, 130, 234. Melville's concern with the emotive origins of religion is also evident in a canto of *Clarel* that ponders the Immaculate Virgin (III.xxxi.1–8), relates Her to the "love feminine" (xxxi.38) of Heaven, and finally confronts the haunting question of whether humans can experience a sense of divine love in isolation from human passion and emotion: "Ah, love, ah wherefore thus unsure? / Linked art thou—locked, with Self impure?" (xxxi. 47–48). For similar reasons, Mel-

This context may help to explain why Pierre feels "irresistibly coerced" (P, 93)[75] to defend Isabel, whom he initially encounters as a *"supernatural light; palpable to the senses, but inscrutable to the soul"* (P, 43; emphasis added). Also, Pierre feels "as in the immediate presence of the spirit" (P, 150) before this girl whose shriek "pealed through and through his soul," as if *"another sense* was touched in him" (P, 48; emphasis added). To the degree, moreover, that Isabel's face somehow mystically appeals to Pierre's "own private and individual *affections"* (P, 49; emphasis added; cf. 143), Melville seems to highlight Pierre's quasi-religious enthusiasm with rhetoric that recalls Jonathan Edwards's *Treatise Concerning Religious Affections* and *A Divine and Supernatural Light.* The first of these works explores "The nature of the affections and their importance in religion"; the second defines the Holy Spirit as a phenomenon palpable to the senses in order to verify the apprehension of the Holy Ghost within the epistemological criteria for authentic knowledge established by John Locke.[76] For better or worse, then, Pierre's early encounter with Isabel conforms to a conversion experience, the seemingly "irresistible" nature of which hides from Pierre the possibility that "the life, the agency of grace, is the life, the agency of emotion."[77] And whether or not Melville specifically had Feuerbach in mind, he makes a similar point by constantly mixing sexual and religious rhetoric to describe Pierre's response to Isabel. For instance, the sentence that mentions the "supernaturalness" of Isabel's

---

ville later has Clarel contemplate the relation of "creative love" (IV.xviii.17) to other legends about the Madonna.

75. A pun on "Irresistible Grace" (one of the Five Points of Calvinism), which signifies man's passive role in the conversion process. The term functions similarly on pp. 49 and 87 of *Pierre.*

76. Edwards, *Works,* V: 7; VI: 176–80. Edwards's strategy is best apprehended as a response to John Locke's chapter entitled "Enthusiasm" in *An Essay Concerning Human Understanding* (1690), in which Locke complained that religious "light ... is nothing but an *ignis fatuus"* and that pretensions to "supernatural light" are contrary to reason: "The question then here is, how do I *know* that God is the revealer of this to me; that this impression is made upon my mind by his Holy Spirit, and that therefore I ought to obey it? If I know not this, how great soever the assurance is that I am possessed with, it is groundless; whatever *light* I pretend to, it is but enthusiasm" (*The Works of John Locke,* 10 vols., 11th ed. [London: T. Davidson, 1812], III: 140–42; emphasis added). As Perry Miller, in *Jonathan Edwards* (New York: W. Sloane, 1949), pp. 52–68, suggests, Edwards meets Locke's epistemological criteria by defining the Holy Spirit as a *new sense.* Edwards then has only to invoke this empiricist premise to answer more current charges of "enthusiasm" leveled against the Great Awakening by Charles Chauncy and other "Old Light" antirevivalists. (Melville several times uses the term "enthusiasm" to describe Pierre's excitement [P, 87, 90, 106, 111, 151, 152, 165, 166, 173, 175].)

77. Feuerbach, p. 186.

face also tells of Pierre's "yielding to the irresistible *climax* of her concealed emotion" (P, 46; emphasis added). Similarly, "a power...seemed *irresistibly* to draw him toward Isabel, but to draw him from another quarter—*wantonly* as it were" (P, 151; emphasis added). Also, the same paragraph that capitalizes upon the sensory emphasis of *A Divine and Supernatural Light* tells how "the face haunted [Pierre] as some imploring, and beauteous, *impassioned* ideal Madonna's haunts the morbidly longing and enthusiastic, but ever-baffled artist" (P, 48; emphasis added). Moreover, Pierre's allegiance to his duty "foetally form[s] in him" after he receives "impregnations from high *enthusiasms*" (P, 106; emphasis added). Appropriate, then, is Melville's pun: "[I]n a *transcendent* degree, womanly beauty, and not womanly ugliness, invited [Pierre] to champion the right" (P, 107; emphasis added). Although Pierre early believes that "piety hath juggled me, and taught me to revere, where I should spurn" (P, 66), his is actually an "*impulsive* subservience to the *god-like* dictation of events themselves" (P, 88; emphasis added), a "moody" (P, 135) perception of seemingly divine mandates that, like Pierre's final dream of Enceladus, Melville may have associated with the primal empire of passion.[78]

However tenuous the assumptions of Transcendental thought, one would not wish to overlook Melville's awareness of an implicit subjectivism in the moral sentiment. As he says in *Pierre*, "From without, no wonderful effect is wrought within ourselves, unless some interior, responding wonder meets it" (P, 51). More than a grain of truth, after all, exists in the anti-empiricist logic espoused in the *Democratic Review* by an advocate of Bailey's *Festus*:

A moral evil...is—destitution of soul. While feeling remains, while any native sentiment exists, there is always a foundation upon which truth and duty can rear their beautiful and holy temples. We need not despair of ourselves or others until the fountain of pure emotion is exhausted in the heart. It is vain to hope for the renovation and progress either of the individual or society through systems of faith merely addressed to the reason, or rules of life that hem in *action*, but have no influence upon *motive*. Many of the

---

78. "Under the character of the Titans," claimed a critic of Keats's "Hyperion," "the primeval empire of passion is repeated" (J. D. W., "The 'Hyperion' of John Keats," *American Whig Review*, 14 [Oct. 1851], 313). Worth considering, as well, for its correspondence to the moodiness of Pierre's seemingly prophetic intuitions is Spinoza's *Theologico-Political Treatise*, which attributes to "changing moods" so-called prophetic insights about God's character. See Ernst Cassirer, *The Philosophy of the Enlightenment*, trans. Fritz C. A. Koelln and James P. Pettegrove (Princeton, N.J.: Princeton Univ. Press, 1951), pp. 188–89.

richest spirits that abide in the world can only become disinterested, reverent of themselves, patient and faithful in duty, and hopeful of immortality, through the free, powerful and happy indulgence of their sympathies. Absolute self-denial of lofty enthusiasm is, in their case, a frightful alternative.[79]

From this angle, then, Pierre's dilemma embodies the ambiguities confronted by horological man in distinguishing a valid respect for the moral *sentiment*—which, by definition, is subjective—from sentimental impulsiveness. Phrased otherwise, Pierre embodies Melville's "problematic 'Being,'" a phrase used by one critic to characterize Melville's encounter with Coleridge's definition of the autonomous man. Says Coleridge, in *Theory of Life* (1848):

> In Man the centripetal and individualizing tendency of all Nature is itself concentred and individualized—he is a revelation of Nature! Henceforward, he is referred to himself, delivered up to his own charge; and he who stands the most on himself, and stands the firmest, is the truest, because the most individual, Man. In social and political life this acme is inter-dependence; in moral life it is independence; in intellectual life it is genius.[80]

Indeed, the subjective foundations of genius comprise what Melville surely would have recognized as the necessary inspiration for all great works of art, including *Pierre*. And in this respect, Melville conspicuously oscillates in Emerson's rainbow.[81] But even here the question returns to horological versus chronometrical perspectives on the artistic mandate, which brings us to *Pierre*'s exploration of the tie between Transcendentalism and authorship.

Certain studies, in attacking *Pierre*'s unity—and specifically, the pertinence of the novel's late "author" chapters to the book's larger concerns—overlook the interplay between "subjective Transcendentalism" and "literary Transcendentalism." The oversight is largely the product of a too-facile biographical reading: because of disappointments over the terms of his contract for *Pierre*—which coincided with hostile reviews of *Moby-Dick*—Melville

---

79. "Festus," *Democratic Review*, 17 (Dec. 1845), 460.

80. Quoted in Sanford E. Marovitz's discussion of "Melville's Problematic 'Being,'" *ESQ: A Journal of the American Renaissance*, 28 (1982), 18.

81. Sealts ("Melville and Emerson's Rainbow," pp. 62–65) details Melville's respect for noble thinking. The conclusion of my book elaborates upon this dimension of Melville's outlook.

is supposed to have been "diverted from the exploration of Pierre's psyche into a psychological analysis of his own literary career." Another study in this vein concludes that "Pierre's incestuous passion, once central to the book, becomes the subject of offhand allusion"; that Pierre's status as an author "deprived Melville of a full sense of what he was doing, in the second half and in the novel as a whole"; and that Pierre's new profession offered "nothing, in short, to help [Melville] hold to the pervading idea that impelled the first half of the book."[82] Although seemingly irrelevant, Pierre's decision to become a writer is both thematically and structurally consistent with the book's early concerns. As Brook Thomas shows, a parallel exists between *Pierre*'s emphases on incestuous and artistic procreation; Edgar A. Dryden, moreover, illustrates the "intertextual" dimension of "human relations" in *Pierre*.[83] Remaining to be addressed, however, is the way Melville's encounter with "Young America in Literature" (to borrow the title of Book XVII) is a logical outgrowth of *Pierre*'s earlier attention to subjective Transcendentalism, or the mind's incestuous union with its own desires and aspirations.

The tie between authorship and Transcendentalism surfaces in the *Boston Quarterly Review*'s celebration of Emerson's "American Scholar," the closing line of which the *Review* reiterates: "A nation of men will for the first time exist, because each believes himself inspired by the Divine Soul which also inspires all men." A "truly American literature" will be the vehicle for uttering the truths inspired in this way; and the scholar/author will be the only suitable prophet: "The theme proposed by the orator is the 'AMERICAN SCHOLAR.' Why did he not say AUTHOR?" And such authors, of whom Pierre may seem a parody,

> will utter when they are filled with the spirit.... And whenever and however any one is filled to overflowing with this grand idea of God in the soul of man, he will utter it—he must utter it. He will be an American Author. He may prophesy from the pulpit, at the Lyceum, in the schoolhouse, in the daily press, in books, in public addresses. But the burden of the prophecy will be the same: "Man measures man the world over:" Man's spirit, is from God: We are brethren.

---

82. Hershel Parker, p. 19; Parker and Higgins, pp. 188, 192, 193.
83. Brook Thomas, "The Writer's Procreative Urge in *Pierre*: Fictional Freedom or Convoluted Incest?" *Studies in the Novel*, 11 (Winter 1979), 419, 422; Dryden, p. 163. Eric J. Sundquist, in *Home as Found: Authority and Genealogy in Nineteenth-Century American Fiction* (Baltimore, Md.: Johns Hopkins Univ. Press, 1979), pp. 177–85, also treats the relation in *Pierre* between writing and incest.

Not unexpectedly, the tendency of this outlook is chronometrical sympathy and fellow-feeling, like that which Pierre initially feels as a result of Isabel's musical appeal:

> A man must live the life of Jesus, according to his power, would he be a truly American author; yes! he must live a self-forgetting minister to men, in the charities of home and acquaintance—in thankless and unnoticed sympathy,—in painful toil amid great enterprises. . . . When his heart is tuned to unison, with every chord that vibrates through the moral universe, and responds to the music of love through his whole being, let him pour out the joy of a spirit communing with the All Holy, of an Immortal stepping onward hand in hand with growing spirits on a brightening pathway to heaven.[84]

In a related context, Merton M. Sealts, Jr., suggests that *writing*—considered as an act of creativity—becomes an almost sanctifying evidence of Divine inspiration for Emerson: "'To create, to create' is ultimately 'the proof of a Divine presence,' Emerson had written in July of 1837. 'Whoever creates is God, and whatever talents are, <exhibited> if the man create not,. the pure efflux of Deity is not his.'" What follows, as suggested above, is an outlook in which *writing* becomes the ultimate bridge between the chronometrical and the horological. "Implicit," as Sealts says, "in Emerson's account of this process is his desire, in common with all men of a Transcendental persuasion, to bridge two worlds, the temporal and the eternal, *transcending* the realm of the here and now by viewing it in terms of an intellectual or spiritual world beyond it."[85]

Thus, far from having nothing in common with the novel's early concerns, Pierre's declaration, "I will write such things—I will gospelize the world anew, and show them deeper secrets than the Apocalypse!—I will write it, I will write it!" (P, 273) is a consistent outcome of the book's larger emphasis on Transcendental intuition. Still, whatever the *Boston Quarterly Review*'s praise for the Emersonian precept that "the deeper [a scholar] dives into his privatest, secretest presentiment,—to his wonder he finds this is the most . . . public, and uni-

---

84. "Emerson's Phi Beta Kappa Oration," *Boston Quarterly Review*, 1 (Jan. 1838), 108, 113–15, 116–17.

85. Merton M. Sealts, Jr., "Emerson on the Scholar," *PMLA*, 85 (March 1970), 195, 191. Sealts quotes *The Journals and Miscellaneous Notebooks of Ralph Waldo Emerson*, ed. William H. Gilman et al. (Cambridge: Belknap Press of Harvard Univ. Press, 1960–), V: 341. On the relation between writing and Transcendentalism, also see B. R. McElderry, Jr., "Emerson's Second Address on the American Scholar," *Personalist*, 39 (Autumn 1958), 371–72.

versally true,"[86] Pierre's *"Presentiment and Verification"* (P, 43) falls somewhat wide of objective truth. And that Pierre's is a peculiarly Emersonian mode of subjectivity is evident from the way Melville's narrator enumerates the ultimate truths to which Pierre's mind must open more completely if he is to be a successful author:

> He did not see... [that] the heavy unmalleable element of mere book-knowledge would not congenially weld with ... spontaneous creative thought. He would climb Parnassus with a pile of folios on his back. He did not see, that it was nothing at all to him, what other men had written; that though Plato was indeed a transcendently great man in himself, yet Plato must not be transcendently great to him (Pierre), so long as he (Pierre himself) would also do something transcendently great. He did not see that there is no such thing as a standard for the *creative* spirit; that no one great book must ever be separately regarded, and permitted to domineer with its own uniqueness upon the *creative mind*; but that all existing great works must be federated in the fancy; and so regarded as a miscellaneous whole; and then,—without dictating to his own mind, or unduly biasing it any way,—thus combined, they would prove simply an exhilarative and provocative to him. He did not see, that even when thus combined, all was but one small mite, compared to the latent infiniteness and inexhaustibility in himself.... (P, 283–84; emphasis added)

Mixed as it is with explicit allusions to *transcendent* issues, this description of the self-centered basis of both writing and "the creative mind" corresponds to any number of passages from Emerson's "American Scholar," including those quoted by the *Boston Quarterly Review* in its celebration of Emersonian genius:

> "Hence arises a mischief. The sacredness which attaches to the act of creation—the act of thought,—is transferred to the record...." "Instantly, the book becomes noxious. Colleges are built on it. Books are written on it by thinkers, not by Man Thinking. Meek young men grow up in libraries, believing it their duty to accept the views which Cicero, which Locke, which Bacon, have given, forgetful that Cicero, Locke, and Bacon were only young men in libraries when they wrote these books." "Books are good only to inspire. I had better never see a book than to be warped by its attraction clean out of my own orbit, and made a satellite instead of a system." "The soul active sees absolute truth; and utters truth, or creates...." "Books are for the scholar's idle

---

86. "Emerson's Phi Beta Kappa Oration," p. 109.

times. Then he can read God directly, the hour is too precious to be wasted in other men's transcripts of their readings." "One must be an inventor to read well. There is then creative reading, as well as creative writing."[87]

Yet, rather than concur that "I had better never see a book than to be warped by its attraction clean out of my own orbit, and made a satellite instead of a system," the narrator of *Pierre* finally retracts his enthusiasm for such extreme subjectivity: "Better," he says, "might one be pushed off into the material spaces beyond the uttermost orbit of our sun, than once feel himself fairly afloat in himself!" (P, 284).[88] It is the lesson of Swift's "A Tale of a Tub": ultimate subjectivity is madness.

Thus, whatever its dramatization of the intensely procreative and subjective bases of art, *Pierre* finally challenges what Lawrence Buell defines as the distinguishing feature of "literary Transcendentalism," the writer's "basic faith ... that if only he looks far enough inward ... he will reach the unconscious universal."[89] Also, if we can judge from "Bartleby," Melville regarded as a subjective fiction the idealist (i.e., Transcendentalist) effort to conflate mind with reality; the outcome resembled the intentional consignment of a letter to the Dead Letter Office. *Pierre*, too, challenges Transcendental notions of an "internal universal," and in ways that coincide with what we shall now explore as the book's inquiry into the political subjectivism of Transcendental thought.[90]

---

87. "Emerson's Phi Beta Kappa Oration," p. 111.

88. The narrator's shifting stance is possibly explained by Raymond J. Nelson, who holds that Pierre himself is the "author" of his own book, and that Pierre periodically betrays skepticism about assumptions and events that brought about his calamity. See "The Art of Herman Melville. The Author of *Pierre*," *Yale Review*, 59 (Winter 1970), 197–214. Sundquist (pp. 178–82) offers a similar reading.

89. See the chapter titled "Transcendentalist Self-Examination and Autobiographical Tradition," in Lawrence Buell, *Literary Transcendentalism: Style and Vision in the American Renaissance* (Ithaca, N.Y.: Cornell Univ. Press, 1973), p. 271; cf. p. 283. Sacvan Bercovitch, therefore, seems correct in regarding Pierre's novel as an instance of the Emersonian effort to create "auto-American-biography." See his "Emerson the Prophet: Romanticism, Puritanism, and Auto-American-Biography," in David Levin, ed., *Emerson: Prophecy, Metamorphosis, and Influence* (New York: Columbia Univ. Press, 1975), pp. 23–24.

90. See Sten, pp. 38–39. (Cf. Blansett, p. 102, for a related observation about Melville's response to "The American Scholar.") My use of the term "internal universal" is indebted to Bercovitch's discussion of Emerson in *The Puritan Origins of the American Self* (New Haven: Yale Univ. Press, 1975), p. 171.

As Jonathan Ashley Saxton remarked, "[B]esides its intellectual and religious aspects, [Transcendentalism] has social and political relations of the highest importance."[91] Certainly any discussion of *Pierre* would be incomplete without some attention to the way it explores, from a rather conservative stance, the political tendencies of both subjective Transcendentalism and of Young Americanism. Although an acknowledged difference exists between "Young America in Literature" and "Young America" in politics (an ultra-Democratic and interventionist outlook of the early 1850's), John Stafford has shown that the groups, with individual reservations, shared common assumptions. In fact, George Washington Peck called Young Americans "in our literature the exact counterpart of the Democratic party in our politics." Moreover, Henry Wadsworth Longfellow complained, "The *Loco-focos* are organizing a new politico-literary system. They shout Hosannas to every *loco-foco* authorling, and speak coolly of, if they do not abuse, every other. They puff *Bryant* loud and long; likewise my good friend Hawthorne...; also a Mr. O'Sullivan, once Editor of the 'Democratic Review'...."[92] Only a year after the politically oriented *Democratic Review* called for "all history...to be re-written...in the light of the democratic principle," the more literary *Boston Quarterly Review* expressed admiration for the way "the writings of French or even German scholars breathe altogether more of a democratic spirit than do those of the English.... The study of French and German literature will arrest [this aristocratic] tendency... [and] will furnish us new elements, and a broader and more democratic basis for our own."[93] To be Young American—whether in politics or in literature—was to be democratic; and Pierre possesses his fair share of Loco-focoism.

Important for our understanding of Pierre's democratic leanings is what Arthur M. Schlesinger, Jr., defines as the similarity between the Concord and Jacksonian frames of mind:

---

91. Saxton, p. 99.

92. For Stafford's remarks on the similarities between Young American political and literary concerns, see his "William A. Jones, Democratic Literary Critic," *Huntington Library Quarterly*, 12 (May 1949), 294. Peck's remark (quoted by Stafford, p. 300) is from "Hudson's Lectures," *American Whig Review*, 8 (July 1846), 40. Longfellow's comment (the first part of which Stafford [p. 295, n. 16] quotes) is from a letter of 23 July 1839 to George W. Greene, originally quoted in the "Notes" of *The American Notebooks by Nathaniel Hawthorne*, ed. Randall Stewart (New Haven, Conn.: Yale Univ. Press, 1932), p. 288, n. 62.

93. "Introduction," *Democratic Review*, 1 (Oct. 1837), 14; "Specimens of Foreign Literature," *Boston Quarterly Review*, 1 (Oct. 1838), 438–39.

Both democrat and transcendentalist agreed in asserting the rights of free mind against the pretensions of precedents or institutions. Both shared a living faith in the integrity and perfectibility of man. Both proclaimed self-reliance. Both detested special groups claiming authority to mediate between the common man and the truth. Both aimed to plant the individual squarely on his instincts, responsible only to himself and God.[94]

Alexis de Tocqueville seems also to have perceived the Transcendental tendencies of democracy: "[N]othing is more repugnant to the human mind in an age of equality than the idea of subjection to forms. Men living at such times.... are unmoved by ceremonial observances, and they are predisposed to attach a secondary importance to the details of public worship." Moreover, the compatibility of Transcendentalism and Jacksonianism has impressed a more recent historian, who shows that "Jacksonians took the same ground as Transcendentalists: against 'Understanding,' or methodical thought, they appealed to 'Reason,' that is, intuition."[95]

Whereas, then, a contributor to the *Dial* could describe the typical Unitarian as a "Whig in his Politics,...and a conservative in everything," the *American Whig Review* could smugly respond that Transcendentalism "adopts a philanthropic, and usually a democratic phrase." The Transcendentalists, however, were hardly abashed at the charge. "Democracy is better for us," wrote Emerson, "because the religious sentiment of the present time accords better with it." And in much the same way, the *Boston Quarterly Review* regarded democracy as the by-product of intuitive epistemology: "The democrat is...he who believes that Reason, the light which shines out from God's throne, shines into the heart of every man.... It is only on the reality of this inner light, and on the fact, that it is universal, in all men, and in every man, that you can found a democracy."[96] Perhaps to be expected, then, was the messianic application of these ideas by such democrats as George Bancroft and Jonathan Ashley

---

94. Arthur M. Schlesinger, Jr., *The Age of Jackson* (Boston: Little, Brown, 1946), p. 381.

95. Alexis de Tocqueville, *Democracy in America*, trans. Henry Reeve, part II (New York: J. & H. G. Langley, 1840), p. 25; John William Ward, *Andrew Jackson—Symbol for an Age* (London: Oxford Univ. Press, 1953), p. 50; cf. pp. 53, 56–57, 74, 76.

96. W. D. Wilson, "The Unitarian Movement in New England," *Dial*, 1 (April 1841), 417; "The Idealist: A Socratic Dialogue," *American Whig Review*, 3 (March 1846), 258; Emerson, "Politics" (*Essays, Second Series*), in *Works*, III: 207; "Norton on the Evidences of Christianity," *Boston Quarterly Review*, 2 (Jan. 1839), 111. Cf. Emerson's belief that "the rights of all persons are equal, in virtue to their access to reason" ("Politics," p. 201).

Saxton, the first of whom thought that "the possession of this higher faculty...renders advancement possible"; the second, that all "political progress" presupposes egalitarianism "based, like the faith in the All-perfect, in the intuitions of man's soul."[97] Less optimistically, though, the *American Whig Review* cautioned, "[W]hen men have cast off authority in religious matters, they are but a step from casting it off in civil matters." The *Whig* also warned of a direct tie between the "spiritual revolution" of Kantian metaphysics and the "material revolution in France": "On both sides of the Rhine do we see the same rupture with the past; all respect for tradition is renounced." Nor did this lesson go unnoticed by Emerson, whose Divinity School Address calls for the demise of that "eastern monarchy of ... Christianity" at Cambridge, Massachusetts, and proclaims, "Wherever a man comes, there comes revolution."[98]

Related to the political tendencies of intuitive thought is the "transcendental" nature of Pierre's "usurper mood" (P, 180). More obviously, of course, Charles Millthorpe, Pierre's estranged boyhood companion, preoccupies himself with "stumping the State" and with publishing his "Ultimate Transcendentals" (P, 280). But in a subtler way, Pierre's career embodies the Transcendental radicalism of which Jonathan Ashley Saxton spoke in discoursing upon social reform in a country "whose very existence is transcendental; whose right to be a nation was ...legitimated upon the intuitive truth of the principle of the equality and brotherhood of universal man."[99] Perhaps for similar reasons, Melville emphasizes Pierre's Revolutionary family background, his "Fourth of July morning" strolls, and his readings in "the History of the Revolutionary War"—and all in the same paragaph cautioning that readers "will pronounce Pierre a thorough-going Democrat in time; perhaps a little too Radical altogether" (P, 12–13).[100]

---

97. George Bancroft, "On the Progress of Civilization," *Boston Quarterly Review*, 1 (Oct. 1838), 390; Saxton, pp. 111, 113.

98. "Religious Union of Associationists," *American Whig Review*, 5 (May 1847), 498; "More Gossip from a New Contributor," *American Whig Review*, 6 (Sept. 1847), 321; Emerson, Divinity School Address, in *Works*, I: 130, 144. For the revolutionary tendencies of Transcendental thought, see Henry Alonzo Myers, *Are All Men Equal?* (Ithaca, N.Y.: Cornell Univ. Press, 1945), pp. 38, 40; Stephen E. Whicher, *Freedom and Fate: An Inner Life of Ralph Waldo Emerson* (Philadelphia: Univ. of Pennsylvania Press, 1953), p. 56.

99. Saxton, p. 101. Since Saxton here addresses social reform in the area of slavery, my emphasis on *Pierre*'s encounter with the democratic and revolutionary tendencies of Transcendentalism is consistent with what Carolyn L. Karcher, in *Shadow Over the Promised Land* (Baton Rouge: Louisiana State Univ. Press, 1980), pp. 101–2, has recognized as abolitionist overtones in Pierre's effort to assist Isabel.

100. For discussions of Pierre's democratic spirit in rebelling against his mother's

In considering the political aspect of Pierre's response to Isabel, we should note a possible connection with "that transcendental French Revolution," the inspiration of which lay in the inequalities "by which man had so long been defrauded of his *birthright*."[101] Pierre's "great life-revolution, the receipt of Isabel's letter" (P, 225; cf. 92) may receive at least some of its impetus from Pierre's recollection that Isabel's mother supposedly escaped from France during the Reign of Terror; and Pierre claims to "know all about . . . the French Revolution" from "the little history" (P, 75) of the affair given him by Aunt Dorothea. But whatever the historically definable reasons for the French uprising, Melville emphasizes the subjective fallacy of Pierre's more private revolt by remarking that "there is a dark, mad mystery in some hearts, which, sometimes, during the tyranny of a usurper *mood*, leads them to be all eagerness to cast off the most intense beloved bond, as a hindrance to the attainment of whatever *transcendental* object that usurper *mood* so tyranically suggests" (P, 180; emphasis added).[102]

Pierre's political and authorial concerns may, then, ultimately take into account Emerson's progression from denying the authority of historical Christianity to denying the objective status of history itself: "All history becomes subjective," wrote Emerson; "in other words there is properly no history, only biography."[103] Thus, the suggestion that "Pierre assumes that as an author he will wield an authority that is not subject to confining and restricting definitions from the past"[104] should not be considered in isolation from the more generally Young American and Transcendental effort to obliterate the authority of the Past. The attempt, after all, is evident in John L. O'Sullivan's views on "The Great Nation of Futurity"; in the *Dial*'s pronouncement that "The Future Is Better than the Past"; in Walt Whitman's belief that "mere precedent is nothing, and will oftener warrant wrong than right"; and in Jonathan Ashley Saxton's conviction that "all monuments, from their very nature and design, belong to the past almost from the moment of

---

domination, in abandoning the rights to a nearly feudal estate, and in his inconstancy to Lucy, see Stern, p. 172; Murray, pp. xxxiii, xcix.

101. Saxton, p. 105 (emphasis added); cf. p. 110.

102. Worth noting here is the way Melville points out the revolutionary tendencies of Transcendentalism in *Clarel* (IV.xx.99–136), especially in Ungar's reference to the French Revolutionaries as "Transcended rebel angels!" (135). Possibly Melville knew Thomas Carlyle's thoughts about how "frightful it is when a Nation, rending asunder its Constitutions and Regulations. . . , becomes *trans*cendental; and must now seek its wild way through the New, Chaotic, . . . in that domain of what is called the Passions; of what we call the Miracles and the Portents!" (*The French Revolution* [1837], in *Thomas Carlyle's Works*, 18 vols. [London: Chapman & Hall, 1904–06], I: 514).

103. Emerson, "History" (*Essays, First Series*), in *Works*, II: 10.

104. Dryden, p. 151.

their erection. As Humanity by the laws of its being, must continue to advance, it will leave its forms and institutions, of which permanence is necessarily a chief object, behind it."[105] And highly appropriate for its bearing on *Pierre* is the way these categories imply a merging of the horological and chronometrical; as one scholar of Emerson's "History" puts it, "That this course of thought involves the reduction of history to an illusion and of experience to a pin-point present, and finally the obliteration of the distinction between contingent and absolute Being, Emerson is well aware."[106]

Pierre likewise regrets having "hoarded up momentoes and monuments of the past; [and having] been a worshipper of all heir-looms" (P, 197) and almost anarchically rejects time-proven values and hereditary persuasions:

> Nor now, though profoundly sensible that his whole previous moral being was overturned, and that for him the fair structure of the world must, in some then unknown way, be entirely rebuilded again, from the lowermost corner stone up; nor now did Pierre torment himself with the thought of that last desolation; and how the desolate place was to be made flourishing again. He seemed to feel that in his deepest soul, lurked an indefinite but potential faith, which could rule in the interregnum of all hereditary beliefs, and circumstantial persuasions. Not wholly, he felt, was his soul in anarchy. (P, 87)

Pierre's attitude here may be extreme enough to warrant Edmund Burke's outcries against revolutionaries who, "unmindful of what they have received from their ancestors, . . . think it among their rights to cut off the entail, or commit waste on the inheritance, by destroying at their pleasure the whole original fabric of their society."[107] Indeed, in his failure to consider "how the desolate place was to be made flourishing again," Pierre dramatizes Melville's most essential quarrel with

---

105. John L. O'Sullivan, "The Great Nation of Futurity," *Democratic Review*, 6 (Nov. 1839), 426–30; Clapp, pp. 57–58; Whitman, "Stark Democracy's Destructiveness," in *The Gathering of the Forces by Walt Whitman: Editorials, Essays, Literary and Dramatic Reviews . . . Written by Walt Whitman as Editor of the "Brooklyn Daily Eagle" in 1846 and 1847*, ed. Cleveland Rodgers and John Black, 2 vols. (New York: G. P. Putnam's Sons, 1920), II: 14; Saxton, p. 106.

106. Robert A. Caponigri, "Brownson and Emerson: Nature and History," *New England Quarterly*, 18 (Sept. 1945), 371.

107. Burke, *Reflections on the Revolution in France* (1790), in *The Works of the Right Honourable Edmund Burke*, 8 vols. (London: Henry G. Bohn, 1854–58), II: 367. As early as *Mardi* (pp. 78–79) Melville alludes to Burke's *Reflections*. We shall see below that *Billy Budd* more directly illustrates Melville's encounter with Burkean conservatism.

Emersonian radicalism: "[N]ever will the pullers-down be able to cope with the builders-up. And this pulling down is easy enough—a keg of powder blew up Block's Monument—but the man who applied the match, could not, alone, build such a pile to save his soul from the sharkmaw of the Devil" (L, 79). And *Pierre* shows that the motives for such destructiveness often originate in the innermost desires and impulses of the human heart rather than in any Transcendental correspondence between the heavens and human nature.

In this respect, *Pierre's* preoccupation with the human condition foreshadows the concerns of *The Confidence-Man*. Emerson, we know, held that "the theological problems of original sin, origin of evil, predestination and the like.... never ... darkened across any man's road who did not go out of his way to seek them." But in its demonstration that behavior is often determined by "an infinite series of infinitely involved and untraceable foregoing occurrences" (P, 67), *Pierre* comes closer to Jonathan Edwards's outlook on human nature.[108] Moreover, in its emphasis on the ambiguities surrounding truth and moral distinctions, as well as in its skepticism concerning disinterested love and chronometrical standards of morality, *Pierre* offers a formidable challenge to one of the most popular Transcendental arguments for human regeneracy. "Consider," said George Ripley, in his discourse on "The Divine Elements in Human Nature," "these four principles of human nature, the power of perceiving Truth—of recognising moral distinctions—of exercising disinterested love—and of aspiring after illimitable perfection, and tell me, if we were not made to become partakers of the Divine Nature?"[109] Readers of *Pierre* would probably be hard-pressed to respond in the affirmative; at best, perhaps, we might concur that "if the human heart contains the germs of the noblest plants, it also contains the germs of the vilest weeds."[110] These issues, and the christological and political interplay among them, appear to have remained prime concerns of Melville's in *The Confidence-Man, Clarel,* and *Billy Budd.*

---

108. Emerson, "Spiritual Laws" (*Essays, First Series*), in *Works,* II: 132. I have in mind Edwards's treatise on *The Freedom of the Will* (*Works,* II: 11–300), which supports a Calvinist outlook by denying man's essential freedom. All actions, argues Edwards, result from preconditioned motives. Melville, as existing scholarship shows, drew upon *Freedom of the Will* in "Bartleby." See Allan Moore Emery, "The Alternatives of Melville's 'Bartleby,'" *Nineteenth-Century Fiction,* 31 (Sept. 1976), 170–87.

109. Ripley, *Discourses on the Philosophy of Religion,* p. 40.

110. Hudson, "Festus," *American Whig Review,* 5 (Feb. 1847), 141–42.

C H A P T E R VI

"The Cross Scarce Needs a Word": *The Confidence-Man* and *Clarel*

An appropriate introduction to the April 1 charade aboard Melville's *Fidèle* is Walt Whitman's amusement over celebrating April Fools' Day only once a year: "AHA! *this* is all Fools' day, is it? What right or reason has anyone to select out *one* day from the whole year, and give it such a name? Just as if our world was weak and wicked a three hundred and sixty-fifth fraction of its existence only." Less skeptical, however, was George Bancroft, who, in "The Progress of Mankind" (1854), applauded the way "the course of civilization flows on like a mighty river through a boundless valley, calling to the streams from every side to swell its current, which is always growing wider, and deeper, and clearer, as it rolls along. Let us trust ourselves," he adds, "upon its bosom without fear; nay, rather with *confidence and joy*."[1] Whether or not Melville knew Bancroft's essay, *The Confidence-Man*'s description of "the dashing and all-fusing spirit of the West, whose type is the Mississippi itself, which, uniting the streams of the most distant and opposite zones, pours them along, helter-skelter, in one cosmopolitan and confident tide" (CM, 6) invokes the progressive attitudes that the book finally subverts. These attitudes resemble those in the opening issue of the *Democratic Review*, which foreshadows the concerns of *The Confidence-Man* by declaring democracy

> the cause of Humanity. It has faith in human nature. It believes in its essential equality and fundamental goodness....It is the

1. Whitman, "Motley's Your Only Wear," *Brooklyn Daily Eagle* (1 April 1846), in *The Gathering of the Forces by Walt Whitman: Editorials, Essays, Literary and Dramatic Reviews ... Written by Walt Whitman as Editor of the "Brooklyn Daily Eagle" in 1846 and 1847*, ed. Cleveland Rodgers and John Black, 2 vols. (New York: G. P. Putnam's Sons, 1920), II: 96; George Bancroft, *Literary and Historical Miscellanies* (New York: Harper & Brothers, 1855), p. 516 (emphasis added).

cause of philanthropy.... It is, moreover, a cheerful creed, a creed of high hope and universal love, noble and ennobling; while all others... imply a distrust of mankind, and the natural moral principles infused into it by its creator.[2]

This celebration of democracy and human nature is crucial for our purposes because it closely approaches the liberal Christian assumptions satirized by William R. Weeks's *The Pilgrim's Progress in the Nineteenth Century*, in which a character named "Liberal" declares,

[T]here is certainly something very pleasant in thinking of others as favorably as we can.... If a stranger comes to my house, and calls himself a pilgrim, I am unwilling to be suspicious of him, and by a severe scrutiny to give him reason to believe that I am disposed to think every man an impostor. I am rather disposed to treat every man as if I thought him honest, till he proves himself otherwise.[3]

Ample precedent, then, exists for the "fresh and liberal construction" (CM, 46) espoused by the Confidence-Man in gulling his victims into what Ernest Lee Tuveson describes as a creed of *tout est bien*, the substance of which "is that for millennia mankind has been laboring under a monstrous delusion: it has mistakenly thought that evil is integral to nature and that evil is ingrained in the human heart."[4] This view coincides with the Unitarian outlook that the Confidence-Man offers up in his glorification of human nature, in his rejection of "Saint Augustine on Original Sin" (CM, 109), and in his at least nominal disbelief in imputed sin (CM, 107). There is also a Unitarian ring to the Confidence-Man's remark that "each member of the human guild is worthy of respect" (CM, 171); indeed, "Men have as yet no just respect for themselves," claimed William Ellery Channing, "and of consequence no just respect for others."[5] The Confidence-

---

2. "Introduction," *Democratic Review*, 1 (Oct. 1837), 11.

3. William R. Weeks, *The Pilgrim's Progress in the Nineteenth Century* (New York: M. W. Dodd, 1848), pp. 153–54. This book was an expanded version of a satire on liberal Christianity first published in the *Utica Christian Repository* (1824–26). See David E. Smith's informative chapter on Weeks in *John Bunyan in America* (Bloomington: Indiana Univ. Press, 1966), pp. 20–25. For the specifically Unitarian associations of the term "Liberal Christian," see Clarence H. Faust, "The Background of the Unitarian Opposition to Transcendentalism," *Modern Philology*, 35 (Feb. 1938), 311.

4. Ernest Lee Tuveson, "The Creed of the Confidence-Man," *English Literary History*, 33 (June 1966), 253.

5. Channing, "Honor Due All Men," in *The Works of William E. Channing, D.D.* (Boston: American Unitarian Assoc., 1895), p. 67.

Man's thoughts on the "final benignity" of "heaven's law" (CM, 84) and the possibility that "mankind ... present as pure a moral specta- cle as the purest angel could wish" (CM, 103) bring to mind Armi- nian ideas about God's benevolence and the absurdity of depreciating moral virtue.[6] Satirized, too, as shown by current scholarship, are the liberal ideas of William Cullen Bryant, Theodore Parker, and Horace Greeley— as well as the bastardized forms of Christianity that Orestes A. Brownson came to think characteristic of the cults which had ear- lier captured his Transcendental sympathies.[7]

Of course, Melville also dramatizes how misanthropy can be just as harmful as naive liberal confidence and how a supposedly "true sight of sin" can sustain proslavery apologetics and perpetuate modes of historiography that justify the extermination of Indians.[8] Even- handedly, however, *The Confidence-Man* shows that a failure to acknowledge depravity has serious practical consequences and impor-

---

6. See, for example, Charles Chauncy, *The Benevolence of the Deity* (1784); Jona- than Mayhew, *Two Sermons on the Nature, Extent, and the Perfection of the Divine Goodness* (1763); Lemuel Briant, *The Absurdity and Blasphemy of Depreciating Moral Virtue* (1749).

Melville's general familiarity with both the orthodox and liberal Christian tradi- tions is suggested by his mother's membership in the Dutch Reformed Church and by his paternal grandfather's and father's Arminian and Unitarian leanings. See William H. Gilman, *Melville's Early Life and "Redburn"* (New York: New York Univ. Press, 1951), pp. 21–23, 38; Newton Arvin, *Herman Melville* (New York: William Sloane, 1950), pp. 30–35. Moreover, as Merton M. Sealts, Jr., shows, in *Melville's Reading: A Check-List of Books Owned and Borrowed* (Madison: Univ. of Wisconsin Press, 1966), item 496, in 1851 Melville acquired John Taylor's *The Scripture Doctrine of Original Sin Proposed to Free and Candid Examination* (1710), which became a primer for New England Arminians, later evoking Jonathan Edwards's *The Great Doctrine of Original Sin Defended* (1758). For further suggestions about Melville's familiarity with debates surrounding orthodox and liberal Christianity, see T. Walter Herbert, Jr., *"Moby-Dick" and Calvinism: A World Dismantled* (New Brunswick, N.J.: Rutgers Univ. Press, 1977), pp. 23–68.

7. See Helen P. Trimpi, "Three of Melville's Confidence Men: William Cullen Bry- ant, Theodore Parker, and Horace Greeley," *Texas Studies in Literature and Language*, 21 (Fall 1979), 368–95; Carolyn L. Karcher, "Spiritualism and Philanthropy in Brown- son's *The Spirit Rapper* and Melville's *The Confidence-Man*," *ESQ: A Journal of the American Renaissance*, 25 (1979), 26–36. Of course, studies such as these presuppose the by now generally accepted view that part of *The Confidence-Man*'s satire is leveled at a specifically Emersonian variety of liberalism. See Egbert S. Oliver, "Melville's Picture of Emerson and Thoreau in 'The Confidence-Man,'" *College English*, 8 (Nov. 1946), 61–72; Elizabeth S. Foster, "Introduction" and "Explanatory Notes" to *The Confidence-Man: His Masquerade* (New York: Hendricks House, 1954), pp. lxxiii–lxxxii, 351–61.

8. See Carolyn L. Karcher, *Shadow Over the Promised Land: Slavery, Race, and Violence in Melville's America* (Baton Rouge: Louisiana State Univ. Press, 1980), pp. 217, 243; Joyce Sparer Adler, *War in Melville's Imagination* (New York: New York Univ. Press, 1981), pp. 111–32, esp. 119–21.

tant doctrinal ramifications for the liberal Christian outlook more generally characteristic of nineteenth-century *Fidèle*. To these concerns let us now turn in a discussion of the book's epistemological drama, which first undermines the foundations of liberal confidence in man's faculties of perception but which then shows many of the *Fidèle*'s company to teeter on the brink of both infidelity and philosophical skepticism because they willingly ignore whatever "moral evidence" is proffered them concerning the reality of evil.

To understand the impact of *The Confidence-Man*'s skeptical epistemology, recall how liberal Christian claims to regeneracy presuppose the mind's ability to distinguish truth. "To reject human nature and declare it unworthy of confidence," claimed Orestes A. Brownson, "is—whether we know it or not—to reject all grounds of certainty, and to declare that we have no means for distinguishing truth from falsehood."[9] Nineteenth-century progressivist and liberal religious thought generally embraced the assumption that "the progress of man consists in this, that he himself arrives at the perception of truth"[10] and that

> [t]o confide in God, we must first confide in the faculties by which He is apprehended. . . . A trust in our ability to distinguish between truth and falsehood is implied in every act of belief. . . . In affirming the existence and perfections of God, we suppose and affirm the existence in ourselves of faculties which correspond to these sublime objects, and which are fitted to discern them. Religion is a conviction and an act of the human soul, so that in denying confidence to the one, we subvert the truth and claims of the other.[11]

Indicative of Melville's familarity with ideas such as these is the section of *Mardi* in which the Old Man of (Unitarian/Transcendentalist) Serenia says, "[M]en's faculties are Oro-given"; in fact, his belief that "to do [God's] bidding, then, some new faculty must be vouchsafed, whereby to apprehend aright" (M, 626) may even echo Channing's remark, "To confide in God, we must first confide in the faculties by which He is apprehended." Yet *The Confidence-Man*'s dramatization of man's inability to detect fraud—a point mirrored in the book's evasive and often confusing form—shows human nature to be unworthy

9. *New Views of Christianity* (1836), in *The Works of Orestes A. Brownson*, ed. Henry F. Brownson, 20 vols. (Detroit: Thorndike Nourse, 1882–87), IV: 34.

10. Bancroft, p. 484.

11. Channing, "The Moral Argument Against Calvinism" (1809), in *Works*, p. 462.

of confidence when judged in the context of rationalistic liberal criteria for regeneracy. Aptly, then, the Confidence-Man acts out the dictum, expressed earlier in *Pierre*, that persons who "slide into the most practically Calvinistic view of humanity . . . hold every man at bottom a fit subject for the coarsest ribaldry and jest" (P, 232).

The exact mechanism by which Melville unsettles liberal confidence in the faculties of the human mind is best approached by way of one critic's remark that "the paramount issue" of *The Confidence-Man* "is the quality, the how and why, of belief."[12] Still, neither this dimension of the text nor what other scholars discuss as the debasement and manipulation of language in *The Confidence-Man*[13] can be fully understood without reference to a definition of "confidence" that has lain dormant in the midst of otherwise fruitful inquiries into Melville's knowledge of actual confidence men or literary types of the Confidence-Man.[14] The book's assault upon man's ability to distinguish truth dismantles the logic of "moral certainty"; in considering this issue it is useful to examine *An Essay Concerning Human Understanding* (1690), in which John Locke shows it "impossible for us to know, that this or that quality or idea has a necessary connexion with a real essence, of which we have no idea at all." For this reason, "few general propositions [are] to be made concerning substances, which can carry with them undoubted certainty."[15] Although Locke was not the first philoso-

---

12. Warwick Wadlington, *The Confidence Game in American Literature* (Princeton, N.J.: Princeton Univ. Press, 1975), p. 147; cf. p. 145. More recently, Gary Lindberg, in *The Confidence Man in American Literature* (New York and Oxford: Oxford Univ. Press, 1982), pp. 28–34, offers an illuminating discussion of the relation between belief and the forging of identity in *The Confidence-Man*.

13. See, for example, Cecelia Tichi, "Melville's Craft and Theme of Language Debased in *The Confidence-Man*," *English Literary History*, 39 (Dec. 1972), 639–58; Henry Sussman, "The Deconstructor as Politician in Melville's *The Confidence-Man*," *Glyph: Johns Hopkins Textual Studies*, 4 (1978), 32–56; Steven E. Kemper, *"The Confidence-Man*: A Knavishly Packed Deck," *Studies in American Fiction*, 8 (Spring 1980), 23–35; William M. Ramsey, "The Moot Points of Melville's Indian-Hating," *American Literature*, 52 (May 1980), 224–35; Philip F. Gura, *Wisdom of Words: Language, Theology and Literature in the New England Renaissance* (Middletown, Conn.: Wesleyan Univ. Press, 1981), pp. 150–53.

14. See Johannes D. Bergmann, "The Original Confidence-Man," *American Quarterly*, 21 (Fall 1969), 560–77; Paschal Reeves, "The 'Deaf Mute' Confidence Man: Melville's Impostor in Action," *Modern Language Notes*, 75 (Jan. 1960), 18–20; John W. Shroeder, "Sources and Symbols for Melville's Confidence-Man," *PMLA*, 66 (June, 1951), 363–80; H. Bruce Franklin, *The Wake of the Gods: Melville's Mythology* (Stanford, Calif: Stanford Univ. Press, 1963), pp. 153–87; Thomas L. McHaney, *"The Confidence-Man* and Satan's Disguises in *Paradise Lost*," *Nineteenth-Century Fiction*, 30 (Sept. 1975), 200–206.

15. Locke, *An Essay Concerning Human Understanding* (1690), in *The Works of*

pher to acknowledge this gap between perception and knowledge,[16] he
was among the earliest to formulate a theory of "moral certainty," in
which sensory experience was thought to offer degrees of *confidence*—
confidence that accepts probability as a reliable guide in the absence of
absolute knowledge. Thus, while sensory experience can never be an entirely accurate index to knowledge, Locke believed it offered "an assurance that deserves the name of knowledge. If we persuade ourselves,
that our faculties act and inform us right, concerning the existence of
those objects that affect them, it cannot pass for an ill-grounded *confidence*" (IV.11.3; emphasis added). Moreover, according to Locke,
"[T]he confidence that our faculties do not herein deceive us is the
greatest assurance we are capable of, concerning the existence of material beings" (IV.11.3). And while *confidence* may not be *knowledge*, its
foundation in probability allows for practical certainty:

> And therefore though it be highly probable, that millions of men
> do now exist, yet, whilst I am alone writing this, I have not that
> certainty of it which we strictly call knowledge; though the great
> likelihood of it puts me past doubt, and it be reasonable for me to
> do several things upon the confidence that there are men...now
> in the world: but this is probability, not knowledge. (IV.11.9)

From here, Locke proceeds to define *Judgment* as "the faculty which God
has given man to supply the want of clear and certain knowledge";
judgment exercised upon "truths delivered in words" is "called assent
or dissent" (IV.14.3), and the highest degree of assent is *confidence*:

> Our knowledge, as has been shown, being very narrow, and
> we not happy enough to find certain truth in everything which we
> have occasion to consider; most of the propositions we think, rea-
> son, discourse, nay act upon, are such, as we cannot have un-
> doubted knowledge of their truth; yet some of them border so near
> upon certainty, that we make no doubt at all about them; but as-
> sent to them as firmly, and act, according to that assent, as resolute-
> ly, as if they were infallibly demonstrated, and that our knowledge

---

John Locke, 10 vols. (London: T. Davison, 1812), book IV, chapter 6, parts 5 and 7.
Further citations will appear parenthetically. For Melville's familiarity with Locke's
Essay, see Robert Zoellner, *The Salt-Sea Mastodon: A Reading of "Moby-Dick"* (Los
Angeles: Univ. of California Press, 1973), pp. 1–28.

  16. Richard Popkin, in *The History of Scepticism from Erasmus to Descartes* (1964;
rpt. New York: Harper & Row, 1968), p. 103, says that "Bayle, in his article on Pyrrho,
credited Gassendi [1592–1655] with having introduced Sextus Empiricus into modern
thought, and thereby having opened our eyes to the fact that 'the qualities of bodies that
strike our senses are only appearances.'"

of them was perfect and certain. But there being degrees herein from the very neighbourhood of certainty and demonstration, quite down to improbability and unlikeness, even to the confines of impossibility; and also degrees of assent from full assurance and *confidence*, quite down to conjecture, doubt, and *distrust*. (IV.15.2; emphasis added)

The last segment of this passage anticipates the range of trust aboard the *Fidèle*, from full assurance and confidence quite down to the barber's sign of "NO TRUST." Melville had already revealingly capitalized upon the rhetoric of moral certainty in Ishmael's remark that, while "the certainty [involved in calculating the age of a whale]... is far from demonstrable, yet it has the savor of analogical probability" (MD, 282). And in *Mardi* Taji uses a form of the word "confidence" in the precise sense mentioned by Locke.[17] Good reason, therefore, exists for probing deeper into the backgrounds of this concept, the rationalistic premises of which are so crucial to the assault upon liberal optimism in *The Confidence-Man*.[18]

In the nineteenth century the most detailed discourse on moral evidence was James Edward Gambier's *Introduction to the Study of Moral Evidence; or that Species of Reasoning which Relates to Matters of Fact and Practice* (1806). Gambier inquires into the probable certainty entailed in "Personal observation," "Testimony," "Observations of others," "Report," and "Analogy"—techniques that all surface in the wiles of Melville's Confidence-Man. Like Locke (whose theory of probability he cites [p. iii]), Gambier discusses "moral certainty" in terms of "confidence" and "complete confidence." He investigates this subject not only for its bearing on "the Truth of Christianity" but for its relation as well to everyday life, such as that aboard Melville's *Fidèle*: "[I]n our transactions with men who are as yet strangers to us, we deal with

---

17. See Taji's description of a sailor's susceptibility to "skeptical" surmises in a "calm": "At first he is taken by surprise, never having dreamt of a state of existence where existence itself seems suspended.... His faith in Malte Brun ... begins to fail; for the geography, which from his boyhood he had implicitly *confided* in, always assured him, that though expatiating all over the globe, the sea was at least margined by land. That over against America, for example, was Asia. But it is a calm, and he grows madly skeptical" (M, 9; emphasis added).

18. Although I concentrate below on the Lockean heritage of predominantly nineteenth-century ideas about moral evidence, germane to the evolution of the concept is Peter Ramus's distinction between "artificial" and "inartificial" arguments (see Perry Miller, *The New England Mind: The Seventeenth Century* [1939; rpt. Boston: Beacon Press, 1961], pp. 129–30) and the preoccupation of seventeenth- and early-eighteenth-century continental Deists and logicians with theories of probability (see Garry Wills, *Inventing America: Jefferson's Declaration of Independence* [New York: Doubleday, 1978], pp. 139–40).

them with confidence or distrust, according to what we know, from our own experience or that of others, of the honesty or dishonesty of persons under similar circumstances."[19] Sixteen years later, yet another Englishman spoke of "confidence" in this way, claiming that "we are called upon to arm the victim of sophistry with an honest confidence in the reality of human knowledge, and the worth of that conviction which is derived from the calculation of probabilities. This is the object, and ... the effect of the study of moral evidence."[20]

Americans, too, capitalized upon the rhetoric of moral certainty. Andrews Norton, for instance, responded to the intuitionalist thrust of Emerson's Divinity School Address by insisting, "There can be no intuition, no direct perception of the truth of Christianity, no metaphysical certainty"; men "must act on probabilities alone. . . . It would be . . . insanity . . . to shake our confidence in the facts, of which human testimony and our experiences assure us."[21] Likewise compatible with the concerns of *The Confidence-Man* is Lyman Beecher's *Lectures on Scepticism* (1835). In response to infidel attacks upon both probability and human testimony as reliable indices to epistemological certitude or religious belief in miracles, Beecher maintains:

> The difference between demonstration and moral certainty, is, that in one case the mind sees the object of comparison, and sees the result, which, of course, is knowledge; but in the other, derives its confidence from the perception of probabilities multiplied till they produce *confidence, or moral certainty.* On the whole, consciousness, intuition, the senses, the evidence of testimony, and analogy, all rest on the supposition, that things are as they seem to be, and will continue to manifest the same attributes and results.

"Scepticism," says Beecher, is that "state of mind in which these constitutional grounds of certainty fail to produce confidence."[22] We have but to proceed to *The Confidence-Man* to see how its epistemological assumptions exploit the rhetoric of moral certainty, first to undermine

---

19. I quote from James Edward Gambier, *An Introduction to the Study of Moral Evidence* (1806), 3rd ed. (London: R. Gilbert, 1824), pp. xiv–xv, 60, 61, vii, 64.

20. Walter A. Shirley, "The Study of Moral Evidence" (1822), *Oxford English Prize Essays*, 4 (1836), 33.

21. Andrews Norton, *A Discourse on the Latest Form of Infidelity* (Cambridge, Mass.: John Owen, 1839), pp. 32–33.

22. Lyman Beecher, *Lectures on Scepticism, Delivered in the Park Street Church, Boston, and in the Second Presbyterian Church, Cincinnati* (Cincinnati: Corey and Fairbank, 1835), pp. 10–11; emphasis added. Subsequent quotations from *Lectures* will be cited parenthetically.

the moral argument against Calvinism by pointing out the ambiguities surrounding the perception of truth—and then to enmesh in a web of theological skepticism those persons aboard the *Fidèle* who refuse to acknowledge the genuineness of whatever evidence exists for recognizing human iniquity.

The Confidence-Man's ironic use of moral certainty to question the mind's capacity for distinguishing truth is evident, for instance, in chapter 10, where a merchant wishes to purchase stock in the Black Rapids Coal Company. Significantly, the Confidence-Man cautions his victim about the company's Transfer Book: "[H]ow do you know that it may not be a bogus one?... It might suggest doubts." Refusing, however, to examine the book, the merchant justifies his faith by distinguishing between knowledge and moral certainty: "Doubts, may be, it might suggest, but *not knowledge;* for how, by examining the book, should I think I knew any more than I now think I do; since, if it be the true book, I think it so already; and since if it be otherwise, then *I have never seen* the true one, and don't know what that ought to look like" (CM, 48; emphasis added). The merchant's position here corresponds to Beecher's explanation that "the difference between demonstration and moral certainty, is, that in one case the mind *sees the object of comparison,* and sees the result, which, of course, is *knowledge;* but in the other, derives its confidence from the perception of probabilities multiplied till they produce confidence, or moral certainty" (p. 10; emphasis added). The "true book" to which the merchant alludes has much in common with Beecher's "object of comparison," while his overall confidence rests beyond evidence, in probability, or moral certainty. Appropriately, the Confidence-Man responds, "Your logic I will not criticize, but your confidence I admire" (CM, 48).

The Confidence-Man himself distinguishes between primary evidence and probability by trying to convince the one-legged customhouse officer of Black Guinea's innocence: "I think that without personal proof I can convince you of your mistake. For I put it to you, is it reasonable to suppose that a man with brains, sufficient to act such a part as you say, would take all that trouble, and run all that hazard, for the mere sake of those few paltry coppers...?" (CM, 27–28). Prevalent here is the erroneous belief that moral evidence always affords a degree of predictability that, in the absence of primary demonstration, merits confidence or assent. This assumption also informs the Herb Doctor's discourse with the sickly miser, to whom he proffers medicine. "What herbs?" asks his incapacitated victim, "and the nature of them? And the reasons for giving them?" Insisting these matters "cannot be made known," the Confidence-Man chides the sickly miser for being "sick, and a philosopher." A "sick philosopher," he claims, "is incurable . . . because he has no confidence" (CM, 68). Interestingly, this exchange finds an analog in Beecher's description of the philosophical sick man, who, rejecting moral evidence, settles for nothing short of demonstrative certainty in both prognosis and prescription:

> Let one of these philosophers put in practice his own maxim, and we shall perceive his folly. He sends for his physician—Sir, can you demonstrate that I am sick, and what ails me, and what will cure me? Not exactly,—but I perceive symptoms of indisposition upon you. I know by observation what disease they indicate; and by experience, I have ascertained the remedy. None of your quackery—I am not a man to be imposed upon. Demonstrate to me . . . what will cure me, or I have no further occasion for your services. (pp. 19–20)

Although Melville's sick man initially evades the Confidence-Man's appeals, he, like the merchant of chapter 10, eventually surrenders his wish for demonstrative knowledge and joins the ranks of the duped: "The sick man's *knowledge* did not warrant him to gainsay [this talk of confidence]. But he seemed not grieved at it; glad to be confuted in a way tending towards his wish" (CM, 68; emphasis added).

Subject, as well, to the ambiguities of moral evidence is Mr. Roberts, in "Renewal of an Old Acquaintance" (ch. 4). "[Y]ou have a faithless memory," says the Confidence-Man, "but trust in the faithfulness of mine" (CM, 16). Locke, we may recall, had pronounced it "unavoidable that the memory be relied on . . . and that men be persuaded of several opinions, whereof the proofs are not actually in their thoughts; nay, which perhaps they are not able actually to recall" (IV.16.2). Moreover, Melville alerts us to the morally certain context of the Confidence-Man's plea by having his trickster lecture Roberts on the distinction between demonstrative knowledge and "implicit reliance" on the testimony of others:

> In my boyhood I was kicked by a horse, and lay insensible for a long time. Upon recovering, what a blank! No faintest trace in regard to how I had come near the horse, or what horse it was, or where it was, or that it was horse at all that had brought me to that pass. For the knowledge of those particulars I am indebted solely to my friends, in whose statements, I need not say, I place implicit reliance, since particulars of some sort there must have been, and why should they deceive me? (CM, 16)

When at the beginning of the chapter the Confidence-Man asks, "Don't you know me?" Roberts replies, "No, certainly" (CM, 14). Yet before the encounter ends, the Confidence-Man alters Roberts's belief affirmatively through the agency of moral certainty—but this to Roberts's misfortune: "[H]e drew from his wallet a bank note, but after a while . . . changed it for another, probably of a somewhat larger amount" (CM, 18).

This use of moral certainty to undermine confidence also functions in Pitch's susceptibility to analogical reasoning (CM, 104, 113) and in the Confidence-Man's encounter with the merchant. The latter learns the potentially specious nature of moral certainty by investing trust in "the man with the weed, whose story, as narrated by himself, and confirmed and filled out by the testimony of a certain man in a gray coat, whom the merchant had afterwards met, he now proceeded to give" (CM, 50). Regrettably, the merchant here places faith in the Lockean premise that assent is properly bestowed when based upon either "the testimony of others, vouching their observation and experience" (IV.15.4) or "the concurrent testimony of unsuspected witnesses" (IV.16.8). Thus, the Confidence-Man consistently deceives his victims with *moral evidence*, a variety of logic espoused regularly both by philosophers intent upon demonstrating man's ability to distinguish truth and by Unitarian theologians wishing to ascertain the verity of a religion having historical evidences (i.e., a variety of "moral evidence" based upon recorded testimonies) that were thought to confirm its probable authenticity.[23]

In *The Confidence-Man*, however, the failure of moral evidence to function reliably has a twofold implication for Melville's quarrel with liberal optimism about human regeneracy. As suggested, by dramatizing the mind's inability to distinguish truth from falsehood, the book challenges the rationalist grounds on which liberals rejected Calvinist ideas about depravity. Here, then, *The Confidence-Man* comprises a theoretical quarrel with liberal notions of certitude, though one with very real consequences for many of the *Fidèle*'s passengers. More practically, however, *The Confidence-Man* shows that while enough moral evidence of depravity may exist to justify suspicion of human nature, the liberal imagination too often engages in voluntary skepticism by disclaiming both the reality of depravity and the legitimacy of moral evidence confirming its existence. As will become evident below, this self-imposed liberal skepticism helps to illustrate the orthodox charge that the failure to acknowledge depravity denigrates the integrity of

23. For a discussion of how liberal Christians used moral evidence to verify the authenticity of Scripture, see Conrad Wright, *The Beginnings of Unitarianism in America* (Boston: Starr King Press, 1955), pp. 150–60. Cf. Norton (as quoted above); Channing, *Works*, pp. 188–232.

New Testament Scripture, the authenticity and genuineness of which the liberals otherwise championed, almost totally on the grounds of moral evidence. Indeed, *The Confidence-Man*'s "Story of the Gentleman-Madman" depicts the contemporary Pontius less as displaying vindictive atheism than as revealing an epistemological lassitude to moral evidence of human iniquity. Regarded theologically, this episode illustrates the orthodox (Calvinist) sentiment that liberal Christians denounced in lamenting the "profligacy of those, who ... insinuate that Unitarians do not believe in inspiration, or in the Bible as containing the Christian revelation, or that their views on these and the kindred subjects are essentially *novel* or particular."[24] My discussion of the Charlemont episode will, therefore, go beyond what one critic has established as Charlemont's farcical identification with Christ to detail how the story links liberal emphasis on human regeneracy to a more literary *novelization*, or reductive fictionalizing, of Christian revelation. As one of America's more Calvinistic historians says, in Arminian and Unitarian thought "the righteousness of the Lamb, the infinity of human sinfulness, sanctification by the Spirit, without which the historical theories of the Atonement *lose all semblance of empirical reality*, hardly come into the picture."[25] The alleged denigration of the Savior is also the issue at stake when the Cosmopolitan, with calculated irony, convinces Charlie Noble that the story of Charlemont is "a story which I told with the purpose of every *story-teller*—to amuse" (CM, 160; emphasis added). However, this phase of our discussion is best introduced and illustrated by Melville's later preoccupation in the poem *Clarel* (1876) with the way Derwent's shallow optimism corresponds to a persistent evasion of matters pertaining to a crucified Christ. Thus, although *Clarel* deviates in genre and is outside the chronology of our immediate focus, its thematic emphases are crucial for our analysis of theology aboard the *Fidèle*.

A s the canto "In Confidence" (*Clarel*, III.xxi)—where Derwent seeks to justify his liberal Anglicanism to Clarel—might suggest, more than a casual resemblance exists between the Confidence-Man and this "liberal priest" (II.xxiv.36) of "genial spirits" (II.xxxix.43), whom Mortmain rightly disparages as a

---

24. "Unitarianism Vindicated Against the Charge of Skeptical and Infidel Tendencies," *Christian Examiner*, 11 (Nov. 1831), p. 188; emphasis added.

25. Joseph Haroutunian, *Piety Versus Moralism: The Passing of the New England Theology* (New York: Henry Holt, 1932), p. 199; emphasis added.

"Doctor of consolation" (III.vi.13). An apostle of modernism, who keeps "abreast ... with the age, the year, / And each bright optimistic mind" (II.1.36–37), Derwent not surprisingly argues against Calvinistic notions of eternal perdition (IV.xxiii). Moreover, with mannerisms reminiscent of his Cosmopolitan predecessor,

> ... he would so transmit a charm
> Along the nerve, which might insure,
> However cynic challenge ran,
> Faith genial in at least one man
> Fraternal in love's overture. (IV.xxiii.73–77)

Far, too, from seeking evidence of imputed sin, Derwent reiterates the Confidence-Man's creed of *tout est bien*:

> What's good to see
> Better than Adam's humanity
> When genial lodged! (IV.xxvi.1–3)

It is problematic, though, that we first encounter Derwent's "random cheer" (II.i.18, 24) on the Via Dolorosa, itself a reminder of a crucified Christ who "shared all of man except sin and mirth" (I.iii.11), and whose suffering Clarel thinks "cause ... / ... to check the hilarious heart" (I.iv.28). Derwent, nevertheless, perceives in the Crucifixion only the "cheerful hope" (II.iii.134) it seems to promise mankind. Thus, Clarel later labels Derwent's faith "an over-easy glove" (II.xxii.147) because, among other reasons, Derwent disregards the Anselmic scheme of redemption, in which an infinite God suffering upon the Cross makes sense only in terms of atonement for man's infinite sin.[26] Indeed, something like this idea functions in an ex-

---

26. For a review of the way liberal Christians traditionally rejected the Anselmic view of atonement, see Wright, p. 218. In *The Pilgrim's Progress in the Nineteenth Century,* Weeks had already suggested that glorification of human nature tended to "rob" Christians of their Savior, since the liberals no longer felt any need of atonement for their sins (pp. 50, 54). Much to the same point is a passage in Hawthorne's "The Celestial Railroad" (1844), in which a group of liberally disposed pilgrims arrives at the Slough of Despond, Bunyan's metaphor for insurmountable conviction of sin. However, Hawthorne's travelers pass over this obstacle because it has been solidified, among other items, with "books of morality" and "essays of modern clergymen." Yet Hawthorne dramatizes how a failure to acknowledge depravity renders the Crucifixion anachronistic. For after depositing their (sinful) burdens in the baggage car, the pilgrims simply rush "by the place where Christian's burden fell from his shoulders [in John Bunyan's *Pilgrim's Progress*] at the sight of the Cross." Descanting "upon the inestimable advantages resulting from the safety of our baggage," they obviously sense no personal need for atonement. *The Complete Works of Nathaniel Hawthorne,* ed.

change in which Rolfe asks Derwent to explain the concept of *manliness*. Blithely, the priest responds,

> "Why,
> To be man-like"—and here the chest
> Bold out he threw—"man at his best!" (IV.xiv.101–3)

Rolfe, however, less flatteringly remarks that

> ... even at best, one might reply,
> Man is that thing of sad renown
> Which moved a deity to come down
> And save him. (IV.xiv.104–7)

Similarly, after Derwent at one point alludes in a calm and genial way to Christ's redemptive powers, Ungar becomes infuriated by the priest's failure to fathom the really tragic implications of redemption for human nature:

> ... visibly the red blood shot
> Into his thin-skinned scar, and sent,
> As seemed, a pulse of argument
> Confirming so some angry sense
> Of evil, and malevolence
> In man toward man. (IV.xiii.225–30)

Thus, from an orthodox perspective, only man's fallen stature lends significance to a crucified Christ, a point that Melville indirectly stresses when Clarel imagines how Ruth's beautiful charm "wins Eden back," causing "tales abstruse / Of Christ, the crucified, Pain's Lord," to "seem foreign—forged—incongruous" (I.xxviii.1–11).

That Derwent's liberality evades and denigrates the importance of the Crucifixion is evident from a passage in which Mortmain interrupts the Anglican's light-hearted discourse to point out Gethsemane, where Judas betrayed Christ. Derwent, however, wishes to hurry past this somber monument of human turpitude, leading Mortmain to distinguish between Christians who have a merely nominal sense of Christ's mission and those who possess the courage to acknowledge its indicting implications for humanity:

> Be some who with the god will sup,

George Parsons Lathrop, 12 vols. (Cambridge, Mass.: Houghton Mifflin, 1883), II: 213, 218.

Happy to share his paschal wine.
'Tis well. But the ensuing cup,
The bitter cup? (II.iii.123–26)

Outraged, as well, by Derwent's membership among the "laureates of man's fallen tribe" (II.iii.174), Mortmain stresses how "'Twas *human* that unanimous cry, / 'We're fixed to hate him—crucify!' " (II.iii.153–154). And turning toward Gethsemane, Mortmain further illustrates the irony of liberalism:

Ye trunks of moan—
Gethsemane olives, do ye hear
The trump of that vain-glorious land
Where human nature they enthrone
Displacing the divine? (II.iii.166–70)

Moreover, in a stanza that we shall find relevant both for "The Story of the Gentleman-Madman" and the Confidence-Man's parody of Christ, Mortmain responds to Derwent's view that Christ was a "Pontiff of optimists supreme" by showing theories of *tout est bien* to be Pontius-like in tendency:

Leave thy carmine! From thorns that streak
Ruddies enough that tortured cheek.
'Twas Shaftesbury first assumed your tone,
Trying to cheerfulize Christ's moan. (II.vi.138–43)

Thus, while existing scholarship accounts for the shallowness of Derwent's geniality,[27] the point to be stressed here is Melville's persistence in dramatizing the way liberalism renders the traditional implications of the Cross meaningless. This issue, we should recall, surfaces both in Melville's poem "The New Rosicrucians"[28] and the stanza in which Derwent advises Clarel to avoid the anxiety attendant upon indulging in his era's numerous religious debates. Resorting to cliché, Derwent counsels, "For time 'tis well to bear a Cross" (III.xxi.145), adding that Clarel should resolve to "throw all this burden upon HIM" (III.xxi.159). But after momentarily pondering the implications (for hu-

27. See, for example, Vincent Kenny, *Herman Melville's "Clarel": A Spiritual Autobiography* (Hamden, Conn.: Archon, 1973), pp. 168–71; Joseph G. Knapp, *Tortured Synthesis: The Meaning of Melville's "Clarel"* (New York: Philosophical Library, 1971), 34–52. See also, however, pp. 70–73 of Knapp's text for an informative discussion of Mortmain's understanding of the relation between evil and Christianity.

28. See Howard P. Vincent, ed., *Collected Poems of Herman Melville* (Chicago: Packard, 1947), p. 297.

man nature) of what he has just said, Derwent "chang[es] trim" (III.xxi.160), thereafter proffering consolation less prejudicial to his liberal ideology. And Melville again illustrates this point in Derwent's later encounter with

> A crucifixion in tattoo,
> With trickling blood-drops strange to see.
> Above that emblem of the loss,
> Twin curving palm-boughs draping met. . . .
> Over an equi-limbed small cross
> And three tri-spiked and sister crowns. (IV.ii.51–57)

Agath, who wears the tattoo, confesses to having been initially indifferent to these symbols, though recently, he adds, they have come to possess a deep meaning. Derwent, however, offers an at best patronizing view of such archaic and monastic superstition: " 'Ah—yes,' sighed Derwent; 'yes indeed! / But 'tis the *Ensign* now we heed' " (IV.ii.81–82). Yet in thus recognizing the merely emblematic quality of the Cross, Derwent disowns any authentic conviction about its efficacy for human sinners, a point evident in the double entendre that Melville assigns to Derwent's hasty explanation of the Cross in Agath's tattoo:

> "Come, come," cried Derwent; "dull ye bide!
> By palm-leaves here are signified
> Judaea, as on the Roman gem;
> *The cross scarce needs a word, agree*;
> The crowns are for the magi three;
> This star—the star of Bethlehem." (IV.ii. 131–37;
> emphasis added)

At the Franciscan convent, as well, Derwent fails to appreciate the significance of the cross, this time associated with a marble shell that holds the holy water with which the monks "make the sign, / The Cross's sign, ere they slip / And bend the knee"(V.xvi.36–38). "*Save me*, what now?" (IV.xvi.28; emphasis added), Derwent mocks, again insensitive to the way some Christians believe in a salvation made possible by a crucified Christ in behalf of an undeserving and iniquitous humanity. Derwent displays a similar ignorance when shown around the Franciscan convent by Brother Salvaterra, whose name the liberal cleric thinks "Silver in every syllable!" Rolfe, however, adds, "And import too" (IV.xvi.75–76), with reference to the meaning of the name (savior of the earth). The seriousness of this point is apparently lost upon Derwent, who blithely sings, "*Me save from sin, and all from error!* / So prays good brother Salvaterra"

(IV.xvi.81–82). Appropriately, a seemingly mad Franciscan Monk named Cyril at one point interrupts Derwent's revelry and proclaims, "*Lachryma Christi* makes ye glad!" (III.xxv.101). Although "The Tears of Christ" was actually a brand of wine,[29] Melville here suggests—as he will again in "The Story of the Gentleman-Madman"— that because Christ saw in human nature "what made him weep," a facile liberalism constitutes an affront to the significance of the Crucifixion. Indeed, as Derwent exclaims after breathing "the liberal air" outside the convent, "Ah, Salvaterra, / So winning in thy dulcet error" (IV.xvi.127–31). Here, too, there is a double entendre. Most obviously, Derwent rejects what he thinks to be the error of this Roman Catholic priest in crediting the superstitious "witcheries" (IV.xvi.128) of a religion that magnifies and then institutionalizes the shortcomings of human nature. But by recalling the literal meaning of "Salvaterra," we may observe Derwent unwittingly indicting the Savior of having somehow erred in his "fervid" (IV.xvi.131) devotion to saving a humanity which may not, after all, have been all *that* bad. Unnecessary, by implication, was Christ's Agony on the Cross. And viewed from the vantage of the *Fidèle*'s liberal society, the enormity of this erroneous assumption might suggest that it was instigated by someone not completely in control of his judgment. This is very much the point of "The Story of the Gentleman-Madman" in *The Confidence-Man*.

T̲he correspondence between the christological concerns of *Clarel* and "The Story of the Gentleman-Madman" is illuminated by what one critic has shown to be the quixotic dimension of *The Confidence-Man*'s madly subversive approach to Scripture:

> In *Don Quixote* the chivalric romances are errant texts, without any claims to authority outside Quixote's subversive madness. In *The Confidence-Man* the structural equivalent of the chivalric romances is the Bible.... The Old and New Testaments are both criticized and defended, in the same way that the chivalric romances are denounced and vindicated in *Don Quixote*. The notions that a particular body of writings is "realistic" or "unrealistic," that certain texts are "good" or "bad," and that certain doctrines in them are "correct" or "incorrect" are set forth, con-

---

29. See Bezanson's note (p. 628) to III.xxv.101. Melville uses the word more conventionally in a section of *Mardi* in which Media talks of "lachrymose rivulets, and inconsolable lagoons" (M, 453).

tradicted, and convoluted, until the apparent rhetorical purpose of the narrative is overwhelmed in the speculative complication.[30]

While an implied comparison with *Don Quixote* may be the vehicle of Melville's satire, I would suggest that his tenor remains something like what, in "Unitarian Christianity" (1819), William Ellery Channing called "our leading principle in interpreting Scripture ... [:] that the Bible is a book written for men, in the language of men, and that its meaning is to be sought in the same manner as that of other books." Of course, Channing did establish literary criteria for biblical studies, at least partly to discourage any fundamentalist tendencies to dwell on human depravity. The Bible's language, he claims, "is singularly glowing, bold, and figurative, demanding more frequent departures from the literal sense...."[31] The issue of literalism was, we know, among the most contested points between Unitarians and Andover Calvinists,[32] the latter of whom may later have been particularly appalled at Emerson's call for Scripture to be read solely as inspirational literature.[33]

A sardonic and reductive outlook on this symbolic approach to Scripture is offered up in the Confidence-Man's story of Charlemont, the allegorical meaning of which comes close to justifying the orthodox charge that liberals *"explain away"* the Scripture truths of *"Original Sin"* and "the Redeemer's Atonement."[34] Granted, the story is both an interpolated and mockingly secularized rendition of the Crucifixion, but the interpolated form of this episode achieves an understatement of theme that aptly mirrors what the orthodox would have regarded as the

---

30. Walter L. Reed, *An Exemplary History of the Novel: The Quixotic versus the Picaresque* (Chicago: Univ. of Chicago Press, 1981), p. 214.

31. Channing, *Works*, pp. 367–68. Five years after Channing penned this remark, Walter Balfour, a Universalist, composed his well-known expurgation of the Bible, *An Inquiry into the Scriptural Import of the Words SHEOL, HADES, TARTARUS, and GEHENNA: All Translated HELL, in the Common English Version* (1824; rpt. Boston: Benjamin B. Mussey, 1832), which advances that

> our English word hell, in its primitive signification, perfectly corresponded to Hades and Sheol, and did not, as it now does, signify a place of misery. It denoted only what was secret and concealed. What we wish to be noticed here, is, that people generally have connected the idea of misery with the word *hell*, but it is evident that it is a very false association. It is beyond all controversy, that the word *hell* is changed from its original signification to express this idea. (p. 17)

32. See Jerry Wayne Brown, *The Rise of Biblical Criticism in America, 1800–1870* (Middletown, Conn.: Wesleyan Univ. Press, 1969), p. 65.

33. See Lawrence Buell, *Literary Transcendentalism: Style and Vision in the American Renaissance* (Ithaca, N.Y.: Cornell Univ. Press, 1973), p. 31.

34. Peter Clark, *The Scripture Doctrine of Original Sin, stated and defended* (Boston: S. Kneeland, 1758), p. 114.

diminutive effects of liberal optimism upon Christian Revelation. Here, no less than in Hawthorne's "Story Teller," both the meaning and form of a frame-narrative parody the self-proclaimed reductive effort of liberal Christians to humanize Christ and to render the Bible a mere book, to be analyzed like any other book.[35] In addition, Melville examines the tendency of liberal Christians to regard as fictitious the motives that, from an orthodox outlook, inspired Christ to mediate between iniquitous humanity and an angry God.

The mechanism of this exposé is best approached by way of Carolyn L. Karcher's identification of Charlemont and Christ.[36] In a manner reminiscent of Christ (who entered his ministry at age thirty), Charlemont, at age twenty-nine, "cut dead" all friendships, disowned his property, and disappeared. Years later, though, he reappears, and "not only was he alive, but he was himself again." Appropriately, the Cosmopolitan describes how "the world feels a return of love for one who returns to it as he did." Moreover, asked to account for the "mystery" of his disappearance and unexpected resurrection, Charlemont aptly sips some wine and explains his behavior in terms recalling an *imitatio Christi* predicated upon the orthodox scheme of atonement:

> If ever, in days to come, you shall see ruin at hand, and, thinking you understand mankind, shall tremble for your friendships, and tremble for your pride; and, partly through love for the one and fear for the other, shall resolve to be before-hand with the world, and *save it from a sin by prospectively taking that sin to yourself*, then will you do as one I now dream of once did, and like him will you suffer. (CM, 159–60; emphasis added)

The motive, in short, for Christ's self-sacrifice is man's sinfulness. But when the Cosmopolitan narrates the story of Charlemont, he reduces it to just that—an amusing story—by getting his auditor to agree that Charlemont's "motive" was *not* "a sort of one at all justified by the nature of human society." And here the Cosmopolitan is less a satirized proponent of liberal theology than he is the agent of its ironic exposure. Reinforcing and then exploiting the liberal mood of his audience, the Cosmopolitan insists the story must be fictional since

---

35. See my "Triumph of Infidelity in Hawthorne's *The Story Teller*," *Studies in American Fiction*, 7 (Spring 1979), pp. 49–60. In exploring *The Confidence-Man's* treatment of *fiction* within these religious categories, I differ from Lindberg (p. 28), who divorces the book's fictional and theological concerns in his discussion of belief and the formation of identity in *The Confidence-Man*.

36. Karcher, "The Story of Charlemont: A Dramatization of Melville's Concepts of Fiction in *The Confidence-Man: His Masquerade*," *Nineteenth-Century Fiction*, 21 (June 1966), 73–84.

Charlemont's recognition of sin scarcely corresponds to anything in real life:

> "Well, what do you think of the story of Charlemont?" mildly asked he who had told it.
>
> "A very strange one," answered the auditor, who had been such not without perfect ease, *"but is it true?"*
>
> *"Of course not; it is a story which I told with the purpose of every story-teller—to amuse.* Hence, if it seem strange to you, that strangeness is the romance; it is what contrasts it with real life; it is the invention, in brief, the fiction as opposed to the fact. For do but ask yourself, my dear Charlie," lovingly leaning over towards him, "I rest it with your own heart now, whether such a forereaching motive as Charlemont hinted he had acted on in his change—*whether such a motive, I say, were a sort of one at all justified by the nature of human society?"* (CM, 160; emphasis added)

The implication of this exchange is that the Crucifixion has little meaning in isolation from the sin for which Christ sought to atone. Indeed, after reading Emerson's remark that "the good, compared to the evil which [a person] sees, is as his own good to his own evil," Melville entered a telling annotation on the relation between *Lachryma Christi* and human turpitude: "A perfectly good being, therefore, would see no evil.—But what did Christ see?—He saw what made him weep." Unlike the Cosmopolitan, who contrivingly and ironically echoes the *Fidèle*'s liberality to illustrate its reductionist doctrinal tendencies, Melville here hints that Charlemont's motive *is* justified by the nature of human society: "[R]ead the Sermon on the Mount," he further annotated, "and consider what it implies."[37]

The point, then, of "The Story of the Gentleman-Madman" resembles the position of orthodox Protestants who held that "till the infinite evil of sin is seen, an incarnate God dying on the Cross, is an incredible story,"[38] or, as the Cosmopolitan says, a "fiction ... op-

---

37. Quoted in William Braswell, "Melville as a Critic of Emerson," *American Literature*, 9 (Nov. 1937), 330.

It is possible that William Gilmore Simms's *Charlemont, or the Pride of the Village* (1856) may have suggested the name Melville assigns his Gentleman-Madman. In Simms's story, a confidence man named Alfred Stevens ingratiates himself with the community of Charlemont, and especially with the pride-filled, intellectual belle of the village, Margaret Cooper, whom he seduces and then abandons. That Stevens chooses to masquerade as a regenerate Christian preparing for the ministry may have been particularly appealing to Melville, whose "The Story of the Gentleman-Madman" dramatizes the sinfulness upon which so much of Christian doctrine is predicated.

38. Joseph Bellamy (in a letter to Ezra Stiles), in Isabel M. Calder, ed., *Letters and*

posed to ... fact." And while Melville doubtless felt little fervor for organized Trinitarianism, the meaning of his chapter on Charlemont approaches the more general significance of the following line, marked by Melville in his copy of Schopenhauer's *Studies in Pessimism*: "Accordingly, the sole thing that reconciles me to the Old Testament is the story of the Fall. In my eyes, it is the only metaphysical truth in that book, even though it appears in the form of an allegory."[39] To Melville's mind, it would seem, at least one of the things that imbued the New Testament's record of the Crucifixion with significance was the event of the Fall in the Old Testament. Thus, the story of Charlemont brings into focus still another phase of Melville's quarrel with liberal Christianity by showing that its whitewash of human nature degrades Christ's Agony on the Cross to a mission inspired by the delusions and "dulcet error" of a Gentleman-Madman.

Perhaps understandably, then, orthodox Protestants thought it "lament[able] that there should be any one ... so little acquainted with the *Plague of his own Heart*, as to make light of this sad Effect of Man's Apostasy; yea, to reject the Notion with Contempt, and finally, to represent it as a dangerous and hurtful Doctrine."[40] Yet this very outlook characterizes many of the *Fidèle*'s passengers, whose liberalism finds articulation in the Confidence-Man's habit of labeling as unchristian any recognition of sin: "[W]hen the whole world shall have been genialized, it will be as out of place to talk of murderers, as in a Christianized world to talk of sinners" (CM, 153). The assumption here is quite similar to the informing premise of John Lowell's *Are You a Christian or a Calvinist?* (1815)—a text Melville might have read as early as 1842—which refutes the orthodox charge that "the liberal clergy creep silently into orthodox churches, preach negatively (that is, are silent) on certain controverted points, ... and simply by *not hearing* these doctrines, for some time, (that is, 'after a while') when they hear them anew they are shocked at them, and consider the man who utters them a monster! ! !"[41] Although Melville need not have been thinking

---

Papers of Ezra Stiles (New Haven: Yale Univ. Press, 1933), p. 21; quoted by Wright, p. 200. In a related vein, see Jonathan Edwards's belief that "If all mankind ... have such sufficient power to do their whole duty, without being sinful *in any degree*, then they have sufficient power to obtain righteousness by the law: and then, according to the apostle, Paul, *Christ is dead in vain*, Gal. ii. 21." *The Great Scripture Doctrine of Original Sin Defended* (1758), in *The Works of President Edwards*, ed. Sereno E. Dwight, 10 vols. (New York: S. Converse, 1829–30), II: 516.

39. Quoted by Nathalia Wright, *Melville's Use of the Bible* (Durham, N.C.: Duke Univ. Press, 1949), p. 16.

40. Clark, p. 3.

41. John Lowell, *Are You a Christian or a Calvinist? Do You Prefer the Authority*

specifically of either this pamphlet or this particular passage, *The Confidence-Man* still makes the same point in dramatizing the liberal belief that "views ... injurious to human nature" constitute "unsuspected heresy ... in the heart of Christendom" (CM, 23).[42] Even the Methodist minister aboard the *Fidèle* labels as a "godless reprobate" (CM, 11) the discharged customhouse officer who questions Black Guinea's authenticity. Nor can the Man in Gray abide the custom officer's talk about "deception and deviltry"; he, too, refers to the propagator of such ideas as "a man to be put down in any Christian community" (CM, 28). But since, as our discussion of both *Clarel* and the story of Charlemont has shown, recognition of iniquity is appropriate to the Christian world view, Melville could scarcely have endowed the *Fidèle*'s chief realist with a more suitable identity than that of a discharged customhouse official, "suspecting everything and everybody" (CM, 8). "The people ... and the people's representatives in Congress," proclaimed the *American Whig Review*, "have but little confidence in humanity, else they would not go to the expense of revenue cutters and custom-houses. They would content themselves with imposing a certain tariff, and leaving it to the conscience of the importers to pay it fully and promptly."[43]

Interestingly, the article just quoted ends by distinguishing between the abstract and the practical precepts involved in allotting confidence: "If a virtuous people elect virtuous rulers, all confidence should be placed in these rulers, and yet it is a democratic rule to entertain no such confidence."[44] The ability to discriminate between abstract and

---

of Christ to that of the Genevan Reformer? (Boston: Wells and Lilly, 1815), p. 48. Lowell quotes a derisive summary of Unitarianism from the *Panoplist*, an orthodox journal. Wilson Heflin, in "New Light on Cruise of Herman Melville in the *Charles and Henry*," *Historic Nantucket*, 22 (Oct. 1974), 13, 16–17, has shown this book to have been in the library of the *Charles and Henry* during Melville's stay aboard that ship from November 1842 to April 1843.

42. Indeed, one liberal minister actually defined Calvinistic emphasis on human turpitude as the "orthodox heresy." See William Hart, *Brief Remarks on a Number of False Propositions, and dangerous Errors ... Collected out of sundry Discourses ... by Dr. Whitaker and Mr. Hopkins* (New London, Conn.: Timothy Green, 1769), p. 48.

43. "Political Paradoxes," *American Whig Review*, 12 (July 1850), 3. In terms highly suggestive for *The Confidence-Man*, the article goes on to remark:

Governments established upon the *confidence* principle never last beyond the cooling of a first enthusiasm; those on the other hand which are based upon the "laws of human nature," last while their foundations remain. It is good and amiable to place confidence in *the people*, but by no means so to place the same confidence in that mixture of rogues and swindlers which form no small and mischievous minority of every community, and whose want of *confidence* gives them a temporary advantage. (p. 4)

44. "Political Paradoxes," p. 4. The author here seems to allude to the negative view of human nature implied by checks and balances in government.

practical considerations in the awarding of confidence is central, as well, to a crucial aspect of *The Confidence-Man*'s epistemological drama. For while many of the book's episodes belie liberal confidence in the faculties by illustrating man's inability always to distinguish truth attested by moral evidence, *The Confidence-Man*'s more "practical" dimension defines as both philosophically and theologically unsound the liberalism that *ignores* moral evidence of iniquity. As Leonard Woods had already argued in his famous *Letters to Unitarians* (1820), "[W]e receive the doctrine of man's native corruption upon its own proper evidence, as we receive any other truth; and ... it is totally unphilosophical ... to suffer this evidence to be obscured...." To disown the doctrine of depravity, he says, is to ignore moral evidence as convincing as that which confirms "the law of gravitation."[45] Even Gambier's book on moral evidence repudiates the belief that "in order to [have] peace of mind, we should learn to view everything on its best side, and in the fairest light." And greatly suggestive for the invitational outlook of Melville's deaf-mute is Gambier's displeasure with the idea of imitating "that divine charity, which thinketh no evil, believeth all things, and hopeth all things." For Gambier, the "desire to see a thing in *its brightest light* and on *its best side,* is not a desire to see it as it really is, compounded of good and evil in certain proportions."[46] When, in *The Confidence-Man,* William Cream arrives at a similar conclusion, he reinstates his sign of "NO TRUST" and tears up the contract into which he had entered with the Confidence-Man; for "in all human probability"—in short, according to the best available moral evidence—"he would never again see the person who had drawn it" (CM, 204). Still, only Pitch, the auburn-haired gentleman, and the discharged customhouse officer join the barber in entertaining moral evidence of man's depravity.[47] The rest of the passengers practice a self-imposed

---

45. Woods, *The Works of Leonard Woods, D.D.,* 5 vols. (Boston: John P. Jewett & Co., 1851), IV: 38. For an overview of Woods's strategy here, see Haroutunian, pp. 208–9.

46. Gambier, pp. 74–75.

47. Note especially the auburn-haired gentleman's distrust of the Confidence-Man: "I suspect him for something." In response he is told, "Suspicion. We want knowledge." His reply, however, entails a consideration of suspicion as a reliable mode of moral certainty: "Well, suspect first and know next. True knowledge comes but by suspicion or revelation" (CM, 78). This, in turn, anticipates a passage in *Billy Budd* in which Melville seems to pun upon the necessity of accepting moral evidence of depravity:

> that promiscuous commerce with mankind ... soon teaches one that unless upon occasion he exercise a distrust keen in proportion to the fairness of the appearance, some foul turn may be served him. A ruled *undemonstrative distrustfulness* is so habitual, not with businessmen so much as with men who know their kind in less

skepticism that implicates them in liberal perceptions about Charlemont's deluded mentality.

Consider, for instance, Charlie Noble's willingness to dismiss moral evidence suggestive of human degeneracy:

> "Like you," said the stranger, "I can't understand the misanthrope.... Cheating, backbiting, superciliousness, disdain, hardheartedness, and all that brood, *I know but by report*.[48] Cold regards tossed over the sinister shoulder of a former friend, ingratitude in a beneficiary, treachery in a confidant—*such things may be; but I must take somebody's word for it*. Now the bridge that has carried me so well over, shall I not praise it?" (CM, 137; emphasis added)

In his discussion with the barber, the Confidence-Man, too, offers up moral evidence of depravity, but only to echo the majority sentiment aboard the *Fidèle* that such evidence is misleading:

> I think I understand ... and much *the same thing* I have heard from persons in pursuits different from yours—from the lawyer, from the congressman, from the editor, not to mention *others*, each, with a strange kind of melancholy vanity, claiming for his vocation the distinction of affording the surest inlets to the conviction that man is no better than he should be. All of which *testimony*, if reliable, would, by *mutual corroboration*, justify some disturbance in a good man's mind. But, no, no; it is a *mistake*—all a *mistake*. (CM, 198; emphasis added)

Judged, however, by the standards of moral certainty, this evidence ought "practically" to be reliable. As Gambier says,

> The third species of moral evidence, is of a mixt [*sic*] kind, possessing partly the nature of personal observation, and partly that of *testimony*. It is that by which we learn from *others*, those general conclusions which they have deduced by the observation of a variety of facts of *the same kind....*
> The number of our informers is another circumstance by which the credibility of their information is regulated. This depends ... on its being less probable, that several persons would be *mistaken* in the general conclusions which they have drawn from their observations, than one.[49]

---

shallow relations than business, namely *certain* men of the world, that they come at last to employ it all but unconsciously. (BB, 87; emphasis added)

48. "A fifth kind of moral evidence, is *Report*" (Gambier, p. 53).

49. Gambier, pp. 42, 44–45; emphasis added. Joel Porte, in *The Romance in Ameri-*

With respect to these standards, the Confidence-Man proffers adequate moral evidence of human iniquity, but only to lead his victims into a maze of philosophical skepticism by encouraging them to deny the legitimacy of this evidence.

By illustrating the skeptical indulgences of the *Fidèle*'s liberal passengers, Melville clarifies the epistemological assumptions that ultimately transform the Agony of Charlemont into a "fiction as opposed to . . . fact" (CM, 160). But the incidents described above are more or less preparatory to *The Confidence-Man*'s concern with the even greater skepticism of liberals who profess that the Scriptures contain little or no evidence to support any Calvinistic assumptions about degeneracy. Much to the point of this concern is a passage from *Pierre* that posits the Bible's attention to iniquity as a variety of moral evidence:

> The sense of [humanity's corruption] is so overpowering, that at first the youth is apt to refuse the evidence of his own senses; even as he does that same evidence in the matter of movement of the visible sun in the heavens, which with his own eyes he plainly sees to go round the world, but nevertheless on the authority of other persons,—the Copernican astronomers, whom he never saw— he believes it *not* to go round the world, but the world round it. Just so, too, he hears good and wise people sincerely say: This world only *seems* to be saturated and soaking with lies; but in reality it does not so lie soaking and saturate; along with some lies, there is much truth in this world. But again he *refers to his Bible, and there he reads most explicitly, that this world is unconditionally depraved and accursed.* (**P**, 208; emphasis added)

Quite probably, however, Melville would have known some version of the standard Unitarian claim that the Bible contains no evidence of human depravity, that when "we bring every doctrine and every duty to the test of Scripture[,] the reason of our rejecting certain [Calvinist] doctrines, is, that we cannot find them taught in the Bible; if we did, we should embrace and avow them, as readily as we now disown and cast them away."[50] The most general liberal assumption that "I find

---

ca: Studies in Cooper, Poe, Hawthorne, Melville, and James (Middletown, Conn.: Wesleyan Univ. Press, 1969), pp. 163–65, observes a similar strategy in the Confidence-Man's effort to establish Goneril's "natural depravity" in order to see if he can later "explain away a tale that he himself created!"

50. William Peabody, *"Come and see,"* or *the duty of those who dread the sentiment of other Christians* (1823; American Unitarian Assoc. tract [ser. 1], no. 71), pp. 5–6; quoted by Faust (p. 312) in an excellent discussion of liberal disclaimers of scriptural allusions to depravity.

nothing in the scriptures that implies either [total depravity or imputed sin]; and, beyond them I do not chuse [sic] to be wise"[51] seems parodied in *The Confidence-Man*'s treatment of the Bible's so-called "apocryphal" Wisdom Books. Indeed, when the Confidence-Man hears that the passage "An enemy speaketh sweetly with his lips" (CM, 202) is scriptural, he rushes to a cabin housing the ship's Bible. There, an old man tells him the passage is from Ecclesiasticus (12:16); but since that book is Apocryphal, it need not be credited with moral certainty:

> "Ah!" cried the old man, brightening up, "now I know. Look," turning the leaves forward and back, till all the Old Testament lay flat on one side and all the New Testament flat on the other, while in his fingers he supported vertically the portion between, "look, sir, all this to the right is *certain* truth, and all this to the left is *certain* truth, but all I hold in my hand here is apocrypha." (CM, 208; emphasis added)[52]

The "uncertain credit" by means of which the Wisdom Books are here denied their wisdom ("[I]t ain't wisdom; it's apocrypha" [CM, 209]) captures the largest skeptical tendency aboard a *Fidèle* in which discouraging knowledge is deprived of epistemological integrity. Confronted, for example, by "St. Augustine on Original Sin," the Confidence-Man echoes the ship's predominantly liberal mood by refusing to regard this topic as a legitimate branch of knowledge: "St. Augustine? What should I, or you, either, know of him? Seems to me ... that ... you know a good deal more than you ought to know, or than you have a right to know.... [T]his knowledge of yours, which you haven't enough knowledge to know how to make a right use of, it should be taken from you" (CM, 108–109; cf. p. 117). Still, the suggestion here is that one cannot function in the world without throwing in knowledge

---

51. Jonathan Mayhew, *Christian Sobriety* (Boston: Draper, 1763), p. 75.

52. That Melville has in mind the concept of moral certainty is suggested by his ability elsewhere to manipulate the concept—for example, in the encounter between the Confidence-Man and the barber:

"Cash again! What do you mean?"

"Why, in this paper here, you engage, sir, to insure me against a certain [*] loss, and—"

"Certain? Is it so certain [**] you are going to lose?"

"Why, that way of taking the word may not be amiss, but I didn't mean it so, I meant a *certain* loss; you understand, a CERTAIN loss; that is to say, a certain loss." (CM, 203)

Here the Confidence-Man accommodates the barber's neutral adjective (*) to his own preoccupation with moral certainty (**).

of something like original sin. And the epistemological thrust of this mandate anticipates the enthusiasm with which Melville later read, underscored, and annotated the following passage in Madame de Staël's *Germany*: "It cannot be denied that there is in Goethe's book [*Elective Affinities*] a profound knowledge of the human heart, but it is a discouraging knowledge." Melville's annotation reads: "What inadvertence! And what an admission!—'Profound Knowledge' and 'discouraging knowledge.'"[53] As the story of Charlemont shows, the epistemological point of this insight is pertinent, as well, for the integrity of a religion having a crucified Savior whose tears are relegated to "uncertain" status by liberal evasion of human iniquity.

In *The Confidence-Man*, however, Melville seeks to vindicate neither a conservative Calvinist Christology nor the doctrine of vicarious atonement; rather, by allegorizing an essentially Calvinist outlook, he corroborates something like Pierre Bayle's belief that "the principal Character of a good System is to give an account of Matters of Fact, and that bare incapacity of explaining them, is a proof that an Hypothesis is not good, however beautiful soever it appears."[54] From this angle, the Confidence-Man aptly becomes a revealer of truths about human iniquity that are consistent with his early posture as a crucified Christ: "Gradually overtaken by slumber, his flaxen head drooped, his whole lamb-like figure relaxed, and, half reclining against the ladder's foot, lay motionless" (CM, 4). Not surprisingly, a "cross-wise balcony" (CM, 5) intersects the ladder.[55] Also Christ-like is the Confidence-Man's status as a "bridegroom tripping to the bridal chamber" (CM, 207), as is his "original character" (CM, 205), which, for Lawrance Thompson, recalls Carlyle's description of the *"original* man," who "comes to us at firsthand. A messenger he, sent from the Infinite Unknown with tidings to us. We may call him Poet, Prophet, God.... Really, his utterances, are they not a kind of 'revelation'...?"[56] Melville, however, knew that Christ's revelation was not entirely joyful; as Mohi says in *Mardi*, "according to all one hears in [orthodox]

---

53. See Jay Leyda, ed., *The Melville Log: A Documentary Life of Herman Melville, 1819–1891*, 2 vols. (New York: Harcourt, Brace, 1951), II: 651.

54. Pierre Bayle, *An Historical and Critical Dictionary*, trans. Jacob Tonson, 4 vols. (London: Harper, 1710), III: 2151 (misnumbered 1151).

55. Foster, "Introduction," p. li, first explained the cross-wise balcony.

56. The passage, quoted by Lawrance Thompson in *Melville's Quarrel with God* (Princeton, N.J.: Princeton Univ. Press, 1952), pp. 298–99, is from Thomas Carlyle's *On Heroes, Hero-Worship, and the Heroic in History* (1841), which Melville borrowed from Duyckinck in 1850. See Sealts, *Melville's Reading*, item 122. For the Christly significance of the bridegroom, see Hershel Parker's editorial note to p. 207 of the Norton critical edition of *The Confidence-Man*.

Maramma, the great end of [Alma's, i.e., Christ's] mission seems to have been the revealing to us Mardians the existence of horrors most hard to escape" (M, 350). Among these is the corruption of human nature; in the words of R. W. B. Lewis, "[T]he Confidence Man is not a bringer of darkness; he is the one who reveals the darkness in ourselves."[57] And with respect to *The Confidence-Man*'s concern with the relation of human depravity to a crucified Christ, Melville could scarcely have chosen a better day than April 1 to stage this revelation. For All Fools' Day "is never far from the Passion–Week," and "the old custom of sending persons on needless (or fools') errands is nothing but a travesty of the sending hither and thither of the Savior from Annas to Caiaphas, and from Pilate to Herod."[58] Thus, whereas the April 1 editorial of Walt Whitman, from which I quote above, finally begs "the sour-tempered grumbler at humanity, . . . the man whose actions sing, 'love not'" to adopt a "more genial philosophy,"[59] Melville's *The Confidence-Man* persists in encouraging at least enough misanthropy to counterbalance the assumption that "the Cross scarce needs a word."

What, though, are we to make of the Deaf Mute's authentically Christ-like injunctions?

> Charity thinketh no evil.
> Charity suffereth long, and is kind.
> Charity endureth all things.
> Charity believeth all things.
> Charity never faileth [1 Cor. 13]. (CM, 2–3)

Ernest Lee Tuveson is correct, I think, in suggesting that "Paul . . . is talking about those who have been baptized of the spirit, not of the natural man, subject to original sin. The Confidence-Man is inducing his subjects to believe that these gifts of grace are innate in all of us."[60] However, in *The Confidence-Man* the customhouse officer remarks that "charity is one thing, and truth is another" (CM, 11), as

---

57. R. W. B. Lewis, *Trials of the Word: Essays in American Literature and the Humanistic Tradition* (New Haven, Conn.: Yale Univ. Press, 1965), p. 76.

58. Fred[eric]k W[illia]m Hackwood, *Christ Lore: Being the Legends, Traditions, Myths, Symbols, Customs and Superstititions of the Christian Church* (London: Elliot Stock, 1902), p. 95. While we cannot know for sure if Melville was aware of this explanation for All Fools' Day, existing scholarship argues convincingly that he elsewhere exploits the literary possibilities surrounding Caiaphas and Pilate. See Philip D. Beidler, "*Billy Budd:* Melville's Valedictory to Emerson," *ESQ: A Journal of the American Renaissance*, 24 (1978), 221–23.

59. Whitman, "Motley's Your Only Wear," in *Gathering of the Forces*, II: 97–98.

60. Tuveson, p. 255.

did Horace Bushnell, when in 1858 he claimed that charity is one thing and liberalism quite another:

> Christ is no liberal, never takes the ground or boasts the distinction of a liberal among his countrymen, because it is not a part of his infirmity, in discovering an error here, to fly to an excess there. His ground is charity, not liberality; and the two are as wide apart in their practical implications, as adhering to all truth and being loose in all. Charity holds fast the minutest atoms of truth, as being precious and divine, offended by even so much as a thought of laxity. Liberality loosens the terms of truth; permitting easily and with careless magnanimity variations from it; consenting, as it were, in its own sovereignty, to overlook or allow them; and subsiding thus, ere long, into a licentious indifference to all truth, and a general defect of responsibility in regard to it. Charity extends allowance to men; liberality, to falsities themselves.[61]

Although Melville could obviously not have known this passage when he wrote *The Confidence-Man,* he certainly anticipates its leading point. Moreover, Bushnell's insistence that Christ was no liberal has the added benefit of providing us with a category suitable to what we shall now explore as the "politics of crucifixion" in *Billy Budd,* distinguishing between what that book's crucifixion motif means for its conservative narrator and, more complexly, what it may have signified for Melville about the agony of human consciousness.

---

61. Horace Bushnell, *Nature and the Supernatural* (1858; rpt. New York: Charles Scribner's Sons, 1892), pp. 312–13.

C H A P T E R   VII

The Cross of Consciousness: *Billy Budd*

Though not as preoccupied as *The Confidence-Man* with moral certainty, *Billy Budd* still shows that an "undemonstrative distrustfulness" is essential for survival: "[U]nless upon occasion [a person] exercise a distrust keen in proportion to the fairness of the appearance, some foul turn may be served him" (BB, 87). Billy, however, initially has neither a direct apprehension of evil nor any inclination to heed moral evidence of its existence. His is a simple-minded innocence, oblivious to what Melville elsewhere called "that Calvinistic sense of Innate Depravity and Original Sin, from whose visitations, in some shape or other, no deeply thinking mind is always and wholly free."[1] Whereas, however, *The Confidence-Man* addresses the epistemology and the theological consequences of evading evil, *Billy Budd* takes up the political ramifications of liberality. Billy, after all, begins his service aboard a ship named the *Rights of Man*, the Dundee owner of which is a "staunch admirer of Thomas Paine" and is said to resemble "Stephen Girard of Philadelphia, whose sympathies, alike with his native land and its liberal philosophers, he evinced by naming his ships after Voltaire, Diderot, and so forth" (BB, 48). Of course, the place of Enlightenment thought in *Billy Budd* has not gone undetected. Existing studies have finally gone beyond such categories as "acceptance" and "resistance," in relation to Melville's reflections on evil and suffering, to address the book's encounter with the outlooks of Rousseau, Hobbes, Paine, and Burke.[2] Yet Melville need

---

1. Melville, "Hawthorne and His Mosses," *Literary World*, 7 (17 Aug. 1850), 126.

2. For the standard "acceptance" and "resistance" studies, see Sealts's and Hayford's "Editor's Introduction," pp. 24–27, to the edition of *Billy Budd* cited in this book. Philosophical and political readings of *Billy Budd* include John B. Noone's "*Billy Budd*: Two Concepts of Nature," *American Literature*, 29 (Nov. 1957), 249–62; Ray B. Browne, "*Billy Budd*: Gospel of Democracy," *Nineteenth-Century Fiction*, 17 (March 1963), 321–37; Milton R. Stern, "Introduction," *Billy Budd, Sailor: An Inside Narrative*

not have been thinking only about natural rights theories of the eighteenth century. As late as 1845 one popular book, *Essays on Human Rights and Their Political Guaranties*, held "that the laws shall be merely declaratory of natural rights and natural wrongs, and that whatever is indifferent to the laws of nature shall be left unnoticed by human legislation."[3] Similarly minded was Henry David Thoreau, who wrote, "[W]e should be men first, and subjects afterward. It is not desirable to cultivate a respect for the law, so much as for the right." "Is it not possible," he asks, "to take a step further towards recognizing and organizing the rights of man?" Also, with rhetoric particularly appropriate to the sort of liberalism that Captain Vere will refute, Thoreau adds, "There will never be a really free and enlightened State, until the State comes to recognize the individual as a higher and independent power, from which all its own power and authority are derived, and treats him accordingly."[4]

However, not everybody in the nineteenth century was as enthusiastic about the rights of man; James Fenimore Cooper thought that "they who fancy it possible to frame the institutions of a country, on the pure principles of abstract justice, as these principles exist in theories, know little of human nature, or of the restraints that are necessary to society."[5] In *Clarel*, moreover, Mortmain's obsession with human depravity finds a political analog in his exaggerated views about authoritarianism:

> Man's vicious; snaffle him with kings;
> Or, if kings cease to curb, devise
> Severer bit. (II.iii.189–91)

Significantly, Mortmain formulates this statement when he and his companions pass the Garden of Gethsemane, where Judas betrayed Christ. Mortmain's proclamation anticipates the "politics of crucifixion" in *Billy Budd*; for Melville's conservative narrator finally posits

---

(Indianapolis, Ind.: Bobbs–Merrill, 1975), pp. vii–xliv. Of major value is Thomas J. Scorza's *In The Time Before Steamships: "Billy Budd," The Limits of Politics, and Modernity* (DeKalb, Ill.: Northern Illinois Univ. Press, 1979).

3. E. P. Hurlbut, *Essays on Human Rights and Their Political Guaranties* (New York: Greeley & McElrath, 1845), p. 10; cf. p. 26. *The National Union Catalogue* (pre-1956) lists six editions of this book published between 1845 and 1853. *Essays* would have been widely known after being severely criticized in the lead articles of both the October and November issues of the *American Whig Review*, 2 (1845), 327–40; 437–51.

4. Henry David Thoreau, "Resistance to Civil Government," in *Aesthetic Papers*, ed. Elizabeth P. Peabody (New York: G. P. Putnam, 1849), pp. 190, 211.

5. James Fenimore Cooper, *The American Democrat* (1838), ed. H. L. Mencken (New York: Alfred A. Knopf, 1931), p. 40.

Billy's hanging as an atoning sacrifice that illuminates the relation between turpitude and the need for social control and authority.[6] And here, *Billy Budd*'s narrative outlook conforms to the conservative stance that "the state of freedom . . . is identified with the possession of reason or of the governing power; and as all are equal through obedience to the law, all are free through the fulfillment of the law."[7]

Still, the significance of *Billy Budd*'s crucifixion motif finally transcends the narrator's conservative politics to encompass the psychological anguish of individuals caught between such opposing forces as primitivism and civilization, freedom and law, tyranny and democracy, and—to draw upon existential categories—Being and Nothingness, the tormenting problem of consciousness itself. Nor is an existential reading inconsistent with the way Vere's dilemma finds a precise historical analog in the *Somers* affair of 1842, in which Captain Alexander Slidell Mackenzie and Melville's cousin, Lieutenant Guert Gansevoort, were among the officers who sentenced to death three allegedly mutinous sailors, including Philip Spencer, son of the nation's Secretary of War. As Harrison Hayford shows, the case set radical Democrats against conservative Whigs and raised many questions about the rights of both captains and common sailors.[8] In *Billy Budd*, however, the narrator's encounter with the *Somers* affair, as well as that incident's political ramifications, subserve a more pressing concern: the anguish of choosing one's destiny in the face of "nothingness," or almost limitless possibility. Regrettably, conservative Whig assessments of Mackenzie's heroism dominate the narrator's outlook, allowing both him and the captain whose perspective he renders to evade a truly conscientious encounter with alternatives to Billy's execution.

Important in this respect is the way "the military forms adhered to by Captain Vere may be representing—standing in for—the literary forms being advanced by the putative Author of the work."[9] Yet to understand more completely the relation between narrative form and philosophical outlook in *Billy Budd*, we must supplement this observa-

---

6. See Richard Harter Fogle, "*Billy Budd*: The Order of the Fall," *Nineteenth-Century Fiction*, 15 (Dec. 1960), 189–205.

7. "Political Paradoxes: 'Men are Born Free and Equal,'" *American Whig Review*, 12 (July 1850), 15–16.

8. Harrison Hayford, ed., *The Somers Mutiny Affair* (Englewood Cliffs, N.J.: Prentice-Hall, 1959), pp. 156–57. Also see Charles Roberts Anderson, "The Genesis of *Billy Budd*," *American Literature*, 12 (Nov. 1940), 329–46.

9. Walter L. Reed, "The Measured Forms of Captain Vere," *Modern Fiction Studies*, 23 (Summer 1977). Crucial is Reed's observation that "the burden of formalization is shifted from the Author to Captain Vere, and this shifting is not merely an event in the history of the story's composition but is dramatically enacted in the course of the story as it now exists" (p. 232).

tion with a contextual reassessment of how the *Somers* affair functions in the shift of formalization from the narrator's consciousness to Vere's. For what until now has been regarded merely as an influential historical source for the plot of *Billy Budd* actually figures importantly in the relation between *Billy Budd*'s existential concerns and its narrative outlook. That the narrator is a Burkean conservative who seeks didactically to impose his values upon the reader has been adequately shown elsewhere;[10] remaining to be addressed is the way his reverence for Burke, Arnold, Carlyle, and Captain Mackenzie allows him to shape a narrative having as its *hero* an individual whose timorousness corresponds to, and thereby sanctions, his own reluctance to confront existential possibility. Although the narrator is saddened by the way technology has imperiled the expression of valor and gallantry,[11] the measured forms of his own narrative invite a Thoreauvian concern about whether the more general *mechanism* of society has usurped man's thinking and moral capacities. Thus, Melville ends his literary career pondering one of the same issues with which he began it in *Typee.* There he had dramatized the threat posed to consciousness by primitivism; ironically, his final book posits a "flight from consciousness" as the lamentable by-product of civilization as well.[12]

A s suggested, a major concern of Melville's narrator—and especially in his portrait of Claggart—is the way mechanized society suppresses natural integrity and encourages modes of rational duplicity alien to most primitive societies.[13] Melville's narrator, then, stands opposed to ideas like those advanced in 1845 by E. P. Hurlbut, who described how man "is endowed with faculties which inevitably tend to high civilization and improvement. A faculty improved is still the same faculty. A sentiment enlightened does not lose its original character."[14] Significantly, Hurlbut's assessment of the incorruptible "faculties" corresponds to

---

10. For the narrator's adherence to the ideas of Edmund Burke, see Scorza, pp. xxviii–xxix, 43–45; for his didacticism, Rowland A. Sherrill's *The Prophetic Melville: Experience, Transcendence, and Tragedy* (Athens, Ga.: Univ. of Georgia Press, 1979), pp. 222–38.

11. See Scorza, pp. 46–47.

12. For *Typee*'s concern with the threat posed by primitivism to consciousness and abstract thought, see Milton R. Stern, *The Fine Hammered Steel of Herman Melville* (Urbana, Ill.: Univ. of Illinois Press, 1957), pp. 40–65.

13. See Scorza, pp. 69, 80–81.

14. Hurlbut, *Essays on Human Rights*, p. 10; cf. p. 18.

the more widely known effort of William Ellery Channing to disavow Calvinist ideas about human depravity by appealing to *"the confidence which is due to our rational and moral faculties. . . . "*[15] In *Billy Budd*, however, the narrator's portrait of Claggart challenges the equation between rationality and regeneracy:

> Though the man's even temper and discreet bearing would seem to intimate a mind peculiarly subject to the law of reason, not the less in heart he would seem to riot in complete exemption from that law, having apparently little to do with reason further than to employ it as an ambidexter implement for effecting the irrational. (BB, 76)

The suggestion is that turpitude often lodges "in the heart not the brain" (BB, 77); intellect, therefore, offers no sanctuary against corruption. Indeed, Claggart's status as the only person "intellectually capable of adequately appreciating the moral phenomenon presented in Billy Budd" (BB, 78) serves only to intensify his insidiousness. Also, insofar as the narrator posits "Claggart's conscience [as] . . . lawyer to his will" (BB, 80), describing, too, how this will is motivated by "passion, and passion in its profoundest" (BB, 78), the narrative likewise conflicts with the liberal position on God's "tolerat[ing] no degradation of conscience to the power of impulse and passion. And this is precisely what is commanded by the higher nature of man."[16] It is consistent, then, with the narrator's belief in the "doctrine of man's Fall, a doctrine now popularly ignored" (BB, 52), that Claggart's villainy is described as something like "the paralyzing lurch of the torpedo fish" (BB, 98), which scholarship shows to be symbolic of "cerebral malice or domination."[17] Depravity, Mortmain says in *Clarel* (II.xxvi.34–37), is compatible with

> Things hard to prove: decorum's wile,

---

15. Channing, "The Moral Argument Against Calvinism" (1809), in *The Works of William E. Channing, D.D.* (Boston: American Unitarian Assoc., 1895), p. 462. Melville's wife owned the complete *Works* of Channing (see Merton M. Sealts, Jr., *Melville's Reading: A Check-List of Books Owned and Borrowed* [Madison: Univ. of Wisconsin Press, 1966], item 130). For Melville's familiarity with liberal Christian confidence in the faculties of the mind, see T. Walter Herbert, Jr., *"Moby-Dick" and Calvinism: A World Dismantled* (New Brunswick, N.J.: Rutgers Univ. Press, 1977), p. 76.

16. George Ripley, "The Coincidence of Christianity with the Higher Nature of Man," in *Discourses on the Philosophy of Religion* (Boston: James Munroe, 1836), p. 63.

17. Harold Aspiz, "The 'Lurch of the Torpedo Fish': Electrical Concepts in *Billy Budd*," *ESQ: A Journal of the American Renaissance*, 26 (1980), 132. Cf. Scorza's remark (p. 81) that in *Billy Budd* "intellectuality itself" may be "the ultimate depravity."

> Malice discreet, judicious guile;
> Good done with ill intent—reversed:
> Best deeds designed to serve the worst.

Like Mortmain, however, Melville's narrator has an audience disinclined to believe in the "lexicon which is based on Holy Writ." Knowing, in fact, how lightly his nineteenth-century readers will take any definition of Claggart "tinctured with the biblical element," the narrator turns to Plato's definition of "Natural Depravity." This is "a depravity according to nature" which, "though savoring of Calvinism," applies *not* to all mankind, but only to "individuals" (BB, 75). Still, for all practical purposes the narrator here finds in antiquity confirmation of the most general assumptions behind the Calvinistic tenet of Total Depravity. And his strategy is ironic, since French philosophes and English Deists, intent upon confirming humanistic and progressivist values, more customarily resurrected the sentiments of Classical writers.[18] Like Horace Bushnell, therefore, Melville's narrator appropriates the argumentative strategy of enlightened philosophers to locate "classical" corroboration for truths too often dismissed as the by-product of monastic dyspepsia.[19]

Also supportive of a skeptical view of human nature, and indicative of attitudes germane to the "politics of crucifixion," is the narra-

---

18. As Ernst Cassirer, in *The Philosophy of the Enlightenment* (1932), trans. Fritz C. A. Koelln and James P. Pettegrove (Princeton, N.J.: Princeton Univ. Press, 1951), p. 139, says, "Plato's doctrine of Eros and the Stoic doctrine of self-determination of the will are matched against the Augustinian view of the radical corruption of human nature and its inability to attain divinity by its own efforts." For a more detailed account of ways in which Enlightenment philosophers appealed to Classical writers to discredit the assumptions of Calvinism, see Peter Gay's *The Enlightenment: An Interpretation* (New York: Alfred A. Knopf, 1966), pp. 31–203.

19. Horace Bushnell, *Nature and the Supernatural* (1858; rpt. New York: Charles Scribner's Sons, 1892). Bushnell anticipates (pp. 241–42) the strategy espoused by Melville's narrator in corroborating Calvinistic sentiments without having to appeal to writers tinctured by Scripture. "Suppose," he says, "there might be found some great and profound thinker, who has never come under the impress of Christianity, or even heard of such a thing as a plan of supernatural redemption; a man of the highest culture, least under the power of superstition; a free-thinker as regards the religion of his country and times." Such a man is Plato; but even he, "beginning at the base note of human depravity," says " 'the prime evil is inborn in souls'; 'it is implanted in men to sin' (Leg., p. 731). Again, 'The nature of mankind is greatly degenerated and depraved, all manner of disorders infest human nature ... ' (Politicus, p. 274). He also speaks of 'an evil in nature,' 'a disease in nature,' 'a destruction of harmony in the soul,' and much more to the same effect." (With a difference in emphasis, R. W. B. Lewis, in *The American Adam* [Chicago: Univ. of Chicago Press, 1955], pp. 66–73, and esp. 148, first suggested the importance of Bushnell's views about evil for *Billy Budd*.)

tor's description of Captain Vere as a Burkean conservative struggling to maintain order in the face of both domestic and foreign insurgency:

> It was the summer of 1797. In April of that year had occurred the commotion at Spithead followed in May by a second and yet more serious outbreak in the fleet at the Nore. The latter is known, and without exaggeration in the epithet, as "the Great Mutiny." It was indeed a demonstration more menacing to England than the contemporary manifestoes and conquering and proselyting armies of the French Directory. To the British Empire the Nore Mutiny was what a strike in the fire brigade would be to London threatened by general arson.... *that* was the time when at the mastheads of the three-deckers and seventy-fours moored in her own roadstead—a fleet the right arm of a Power then all but the sole free conservative one of the Old World—the bluejackets, to be numbered by thousands, ran up with huzzas the British colors with the union and cross wiped out; by that cancellation transmuting the flag of founded law and freedom defined, into the enemy's red meteor of unbridled and unbounded revolt. (BB, 54)

Obviously familiar with Edmund Burke's "arraignment of the French Revolution" (BB, 48) (i.e., in *Reflections on the Revolution in France* [1790]), the narrator certainly intimates something about his own conservative bias in describing Vere. Vere, he says, is a man whose "settled convictions were as a dike against those invading waters of novel opinion social, political and otherwise" and whose opposition to the French rests in the fact that their political theories "seemed ... insusceptible of embodiment in lasting institutions, [and] ... at war with the peace of the world and the true welfare of mankind" (BB, 62–63). Aptly, then, the narrator describes Vere as being "absorbed in his *reflections*" (BB, 91; emphasis added), as possessing an "aristocratic" (BB, 60) frame of mind, and as ready to assume "prompt initiative" (BB, 90) in unforeseen difficulties—and especially in "emergencies involving considerations both practical and moral, and when it is imperative promptly to act" (BB, 114). In Burke's words, "prejudice [meaning an inclination based on historical precedent and custom], with its reason, has a motive to give *action* to that reason, and an affection which will give it permanence. Prejudice is of ready application in the *emergency*; it previously engages the mind in a steady course of wisdom and virtue, and does not leave the man hesitating in the moment of decision, sceptical, puzzled, and unresolved."[20] Also Burkean is the

---

20. Burke, *Reflections on the Revolution in France* (1790), in *The Works of the*

narrator's observation that "innocence and guilt personified in Claggart and Budd in effect changed places"; for the "essential right and wrong involved in the matter" only intensify the quandary of a captain "not authorized to determine the matter on that *primitive basis*" (BB, 103; emphasis added). As Burke had already said, "[M]etaphysic rights entering into common life, like rays of light which pierce into a dense medium, are, by the laws of nature, refracted from their straight line. Indeed . . . , the *primitive rights of men* undergo such a variety of refractions and reflections, that it becomes absurd to talk of them as if they continued in the simplicity of their original direction."[21]

Yet these parallels between Burke's arraignment of the French Revolution and the narrator's portrait of Vere are subordinate in importance to the implications that Burke's treatise holds both for human nature and for the "politics of crucifixion" in *Billy Budd*. "[I]n this enlightened age," claims Burke, "we are afraid to put men to live and trade each on his own private stock of reason; because we suspect that this stock in each man is small." To Burke's mind, "the splendour of these triumphs of the rights of men" issues only in an abandonment of "all natural sense of wrong and right." Stressing the sort of distrust of human nature that Melville's narrator will project onto Vere's deliberation of how "the people" might mutiny at any sign of clemency (BB, 112), Burke points to the "treasons, robberies, rapes, assassinations, slaughters, and burnings" in France, all painful reminders of unbridled liberty: "The effect of liberty to individuals is, that they may do what they please: we ought to see what it will please them to do, before we risk congratulations." For Burke, then, customs, traditions, institutions, and usage are necessary restraints in a fallen world, furnishing "the wardrobe of a moral imagination" by covering "the defects of our naked, shivering nature."[22] Or, to draw upon the remark that Melville's narrator attributes to Captain Vere (and note how the narrator never claims that Vere makes this statement on the precise occasion recorded in the narrative), "With mankind, . . . forms, measured forms, are everything; and that is the import couched in the story of Orpheus with his lyre spellbinding the wild denizens of the wood" (BB, 128).

The assertion that Vere has once drawn upon this legend to de-

---

Right Honorable Edmund Burke, 8 vols. (London: Henry G. Bohn, 1854–58), II: 359; emphasis added. For other correspondences between Vere's and Burke's dispositions, see Browne, pp. 326–37. Burke's respect for social institutions is discussed by Peter J. Stanlis, *Edmund Burke and the Natural Law* (Ann Arbor: Univ. of Michigan Press, 1958), pp. 130–32.

21. Burke, *Reflections*, p. 334; emphasis added.
22. Burke, *Reflections*, pp. 359, 354, 313, 283, 349.

scribe "the disruption of *forms* going on across the Channel" (emphasis added) suggests the narrator's debt to Thomas Carlyle's concern, in *The French Revolution: A History* (1837), with sanscullotist regicide, the September Massacres, and the "total destruction of social order in this world." In fact, by calling for "the Lyre of some Orpheus, to constrain, with touch of melodious strings, these mad masses into Order," Carlyle anticipates—and, probably, helps to formulate—the words that Melville's narrator attributes to Vere.[23] Also, by equating revolutionary fervor with "the Fanaticism of 'making away with formulas, *de humer les formules,*'" Carlyle may likewise facilitate the narrator's enunciation of Vere's concern with measured forms: "The world of formulas," says Carlyle, "the *formed* regulated world, which all habitable world is,—must need hate such Fanaticism like death; and be at deadly variance with it." Insisting, moreover, that "man lives not except with formulas; with customs, *ways* of doing and living," Carlyle possibly inspires what Melville's narrator might regard as the most *virtuous* significance of Vere's name: "[I]t were perhaps edifying to remark ... what a singular thing Customs (in Latin, *Mores*) are; and how fitly the Virtue, *Vir-tus,* Manhood or Worth, that is a man, is called his *Morality* or *Customariness.*"[24]

Implicit, of course, in this conservatism is the same distrust of human nature that characterizes Burke's *Reflections*: "Satan has his place in all hearts," remarks Carlyle, and "though it is not Satan's world this that we live in, Satan always has his place in it."[25] This opinion resembles the narrator's assessment of how Billy's stutter confirms that the "arch interferer, the envious marplot of Eden, still has more or less to do with every human consignment" (BB, 53). Also, insofar as Billy's deathblow to Claggart recalls the blind and passionate fury of the proletariat in the French Revolution,[26] Melville's narrator may intend

---

23. Carlyle, *The French Revolution: A History* (1837), in *Thomas Carlyle's Works,* 18 vols. (London: Chapman, 1904–06), I: 609, 229. Elsewhere in *The French Revolution* Carlyle refers to "Orphic witchery, struggling to recivilise mankind" (p. 762) and to the civilizing charm of "the Orphic fiddle-bow" (p. 760).

To my knowledge, *Billy Budd*'s debt to Carlyle's *French Revolution* has received no critical mention beyond a brief note by Hayford and Sealts (BB, 136), who suggest that Carlyle's *French Revolution* may be implicated in the narrator's allusion to Anacharsis Clootz. In his "Thomas Carlyle and Herman Melville: Parallels, Obliques, and Perpendiculars," Diss., Univ. of North Carolina, 1964, Bruce L. Grenberg argues for the general influence of Carlyle's *History* on Melville's writing from *Typee* through *Pierre*.

24. Carlyle, *French Revolution*, pp. 181, 570, 553.

25. Carlyle, *French Revolution*, pp. 156, 549.

26. Oliver Snyder, "A Note on Billy Budd," *Accent*, 11 (Winter 1951), 58–60, argues convincingly for this analog.

to present Billy as dramatizing a belief similar to Carlyle's that human shortcomings range from the pardonable theatricalities of "a tongue which with sincerity *stammers*" to the awesome, "unpremeditated outbursts of Nature" evinced by mobs. Thus, the narrator seems to shape his reconstruction of Billy's outburst with a full range of overtones identical to Carlyle's skepticism about "Anacharsis Clootz and the Collective sinful Posterity of Adam."[27]

The way in which Melville's narrator likewise evokes the biblical Fall and the identity of Adam (BB, 94) to gloss Billy's character foreshadows his later regard for Billy as the "Second Adam," whose crucifixion benefits the collective humanity aboard the *Bellipotent*. Still, this tendency to impose biblical categories—and especially those of crucifixion and redemption—upon his narration of events may well indicate that the narrator himself is unsettled by the tragedy that he has the duty to relate—and that the compensatory outlook with which he structures his account of Billy's death tells us more about his own quest for peace of mind than about what actually transpired aboard the *Bellipotent*. Moreover, the narrator continues to fashion his sense of Vere's integrity with reference to conservative intellectual contexts that allow him cathartically to resolve his own anguish by viewing Billy's death redemptively. His remark, therefore, that Captain Vere "disinterestedly" (BB, 63) opposed the French Revolution may, as Hayford and Sealts suggest, evoke Matthew Arnold's definition, in *Culture and Anarchy* (1869), of culture as "the disinterested endeavour after man's perfection." Melville actually read and marked sections of this book, as well as of Arnold's *Literature and Dogma* (1873). And both clarify some of the conservative assumptions surrounding the narrator's assessment of Vere's character.[28]

Compatible, for instance, with the narrator's description of Vere's having a "marked leaning toward everything intellectual," and particularly "books treating of actual men and events no matter what era" (BB, 62), is Arnold's definition of culture as the "getting to know,

---

27. Carlyle, *French Revolution*, p. 290 (italics are textual).

28. The quotation about disinterestedness is from Matthew Arnold, *Culture and Anarchy* (New York: Macmillan, 1883), p. xxxiv; this work is cited henceforth parenthetically as "C & A." As Sealts, *Melville's Reading* (item 16) shows, Melville read and marked this edition. Below I quote as well from Arnold's *Literature and Dogma* (New York: Macmillan, 1883), abbreviated parenthetically as "L & D." (Melville owned the 1881 Macmillan edition. See Sealts, item 18.) With a major difference in emphasis, R. A. Yoder, in "Poetry and Science: 'Two Distinct Branches of Knowledge' in *Billy Budd*," *Southern Review: An Australian Journal of Literary Studies* (Univ. of Adelaide), 3, no. 3 (1969), 232–34, explores the implications of Arnold's *Literature and Dogma* for the aesthetic outlook of *Billy Budd*.

whether through reading, observing, or thinking, the best that can at present be known in the world, ... and thus to get a basis for a less confused action ... than we have at present" (C & A, 150). The narrator evidently regards Vere as someone able to surmount confusion, especially the variety entailed in a "clash of military duty and moral scruple—scruple vitalized by compassion." Vere, the narrator conceives, shows himself "mindful of paramount obligations" which dictate that he "strive against scruples that may tend to enervate decision" (BB, 110)—here positing Vere's heroic ability to rise above compassion in a way corresponding to Arnold's definition of manly stability:

> The very words *mind, memory, remain,* come probably, all from the same root, from the notion of staying, attending. Possibly even the word *man* comes from the same; so entirely does the idea of humanity, of intelligence, of looking before and after, of raising oneself out of the flux of things, rest upon the idea of steadying oneself, concentrating oneself, making order in the chaos of one's impressions by attending to one impression rather than the other. The rules of conduct, of morality, were themselves, philosophers suppose, reached in this way;—the notion of a whole self as opposed to a partial self, a best self to an inferior, to a momentary self a permanent self requiring the restraint of impulses a man would naturally have indulged;—because, by *attending* to his life, man found it had a scope beyond the wants of the present moment. (L & D, 21-22)

Both for Arnold and for Melville's narrator, therefore, among the main benefits of culture is its intolerance of unbridled popular will: "[C]ulture ... shows us that there is nothing so very blessed in merely doing as one likes, ... that the really blessed thing is to like what right reason ordains, and to follow her authority ..." (C & A, 52). Moreover, Vere's alleged fear of "the people" corresponds to Arnold's outcry against the anarchical tendencies of the *"Populace,"* "now issuing from its hiding place to assert an Englishman's heaven-born privilege of doing as he likes, ... marching where it likes, bawling what it likes, [and] breaking what it likes" (C & A, 81). Significantly, for our purposes, Arnold cites *conscription* as the obligation most "at variance with our English notion of the prime right and blessedness of doing as one likes" (C & A, 45)—and even defines the "aristocratic" version of "doing as one likes" in a way that helps to explain why Melville's narrator mentions in such close proximity Billy's "noble descent" and his status as an "upright barbarian" (BB, 52), *barbarism* being a term that Melville more customarily uses in connection with

imperialist racism.[29] In *Culture and Anarchy*, however, there is a definition of *barbarism* compatible with the political concerns relating to
human rights in *Billy Budd*:

> I have in my own mind often indulged myself with the fancy of
> employing, in order to designate our aristocratic class, the name
> of *The Barbarians*. The Barbarians, to whom we all owe so
> much, and who reinvigorated and renewed our worn-out Eu-
> rope, had, as is well known, eminent merits; and in this country,
> where we are for the most part sprung from the Barbarians, we
> have never had the prejudice against them which prevails among
> the races of Latin origin. The Barbarians brought with them that
> staunch individualism, as the modern phrase is, and that passion
> for doing as one likes, for the assertion of personal liberty, which
> appears ... the central idea of English life.... (C & A, 77)

Aboard the *Rights of Man*, then, Billy was at liberty to do as he liked
by barbarously drubbing Red Whiskers (BB, 47); in the more complex
society of the *Bellipotent*, however, the same bellicosity leads to the
sort of encounter with Vere that Arnold would regard as inevitable:
"[T]he framework of society ... is sacred; and whoever administers
it, ... we steadily and with undivided heart support them in repress-
ing anarchy and disorder" (C & A, 196). Pertinent, too, for the stance
espoused by Melville's narrator on the "politics of crucifixion" is the
way Arnold equates religion and obedience in distinguishing between
Hellenism—the governing idea of which is *"spontaneity of consciousness"*—and Hebraism, characterized by "conduct and obedience" and
"strictness of conscience" (C & A, 112–13). According to Arnold, the
"object of religion" is simply *"Conduct"* (L & D, 16).

These views certainly anticipate the outlook of Melville's narrator concerning the place of authority and religion aboard the potentially chaotic world of the *Bellipotent*. Also important is the way the
narrator corroborates his own ideas about "the doctrine of man's
Fall" (BB, 52) by sympathetically imagining Vere's decision to hang
Billy to have been inspired by a belief that the depraved crew would
otherwise mutiny: "[M]ost of them are familiar with our naval usage
and tradition," the narrator imagines Vere to say, "and how would
they take it?... Will they not revert to the recent outbreak at the Nore?
Ay" (BB, 112). Here, as elsewhere, not a word of dialogue in *Billy
Budd* is reliable, since the narrator customarily imposes his own
skepticism about human nature upon what he imagines to be a disinterested account of what in all likelihood transpired. For example, the

---

29. See chapter IV above.

narrator—and not Vere—stresses the crew's turpitude by imagining
that the sailors listen to the death sentence "like ... a seated congregation of believers in hell listening to the clergyman's announcement of
his Calvinistic text" (BB, 117). And this projected sentiment is consistent with the way the narrator elsewhere suggests the crew's depravity
by comparing their restlessness at Billy's hanging to the "animal greed
for prey" (BB, 127) displayed by the screaming seafowl that supposedly
fly overhead at the same moment. Responding, to the narrator's mind,
as "mobs ashore are liable to" (BB, 126), the sailors supposedly
indulge in a slight "encroachment," the insurrectionist tendencies of
which Vere is said to quell by ordering his famous drumbeat to quarters: " 'With mankind,' he would say, 'forms, measured forms, are
everything' " (BB, 128).

The narrator, then, would doubtless laud the critical view that
"Vere's estimate of the situation ... is correct. A fallen and corrupted
world can only be governed by the stern provisions of the Mutiny Act,
carried out with the utmost speed and decision."[30] Yet Vere does not
necessarily make his remark about measured forms at this specific
juncture; the narrator's phrase "he would say" only gives that impression. Moreover, the narrator *imagines* that Billy's face was "a crucifixion to behold" (BB, 99) and imbues with Christly significance the
clouds that are said to hover over the *Bellipotent* at the moment of
Billy's death. "[I]t chanced that the vapory fleece hanging low in the
East was shot through with a soft glory as of the fleece of the Lamb of
God seen in the mystical vision, and simultaneously therewith,
watched by the wedged mass of upturned faces, Billy ascended; and,
ascending, took the full rose of the dawn" (BB, 124). Significantly,
this is a reference to John 1:29: "the Lamb of God, which taketh away
the sin of the world"—an allusion that reinforces the depraved view
of humanity implicit in the narrator's sense of the "politics of crucifixion." And neither does the fact that the *Bellipotent*'s chaplain
cannot bring Billy to any "dogma[tic]" view of "salvation and a Savior" (BB, 121) present a contradiction here, since the narrative suggests that Billy possesses what, in *Literature and Dogma*, Arnold
defines as the nondogmatic or genuine method and secret of Jesus:
"righteousness" (L & D, 328), by which Arnold means *"conduct"*:
"The saviour of Israel is he who makes Israel use his conscience
simply and sincerely, who makes him change and sweeten his temper,

---

30. Fogle, p. 198. Cf. Wendell Glick, "Expediency and Absolute Morality in *Billy
Budd*," *PMLA*, 68 (March 1953), 105–6; Christopher W. Sten, "Vere's Use of the
'Forms': Means and Ends in *Billy Budd*," *American Literature*, 47 (March 1975), 37–51;
Stern, *Billy Budd*, pp. xxii–xxxiv.

conquer and annul his sensuality" (L & D, 91). By speculating, moreover, that Captain Vere may even explain his "actuating motives"
(BB, 115) to Billy, the narrator would have us believe Billy's Christ-
like "God bless Captain Vere" (BB, 123) to comprise a truly *pardonable* acquiescence in this social and political drama.[31]

Still, whatever the strengths or shortcomings of such conservatism, *Billy Budd* is less concerned with the benefits of one political
outlook over another than with the futility of processes by which
people generally seek to make sense of, and impose order upon, the
chaos of history. For while the narrator regards himself as an un-
biased historian who would never compromise truth for the sake of
fictional symmetry (BB, 128), Milton R. Stern has shown elements of
the narrative to be ethnically biased. William Bysshe Stein, moreover,
seems correctly to remark that in the following passage the narrator's
"first approach to an understanding of Claggart's corruption depends
upon an absurd combination of historical fact and pseudo-science":

> The face was a notable one; the features all except the chin cleanly
> cut as those on a Greek medallion; yet the chin, beardless as
> Tecumseh's, had something of strange protuberant heaviness in
> its make that recalled the prints of the Reverend Dr. Titus Oates,
> the historic deponent with the clerical drawl in the time of
> Charles II and the fraud of the alleged Popish Plot. It served
> Claggart in his office that his eye could cast a tutoring glance.
> His brow was of the sort phrenologically associated with the
> more than average intellect; silken jet curls partly clustered over
> it, making a foil to the pallor below.... This complexion...
> seemed to hint of something defective or abnormal in the consti-
> tution and blood. (BB, 64)[32]

---

31. W. H. Auden, in *The Enchafed Flood, or the Romantic Iconography of the Sea*
(New York: Random House, 1950), pp. 146–47, best describes what I take to be the
narrator's typological outlook by remarking that Vere's closeted interview transforms
Billy from "the unconscious Adam into the conscious Christ," or the Second Adam. Yet
in believing that Billy "must know what sin is, or else his suffering is not redemptive,"
Auden actually tells us more about the narrator's outlook, anxieties, and projections
than about the interior workings of Billy's mind.

32. For Stern's remarks about cultural relativism and anti-Catholicism, see his edition of *Billy Budd*, pp. 41, n. 2, 81, n. 3. (Again, however, I would attribute these
prejudicial features to the narrator rather than to the "conservative Melville" whom
Stern equates with the narrative voice in *Billy Budd*.) William Bysshe Stein's remark is
from his " 'Billy Budd': The Nightmare of History," *Criticism*, 3 (Summer 1961),
244–45. Although I fully agree that Melville has created an unreliable narrator, I take
issue with both Stein's thoughts about the narrator's status as a "grimacing trickster"
(p. 248; cf. pp. 240–41) and Stanton Garner's deduction, in "Fraud as Fact in Herman
Melville's *Billy Budd*," *San Jose Studies*, 4 (May 1978), 83–105, about the narrator's

The narrator's proneness here to displace objective description with personal prejudices and preoccupations corresponds to the most crucial point about the ballad that concludes *Billy Budd*. As one critic observes, it "attributes to Billy an unreflective, unexplained sense of life and death intermingling, of consciousness after death.... Diminished rather than climactic, these last lines relate Billy to all other men through a primitive reaction in the face of death, a refusal to believe in the destructibility of consciousness."[33] The ballad, therefore, reveals just as much—and probably more—about the aspirations of the poetic foretopman who composed it than it does about Billy, whose status becomes more and more like the doubloon in *Moby-Dick*, in which every man reads the projections of his own fears, aspirations, and hopes.[34]

Important in this respect is the narrator's remark that the supposedly flawed account of Claggart's death recorded in a naval chronicle of the time "is *all* that hitherto has stood in human record to attest what manner of men respectively were John Claggart and Billy Budd " (BB, 131; emphasis added). Thus, the narrator's description of Billy's face as "a crucifixion to behold" tells us more about how the narrator reconciles himself to his conception of Billy's anguish than it does about Billy's innermost thoughts, which are irretrievable. Lacking historical corroboration for his views, the narrator everywhere im-

---

self-conscious effort to deceive the reader. Whatever the narrator's erroneous statements—and Garner shows them to be numerous—he still strives, as Yoder (p. 226) argues, to "give a balanced and objective account of Billy." The narrator's unreliability tells us more about the general futility of trying to make sense of the nightmare of Billy's death, and history generally, than it does about the narrator's integrity. In fact, the narrator's struggle to impose order on the ambiguities and uncertainties surrounding Billy's tragedy shows up in the text's "or" constructions, "may / might" constructions, direct and rhetorical questions, and combinations forms (for this emphasis, see Edward M. Cifelli, "*Billy Budd*: Boggy Ground to Build On," *Studies in Short Fiction*, 15 [Fall 1976], p. 464). And more important than what Melville's late pencil revisons teach us about Melville's sympathy for Vere (see Cifelli, p. 469) is what they suggest about Melville's effort to have the text's rhetorical patterns reflect the uncertainties and ambiguities that the narrator seeks to surmount by glorifying Vere.

33. Yoder, pp. 230–31.

34. In this vein, see Vern Wagner, "Billy Budd as Moby-Dick: An Alternate Reading," in *Studies in Honor of John Wilcox*, ed. A. Dayle Wallace and Woodburn O. Ross (Detroit: Wayne State Univ. Press, 1958), pp. 157–74; Paul Brodtkorb, Jr., "The Definitive *Billy Budd*: 'But Aren't It All Sham?'" *PMLA*, 82 (Dec. 1967), 604. Also useful for its reflections on the way *Billy Budd*'s narrative technique reflects the futility of seeking faithfully to represent historical truth is William T. Stafford's "Truth's Ragged Edges: Melville's Loyalties in *Billy Budd*—The Commitment of Form in the Digressions," in *Books Speaking to Books: A Contextual Approach to American Fiction* (Chapel Hill: Univ. of North Carolina Press, 1981), pp. 105–14.

bues his script with elements derived from both personal introspection and psychological projection. For instance, his narrative approaches spiritual autobiography in the chapter dealing with his own encounter with the honest scholar ("At the time, my experience was such that I did not quite see the drift of all this. It may be that I see it now" [BB, 75]). And elsewhere the narrative shows the value that the narrator ascribes to Vere's gestures to be foreign to the captain's consciousness: "[H]e to-and-fro paced the cabin athwart; in the returning ascent to windward climbing the slant deck in the ship's lee roll; *without knowing it symbolizing* thus in his action a mind resolute to surmount difficulties even if against primitive instincts strong as the wind and the sea" (BB, 109; emphasis added). Vere, of course, regularly walks this way aboard a wave-tossed ship; the subconscious motive imputed to his gait is merely a projection of the narrator's conservatism.

This imposition of values is seen also in the way the narrator places the ballad "Billy in the Darbies" at the end of his narrative, though earlier using it, as well as the allegedly corrupt "News from the Mediterranean," as inspiration for recreating the chain of events leading to Billy's death. For just as important as any inquiry into how Melville expanded a poem into a novel is the respect that the narrator shows for *poetic knowledge.*[35] Here rests a factor important both for the narrator's self-proclaimed status as a reliable historian and for his inevitable failure to recover anything beyond his own poetic sense of what really happened aboard the *Bellipotent.* In fact, the point becomes clear with respect to what, in reference to nineteenth-century historiography, Hayden White defines as the relations among history, poetry, and "prefigurative" outlooks:

> Historical accounts purport to be verbal models, or icons, of specific segments of the historical process. But such models are needed because the documentary record does not figure forth an unambiguous image of the structure of events attested in them. In order to figure "what *really* happened" in the past, therefore, the historian must first *pre*figure as a possible object of knowledge the whole set of events reported in the documents. This prefigurative act is *poetic* inasmuch as it is precognitive and precritical in the economy of the historian's own consciousness. It is also poetic insofar as it is constitutive of the structure that will subsequently be imaged in the verbal model offered by the historian as a representation and explanation of "what *really* happened" in the past.

---

35. For an excellent discussion of the way poetic knowledge functions in *Billy Budd*, see Yoder, pp. 228–34.

Moreover, we may appropriate White's remark that the historian "creates his object of analysis and predetermines the modality of the conceptual strategies he will use to explain it"[36] to argue that, in *Billy Budd*, Vere's conservative estimate of how his crew will riot if they deduce that an act of mutiny can go unpunished is actually to be attributed to the narrator himself, an arch conservative. The narrator, we know, would have us think that Vere acts heroically in confronting this emergency with unflinching resolve. But the narrator fails *poetically* to imagine and articulate either Vere's dilemma or the moral consequences of its outcome within categories other than those already defining the Judeo-Christian heritage of sacrifice and atonement. And this failure of imagination leads him to create a protagonist whose tendency to indulge in evasive deliberation corresponds to his own (i.e., the narrator's) flight from the full range of possibilities open to consciousness. Moreover, this particular mode of "bad faith" has everything to do with the narrator's use of the *Somers* affair in creating an "Appleton House" portrait of Vere.

T he narrator's sympathy for Vere is indicated by his effort to explain—and to some degree, therefore, to vindicate—Vere's decision: "Feeling that unless quick action was taken on it, the deed of the foretopman, so soon as it should be known on the gun decks, would tend to awaken the slumbering embers of the Nore among the crew, a sense of the urgency of the case overruled in Captain Vere every other consideration" (BB, 104). As Thomas Scorza says, Vere "can only be said to have erred *if* his fears of rekindled mutiny can be shown to be ill-founded.... In light of ... the narrator's own remarks ..., it would seem impossible to fault the sense of Vere's judgment without appeals beyond the universe of the story."[37] Still, since the narrator is the artificer of a universe having a radical correspondence to his own conservative biases, we might entertain a "noble doubt"—if we may draw upon this Emersonian idiom—about the objective status of the events he describes. And critical to the narrator's re-creation of Vere's dilemma is his compassionate allusion to a similar incident aboard the *Somers*:

Not unlikely [Vere and his officers] were brought to something

---

36. Hayden White, *Metahistory: The Historical Imagination in Nineteenth-Century Europe* (Baltimore, Md.: Johns Hopkins Univ. Press, 1973), pp. 30–31. I here cite White as a means of supplementing Yoder's account of poetic knowledge in *Billy Budd*.

37. Scorza, p. 128.

more or less akin to that harassed frame of mind which in the
year 1842 actuated the commander of the U.S. brig-of-war *Somers*
to resolve, under the so-called Articles of War,... upon the execution at sea of a midshipman and two sailors as mutineers designing the seizure of the brig. Which resolution was carried out
though in a time of peace and within not many days' sail of
home. An act vindicated by a naval court of inquiry subsequently
convened ashore. History, and here cited without comment. True,
the circumstances on board the *Somers* were different from those
on board the *Bellipotent*. But the urgency felt, well-warranted or
otherwise, was much the same. (BB, 113–14)

That the narrator draws prejudicially upon the *Somers* incident to defend Vere is evident from the way he refers to Mackenzie's *vindication*
as "history, and here cited without comment," for the naval court in
fact neither vindicated Mackenzie nor acquitted him outright of the
charges of murder brought against him by Spencer's father. Rather,
much to the consternation of conservative Whigs, the court merely
"decide[d] that the charge against him is not proved"—and issued this
decision "instead of a declaration that he is not guilty."[38]

The narrator's sense of Mackenzie's having been "vindicated" corresponds to the conservative interpretation of the court's ruling as an
"honorable acquittal."[39] Yet even White-Jacket, we should recall,
suspected that the three men died "merely because, in the Captain's
judgment, it became necessary to hang them" (WJ, 313). The narrator
of *Billy Budd* evades this radical outlook, as well as the charges of
murder and negligence leveled by Gail Hamilton at both Mackenzie
and Melville's cousin as late as 1889 in three consecutive issues of the
Cosmopolitan.[40] Instead, Melville's narrator allies himself with the conservative assessment of Charles Sumner, whose defense of Mackenzie
begins—quite suggestively, for our purposes—with a review of the
most menacing mutinies of the eighteenth and nineteenth centuries,

---

38. "Intelligence and Miscellany," *Law Reporter*, 6 (May 1843), 47.

39. Charles Sumner, "The Mutiny of the Somers," *North American Review*, 57
(July 1843), 225.

40. Gail Hamilton, "The Murder of Philip Spencer," *Cosmopolitan*, 7 (June, July,
Aug. 1889), 133–40, 248–56, 345–54. Interestingly, Melville's narrator fails to consider
Hamilton's accusation that the charges brought against Spencer were largely inspired
by the vivid imaginations of the officers (pp. 136, 346). In fact, by imagining that the
crew of the *Bellipotent* would have mutinied had Vere not hanged Billy, the narrator of
Billy Budd may repeat the logical error that Hamilton ascribes to Mackenzie: "His
unvarying habit was to assume a theory of the mutiny, and then to swear to it before
the court as if it were a fact. He had a theory in his own mind that these boys were
planning murder, and on oath before the court he speaks exactly as if the plan of
murder were proven by detail in the paper before him" (p. 249).

and most prominently those at Spithead and Nore: "Perhaps no event during the reign of George the Third seemed, for a while, more to endanger the empire, or threw the people into a deeper consternation."[41] Here, then, is an apologia for the *Somers* affair that invokes for conservative purposes the same incidents of mutiny that function so conspicuously in the way Melville's narrator condones the behavior of Vere. Also, the narrator's nonchalance about whether the urgency felt by Mackenzie was "well-warranted or otherwise" (BB, 114) corresponds to Sumner's belief that "it is not necessary that the danger should in *reality* be imminent; it is sufficient, if there are reasonable grounds to believe that there is a design to destroy life, although it should afterwards appear that no such design existed."[42] Neither, with reference to Sumner's views, is the narrator's exculpation of Vere inconsistent with the remark that the captain's handling of the trial was slightly reminiscent of "the policy adopted in those tragedies of the palace which have occurred more than once in the capital founded by Peter the Barbarian" (BB, 103); for as Sumner says, Mackenzie "was invested with a duty not unlike that of the dictator (It is said that the first cause of creating a dictator, was the fear of a domestic sedition. Liv. II.18,20, III.20. Cic. de Leg. III.3.), *to see that the ship received no detriment.*"[43]

This defense of Mackenzie, as well as the sympathy shown by Melville's narrator for the promptness that Vere exhibits in a crisis, may owe something to an issue of the *Law Reporter* that Sumner twice cites (pp. 225, 228) to fortify his argument. *"There can be little democracy in war,"* claims its article on the *Somers;* "exigencies occur, which leave brief time for thought, and a moment's hesitation may determine the issue of a battle, or the catastrophe of a wreck. The responsibility

---

41. Sumner, p. 200. As the title page of Sumner's article suggests, the piece purports to be a commentary on two publications—the first, *Case of the Somers Mutiny: Defense of Alexander Slidell Mackenzie, Commander of the U.S. Brig Somers, before the Court-Martial held at the Navy-Yard, Brooklyn* (New York: Tribune Office, 1843); the second, *History of the Mutiny at Spithead and the Nore, with an Inquiry into its Origin and Treatment,* Family Library, no. LXXX (London: Thomas Tegg, 1842). Since Melville personally knew Sumner (see chapter III, note 28, above) and was obviously concerned with the part his cousin, Guert, played in the *Somers* affair, he more than likely early read this article, which (p. 222) reprints the statement signed by "Guert Gansevoort, Lieutenant" in justification of the hangings. Moreover, Melville would probably have been reminded about Sumner's views by Gail Hamilton's hostile response (p. 354) to this defense of Mackenzie. (In discussing the coincidence between Sumner's views and the assumptions of Melville's narrator, I use as a point of departure William J. Kimball's more general observations about "Charles Sumner's Contribution to Chapter XVIII of *Billy Budd,*" *South Atlantic Bulletin,* 23, no. 4 [Nov. 1967], 13–14.)

42. Sumner, p. 232.

43. Sumner, p. 229. I have inserted in parentheses the footnote that Sumner offers to support his assertion.

is awful, and the power corresponding to it is tremendous." Also, insofar as the narrator imagines Vere to say that Billy's innocence may be
acquitted at "the Last Assizes," but not under "the Mutiny Act, War's
child" (BB, 111, 112), a suggestive analog exists between the following
passage from the *Law Reporter* and the logic with which the narrator
fashions Vere's speech to the drumhead court:

> It is against all our notions of justice, and all our religious sen-
> timents, that a man should hold by his own breath despotic
> power over human life; but war in all its branches, in all its con-
> ditions, in all its forms, is equally adverse to moral feeling and re-
> ligious duty.... Hence comes martial law and the law of war,
> softened indeed in the civilization of the world, and impressed, to
> some extent, with the improvements of the age, stern, severe, sud-
> den in its decision, prompt in its exercise, yet a necessary part of
> that great system of wrong, which the violence of human passions
> has contrived for the propagation of human wretchedness, and
> which will continue to pour forth its vials of wrath, till the pre-
> dicted time arrives, "when men shall beat their swords into
> ploughshares, and their spears into pruning hooks—when nation
> shall not lift up sword against nation; neither shall they learn
> war any more."

Predictably, then, the narrator's portrait of Vere finally coincides with
the *Law Reporter*'s assessment of Mackenzie's manhood:

> If, under the circumstances of the case, it was proper that the
> deed should be done, the bold and fearless act of the young com-
> mander, who had the resolution to meet the tremendous responsi-
> bility of his most awful situation, with a full knowledge of the
> perils to which it would subject his own life, and the imputations
> it would cast upon his honor, is an exhibition of moral courage
> which more than the exigencies of wreck or battle give the world
> assurance of a man.[44]

Again, the point here, as above, transcends a mere search for Melville's sources; at issue is how conservative vindications of an event
that occurred in 1842 help fashion the narrator's response to one set in
1797—and what this implies about both the integrity of his history
and his tendency to evade the full range of possibilities open to Vere.
We know that the narrator has been reading about the *Somers*—

---

44. "The Case of the Somers," *Law Reporter*, ed. Peleg Chandler, 6 (May 1843), 13,
2. As I argue above (chapter IV), Chandler and the *Law Reporter* may have influenced
Melville's conception of Peleg in *Moby-Dick*.

perhaps these very write-ups; if not, then documents like them. That Vere ends up looking so much like the heroic Mackenzie described by Sumner and the *Law Reporter*, rather than like the scoundrel portrayed by Gail Hamilton, again tells us more about the narrator's encounter with conservative assessments of the *Somers* affair than about what necessarily happened aboard the *Bellipotent*. Indeed, despite the narrator's insistence that his is an "inside narrative," he actually relies heavily upon an incident external to the eighteenth-century universe of Billy Budd and Captain Vere to structure an account of Billy's execution consistent with his own conservative biases.

Vere, then, is less a phenomenally heroic man than he is a projection of the narrator's belief in phenomenal heroism as a courageous commitment to responsibility and duty.[45] By claiming, however, that "the condemned one suffered less than he who mainly had effected the condemnation" (BB, 115), the narrator departs from contemporary accounts of Mackenzie, who was known to possess a self-righteous arrogance about his conduct aboard the *Somers*. Even the *Law Reporter* remarked that "a man who could look back upon the transaction with so much complacency, if not satisfaction, might have proceeded in the execution with rashness, perhaps, if not with unmanly fear." Anticipating, and perhaps even prescribing, the more compassionate attitude that Melville's narrator ascribes to Vere, the *Law Reporter* says, "It would have been better, we think, for his fame—certainly for the estimation of his character by the people, . . . had he expressed those feelings of distress and regret for the terrible occasion which become the heroism of a warrior not less than the humanity of man."[46] Appropriately, then, the narrator portrays in Vere, as one critic says, "just such agony as the strong Abraham would have felt in surrendering all his deepest individual human feelings—and they were very much *there*—to the greater necessities of a larger demand, a higher morality."[47] Significant, as well, is the narrator's description of Vere's "crossing the deck" (BB, 113) after completing his deliberation; for much like the line that tells how Billy's expression "was a crucifixion to behold" (BB, 99), this passage again reveals the narrator's belief that Vere experiences a crucifixion of consciousness by being caught in the midst of life's seemingly irresolvable dichotomies.

Yet for all the narrator's effort to impose a Christly dignity and a humane magnanimity upon both Billy's execution and Vere's

---

45. Here I take issue with Warner Berthoff's "Certain Phenomenal Men: The Example of *Billy-Budd*," *English Literary History*, 27 (Dec. 1960), 334–51.

46. "Case of the Somers," pp. 10, 9.

47. Stern, *Billy Budd*, p. xxxix.

anguish, existing scholarship is probably correct in remarking that "Billy becomes the Adam who does not fall, the Isaac who is not saved, the Christ who does not redeem. One comes away from the book with a sense of the immense futility of Billy's death."[48] And far, too, from enacting a redemptive scenario, Vere, as still another critic says, unwittingly parodies "the passages from the Gospel of John in which Caiaphas, the appointed high priest of the temple, attempting to reconcile an abstract conception of justice with his sense of his own responsibilities as a representative of earthly political authority, determines the fate of an innocent Christ before a similarly untutored and timorous group of subordinates."[49] If accurate, this observation is beyond the cognizance of Melville's narrator; for insofar as the identity of Caiaphas functions in *Billy Budd*, it comprises Melville's critique not merely of Vere but of a narrator whose use of biblical metaphors to structure an interpretation of events directly informs Vere's remark that "the divine judgment of Ananias!" (BB, 100; cf. Acts 5:1–11) has befallen Claggart. Similarly indebted to the narrator's biblical temperament is Vere's exclamation, "Struck dead by an angel of God! Yet the angel must hang!" (BB, 101). In both cases Vere's words simply reflect the narrator's psychological tendency to fall back on retributive religious models as a means of redemption from the nightmare of history and the chaos of reality.

Worth noting, then, is how this projection of values finds an analog in the narrative technique of Marvell's "Appleton House," from which Melville's narrator actually quotes at one point (BB, 61). As Peter Schwenger argues, Marvell contrasts the unassuming purity of the house and its garden with the significance that each assumes after the narrator of the poem imposes meaning on them with metaphors revealing more about his own fallen nature than about the estate. The narrator of *Billy Budd*, it seems to me, echoes what Schwenger calls the "deceptive projection" of "Appleton House" by imposing his own sense of a fallen humanity upon the conceivable limits of Vere's alternatives, and possibly upon what may have been Claggart's unpremeditated hostility in accusing Billy of mutiny.[50] Moreover, Vere's apparent

48. John W. Rathbun, *"Billy Budd* and the Limits of Perception," *Nineteenth-Century Fiction*, 20 (June 1955), 25. The failure of imagery pertaining to Christ in *Billy Budd* is also noted by Scorza, pp. 153–54; Bernard Rosenthal, "Elegy for Jack Chase," *Studies in Romanticism*, 10 (Summer 1971), 229.

49. Philip D. Beidler, *"Billy Budd*: Melville's Valedictory to Emerson," *ESQ: A Journal of the American Renaissance*, 24 (1978), 222.

50. See Peter Schwenger, " 'To Make His Saying True': Deceit in *Appleton House*," *Studies in Philology*, 77 (Jan. 1980), 94–95, 104. With respect to this crucial narrative issue in both Marvell's poem and *Billy Budd*, some inaccuracy, I think, exists in the

heroism may be nothing more than the creation of a narrator who sub-consciously invents heroic precedent to justify his own tendency to flee from what Jean-Paul Sartre would come to call the anguish of consciousness, or the responsibility of confronting *possibility* in the face of *nothingness.*

An appropriate introduction to Vere's and the narrator's agonized encounter with existential "nothingness" is the precisely opposite state of consciousness which Melville describes in "Buddha" (1891):

> Swooning swim to less and less,
>   Aspirant to nothingness!
> Sobs of the worlds, and dole of kinds
>   That dumb endures be—
> Nirvana! absorb us in your skies,
>   Annul us into thee.

This state of mindless annulment, as Walter Sutton has shown, characterizes the *"euthanasia"* (BB, 125) of Billy's spasmless hanging; indeed, Melville knew of Schopenhauer's interchangeable use of the terms *Nirvana* and *euthanasia* to signify "extinction, or nothingness, the ultimate antithesis to ... pain and suffering."[51] Yet insofar as Vere's suffering is said to exceed Billy's, the more torturous "nothingness" into which the captain (and by implication, his narrator) peers is the existential abyss that Melville had already pondered in *Clarel.* There, as Stanley Brodwin says, the "eternal abyss" is

> defined by the ontological reality of death, man's finiteness, and its consequences to man's quest for religious and psychological

---

suggestion that "Vere's assumption of the mantle of the mythic artificer of order has led to nothing less than the fall of a world" (Beidler, p. 223); for Melville's narrator, like Marvell's poet, is finally the source of what Beidler otherwise rightly refers to as Vere's "'creative' formalism" (p. 220). As suggested, moreover, the narrator's projection of evil may extend to Claggart. Terence J. Matheson, in "A New Look at Melville's Claggart," *Studies in Short Fiction*, 17 (Fall 1980), 445–53, raises the fascinating possibility that Claggart "was not personally behind Billy's encounter with the afterguardsman" (p. 450). We must, however, still ask why readers so readily assume Claggart's premeditative guilt. The answer, again, rests in the deceptive projection and innuendo of the narrator.

51. Walter Sutton, "Melville and the Great God Budd," *Prairie Schooner*, 34 (Summer 1960), 129–31. "Buddha" is quoted from *Collected Poems of Herman Melville*, ed. Howard P. Vincent (Chicago: Packard and Co., 1947), p. 232.

security in a world where teleological values are lost, and where absolutes have broken down or lost all meaning.... The abyss that Melville saw on all sides was a death without transfiguration, and an eternity whose essence was nothingness or silence.

Brodwin shows that Clarel seeks to resolve the "complex passion" (I.v.219) of his existential quandary by means of "the Magi-search for the star of God, a traditional and meaningful Christian pattern."[52] Like the narrator of *Billy Budd*, who falls back on similar biblical patterns, Clarel seeks to imbue the "nothingness" of existence with a plenitude that negates negation.

Still, in *Billy Budd* Melville anticipates Jean-Paul Sartre's recognition that consciousness and moral responsibility are synonymous with an incessant, unalleviated encounter with nothingness. This is to say that the "for-itself" (i.e., perception defined by the awareness of *not being* what it perceives) sustains itself exclusively as a negation of the "in-itself" (i.e., the plenitude of mere matter or things.) In short, consciousness *is* negation: "[T]he pure event by which human reality rises as a presence in the world is apprehended by itself as *its* own *lack*. In coming into existence human reality grasps itself as an incomplete being."[53] From this, Sartre deduces that consciousness is the incessant anguish of confronting *possibilities*, themselves contingent upon the mind's perception of itself in antithesis to the definitive plenitude that would otherwise relieve consciousness of both its precarious *lack* and its *freedom*; indeed, "freedom in its foundation coincides with the nothingness which is at the heart of man.... Thus freedom is not *a* being; it is *the being* of man—i.e., his nothingness of being."[54]

These categories are more than suitable for analyzing the dilemma of both Vere and his narrator in their evasion of *possibility*, or the anguish of consciousness; for "anguish," as Sartre says, "is the recognition of a possibility as *my* possibility; that is, it is constituted when consciousness sees itself cut from its essence by nothingness or separated from the future by its very freedom."[55] This, of course, is an alternative disallowed both by Vere's *a priori* judgment concerning

---

52. Stanley Brodwin, "Herman Melville's *Clarel*: An Existential Gospel," *PMLA*, 86 (May 1971), 375, 376, 384.

53. Jean-Paul Sartre, *Being and Nothingness: An Essay on Phenomenological Ontology*, trans. Hazel E. Barnes (New York: Philosophical Library, 1956), p. 89.

54. Sartre, pp. 440–41.

55. Sartre, p. 35. In applying these Sartrean categories to *Billy Budd*, I am in agreement with Sherrill, who (p. 238) speaks more generally about Melville's belief in "the capacity of the deep-diving literary imagination to plunge to the bottom of human experience and to find there what is funded as ontological possibility."

Billy's destiny, and—more significantly—by the limited possibilities imposed upon Vere by a narrator whose prejudicial allegiance to conservative estimates of the *Somers* affair, along with readings in Burke, Arnold, and Carlyle, circumscribes the perceptual range of Vere's deliberations. And even though the narrator renders in eloquent form Vere's articulation before the drumhead court of "certain principles that were *axioms* to himself" (BB, 109; emphasis added), we know from *Mardi* of Melville's readiness to question the integrity of such self-centered assuredness. As Babbalanja says,

> There is no supreme standard yet revealed, whereby to judge of ourselves; "Our very instincts are prejudices," saith Alla Malolla; "Our very axioms, and postulates are far from infallible." "In respect of the universe, mankind is but a sect," saith Diloro: "and first principles but dogmas." What ethics prevail in the Pleiades? What things have the synods in Sagittarius decreed? (M, 574)

At issue, then, is not whether Vere *should have* shown leniency, but whether his decision *not to* was the product of any genuine encounter with opposing possibilities. The narrative's unperturbed account of Vere's pronouncement, long before his axiomatic deliberations with the drumhead court, that "the angel must hang!" (BB, 101) suggests that there was no consideration of alternatives.[56] And consistent with this limitation of possibility is the idea that civil law preempts the mandates of "private conscience." As the narrator has Vere say, "For that law and the rigor of it, we are not responsible. Our vowed responsibility is in this: That however pitilessly that law may operate in any instances, we nevertheless adhere to it." Also, in having Vere pronounce that private conscience should "yield to that imperial one formulated in the code under which alone we officially proceed" and that "in receiving our commissions we in the most important regards ceased to be natural free agents" (BB, 110–11), the narrator becomes an accessory to an ethic eventually judged inadequate at Nuremberg.[57]

Of course, Melville had ample knowledge in his own era of de-

---

56. As Brodtkorb (p. 616) says, "To the mystery of Billy's act, Vere reacts as spontaneously as Billy has done with his prejudgment that is founded on everything his own nature has up to that point become." Cf. Brodtkorb, p. 606, n. 9; Scorza, pp. 141–42; Philip D. Ortego, "The Existential Roots of *Billy Budd*," *Connecticut Review*, 4 (Oct. 1970), 80–87. Perhaps the most eloquent assessment of Vere's evasion of freedom is Marlene Longenecker's "Captain Vere and the Form of Truth," *Studies in Short Fiction*, 14 (Fall 1977), 337–43. Again, my aim has been to attribute the burden of "bad faith" to the narrative voice that speaks for Vere.

57. In this vein, see Geoffrey Clive, " 'The Teleological Suspension of the Ethical' in Nineteenth-Century Literature," *Journal of Religion*, 23 (April 1954), 83.

bates pitting conscience against civil law, particularly in relation to the split between Cotton Whigs and Conscience Whigs. Indeed, the stance that the narrator imposes upon Vere in the passages just quoted is almost identical to conservative Whig arguments offered in defense of Judge Lemuel Shaw, Melville's father-in-law, for subordinating private conscience to constitutional mandate in the surrender of fugitive slaves to their owners.[58] Moreover, from his readings in Carlyle and Arnold, Melville could have come to an assessment of Vere quite different from that of his narrator. Vere, as one critic suggests, is actually deficient when judged according to Carlyle's standards of heroism,[59] and Arnold explicitly cautions against the "deadness and formality" (L & D, 81) that ensue with too scrupulous attention to "*conduct.*" In fact, far from sanctioning blind obedience to measured forms, Arnold concedes that Jesus' method was one of "deliverance from binding traditions and formulas" (L & D, 216). Thus, while Melville's narrator suggests an alliance with Arnold in his mention of Vere's "disinterested" outlook, he does so without the intolerance Arnold expressed for mechanistic formality:

> culture [is] a pursuit of our total perfection by means of getting to know, on all the matters which most concern us, the best which has been thought and said in the world; and through this knowledge, turning a stream of fresh and free thought upon our stock notions and habits, which we now follow staunchly but mechanically, vainly imagining that there is a virtue in following them staunchly which makes up for the mischief of following them mechanically. This, and this alone, is the scope of the following essay. And the culture we recommend is, above all, an inward operation. (C & A, xi)

Accordingly, Vere and his narrator are what Arnold would denominate "victim[s] of Hebraism, of the tendency to cultivate strictness of conscience rather than spontaneity of consciousness" (C & A, 134). And by spontaneity of consciousness, Arnold means Hellenism, which, in mandating tolerance for ideas, foreshadows existential respect for *possibilities*:

> [W]hile Hebraism seizes upon certain plain, capital intimations of the universal order, and rivets itself, one may say, with un-

---

58. See chapter IV above. Also see my discussion of *White-Jacket*'s "Conscience-Whig" allegory in chapter III.

59. Ralph Willett, "Nelson and Vere: Hero and Victim in *Billy Budd, Sailor*," *PMLA*, 82 (Oct. 1967), 369–76.

equalled grandeur and earnestness and intensity on the study and observance of them, the bent of Hellenism is to follow, with flexible activity, the whole play of universal order, to be apprehensive of missing any part of it, of sacrificing one part to another, to slip away from resting in this or that intimation of it, however capital. (C & A, 112–13)

Rigidity and a limited view, however, are exactly what the narrator of *Billy Budd* displays in his complacent narration of events. For all his anguish over industrial mechanization,[60] he fails to see how an unquestioning respect for "the mechanism of discipline" (BB, 126) is subject to something like Thoreau's lament concerning the way people mechanistically abandon their consciousness (or, as Sartre might say, approach the status of the "in-itself") by refusing to question social values:

> The mass of men serve the State thus, not as men mainly, but as machines, with their bodies. They are the standing army, and the militia, jailers, constables, *posse comitatus*, & c. In most cases there is no free exercise whatever of the judgment or of the moral sense; but they put themselves on a level with wood and earth and stones; and wooden men can perhaps be manufactured that will serve the purpose as well.[61]

As remarked above, Melville first pondered the idea of flight from abstract thought in *Typee* (1846). By 1891, he seems to have deduced that a yearning for primitivism was no more antagonistic to thought than were the mechanized customs of civilization, which were auspicious to a surrender of conscious choice and deadly to the generation of *value*. For whatever the narrator's conservative values, his failure to entertain them as *possible* (rather than inevitable) values comprises a formidable obstacle to the process by which values themselves come into being. To draw, once again, upon Sartre:

---

60. See Scorza, pp. 19–22, 50.

61. Thoreau, p. 191. For the possibility of Melville's familiarity with *Aesthetic Papers*, which contained the first published edition of Thoreau's essay, see chapter V, note 29, above. In suggesting that *Billy Budd* offers a Thoreauvian critique of its narrator, I contend that Melville here evinces a more sympathetic—and perhaps more mature—encounter with Thoreau's outlook than he did nearly four decades earlier, when, in "Cock-A-Doodle-Doo!" (1853), he possibly satirized the potentially irresponsible tendencies of civil disobedience. For the latter emphasis, see Allan Moore Emery, "The Cocks of Melville's 'Cock-A-Doodle-Doo!'" *ESQ: A Journal of the American Renaissance*, 28 (1982), 89–103, esp. 96–97, 103. Also see the conclusion to this book, in which I further stress the compatibility of Transcendental thought and Melville's respect for conscience and imagination.

> My freedom is anguished at being the foundation of values while itself without foundation. It is anguished in addition because values, due to the fact that they are essentially revealed to a freedom, can not disclose themselves without being at the same time "put into question," for the possibility of overturning the scale of values appears complementary as *my* possibility. It is anguish before values which is the recognition of the ideality of values.[62]

Melville's narrator is forever trapped within the measured forms of a narrative that, failing to entertain the possibility that things might have been otherwise, is inimical to any generative apprehension of values. But insofar as readers will periodically recognize that "the focus of our anguish in *Billy Budd* is not Billy's innocence but the rejection of human values symbolized by his punishment,"[63] Melville transcends his narrator's stagnant emphasis on the Crucifixion to remind readers of all generations to lay down intellectual complacency and shoulder the cross of consciousness.

---

62. Sartre, p. 38.
63. Charles A. Reich, "Tragedy of Justice in *Billy Budd*," *Yale Review*, 56 (Spring 1967), 383.

C O N C L U S I O N

Perhaps the best way to introduce a concluding statement about Melville's major works is to contrast the concerns of his fiction with "Young American" literary standards of the 1820's, 1830's, and 1840's, the mood of which, as Benjamin T. Spencer remarks, was that "America was a new nation, not a revision of an old one, and that her literature would attain its distinction through reflecting her noble and unique political principle." In this spirit, the opening issue of the *Democratic Review* announced that "the vital principle of an American national literature must be democracy," and William A. Jones, among others, founded a peculiarly democratic school of literary criticism, having as its standard of excellence the carrying of republican progressiveness into literature.[1] Not

---

1. Benjamin T. Spencer, "A National Literature, 1837–1855," *American Literature,* 8 (May 1936), 133; "Introduction," *Democratic Review,* 1 (Oct. 1837), 14; John Stafford, "William A. Jones, Democratic Literary Critic," *Huntington Library Quarterly,* 12 (May 1949), 289–302. Even Melville's "Hawthorne and His Mosses," I suggest, satirizes the idea of carrying "republican progressiveness into Literature as well as into Life" (*Literary World,* 7 [17 Aug. 1850], 126). Scholars have for too long ignored John Seelye's observations, in "The Structure of Encounter: Melville's Review of Hawthorne's *Mosses,"* in *Melville and Hawthorne in the Berkshires,* ed. Howard P. Vincent (Kent, Ohio: Kent State Univ. Press, 1968), pp. 67–68, that Melville has created an independent narrator who spouts Fourth of July oratory in praising Hawthorne. From the Vivenza sections of *Mardi* we know of Melville's reservations concerning the too-zealous carrying of republicanism into life, and one would hardly attribute to Melville the following provincialism of his narrator: "[L]et America first praise mediocrity even, in her own children, before she praises ... the best excellence in the children of any other land" (*Literary World,* 7 [24 Aug. 1850], 145). Here Melville satirizes the same sort of "Young Americanism" against which Edgar Allan Poe complained in lamenting that

so far from being ashamed of the many disgraceful literary failures to which our own inordinate vanities and misapplied patriotism have lately given birth, and so far from deeply lamenting that these daily puerilities are of home manufacture, we

unexpectedly, New World political and literary standards presupposed a *new man* to carry out the democratic mandate; basic, indeed, to William Ellery Channing's "Remarks on National Literature" (1823) is the conviction that "in Europe, we meet kings, nobles, priests, peasants. How much rarer is it to meet *men*; by which we mean beings conscious of their own nature, and conscious of the utter worthlessness of all outward distinctions compared with what is treasured up in our souls." Hence, Channing attaches "special importance to those branches of literature which relate to human nature, and which give it a consciousness of its own powers." America, Channing believed, needed a "literature in which genius will pay supreme if not undivided homage to truth and virtue."[2]

Melville, as we have seen, was more disposed to discourse in Edwardsian fashion upon the "true nature of American virtue," exposing messianic republican rhetoric as hyperbolic:

> "Ho! Mardi's Poor, and Mardi's Strong! ye, who starve or beg; seventh-sons who slave for earth's first-born—here [in Vivenza] is your home; predestinated yours; Come over, Empire-founders! fathers of the wedded tribes to come!—abject now, illustrious evermore:—Ho: Sinew, Brawn, and Thigh!"
>
> "A very fine invocation," said Media, "now Babbalanja, be seated; and tell us whether Dominora and the kings of Porpheero do not own some small portion of this great continent, which just now you poetically pronounced as the spoil of any vagabonds who may choose to settle therein?" (M, 512)

This passage is typical of a strategy evident in nearly all of Melville's novels, which illustrate how man's horological nature subverts the achievement of his idealistic aspirations: In *Typee* through *Mardi* the glorious idea of "civilization" deteriorates into an imperialistic and self-aggrandizing myth; in *Redburn* America's typological identity as the Redeemer Nation is betrayed by the isolationist and selfish tendencies of Jacksonian self-reliance; in *White-Jacket* America's egalitarian ideal is belied by the institution of slavery and by the tyranny of the majority; and in *Moby-Dick* Melville rounds out his quarrel

---

adhere pertinaciously to our original blindly conceived idea, and thus often find ourselves involved in the gross paradox of liking a stupid book the better, because, sure enough, its stupidity is American. (*Southern Literary Messenger*, 2 [April 1836], 326)

2. Channing, "Remarks on National Literature" (1823), in *The Works of William E. Channing, D.D.* (Boston: American Unitarian Assoc., 1895), pp. 133, 129, 134.

with America's political idealism by showing covenant psychology to shadow forth the national modes of racism and violence nominally repudiated by Ishmael. Our investigation of *Pierre* and *The Confidence-Man* has shown further that the difficulty in achieving the chronometrical or Transcendental ideal lies in the inherent shortcomings of human nature; in fact, all the way through *The Confidence-Man* the drift of Melville's major fiction confirms one of Babbalanja's more humorous fables about aspiration and limitation:

> In the fables of Ridendiabola, this is to be found. "A fresh-water Polyp, despising its marine existence, longed to live upon air. But [despite] all it could do, its tentacles or arms still continued to cram its stomach. By a sudden preternatural impulse, however, the Polyp at last turned itself inside out; supposing that after such a proceeding it would have no gastronomic interior. But its body proved ventricle outside as well as in. Again its arms went to work; food was tossed in, and digestion continued." (M, 506)

For all this, however, Merton M. Sealts, Jr., seems correct in claiming that Melville swayed between an obvious skepticism toward shallow idealism and a profound respect for Emerson's dictum to "abstain from dogmatism, and recognize all the opposite negations between which, as walls, [a person's] being is swung."[3] Indeed, this flexible, inclusive approach comes close to the posture that Melville assumed in acknowledging to Hawthorne the legitimacy of the Pantheistic "'all' feeling" but in also complaining, "[W]hat plays the mischief with the truth is that men will insist upon the universal application of a temporary feeling or opinion" (L, 131). Seemingly as much a critique of Transcendentalism as of Pierre's antinomian sensualism, this remark nonetheless conforms to Theodore Parker's criteria for distinguishing Transcendental madness from Transcendental wisdom:

> The danger is that the transcendental moralist shall too much abhor the actual rules of morality; where much is bad and ill-founded, shall deem all worthless. Danger, too, that he take *a transient impulse, personal and fugitive, for a universal law;* follow a passion for a principle, and come to naught; surrender his manhood, his free will to his unreflecting instinct, become sub-

---

3. Emerson, "Intellect," in *The Complete Works of Ralph Waldo Emerson,* ed. Edward Waldo Emerson, 12 vols. (Boston: Houghton Mifflin, 1903–04, II: 342. See the informative revisionist study by Merton M. Sealts, Jr., "Melville and Emerson's Rainbow," *ESQ: A Journal of the American Renaissance,* 26 (1980), 53–78, esp. 64. Sealts's study gives new credibility to Perry Miller's more general argument in "Melville and Transcendentalism," *Virginia Quarterly Review,* 29 (Autumn 1953), 445–75.

ordinate thereto. Men that are transcendental-mad we have seen in morals; to be transcendental-wise, sober, is another thing.[4]

Whereas Transcendental madness exists aplenty in *Pierre*, Transcendental wisdom is to be found in Melville's career-long allegiance to conscience, individual dignity, and the need to insure the existence of *value* by exercising imagination and perspective. Whig conservatism notwithstanding, a slim line separates what we have explored as the "Conscience Whig" and antimajoritarian allegory of *White-Jacket* from the Thoreauvian inquiry, "Can there be not a government in which majorities do not virtually decide right and wrong, but conscience?...I think that we should be men first, and subjects afterward."[5] And still more Transcendental and chronometrical are the antislavery and pacifist emphases of *Mardi*, *White-Jacket*, and *Moby-Dick*; for, if we can believe Theodore Parker,

> This conscience in politics and ethics transcends experience, and *a priori* tells us of the just, the right, the good, the fair; not the relatively right alone, but the absolute right also. As it transcends experience, so it anticipates history; and the ideal justice of conscience is juster than the empirical and contingent justice actually exercised at Washington or at Athens.... In transcendental politics the question of expediency is always subordinate to the question of natural right; it asks not merely about the cost of a war, but its natural justice.[6]

As Sherman Paul says of Transcendental politics, "[I]dea anticipates history,"[7] and ideas, thought, and imagination are finally the elements that Melville praised both in numbering Emerson among "the whole corps of thought-divers, that have been diving & coming up again with bloodshot eyes since the world began" (L, 79) and in

---

4. Theodore Parker, "Transcendentalism; a Lecture" (1876), in the centenary edition of Parker's *Works*, ed. George Willis Cooke, 15 vols. (Boston: American Unitarian Assoc., 1907–11), VI: 31; emphasis added. References to John C. Calhoun, James K. Polk, and the year 1848 suggest that Parker first wrote and delivered the lecture sometime around 1848.

5. Henry David Thoreau, "Resistance to Civil Government" (1848), in *Aesthetic Papers*, ed. Elizabeth P. Peabody (New York: G. P. Putnam, 1849), p. 190. The essay was published posthumously, under the title of "Civil Disobedience," in *A Yankee in Canada* (1866).

6. Parker, p. 26.

7. Sherman Paul, *The Shores of America: Thoreau's Inward Exploration* (Urbana: Univ. of Illinois Press, 1958), p. 244.

annotating upon a page of Emerson's *Poems*, "All this is nobly written, and proceeds from *noble thinking*."[8]

We have seen how in *Billy Budd* a lack of noble thinking and a failure of imagination inhibit the narrator's re-creation of Vere's moral alternatives. More than appropriate to this tragedy is Thoreau's remark that "so thoroughly and sincerely are we compelled to live,... denying the possibility of change. This is the only way, we say; but there are as many ways as there can be drawn radii from one centre.... When one man has reduced a fact of the imagination to be a fact of his understanding, I foresee that all men will at length establish their lives on that basis."[9] Similarly, Melville's concern with the priority of ideas and the imagination finally takes him beyond the political and theological values of his era to depict the devaluation of value that occurs when persons surrender their intellectual independence, deny the possibility of change, or close off interpretation by labeling as "apocryphal" any explanation that accounts for the nature of things. Thus, institutions, creeds, and political parties finally rank in Melville's fiction as transient concerns; conscience and consciousness, as permanent. Perhaps Melville would never have agreed with Thoreau's belief that "if one advances confidently in the direction of his dreams, and endeavors to live the life which he has imagined, he will meet with a success unexpected in common hours,"[10] but he would doubtless have confirmed that the truth falls somewhere in between the Morpheus-induced enthusiasm of China Aster and the devalued intellectual repose of the narrator of *Billy Budd*.

C losely related to Melville's homage to the exercise of imagination is the problem raised by nineteenth-century philosophers and theologians who explored the indeterminate and subjective nature of language. For example, in *A Treatise on Language: or, the Relation which Words Bear to Things*

---

8. Melville's annotation about Emerson's "noble thinking" is noted by William Braswell, in "Melville as a Critic of Emerson," *American Literature*, 9 (Nov. 1937), 321; emphasis added. My sense of *Billy Budd*'s Transcendental meaning stands opposed to Philip D. Beidler's thesis that the book is "a tortured demonstration of the wholesale inadequacy not only of Emersonian theories of cognition and moral action, but of expression as well" ("*Billy Budd*: Melville's Valedictory to Emerson," *ESQ: A Journal of the American Renaissance*, 24 [1978], 219).

9. Thoreau, *Walden* (1854), in *The Writings of Henry D. Thoreau*, ed. J. Lyndon Shanley *et al.* (Princeton, N.J.: Princeton Univ. Press, 1971), p. 11.

10. Thoreau, *Walden*, p. 323.

(1836), Byron Johnson protested the "sophistries of language," which "cannot enable us to penetrate beyond the range of our senses."[11] And in attacking dogmatic theology, Horace Bushnell reemphasized the latent indeterminateness of language: "[W]e discover that ... words, in respect to which there seemed to be such a definite and precise understanding, and which therefore we had taken to be literal names of the thoughts signified, are in fact only more, because more latently, indeterminate."[12] Also, in an earlier statement on the nature of language, Bushnell observed that "language provides only a single form of predicate—a single grammatic formula. And yet it seems to be imagined that we can saddle mere forms of words, and ride them into necessary unambiguous conclusions!"[13] Similarly, Johnson's belief that men impute to nature "classifications, ambiguities, imperfections, and properties" which "truly belong to language alone"[14] is indeed descriptive of the epistemological errors of Tommo, Ahab, Ishmael, Pierre, and the narrator of *Billy Budd*. Melville may even echo linguistic theories such as these in a chapter of *Mardi* that explains how in Ohonoo, the Land of Rogues, live none but honest men; for this suggests that "words are but algebraic signs, conveying no meaning except what you please" (M, 269). Words, as Babbalanja says elsewhere, are "mere substitutions of sounds for inexplicable meanings" (M, 507). Not surprisingly, then, an exchange between Mohi and Babbalanja anticipates the epistemological concerns of *Pierre* and *The Confidence-Man* by highlighting the evasiveness of Truth:

> "But, come now, thou oracle, if all things are deceptive, tell us what is truth?"

---

11. Byron Johnson's *Treatise on Language: or the Relation which Words Bear to Things* (1836), is quoted in Philip F. Gura's informative overview of the linguistic milieu of American Renaissance literature, "Language and Meaning: An American Tradition," *American Literature*, 53 (March 1981), 3. Cf. Gura's *The Wisdom of Words: Language, Theology, and Literature in the New England Renaissance* (Middletown, Conn.: Wesleyan Univ. Press, 1981).

12. Horace Bushnell, "Language and Doctrine," in *Christ in Theology; Being the Answer of the Author, Before the Hartford Central Association of Ministers, October, 1849, for the Doctrines of the Book Entitled "GOD IN CHRIST"* (Hartford, Conn.: Brown and Parsons, 1851), p. 41.

13. Bushnell, "Preliminary Dissertation on the Nature of Language," in *God in Christ: Three Discourses, Delivered at New Haven, Cambridge, and Andover, with a Preliminary Dissertation on Language* (Hartford, Conn.: Brown and Parsons, 1849), p. 62. Although this book appeared too late to have influenced any of Melville's books prior to *Redburn*, his subsequent encounter wth its ideas could have been facilitated by Elizabeth P. Peabody's essay, "Language," in *Aesthetic Papers*, pp. 214–24.

14. Johnson, *Treatise on Language*, p. 53; quoted by Gura, p. 5.

"The old interrogatory; did they not ask it when the world began? But ask no more. As old Bardianna hath it, that question is more final than any answer." (M, 284)

From this inability either to define or to articulate absolute "Truth" we need not, however, deduce "Melville's quarrel with fiction";[15] rather, we may view the indeterminateness of language and the evasiveness of Truth as linguistic and conceptual analogs to the modern phenomenological "nothingness" that, in our discussion of *Billy Budd*, we saw to occasion consciousness itself. As James Guetti says, "[T]he suggestion of an ineffable reality depends upon a recognition of the insufficiency of language and is communicated largely by means of this insufficiency." For Melville, he continues, language cannot penetrate, but only surround "meaning" with "suggestive rhetoric insufficient to define it," but adequate for intimating its existence.[16] In the nineteenth century Horace Bushnell similarly stressed that the *perspective* afforded by the paradoxical and indefinite nature of language comprised the mind's best approximation of Truth:

As ... words ... generally carry something false with them, as well as something true, associating form with the truths represented, when really there is no form; it will ... be necessary, on this account, to multiply words or figures, and thus to present the subject on opposite sides or many sides.... Accordingly we never come so near to a truly well rounded view of any truth, as when it is offered paradoxically; that is, under contradictions; this is, under two or more dictions, which taken as dictions, are contrary to the other.

. . . .

If we find a writer ... multiplying antagonisms, offering cross views, and bringing us round the field to show us how it looks from different points, then we are to presume that he has some truth which it becomes us to know. We are to pass round accordingly with him, take up all his symbols, catch a view of him here, and another there, use one thing to qualify and interpret another, and the other to shed light upon that, and, by a process of this kind, endeavor to comprehend his antagonisms and settle into a complete view of his meaning.[17]

---

15. See Nina Baym's "Melville's Quarrel with Fiction," *PMLA*, 94 (Oct. 1979), 909-23.

16. James Guetti, *The Limits of Metaphor: A Study of Melville, Conrad, and Faulkner* (Ithaca, N.Y.: Cornell Univ. Press, 1967), pp. 3, 44.

17. Bushnell, "Preliminary Dissertation on the Nature of Language," pp. 55, 67.

This, I think, comprises an appropriate gloss on what Melville may have regarded as the synthetic—by which I mean both unreal, or indeterminate, *and* synthesizing—nature of written art. As he says in his poem "Art,"

> In placid hours well-pleased we dream
> Of many a brave unbodied scheme.
> But form to lend, pulsed life create,
> What unlike things must meet and mate:
> A flame to melt—a wind to freeze;
> Sad patience—joyous energies;
> Humility—yet pride and scorn;
> Instinct and study; love and hate;
> Audacity—reverence. These must mate,
> And fuse with Jacob's mystic heart,
> To wrestle with the angel—Art.[18]

Thus, however tangential to Truth, words that impart *perspective* entail the crystalization of consciousness, the illumination of the Sartrian "for-itself," the articulation of man's possible possibilities in a chaotic and indeterminate world. Like Emerson, who finally saw the "slender human word" as man's exclusive chance to exercise free will in an otherwise fated world,[19] Melville in his commitment to literature suggests that writing actually vitalizes the Cartesian *cogito*— much as Art does in his poem "The Great Pyramid":

> Craftsmen, in dateless quarries dim,
> Stones formless into form did trim,
> Usurped on Nature's self with Art,
> And bade this dumb I AM to start,
>   Imposing him.

For this aspect of Bushnell's thought, see Charles Feidelson, Jr., *Symbolism and American Literature* (Chicago: Univ. of Chicago Press, 1953), pp. 151–57.

18. Part of *Timoleon* (1891), "Art" is here quoted from *Collected Poems of Herman Melville*, ed. Howard P. Vincent (Chicago: Packard, 1947), p. 231.

19. As William J. Scheick says, "Emerson's art conveys through the slender human word that dramatic moment between inspiration and thought, that same transitional point of dynamic interaction he time and again spoke of as the will" (*The Slender Human Word: Emerson's Artistry in Prose* [Knoxville: Univ. of Tennessee Press, 1978], p. 145). As Scheick shows elsewhere, the relation between writing and self-determining freedom is also an important concern in Charles Brockden Brown's *Ormond* (1799). See Scheick's "Problem of Origination in Brown's *Ormond*," in *Critical Essays on Charles Brockden Brown*, ed. Bernard Rosenthal (Boston: G. K. Hall, 1981), pp. 136, 139.

Whatever the evasiveness of Truth, Melville still chose "To wrestle with the angel—Art."[20]

A phenomenological reading of Melville is, finally, consistent with the way his major works question such cultural mind sets as "civilization," messianic nationalism, covenant psychology, racial superiority, human perfectibility, and the objective status of history; for by challenging the contemporary order of *knowing*, Melville transcendentally—indeed *idea*listically—entertains the *possibility* that things might be otherwise. And appropriate here is the opinion that "the history of art is the history of violated 'mental set,' for the truly creative artist strives to reach possibilities for knowing or perceiving the world beyond the limitation of culturally determined categories."[21] Mutually consistent, as well, are Melville's existential vision and his somewhat theistical appreciation for "that Calvinistic sense of Innate Depravity and Original Sin, from whose visitations, in some shape or other, no *deeply thinking* mind is always and wholly free" (emphasis added). The link between these a-theist and theist worlds possibly rests in something like Perry Miller's observation that Puritan introspection entailed "the probing [of] every recess of [one's] being,... leaving no place unexplored in which sin might hide"; also involved was the "unmasking [of] every disguise which nature puts on in its frantic effort to pretend holiness without actually surrendering its lusts."[22] To a large degree, Melville's early concern with the "nature of true virtue" in *Typee* through *Mardi*, as well as his criticism of human nature and national claims to regeneracy in *Redburn*, *White-Jacket*, *Moby-Dick*, *Pierre*, and *The Confidence-Man*, correspond to the "true sight of sin" advocated by the Puritans. In *Billy Budd*, however, Melville finally rises from the couch of introspection to the cross of consciousness, transforming Puritan anxiety and the terrors of conscience into existential anguish over consciousness itself.

---

20. "The Great Pyramid" is quoted from *Collected Poems*, p. 255. This poem is also part of *Timoleon*, Melville's last published thoughts on the anguish entailed in bold, original thinking. See Darrel Abel's " 'Laurel Twined With Thorn': The Theme of Melville's *Timoleon*," *Personalist*, 41 (Summer 1960), 330–40. Melville's respect for the indeterminate, obscure, and evasive nature of truths that art seeks to represent owes something to Matthew Arnold's conception of art's imaginative basis. See Shirley M. Dettlaff's informative study, "Ionian Form and Esau's Waste: Melville's View of Art in *Clarel*," *American Literature*, 54 (May 1982), 212–28.

21. Wesley Morris, *Toward a New Historicism* (Princeton, N.J.: Princeton Univ. Press, 1972), p. 215.

22. Perry Miller, *The New England Mind: The Seventeenth Century* (1939; rpt. Boston: Beacon Press, 1961), p. 56.

I N D E X